PRAISE FOR *THE DES[...]*

"A fascinating page-turner. [Moore] walks the tightrope of inviting readers to have empathy for the pirates whose national history includes brutal colonialism while demonstrating the pirates' capacity for torture. Moore's honest writing will speak to readers. Having faced an experience no one ever should, Moore constructs a narrative that makes readers' hearts beat faster."
—Booklist (starred review)

"Among the virtues of this account is that even when discussing sensational happenings, Moore never overdramatizes. This exceptional memoir will attract many readers." —*Library Journal*

"A harrowing and affecting account of two and a half years of captivity at the hands of Somali pirates. A deftly constructed and tautly told rejoinder to Robert Louis Stevenson's *Kidnapped*, sympathetic but also sharp-edged." —*Kirkus Reviews* (starred review)

"When a young man who is good and brave, keenly intelligent and observant, with a lively mind and a learned sense of human and historical complexity, is kidnapped by pirates and kept as a hostage for three years in Somalia's harsh and violent bush, the result is *The Desert and the Sea*. However much you wish Michael Scott Moore had never had cause to write it, this book could not be more engrossing, harrowing, suspenseful, wrenchingly humane, and illuminating."
—Francisco Goldman, author of Say Her Name and
The Interior Circuit: A Mexico City Chronicle

"If you read Michael Scott Moore's book, first clear your schedule, because you won't put it down until you've finished it. *The Desert and the Sea* is an astonishing and harrowing story, told with great humanity, by a writer who ventures where few will ever go."

—Susan Casey, author of *Voices in the Ocean: A Journey into the Wild and Haunting World of Dolphins*

"Highly addictive reading material. Michael Scott Moore delivers an amazing true-life thriller, one of the most suspenseful books written in recent years, that tracks across oceans and underworlds, culminating in a very rewarding, deeply profound end."

—Jeffrey Gettleman, Pulitzer Prize–winner and author of *Love, Africa*

"His account of his nearly three years of captivity is a testament to the strength of one man's indomitable spirit and Moore's great gifts of observation, his evident gifts as a storyteller, his humor, and his wits. Thank heavens he lived to tell the story, which everyone should now read and cheer."

—Tom Barbash, author of *Stay Up With Me*

THE DESERT AND THE SEA

THE DESERT AND THE SEA

977 Days Captive on the Somali Pirate Coast

MICHAEL SCOTT MOORE

HARPER WAVE

An Imprint of HarperCollins*Publishers*

FIRST HARPER WAVE PAPERBACK EDITION PUBLISHED 2019.

Designed by Leah Carlson-Stanisic

Title and part title photograph by Ipatove/Shutterstock, Inc.

Library of Congress Cataloging-in-Publication Data has been applied for.

ISBN 978-0-06-244918-4 (pbk.)

HB 03.01.2024

For my mother
and the rest of my family, living and dead

In Algiers one speaks simply of the existence of two varieties of Islam—one, which is called the Islam of the desert, and a second, which is defined as the Islam of the river (or of the sea). The first is the religion practiced by warlike nomadic tribes struggling to survive in one of the world's most hostile environments, the Sahara. The second Islam is the faith of merchants, itinerant peddlers, people of the road and of the bazaar, for whom openness, compromise, and exchange are not only beneficial to trade, but necessary to life itself.

—RYSZARD KAPUSCINSKI, *Travels with Herodotus*

CONTENTS

THE DESERT AND THE SEA

Prologue

"Michael, I got a problem," said Rolly Tambara.

"What's the matter?"

"A pirate, he kick my Bible."

We sat in the shade of a conveyor belt on the work deck of a hijacked tuna ship. Rolly was my best friend on board—my best friend in the Indian Ocean, where we were anchored, my best friend in Galmudug, the region of Somalia where we'd met, my best friend in the Horn of Africa and maybe for a circumference of three or four thousand miles. He was a fisherman from the Seychelles, an old, wrinkled-eyed Catholic with a stout, short frame and a nearly bald head. He spoke a French-inflected Creole. We'd both been hauled aboard the *Naham 3* after some time as hostages on shore.

"Which pirate?" I said.

"I not know his name."

Rolly had been reading a tattered Bible in another corner of the deck when a Somali came downstairs from the bridge to make tea. While he waited for his water to boil, the pirate sat next to Rolly to inspect his reading material. The sight of a Bible offended him. Unwilling to touch it with his fingers, he leaned back to kick it with his salty bare foot.

"Where'd it go?" I said. "Did you get it back?"

"I run and get it," said Rolly.

"What happened to the pirate?"

"He go back upstairs wit' his tea."

"You don't know his name?"

Rolly shook his head.

"You should tell Tuure," I said.

Ali Tuure* was the pirate leader on this condemned vessel, a stoop-shouldered elderly Somali with ragged hair and a snaggle-toothed smile. His weird sense of humor and sense of (relative) fairness gave him clout among the pirate guards. He walked around like a skeleton and greeted people with a skinny raised hand and a wheezy "*Heeyyyyyy*," like a morbid imitation of the Fonz from *Happy Days*. He didn't like the sight of a Bible, either, but he never tried to impose Islam on his hostages, and he would have hated any display of (relative) disrespect.

Rolly walked across the deck to make his appeal to the Somalis upstairs. It caused a lot of confusion. I mixed a cup of instant coffee and wandered to the shoreward side of the ship. The town of Hobyo lay across the water, and to my nearsighted eyes it looked like a blurry jumble of rocks on the brownish desert shore. Zinc roofs reflected the sun in sharp pinpricks.

The *Naham 3* was a fifty-meter long-liner, flagged in Oman but operated by a Taiwanese company. The hostages consisted of Chinese, Cambodian, Vietnamese, Indonesian, and Filipino fishermen. They sat behind us—chatting, smoking cigarettes, playing cards. We lived like inmates of a floating internment camp. I was a skinny, lost-looking castaway, an American writer in his early forties who could remember a pleasant expatriate life in Berlin like a distant dream. After three or four months of captivity, I had shed about forty-five pounds. The *Naham 3* had a hanging tuna scale, a spring-loaded contraption with a hook, and if you slung a loop of rope around the hook you could dangle from it like a dead fish.

---

* A nickname, pronounced *TOO-ray*.

A Chinese crewman, Jian Zui,* stood by the rail with a cigarette. He had a plump, deadpan face that broke sometimes into a bright grin. He held out his cigarette pack to me.

"No, no."

He tossed the end of his cigarette into the water and looked out at Hobyo. He placed two flat hands together and mimed a dive overboard. It shocked me, in that prison atmosphere, to see him demonstrate such a forbidden act: I glanced around at the Somali gunmen lazing on the upper deck. Jian Zui and I could hardly communicate, but we thought alike—I'd imagined the same escape dozens of times. I wondered if he could swim.

At last he smiled, as if the idea were a lark. He folded his hands to imitate Christian prayer. "Santa Maria," he said, and rolled his eyes to heaven.

Among the Chinese on our ship, "Santa Maria" was slang for "dead." He meant that if we jumped, we might die.

I nodded.

Soon a motorboat came bouncing across the swells. Supply skiffs buzzed out twice a day from Hobyo. "*Moto*," said Jian Zui, and when it pulled alongside our ship, the arriving Somalis tossed up a thick line. Other men lashed it to the railing while both vessels lurched up and down on the water. Three or four Somalis sprang aboard. Another heaved up a heavy sack of khat, a leafy green stimulant plant that Somalis like to chew the way Westerners like to drink alcohol. The pirates argued about who should haul the sack upstairs.

For a few weeks in the summer of 2012 I watched these skiff deliveries with cautious optimism. I had mentioned my location

---

* Also a nickname, pronounced *Jyen-Tsway*. Real name: Leng Wenbing.

in German during a phone call home to California. My mother had asked about a "care package"—*Can we send you a care package, Michael?*—and the optimism in her voice made me dizzy with grief. A care package, to reach this vessel, would have to move through several layers of clan and criminal networks on the savanna. It was a sweetly intended idea, but what would be left of a care package when it came over the rail? A pair of shorts?

I felt a hot pressure behind my eyes.

A plane made a wide circle around Hobyo from the south, and I spotted it before I heard its engines. The gusting breezes on the water were constant, and they swept noises around in unpredictable ways. I couldn't see much without my glasses, but it was probably a European or American surveillance plane. While it made a wide turn over the land, a fierce old Somali with a damaged-looking face came out from the bridge deck and waved his pistol.

"American!" he hollered.

He thought it was a Western plane, too, and he didn't want me standing where it could spot me. A group of young pirates upstairs had moved to the far side of the deck. Low-ranking guards had learned to hide from aircraft to keep from exposing their faces to surveillance.

"American!" the old Somali hollered at me one more time, waving his pistol. This pirate had never shown me anything but hatred, and it burned me with outraged common sense to take an order from him. I lingered near the gunwale, watching the Somalis unload, until I was satisfied that no ludicrous, unlikely care package was on the skiff.

"Ah, Michael," Rolly said from under the conveyor belt, against the gusting breeze. "Not make them angry, Michael."

Part 1

THE RUMOR KITCHEN

My father, who wasn't very original, used to say, "Curiosity killed the cat," and of course I first went to the Horn of Africa out of curiosity. I liked the strange distances of the arid savanna, the rocky desert sound of the languages, the lack of Western pleasantries. Later I wanted to write about a pirate gang jailed in Hamburg. Their marathon trial was famous in Europe; it represented the first proceeding on German soil against any pirate in more than four centuries. I'd reported on it for *Spiegel Online*, where I worked in Berlin, and it seemed to me that a book about the trial and some underreported aspects of Somali piracy might be interesting.

I also went as a student of Ashwin Raman's. He was an Indian documentary maker, a war correspondent for German TV, and I first met him in Djibouti in 2009, while I worked on a series of magazine columns about pirates. Djibouti is a small nation squeezed into East Africa at the mouth of the Red Sea, and its capital was a grid of crumbling French colonial buildings with occasional tent neighborhoods—slums—that smelled like goat. The heat and glare were punishing. The traditional hotel for Europeans and wayward Americans was the expensive Hotel Méridien, just out of town. Drivers who picked me up for appointments in Djibouti were universally baffled that I hadn't reserved a room there. "It's a nice hotel," said a young French expatriate who ferried me to a NATO ship on the first morning. He frowned with one corner of his mouth. "You are the first journalist from Europe I have met who has not stayed there." But I'd avoided the Méridien for the simple reason that it would tell me nothing about Djibouti. "I don't even know where your hotel is," the driver confessed when we got stuck in traffic. "I never come downtown."

I met Ashwin at Camp Lemonnier, an American base outside Djibouti Ville. We toured it together and interviewed the admiral in charge. By sheer coincidence, we both lived in Germany. Also by coincidence, we had both scorned the Méridien. (We were both cheap.) Ashwin's war-zone documentaries had won international broadcast awards, but he used nothing fancier than a palm-size digital camera. "I just film what I see, you know. That's all." On the job he looked like an Indian tourist making films for his grandchildren, but he had a talent for moving in and out of dangerous places. When we met, he had just finished a month of reporting with Somalia's Islamist fighters, al-Shabaab, by pretending to be a Pakistani Muslim.

Ashwin had led a colorful life. When he left India for the first time, in 1968, as a student bound for Oxford, the road to Britain had presented a complicated adventure; there were no suitable long-distance flights. Instead, a cargo boat intended for pilgrims to Mecca, a wooden hajj dhow, had carried him north and west along the fringes of the Arabian Sea. "I don't know if you have ever been on a dhow, but it can be a very peaceful way to travel. We had calm and beautiful sailing until the next stop, Karachi," in Pakistan. Humor rumbled in Ashwin's voice: "Then all these Muslim guys got on, and from there it was total chaos."

He disembarked near the head of the Persian Gulf, in Kuwait, and took a bus to Baghdad. He planned to board a train to Europe, "but when we entered Baghdad, on the first day, we saw a public hanging," he said. "It was one of the first hangings of the new Baathist regime. So it is interesting. I was in Iraq at the beginning of Saddam Hussein's rise to power, and at the very end."

He'd traveled to Iraq five or six times as a filmmaker for German TV, to Afghanistan more than twenty. Something about him reminded me of V. S. Naipaul. He could be impish and kind, but he never said kind things. He was Oxford educated and chronically unimpressed. After a couple of hours at Camp Lemonnier, I had to mention the resemblance.

"I have met Naipaul," he said. "An extremely unpleasant man, I can assure you."

Ashwin wanted to return to Somalia to make a film about pirates and suggested traveling together. The idea flattered me. I needed a mentor for this kind of work. But for now I wasn't making any definite plans; I was getting to know East Africa. One step at a time.

Camp Lemonnier sat on an old French Foreign Legion base behind enormous berms of sand. It resembled an American town built from shipping containers. There were basketball courts and Quonset huts and little paved roads with street signs. Ashwin and I shopped for toothpaste and magazines at the Navy Exchange (a "NAVEX"), which could have been a drugstore airlifted from suburban L.A. It took me back to childhood in California—the fluorescent lights, the mouthwash, the Doritos, the ibuprofen. The Jack Daniel's and greeting cards. Desert heat pressing on an overcooled box of cheap racked clothing and a thousand brands of shampoo. One reason I lived in Berlin was to get away from this kind of thing, but the banality itself—the overpriced junk, all the stuff you could live without—had a pull of its own. The fluorescent lights reminded me of standing in line with my dad once to buy a bottle of something on a hot afternoon in L.A., when he was distracted, unbalanced, and possibly drunk, and he let his hot cigarette burn my arm. He was awfully sorry, and he made it up with some strands of licorice, but maybe these associations had kept me at a safe distance from American drugstores as an adult. At the Djibouti NAVEX, in any case, I caught a taste of the countersentiment, the weird lure of such dysfunctional places. "If I were stuck on a lonely island, I would never feel homesick for Berlin," the German cabarettist Kurt Weill said a few years before his death, in 1950. "I would feel homesick for a drugstore in New York City."

II

I've made my father sound like a dolt, but that's not what I wanted. In the last years of his life, he could be rough mannered and forgetful, but I remember him as an eager and energetic man. He had a rakehell smile and a receding hairline, and our first years together had played out like a dream of suburban family life in the San Fernando Valley, in a big yellow house with a farmlike garden and a Doughboy pool.

He'd met my mom in Germany, during a stint in Europe for Lockheed. He'd spent most of his career as an aerospace engineer in California. When NATO needed a version of the F-104 Starfighter for its European fleet, Lockheed sent a team of engineers from L.A. to listen to the wishes of generals from Italy and France and tweak certain features on the plane. Mom at the time was a tart-humored secretary in her early twenties. She worked in the Lockheed office in Koblenz, a city across the Rhine from her small hometown.

When Dad first checked in for work, he asked for the "restroom," according to family legend. Mom had never encountered this word in English. *The poor man*, she thought—*he must be jet-lagged*. Like a well-mannered receptionist, she ushered him into the conference room and invited him to rest in there.

"You gotta be kidding," Dad said, according to family legend.

"Yes, it's not in use right now," offered Mom.

"In the potted plants?"

"Wherever you like," said Mom, unruffled, and stepped away on clacking heels.

Dad and most of his Lockheed friends returned to California with German wives. Their circle of friends while I was a kid consisted of garrulous Rhineland mothers with a taste for white wine and skeptical, conservative engineer dads. The first person I intended to marry, as a kindergartner, was the daughter of Denis and Sylvia Lyon, friends of my parents from Koblenz. They owned a little dachshund who felt overstimulated whenever guests came over and charged around their desert-suburban home, a miniature reminder of the family's maternal origins.

Dad worked on electrical systems for satellites and passenger jets, but he was also a drunk, so there was a constant tension between our suburban idyll and his alcoholic rage. He tried to kick his addictions only after he and Mom had split—after she kicked him out—and during the hot summer of 1981 he died in a cigarette-smelling bachelor apartment on Reseda Boulevard, near our local Catholic church. Mom said it was a heart attack. A few months later, we moved to a smaller house in Redondo Beach with less lawn, less upkeep, near the beaches, where the inland California winds wouldn't inflame her allergies.

I spent all of my childhood and most of my young adulthood in California, southern as well as northern, but the materialism and the god-awful traffic seemed as irrational to me as the monolithic aerospace and movie industries. As a boy, I had discovered a box in our hallway closet filled with coins my parents had collected from around the world—not just German marks but also French and Swiss francs, Mexican pesos, and British pounds. These currencies seemed wonderfully exotic, and to slake my sudden and powerful wanderlust I started a stamp collection. But the desire to travel never subsided, and when my first marriage ended, in my thirties, I moved to Berlin, hoping to put my idle German passport to use and thinking with a measure of pride that I would never have to deal with Californian banality again. By "banality" I meant marriage and divorce, but also drugstores, U.S. politics, TV news, rush-hour traffic, vast American supermarkets, and everything that reminded me of the painful and tedious past.

The life I established in 2005 was quiet but pleasant, in a bachelor apartment overlooking a tree-grown park in eastern Berlin. I built some of the best friendships of my life in that neighborhood; I learned to love the languid, long-lit summers as well as the frozen winters. But I missed the ocean, and when I learned about an odd little surf scene in Germany, I decided to write a book about surfing, to show how a non-American tradition had evolved into a big American craze and then proliferated around the world. *Sweetness and Blood* became a travelogue about American influence on the world after World War II, both good and bad, as seeded by surfing hippies and wanderers and recreational Marines.

The research took me to West Africa, Cuba, Morocco, Israel, and the Gaza Strip. It introduced me to florid old pirate stories from Africa and the Caribbean. Large-scale piracy had started to flourish off Somalia around this time, and I followed the hijackings with helpless curiosity from the *Spiegel* newsroom in Berlin. It's hard to write one adventurous book without thinking about another, and soon the headlines began to annoy me. Conventional wisdom about Somali pirates focused on their cruelty: "Forget all the romance of eye patches and parrots—these guys are *mean*." I thought: *That must be wrong*. I was as full of pirate romance as the next American kid, but it was clear that the glow of high-seas heroism clinging to

Pirates of the Caribbean was a question of nostalgic Hollywood misti-
ness and lingering military kitsch. Pirates of old, I figured, were
no less mean than Somalis. Of course I was right. What I didn't
realize was how much all pirates had in common.

In the 1980s, Lou Reed wrote a song about "video violence,"
about an irrational pop-fueled world where people were in thrall to
explosions and gunfire on TV. His prophetic bit of doggerel came
before Columbine-style gun massacres were a routine irruption of
evil in everyday American life. It came before the Twin Towers fell,
before the Iraq invasion, before the most lurid scenes of cinematic
imagination had oozed like gore into our headlines. The rise of modern pirates buzzing off Somalia was an example of entropy in my
lifetime, and it seemed important to know why there were pirates
at all.

III

In Djibouti I also boarded a NATO warship and sailed for a few
days in the Gulf of Aden. The ship was a Turkish frigate, the *Gediz*,
which had a good record of catching pirates off northern Somalia,
and its captain, Hasan Özyurt, made frustrated noises because he
couldn't catch more. He grumbled about NATO's rules of engagement; he wanted permission to get tough. Great world powers had
kept the ancient crime of piracy quelled for almost two hundred
years, he said. "It is an embarrassment for our civilization that they
are here."

Captain Özyurt was more or less right. Piracy had never vanished from the planet, but the last severe and famous phase of it
was the Barbary era, when Ottoman rulers on the North African

coast exacted annual tribute from European powers in exchange for restraining their corsairs from sacking Christian merchant ships. By 1800, a number of American leaders wanted to raid the Barbary Coast and whack the "nests of banditti" instead of paying more tributes and ransom. First they had to establish a navy. But by 1815, a fleet of American ships threatened the dey of Algiers, a sponsor of Barbary pirates, with all-out war. The ships imposed a treaty on the pirate regency that exempted the young American nation from paying tribute. The dey relented, and the romantic era of piracy—still a matter of gunpowder, swords, and sail—began to fade.

The more I read, the deeper I sank. American colonists had passed through a startling pirate phase of their own at the end of the 1600s, but they recovered, through raw trade, less than a century later. I could *smell* a book. What if Somalia could move in the same direction? The parallels weren't clean, but the Atlantic seaboard of North America had evolved from an underdeveloped haven for pirates to an antipirate world power within three generations. Americans ended large-scale piracy for most of the modern era after they built a trade of their own to protect.

It would have made an interesting book. But I wavered about going to Somalia, for obvious reasons, until the trial of the ten men in Hamburg. The event attracted media from all over Europe. *Pirates in Germany! In this day and age!* Ten Somalis sat in a single courtroom with twenty public defenders (God help them). The Somalis had been arrested after a gun battle with Dutch commandos while they tried to hijack the MV *Taipan*, a German cargo ship. Some lawyers insisted that their clients were poor, simple, press-ganged fishermen. The notion of Somali pirates as frustrated fishermen was a cliché, but it seemed to work in court, where little could be verified about the men.

This trial tipped the balance. Well—the trial, and something harder to describe. "It is not the fully conscious mind," Graham Greene wrote in *Journey Without Maps*, regarding his first venture beyond Europe, "which chooses West Africa in preference to Switzerland."

The *Taipan* was trundling south around the Horn of Africa in the spring of 2010 when officers on the bridge spotted a wooden fishing dhow some eight miles astern. A dhow is just a painted wooden boat, rigged with a sail or a diesel motor, common enough on the Indian Ocean. This one pulled off at a strange angle. Captain Dierk Eggers thought it wanted to spread fishing nets. Instead, a pair of skiffs launched from behind it and came speeding toward the ship.

Eggers radioed for help. The approaching pirates fired on the bridge with Kalashnikovs. "The bullets came through the steel walls like butter," the captain said in court. "We were in danger for our lives, no question." The *Taipan* had an armored citadel, or safe room, so Eggers and his crew retreated there and locked the door. When the judge in Hamburg asked for a more precise location of the citadel, Eggers hedged. "It was the machine control room," he said reluctantly, and when the judge asked him to be more specific, the old captain gave a long, baleful glance across the courtroom. It was the first time all day he'd looked at the young Somalis.

"It was our great luck," he said, "that the room was so hard to find."

Captain Eggers was long and gaunt, sixty-nine years old, with swept-back white hair still tinted blond. He had white stubble and a coarse, hollow, gentle voice. Because of his experience, he had great authority in court. He wore black jeans and a leather vest.

"There was no talking," Eggers said. "I assumed they would find the safe room and kidnap us. I had no fear of death, but I also didn't want to be a hostage somewhere on the coast of Somalia."

The crew consisted of fifteen men: Russians, Ukrainians, Sri

Lankans, and Germans. They listened as the pirates ransacked the ship. Eggers worried that the dim emergency lights might be visible under the door. Soon the throttle started to ease. The ship slowed and sped up again, "as if someone were testing the controls," said Eggers, and then they felt a hard turn to starboard.

"That was to the west," Eggers said. "Toward Somalia."

The machine room had toilets and a computer that could read radar signals from the bridge. It also had an emergency stop mechanism. Eggers's engineer cut the power. Meanwhile a German spy plane filmed events from a distance of seven miles. No one on the ship was aware of the plane, but we watched footage in court, and the color and detail were vivid. We saw spinning radar instruments, a violent wake, unmanned fire hoses pumping plumes of salt water. A rushing cargo ship is like a moving city—it couldn't have been easy to catch.

Eggers told me in private that he owed his liberty to the citadel's odd location. The pirates raided the cabins for two hours, until the chop of a Dutch helicopter descended on the *Taipan* and Eggers heard "a terrible din of gunfire." New people wandered the halls, yelling in English. "We want to help you, you're safe." But Eggers and his crew were cautious; they thought the Somalis might speak English. Not until they heard voices mumbling in Dutch did they decide to open the door.

By then the Somalis were lying on their bellies, blindfolded and bound, on an open deck of the *Taipan*. The Dutch photographed, questioned, and moved them to the Netherlands. From there they flew to Germany for trial.

I followed the Hamburg case throughout 2011 and made friends with a good-humored and intelligent court interpreter, Abdi Warsame, who also worked for German immigration agencies. He introduced me to Mohammed Sahal Gerlach, a Somali elder in

Berlin. Many of the defendants had grown up in Galkayo, Gerlach's hometown. A few months earlier, Gerlach had guided a TV journalist safely from Galkayo to Hobyo, a pirate nest on the coast, on a reporting tour of the Galmudug region. Ashwin and I were intrigued. We quizzed Gerlach over the next few months and waited for the trial to end. We settled on a fee for security. I found support from two magazines* and a grant from the Pulitzer Center on Crisis Reporting. I wanted to see parts of Somalia relevant to my project that other journalists had seen: I wasn't trying to overreach. But I was a writer, with a weakness for big ideas, and my ideas, more than anything, carried me off to Somalia.

IV

When we arrived in the first days of 2012, our nominal host in Galkayo was Mohamed Ahmed Alin, the regional president of Galmudug. He lived in a beige villa set back from a dusty street, and when we visited him one afternoon, we found his guards leaning against a wall inside his compound, chewing khat under some wilted trees. Our bodyguards joined them. We walked around the president's silver SUV and through a tall doorway. It struck me how much relative wealth and comfort could exist unseen from the desolate streets of Galkayo. The president's compound had high, plain walls, and the raked metal roofs of even the largest homes were low-slung here, like the brims of fedoras.

He met us in his office wearing a pillbox prayer cap, an emblem

---

* *The Atlantic* and *Pacific Standard* (called *Miller-McCune* at the time).

of Sufi devotion. Galmudug was a self-governing swath of central Somalia that wanted to be a federal state. It had sworn allegiance to the weak Transitional Federal Government in Mogadishu—that is, to the idea of a united Somalia—so its leaders could assign government titles and receive government funds. Alin wore bifocals, a trimmed mustache, and a quiet, beleaguered expression.

"You are welcome in Galmudug," he said. "I hope your stay here has been pleasant."

"So far."

Mohammed Gerlach sat with us, translating the Somali into German.

"You are in the Embassy Hotel?" said President Alin.

"Yes."

"And you will soon go to Hobyo?"

Gerlach had arranged our trip, including the excursion to Hobyo, where we planned to interview a pirate. Hobyo belonged to Galmudug, territorially, but Alin said his government lacked both money and military force to keep the pirate gangs suppressed. "Unfortunately, we do not have much influence there," he said. "We are trying, but it is difficult."

Alin sat behind a plain wooden desk and an aging, off-white computer. We heard the guards' chatter from outside. Alin was a cousin of Gerlach's, and Gerlach was a deputy minister of something. They both belonged to the Sa'ad clan. During our interview, it became clear that all "deputy minister" titles attached to Somalis we had met so far, Gerlach included, had emanated along clan lines from this office.

Before the trip, Gerlach had sketched a development idea for Galmudug, a plan to create jobs by installing piers along the pirate coast. He thought legitimate landing spots for cargo would help the economy. This simple vision, practical or not, fit my idea for a book. Piracy was just a brutal form of trade, and it flourished where jobs were scarce, in modern Somalia as well as the colonial United States. When I mentioned Gerlach's idea about piers, President Alin nodded.

"It is what we need in Somalia," he said. Warlords already moved commodities like sugar toward the borders of Kenya and Ethiopia, where their networks could smuggle the merchandise across (and avoid tariffs). The flow of goods already existed. Gerlach and President Alin seemed to believe this illicit trade could develop into legitimate business, and jobs.

"But we cannot do it ourselves," said Alin. "We need help from abroad."

I promised to spread the word. But foreign aid could be tricky in Somalia. "Galkayo" means "where the infidel ran away," and the name is a reminder of anticolonial hatreds, of war with the Italians and British.

The city was about a century old. After five years of high-profile piracy on the distant ocean, this baked-stone crossroads near the heart of Somalia—this loose affiliation of houses with little tradition of electricity, running water, or schools—had sprouted a pair of universities, more than twenty lower schools, competing cell-phone networks, a few ramshackle hotels, internet cafés, even alcohol. It was almost cosmopolitan. People called it a boomtown. There were medical clinics and modern, air-conditioned "hawala" shops with new computer systems.* The sudden prosperity corresponded with an upward arc in pirate fortunes. General opinion at the U.N. and elsewhere held that ransom cash had juiced the economy. "We've

---

* "Hawala" is a Muslim wire-transfer network, cheaper than Western Union and used throughout the world.

seen a lot of construction around Galkayo in the last few years," a U.N. expert on Somalia told me before I left. "In satellite pictures, we can see a lot more lights." New painted villas had sprung up like daisies.

Still, "boomtown" was an exaggeration. Galkayo had no paved streets. The Somali neighborhood of Nairobi known as Eastleigh was more fast-paced and bustling. Eastleigh had risen like a sudden, surprising corner of Manhattan during the same span of years—2005 to 2012—which suggested that the real pirate boomtowns could be found in other parts of East Africa. In Galkayo, lean men lounged outside the hawala shops in patterned skirtlike sarongs, holding weapons. Businesses advertised themselves with colorful paintings right on the walls, instead of shop signs or billboards. And ragged herds of goats bleated in the road, some with phone numbers spray-painted on their fur. The whole place felt cursed by the sun.

Later, we asked Gerlach to show us a power plant across from our hotel, which rumbled all day and night. Tangled power cables ran down every street. But the plant was nothing but an open space between some buildings where a single Somali tended six chugging engines, generators improvised from trucks or farm tractors. It was this man's job to keep the pistons firing. He wore green overalls and smiled in the black-hazed sunlight, pouring diesel fuel from a jerry can into the decrepit, smoking machines.

"All of Galkayo runs on this?" I shouted at Gerlach.

"All of South Galkayo," Gerlach shouted back in German. "North Galkayo has something similar."

Gerlach and his assistant, Hamid, pointed down the road at some low buildings. "That is the line between the towns," they said.

Galkayo straddled a border between Galmudug state and Puntland, to the north, and the street represented an uneasy line of contention where the Sa'ad clan, from Galmudug, fought the Omar Mahmoud, in Puntland.* The street was a front in Somalia's ever-changing civil war. Occasional bursts of mortar fire thumped across it.

Piracy, like the civil war, had unfolded from the chaos following the federal government's collapse in 1991. President Siad Barre, Somalia's last dictator, was a figure like Muammar Qaddafi in Libya—nobody liked him, but no one else could hold the nation together. Without a national navy, Somalis couldn't repel trawlers and other industrial ships from Europe and Asia that had started to rob fish from the coastal sea. Some regional leaders in Puntland organized "coast guards" in the 1990s—armed militiamen on speedboats who collected fees from the interlopers. Foreign fishing crews would sit idle for a day or two while a "license fee" was negotiated; the owners would pay (for example) fifty thousand dollars; and the clan leaders would sign a semiofficial "license to fish."

This small-change arrangement flourished for years, until the armed men learned to nab larger vessels. A Somali gang hijacked a gas tanker in 2005 and held it for about two weeks. By 2007 the problem had international dimensions. The bands of gunmen had evolved into ruthless organized-crime networks with little connection to fishing, and powerful bodies like NATO and the EU arranged groups of warships to protect shipping lanes off the coast.

We left the power plant and passed a khat stall. Robed women under an awning gossiped behind tables of the leafy drug—hundreds

---

* Clans in Somalia since the fall of President Siad Barre had reverted to violence along old contested frontiers, and the border between the Galmudug and Puntland states was also the border between two of Somalia's most powerful clans, the Hawiye and the Darod. Sa'ads are a subclan of the Hawiye; the Omar Mahmoud belong to the Darod.

of dollars' worth of it piled up like parsley in a supermarket. "Khat turns Somalis into pirates," Gerlach commented. "Imagine how much an addiction costs. Twenty dollars a day! Most people here don't have that kind of money."

The main khat flight for Galkayo roared low across the rooftops each morning at sunrise. The leaf grows in mountainous parts of Kenya and Ethiopia, so the fresh stuff had to arrive in the flatlands of Somalia by plane.

Our guards, who had just been paid, lined up in front of a pretty young woman wearing a scarlet robe. She had fine brown skin and a quiet smile. She smiled at me, so I said, "*Salaam-alaikum.*"*

She asked the guards if I was married. "No!" I said, and laughed.

The woman went very shy, very modest and still. When we returned to the hotel, both Gerlach and the guards said she "liked" me. It startled me that a Somali woman could be so frank about a stranger in public. The mood in Galkayo seemed weary, sarcastic, suspicious, but also freewheeling. In some ways the country felt hooded with traditional stricture and religion; in other ways it was like the Wild West.

V

Our Hobyo trip stumbled over some organizational delays, and time itself seemed to drag. The city bathed in a strange malarial heat, a near-body-temperature clamminess that made it hard for me to tell in those first few days whether or not I had a fever. Chewing a stem

---

* "Hi."

of khat scattered those sensations. With the mild narcotic in my blood, I felt bright and clear.

I said so to Ashwin.

"It's your imagination," he answered.

From our balcony, I looked down and noticed one of our guards, Mowliid, pacing the road with a machine gun across his shoulders. His bands of ammunition clinked like jewelry.

"What do you think of our guards?" I said to Ashwin.

"We have paid them a lot of money," he said, still deadpan.

But he considered my question, and after a moment he gave a more serious answer.

"To me they seem loyal," he said. "But I do not like our hotel."

Our room had dust-caked electric fans and mosquito-netted beds. The power flickered on and off; so did the water. Ashwin and I had taken to filling plastic bottles with tap water and lining them up next to the tub, in case the water quit when we needed a shower.

I thought about our plans to leave. We still had no plane tickets. "Has Hamid found a flight for you?" I asked.

"He has two possible dates."

Gerlach's assistant, Hamid, would buy our return tickets at a local airline office. He'd carried our passports down the road to make two or three reservations. After we chose our flights, he would return down the road to cancel the others. (Apparently a security measure.) We had intended to fly in and out of Somalia together, but now Ashwin wanted to visit Mogadishu after our trip to Hobyo. This change would revise our schedules—I would return to Nairobi alone. Technically no problem. But every unexpected thing was a source of stress.

We ate lunch on the hotel patio, where local elders had gathered around the tea tables, old men in robes shuffling with brittle grandeur on aluminum walking sticks. The Embassy Hotel was also full of young expatriates, Somalis who spent most of their time in Europe. They had clan relationships to President Alin and held government titles. "You'll find a lot of people who call themselves 'minister' in Somalia," the court interpreter in Hamburg, Abdi Warsame, had told me. "All Somalis think they know how to do things. It's one reason we have endless civil war," he joked. "In Europe and America, society is ranked according to class, whether you know it or not. In Somalia, ten million people think they can be prime minister."

Gerlach was tall, potbellied, and good natured, with glasses and a genial smile. He'd married a German woman during the 1970s and adopted her last name. Pictures from Somalia in those days showed a more free-spirited place, with women shroud-free, smiling, in blouses and slacks. Somalia had developed as a poor but successful African nation during the early years of postcolonial independence, with a socialist economy and decent schools, but anarchy since the end of Siad Barre had shifted the people toward headscarves and automatic weapons. "Sa'ads helped topple him," said Gerlach. "But I am not satisfied with the outcome."

A plump, youngish Somali with a goatee greeted Gerlach and sat down.

"This is Mohamud Awale," Gerlach said. "He is the mayor of Hobyo."

The title surprised us. We were about 125 miles from Hobyo.

"It is an honorary title," he explained. "Normally I live in London."

"It's difficult to work in Hobyo, isn't it?" Ashwin said.

"Yes, I cannot live there," said the mayor. "The Galmudug government has no influence on the coast. We hope to assert control one day. But for now, we can try to help—they have problems with food, the people are hungry in Hobyo. If we just say it is difficult, and stay outside, it is no good."

"Will you come with us to Hobyo tomorrow?" said Ashwin.

"Yes. It is good for me to show my presence."

"What do you do in London?" said Ashwin.

"I am a bus driver."

Hamid settled next to us. He was a thin but rather groovy-looking character with a gray-flecked goatee and a taste for Royal cigarettes and wide-collared shirts. He served as Gerlach's lieutenant on the ground, his sub-fixer in Galkayo. He'd hired our guards, according to Gerlach, with help from a local elder. Now he had surprising news. He said a rumor had gone around that a pirate lord wanted me kidnapped.

"I have heard that Mohamed Garfanji is offering a fifteen-million-dollar reward for you," he said.

I blinked and felt a deep qualm of fear.

"Do you take it seriously?" I asked.

Gerlach and Hamid conferred. Gerlach shook his head. In German, he mentioned the *Gerüchteküche*, the rumor mill (literally, "rumor kitchen"). He said the rumor was probably false. But in a semiliterate society, lies could have the authority of firm fact, and false information ran like fire through Somalia. *"Die Gerüchteküche ist auch gefährlich"* was how he put it. *The rumor kitchen can also be dangerous.*

"Yes, I know."

"We will have to be careful," he said.

I spent the afternoon considering whether to fly home. Flights to Nairobi didn't run every day, so there would be a delay. Canceling the Hobyo trip would also be complicated. Moving around—keeping the pirates guessing—might also be an improvement over waiting in the hotel.

Later, in our room, I talked it over with Ashwin. "Michael," he said. "Listen. I know it is unnerving. But they are trying to scare us. Maybe they want more money. If Garfanji wanted to kidnap you, he could back up a technical right now in front of this hotel and make his demands."

I nodded. A technical was a cannon-mounted flatbed truck, a battlewagon from the Somali civil war.

"We will be fine," said Ashwin.

"Okay."

"Gerlach says if we are kidnapped, it will cause a clan war."

"That's right."

"It is just a rumor about Garfanji."

"Okay."

I nodded again. We were guests of the president, after all.

VI

Hamid and Gerlach doubled the number of guards for our journey to Hobyo, as a precaution. We set out in the warm hours of the morning with three Land Rovers and one technical raising dust across the bush. Our Land Rover rocked violently. Gerlach pointed at the technical in front of us, indicating a pair of Somali words painted on the tailgate: KIBIR JABIYE. "That means 'to bring down the arrogant.' It is an anti–Siad Barre slogan. Technicals were very important in toppling him. Aidid—you know Aidid?"

"Yes."

General Mohamed Farrah Aidid had led the rebellion against Siad Barre. He was the warlord who challenged the U.N. during the Battle of Mogadishu, in 1993.*

---

* Reconstructed in Mark Bowden's book *Black Hawk Down*.

"Aidid was our clan brother," said Gerlach. "During the rebellion, we put this phrase on some of our trucks."

"I see. A famous Sa'ad."

"Yes, yes."

In the film version of *Black Hawk Down*, Aidid is a villain. In this part of the world he was a hero.

We bounced and swayed in single file along the dusty trail. Gerlach, Ashwin, Hamid, and I had crammed into one car. A handful of expatriate Somalis from our hotel filled another. We also traveled with a Sa'ad elder named Digsi, who had real influence in Galmudug, maybe more than President Alin. He was a squat, bean-shaped man with a dusting of white hair around his head and a comical rear-leaning gait. The young expatriates represented the Galmudug government, but for the Hobyo pirates, Digsi, as a clan figure, would have more significance. He would keep the peace.

The Toyota technical bounced and swayed with several armed Somalis on the flatbed, sitting around a swiveling automatic cannon.

"Are they all Sa'ads?" I asked Gerlach.

"Yes."

Our guard from the hotel, Mowliid, had folded up in the rear of the car. He tapped Gerlach on the shoulder.

"Ah," said Gerlach. "He wants you to know that he is a clan brother of K'naan, the rapper from Canada."

"Really?"

I smiled at Mowliid. They talked back and forth in Somali. Our driver flipped the music on his stereo to a K'naan song.

"The driver is also his clan brother," Gerlach said. "K'naan is the other famous Sa'ad."

At the end of our day of driving, the red sun lit up swirls of distant cloud; the white and reddish dust seemed to glow and burn. We halted the caravan of cars in the road and climbed out to stretch.

We were about to drive into Budbud, a village pronounced with curt vowels,* to spend the night with Digsi's relatives.

"We are taking our time to Hobyo," Gerlach explained. "Young Somalis can drive it in four or five hours, along khat trails. But we can't go that fast."

"What are khat trails?"

"To deliver khat. Every day, from Galkayo to Hobyo," said Gerlach. "Very important for the economy."

Budbud was a sparse community of low, poor buildings and quiet wind. Powdery dust caked between the houses in ridges and dunes. "It's almost desert here," said Gerlach. "The edge of the savanna. And the desert grows every year because of the climate."

Our cars pulled up to a pastel-painted concrete house where a crowd of villagers waited. The men wore turbans and sarongs and looked rougher than people in Galkayo. Some had wild facial hair. Elders wore beards tipped with henna dye. They smiled and shook hands with Digsi while Hamid hustled us into the house.

We settled in a dim bedroom, where blue drapes tossed on the breeze at a corner window. Beauty products cluttered a wooden vanity table, and a satin-covered mattress lay on the floor. No other furniture, not even a chair.

"What goes on, in this room?" I heard Ashwin ask Hamid as they sat against a wall, on a patchwork of frayed rugs.

"We are guests of Digsi's sister. It is her room," said Hamid.

"I see."

"The family will slaughter a goat."

The guards settled around us with their weapons. Mowliid,

---

* As in *put*.

draped in ammunition, flipped down the tripod of his machine gun and angled it at the doorway. It was loaded, so as long as he wore the rounds, he was also leashed to the gun. To make himself comfortable, he had to unwrap the bullets from his shoulders and roll them into a pile on the floor.

"For protection?" I said, pointing at the weapon.

He gave me a wide smile. "Against pirates!" he said, and offered me some limp stems of khat.

I shook my head.

The sunset had left a soft, apocalyptic glow in the village outside. People came to stare at us from the doorway, tall young men with ragged beards and turbans, and we heard the voices of women working over a fire.

"Michael," said Mowliid, pointing at one of the bullets in his ammunition band, which looked to be about .30 caliber. "How much for this? Guess."

"How much money? I don't know," I said.

"One dollar!" he said.

"One dollar each?"

He hefted part of the ammunition pile. "All, five hundred dollars," he said. An average year's salary in Somalia was about $550. Mowliid looked proud to walk around with such a fortune on his shoulders.

The sky turned deep blue, and two broad pans of pasta came through the door. Someone handed around a pitcher of water, to wash our hands. Hamid poured hot glasses of tea from a kettle. Gerlach and Digsi squatted with other Somalis around one dish of pasta and started winding it around their fingers.

"There is no silverware, like in Galkayo," Hamid explained. "We are in a village now."

The pans full of spaghetti had been mixed with fried onion

and chunks of boiled goat. We had to grab the chunks of meat with mitts of pasta.

"Spaghetti's a remnant of Italian colonialism?" I said to Gerlach, guessing it wasn't traditional food.

He laughed. "The only good thing they left behind."

We ate from the same pan on the floor. In the half light I noticed something crawl across the pasta. I have a strong stomach, but it was a fat dung beetle.

"Careful," I said and pointed.

Gerlach raised the alarm in Somali, and the pan went to Digsi and quickly out the door. A new pan came in just as quickly. I was done with food for the evening, but Digsi found a choice joint of goat in his pan and made an elaborate production of handing it across the room.

"This is the best part of the goat—the shoulder," Hamid said to me. "It is an honor to eat it."

"*Mahadsanid*," I said in Somali. *Thank you.*

I split open the meat. It was still piping hot. Digsi nodded and smiled, but the way he singled me out as a guest of honor had something theatrical about it that would remain with me for months to come, as if he wanted to show the other men that he was upholding a Somali tradition of kindness to strangers. It was overceremonial, a perfumed gesture, and my instincts reacted: I felt an unexpected dread. After the meal we rinsed our hands in water from the pitcher, and Digsi handed around a squat bottle of bright-purple cologne. All I wanted was a paper towel or something to wipe off the grease, but Digsi smiled and showed me how to rub my hands and arms with the oversweet stuff, as if the eye-watering odor might dispel the grease from the goat and the day of sweaty travel.

VII

A pair of minarets reared up against the sky, and we fishtailed along a powdery trail that Gerlach referred to as "the Pirate Road," running through low scrub toward Hobyo, with an occasional view of the sea. "This connects Harardhere to Eyl," he said, naming two other pirate towns on the central coast. "Hobyo is between them."

I pointed at the technical raising dust in front of our car. The cannon bounced and swayed. "You think we're being watched by drones?"

Gerlach laughed. "Yes, probably."

We ran past a plain but enormous gray mosque. I noticed a pair of figures standing guard on the roof, between the minarets, their faces wrapped like holy fighters. Each held a grenade-mounted rifle. Mowliid, our guard in the rear, said something to Gerlach.

"There is a rumor that hostages are inside," he translated.

"In the mosque?" I looked out the window.

The mosque and the weapons made me think of al-Shabaab, the terrorist group, which had no firm presence in Hobyo.

"In the mosque, or near it," said Gerlach.

"Those guys look like al-Shabaab," I said.

"They must be pirates. But if they have hostages in the mosque, of course they are desecrating it." Gerlach grew agitated at the whole idea. "Pirates," he declared, "are not real Muslims."

Hobyo at first was just a few low buildings, empty sand, and shrubs, until we passed a mansion to our right, surrounded by a stone-and-plaster compound wall. On top of the gate sat an ostentatious decoration, a plaster sculpture of a car like ours, painted in pastels, with LAND CRUISER written underneath. It was a cliché that young Somalis earned expensive cars if they proved themselves as pirates. The message seemed unambiguous: *Get yer Land Cruisers here!* I mentioned it to Gerlach.

"Yes, that house belongs to a famous pirate boss," he said.

"Which one?"

"I don't know."

We drove through the town and out across a soft, broad beach. The crescent of sand had enormous white skiffs with twin engines tilted, at rest, in the lapping surf. This was the Hobyo waterfront.

We stopped near a natural jetty of sharp black rock, and our guards fanned across the beach. Hamid explained the hopeful Sa'ad vision of developing this curving strand into a harbor. The rock jetty, he said, could become Galmudug's first functioning pier.

But it looked impractical precisely because of the rocks. Waves shattered against them; spray dampened our faces. Hobyo felt deserted, and our guards were tense.

"Do you see that ship?" Hamid said.

He pointed across the bend of water at a large wrecked ship leaning on its side.

"It is a Chinese fishing boat," he said. "Pirates hijacked it in 2010. It has been beached for several months."

"Where are the hostages?"

"Somewhere in Hobyo. Maybe near the mosque we passed."

So hostages lived around us, in a parallel world.

"One hostage killed himself," Hamid went on. "A Chinese man."

"How long has the crew been held?"

"About fifteen months."

Pirates were holding hostages for longer stretches of time, clinging to fantasies of spectacular ransoms, but seafarers on most of the ships belonged to a lost underclass. Ashwin made noises of pity. "The Chinese don't rescue," he mumbled, "and they don't pay ransom. They just leave their people to rot."

Digsi picked his way onto the rocks, wrapped in robes, but nimble. He told us in a stream of insistent Somali that the water here was emptier than it used to be. He pointed from one end of the horizon to the other, and Hamid translated. "He says once you could see hijacked ships lined up here from left to right. Now you see nothing."

The German reporter who had traveled with Gerlach in 2011 had filmed hijacked ships at anchor off another town in Galmudug. He'd said, on TV, that the crowded waterline resembled "the Port of Amsterdam." Digsi wanted to express his pride that pirates held so few ships in his region now.

"Just that wrecked ship on the beach," I commented.

"That's right," said Hamid.

Our guards yelled a warning. They wanted us to return to our cars.

"We are being watched by pirates," Hamid announced.

Two cars had emerged from Hobyo to study us from an elevation of sand. We heard a crackle of gunfire. I darted across the beach for cover, but someone else motioned me into the car. The firework noises made my stomach swirl.

Ashwin, Hamid, Gerlach, and I crowded into the Land Rover and Ashwin said, "Michael, they were not shooting in our direction. You can tell from the sound. I have heard a lot of guns in my time. They were firing into the air."

"Okay."

"It sounded like firecrackers," Ashwin said. "When it sounds like that, it is not aimed at you. It is just warning gunfire."

"Okay," I said, and cleared my throat. "Warning about what?"

Gerlach said, "They think we are in Hobyo to free hostages. They believe we're allied with Operation Atalanta," the European Union's naval mission. "We've explained that we're journalists. We're looking for a peaceful solution. But our guards are ready to fight if necessary."

"Okay," I said.

Our guards wandered the beach, cradling their guns. I couldn't tell *who* was looking for a peaceful solution—no one seemed to be on the phone—but after a few minutes the guards looked more at ease, and one by one they folded into our cars.

"We are being allowed to leave the beach," said Gerlach.

Our caravan drove in single file around the outskirts of Hobyo, past sand bluffs and old fence posts. We came near enough to the beached fishing vessel to see its pale-blue keel and its long streaks of rust. It tilted over the sand, on the edge of the surf, and from Ashwin's close-up footage of the hull we could even make out a name, in English and Chinese: the *Shiuh Fu 1*.

We filed into a row of houses on the edge of Hobyo, where a stout, deep-black man with a sarong and a flamboyant turban waited for us to park. Digsi climbed out to shake hands.

"That man is a bandit," mumbled Gerlach, watching them.

"Who is he?" I asked.

"He is our host," Gerlach said. "From the other Sa'ad family.* They have invited us to lunch."

We stepped into a hot room furnished with gold-threaded sofas. Someone had prepared the room for guests. Bottles of water and cheap mango juice waited on a low table, and cardboard Somali flags lay along each couch, spaced evenly. I muffled a sharp sense of en-

---

* The Sa'ad subclan is divided into a number of smaller subclans, or families. Digsi represented the Ali Nimaale. The Hobyo Sa'ads tended to be Ahmed Nimaale, who, according to Gerlach, had strong pirate affiliations.

trapment, a sudden vulnerability out here on the edge of a country where no one could save me if things went wrong. We picked up the flags and sat. Flies buzzed in the hot marine air.

Our flamboyant host introduced himself as Abduelle and claimed to be the mayor of Hobyo. I glanced around for Mohamud Awale, his rival for that title, but he'd disappeared. In expansive gestures and a husky voice this new mayor gave a speech, which Gerlach translated into German: "We would like to welcome our clan brothers as well as our guests from far away. And we would like to plead with outside powers for urgent aid. We need weapons and logistics to fight the pirates here—anything that can help us fight them—and we would like to plead for coordination between our side and Atalanta. Many people in Somalia doubt whether Atalanta can be effective."

This was a polite reference to a Somali belief that international navies protected illegal fishing boats. I had written about this controversy myself; I had even asked President Alin for more evidence (documents, photographs). But firm proof was elusive in Somalia, and Alin had provided us nothing.

"Does he know we're not from Atalanta?" I asked Gerlach.

"I have explained it to him."

"We urgently need support," said Abduelle, "both military and economic. The tsunami in 2004 has destroyed our way of life."

The Indian Ocean tsunami of 2004 had flooded the coast of Somalia and wrecked a terrible number of houses and fishing boats, whole livelihoods. It had also washed ashore tubs of poisonous waste. Ships run by the Italian mob had dumped many of these tubs off the coast.

"We will relay the message," I said.

I asked Gerlach in what sense Abduelle was the mayor of Hobyo, since two men were vying for the job.

"Abduelle is not an official mayor. He does not have the government title," he told me. "But he has the respect and support of the clans here in Hobyo. Above all, he has support from the pirates."

I nodded. "Where's our mayor? Mohamud Awale?"

"His car is making a tour of Hobyo. It's important for him to be seen. He will join us for lunch."

Soon he arrived, seeming clumsy and uncertain compared with the flamboyant Abduelle. Lunch arrived, too. We had endless piles of spaghetti, steaming sweet tea, whole fried mackerel, and slabs of camel meat. Flies, excited by the food, dive-bombed our lips before we could finish chewing. We batted them away with greasy hands or with Somali flags, but they kept at it. One even landed on my eyeball. I remember thinking the flies in Hobyo were as hungry as the people.

Gerlach and Digsi had promised that a pirate would visit for an interview after lunch. For a long time we sat and swatted flies. Abduelle vanished, and poor uncertain Mohamud Awale told me the name of the pirate boss who owned the mansion with the Land Cruiser sculpture over the door.

"His name is Fatxi."

Fatxi, it turned out, had masterminded the capture of the *Shiuh Fu 1*.

And the name of the pirate we were about to meet?

Awale wasn't sure. After another hour, though, a gangling man wearing khakis and a tan collared shirt, his head wrapped in a red-patterned keffiyeh, stepped through the door. We saw no part of his face besides the bloodshot eyes. He called himself "Mustaf Mohammed Sheikh." Ashwin focused his camera and started the interview. Mustaf Mohammed lost no time declaring himself at war with forces of the West. He said that "white people" had attacked Somalia by trawling its coral reefs and dumping poison on its shores. "As soon as they stop leaving poison on our beaches and taking fish from our seas, we will stop hijacking ships," the pirate said.

Some of his complaints were legitimate, but it wasn't rare for a pirate to invoke a cause. Pirates throughout history have piggybacked on social ideals. For example, Klaus Störtebeker, the fourteenth-century German privateer, named his gang of North Sea bandits the "Likedeelers" because they shared their loot and lived by an ethic of cooperation more equitable than the cruel hierarchies of most European ships. The complaints were real, and so was the justice of resistance, but that didn't keep the pirates from murder and rape. What undercut Mustaf Mohammed's speech to us was the sheer number of impoverished sailors captured in Somalia. At the time of our interview more than seven hundred hostages from India, Bangladesh, Iran, Sri Lanka, Thailand, Yemen, and the Philippines were still being held in cruel conditions. The affected shipping companies, too, were a random assortment—sometimes Danish or Greek, sometimes Liberian, Malaysian, Chinese. The profiteering had little to do with complaints against the West. Pirates just caught what they could.

"Can you swim?" Ashwin asked, and the pirate said, through Gerlach's translation, "Yes."

"I have heard that most pirates cannot swim," persisted Ashwin.

"But that's an important skill for any pirate," said Mustaf Mohammed. "Someone who works with us should be able to swim. Where did you get this information?"

We had it from the trial in Hamburg—Ashwin had borrowed it from me. One day in court, a Dutch naval captain had described the arrest and transfer of the captured Somalis to his frigate. A young pirate had tried to escape by jumping off the deck.

"Could he swim?" the judge had asked.

No, said the Dutch captain, but that wasn't unusual. And then he uttered one of the few memorable lines of the long and tedious trial:

"In my experience," the captain said, "most pirates can't swim."

But Mustaf Mohammed lectured us about his pirates' water skills. "Most people understand what it takes to be a pirate. Courage, speed in boarding a ship with a ladder or a rope," he said. "Above all, a strong will. Those are the criteria."

We nodded. It was my turn to ask a question.

"Would it help if there were piers along the shore of Galmudug," I said, "to promote the economy and create jobs? If there were more jobs here, would you stop hijacking ships?"

"When foreigners stop robbing our fish, stop poisoning our water, and leave us in peace, then we will accept limitations. Not before."

"How did your career as a pirate start?" I asked.

"Someone sank my boat," he said. "My brother was killed, all our equipment—our nets and everything—were destroyed. That was the beginning."

"When?"

"Ten years ago."

"Who did it?" I said.

"Denmark. A Danish ship. A trawler."

Warm sunlight stifled the room; flies swirled over the plates of food. The pirate, with his face covered, seeming anxious, fixed me with his unquiet eyes.

"I have a final question," said Ashwin. "Have you ever kidnapped anyone on land?"

"No, we have never kidnapped any innocent person," said Mustaf Mohammed Sheikh. "We would never do such a thing. If we did such things, we might kidnap you now."

"I understand," said Ashwin.

Throughout the conversation, one elder whispered to the pirate, as if to feed him lines. It was odd. When Mustaf Mohammed left—as he'd arrived, still wearing his keffiyeh, in a pall of portentous self-regard—Ashwin asked the elder what he'd whispered. The old man shook his head.

"He says he was not whispering to the pirate," Gerlach translated.

VIII

Abduelle then presented the Galkayo elders with his bill for lunch. He smiled and vanished again like a Cheshire cat. Digsi, the dignified elder, sat on the floor with his back against the couch and passed the bill up to another man with a look of rueful amusement. I watched the piece of paper move from hand to hand. Abduelle's family, the Sa'ads in Hobyo, were sticking it to Gerlach's family, the Sa'ads from Galkayo. Or so it was explained to us. For the lunchtime spread they wanted $620.

It was an exorbitant price in any part of the world, but Ashwin and I had paid Gerlach thousands of dollars to organize these two weeks in Somalia. We knew that disputes over money could lead to kidnappings, so we paid close attention to this controversy. It seemed to fizzle.

The heat and flies continued into the late afternoon; for "safety reasons," we had to wait for the right moment to leave. At last we filed out to the cars and drove north from Hobyo along the Pirate Road. The plan was to spend a night on the coast, at Idaan,* a beach

---

* Pronounced e-DEN.

north of Hobyo, where Digsi and the other Sa'ads wanted to build another pier.

After sundown, we came to a stretch of washboarded mud that rattled under our tires. The caravan slowed. Our driver made a phone call, and three Somalis emerged from bushes along a ridge, holding flashlights. They swung the beams until our cars steered into a narrow gap leading through the ridge and down to a camp on the sand.

This was Idaan. Our shelter consisted of a round, thatched roof with a single fat post for support. We unloaded our bags and made ourselves comfortable. Gerlach settled into a plastic chair to smoke a cigarette. "It would be nice to spend the end of my life here," he said ruefully. "There is an old canning factory up on the cliff. Hamid and I have discussed buying it. If this place was secure, we could turn the factory into a water treatment plant. Somalia will always need bottled water." He sighed. "I would like to retire here."

Even in the dark, I could sense the allure of this wild coast. Idaan had a deep quiet, a spooky sense of wilderness and desolation.

A young woman shuffled up in her robe to unlock a door set into the earthen wall. It flipped up to reveal a little shop, no more than a closet, packed with snacks and drinks. The guards crowded around to buy cigarettes. They'd been here before. Outside our shelter, their boss gave soft-spoken orders. He was a middle-aged man called Nuur, with a gap in his teeth and an open-collared shirt, who smoked constantly. The skeptical look in his eye, the cigarettes, and his rough beard all reminded me of a friend of my parents. It was a strange association to make in the Somali bush, but it clung to me. Denis Lyon—the father of Sonja, my kindergarten romance—had the same gravelly voice and the same gap in his teeth. The association was dreamlike and surreal and had nothing to do with Denis's character, or Nuur's, but once I had made it, I thought about Denis for a long time. He was a hard-bitten but clever engineer, a no-nonsense Lockheed man with a brownish beard who used to smoke like a chimney and chide his children with good-humored authority. In my father's absence friends like him had become distant surrogate fathers, the last men from a certain generation to remember me as a kid.

When the sun rose in the morning, it revealed a wide cove, where a sandstone riverbed led to a freshwater well near the surf. Nomad shepherds moved herds of camels and goats to the well. Gerlach took us for a walk along the beach, and we found a massive industrial waste canister, yellow and almost cube shaped, seven or eight feet tall, sitting in the shore break.

"This washed up in the tsunami," he said. "It is too heavy for anyone to move."

"Where is it from?" I said.

"We don't know."

It looked like radioactive waste canisters I had seen in photographs. Italian journalists had uncovered collusion between 'Ndrangheta Mafia bosses and warlords in Somalia to bury tons of waste in Somali soil—or sink it in the waters offshore—during the nineties. This container was similar. I wondered if it would hamper Gerlach's dream of a water treatment plant.

We left Idaan late in the morning and drove north. Digsi's car ran far ahead of ours. The landscape was still dry and blasted, and after a while it occurred to me that we weren't headed west, toward Galkayo.

"Where are we going?" I asked Gerlach.

"To Garacad."

The next significant pirate town to the north.

"Does Digsi have influence there?" I asked.

"Not really."

One pirate from the Hamburg trial came from Garacad, but we'd ruled it out as a town to visit. Gerlach had declared it too dangerous.

"Why are we going there?" I said.

"Digsi wants you to see the horizon," Gerlach said. "He wants Ashwin to film it."

The elder hoped Ashwin would film the empty sea at the same spot where the German reporter had compared the waterline to Amsterdam's. Sa'ads in Galmudug were solving their problems, Digsi wanted us to know. Pirates weren't flourishing here.

"Ashwin, was this your idea?"

"No."

I didn't like it. We asked the caravan to turn toward home. Gerlach nodded. Our driver cut across hard mud to the west while Digsi's car struggled over some terrain about half a mile ahead. Gerlach dialed Digsi's phone. The normally cheerful elder grew angry. From the other car, he asked us all to stop. We did—a whole line of vehicles stalled in the bush—and Digsi climbed out to argue with Gerlach. They stood under the strengthening sun and bickered in Somali. Hamid translated some of what he heard. "You cannot treat us like children!" Digsi said. His honor had been wounded. Ashwin watched the argument in a sideview mirror.

"He is not letting go," he said.

At last Gerlach came back to our car and sat next to us, looking miffed. He muttered about bowing to an "illiterate" like Digsi. But he'd won the argument, and our caravan continued to Galkayo.

IX

After this trip to the coastal wilds, Galkayo seemed bustling and familiar, less menacing and unpredictable. The fear and tension I had felt in Hobyo resolved into a strange feeling of affection for the dusty crossroads town. Hamid said the Garfanji rumors had fizzled. But Ashwin and I made up our minds to leave, as soon as possible, because of Gerlach's altercation with Digsi.

The families of the arrested pirates in Hamburg lived in North Galkayo. I still wanted to talk to them, though it wasn't clear that a tour of the north would be safe—I would try, but I wasn't about to take any (more) stupid risks. In any case, I would take the next flight to Nairobi. Ashwin was off to Mogadishu, and our flights fell on separate days.

"Mike, how do you feel?" he asked in our room.

"Much better."

"Do you have enough material?"

I said we would have to see how it went in North Galkayo.

"It does not look promising, to be honest. Sometimes you just have to take what you can get," he said.

"I know."

"Well, do you want me to stay until you fly out?" he offered. "Or should I take this flight to Mogadishu tomorrow?"

The Galkayo airport roads could be dangerous. Two Western aid workers, Jessica Buchanan and Poul Thisted, had been kidnapped on one of them several months before. I didn't like the idea of an extra trip through such a bad stretch of dirt. But Ashwin had nothing to do; he wanted to leave.

We talked to Hamid and forged a plan. Hamid knew a man called Robert at the U.N. who could assemble a strong security detail for an excursion through North Galkayo. The next day—January 21, a Saturday—I would accompany Ashwin to the airport, and we could meet Robert there. After Ashwin flew off, we could leave for North Galkayo under U.N. guard. The gunmen would be Darod clan members from Puntland, rather than the Sa'ad guards we'd used until now. It was a reasonable solution. I felt less nervous than before. I even wrote cheerful messages home about the food, the slabs of watermelon and the wild camel meat.

Saturday morning, we woke early and waited for a ride to the airport. Our regular Hobyo guards were supposed to escort us. They failed to show up. After half an hour, Gerlach said, "Now I am starting to worry," and he called President Alin, who sent a white jeep with a single gunman for the airport dash. There was no clear explanation for this switch in security and transportation. I considered staying at the hotel, but the safest place for either of us was wherever Gerlach happened to be. "If you are kidnapped, I will be kidnapped," he had told us more than once. "And if I am kidnapped, there will be war," meaning a flare-up of violence between subclans.

The "airport road" was actually two or three trails winding out of Galkayo through an arid, boulder-littered landscape. The piles of dusty rock were traditional Sufi graves, and they memorialized Galkayo residents killed in the long civil war.

A Somali sat in a chair beside the airport gate, which wasn't a gate but just a rickety steel barrier, a piece of junk in the dust. The Galkayo airport had strict rules against weapons, in this nation lousy with guns, and he demanded our guard's rifle. The airport was still closed, he said. We were too early. After a moment, he accepted a one-dollar bribe to move the piece of junk and let us park beside the terminal.

The chalk-white building had the lassitude of a lonely bus terminal, and it was, in fact, closed tight. The rising sun cast a fresh young light across the airstrip, and a patio had a number of plastic chairs and some words painted on the wall suggesting that a shuttered window might open soon for refreshments. When it did, we bought glasses of tea.

Other Somalis came to settle in chairs and wait. Hamid's phone rang. Robert, the U.N. man, had bad news.

"He says his security team will not make the appointment," said Hamid.

"Let me talk to him."

Robert, who spoke European-accented English, sounded gentle and concerned. He had to apologize—his security team had an urgent job somewhere else. He'd been doing Hamid a favor. He wasn't contracted to help.

"We won't make it to North Galkayo today," I told Hamid. "We can't do it with the security we have."

"Maybe tomorrow," he agreed and lit a cigarette.

The tense prospect of a visit to North Galkayo had eased, but now we had just a single guard, in the president's jeep, for the trip back to our hotel. I blinked away a bad intuition and took a sip of tea.

Hamid asked for my email address. I gave him a card from *Spiegel Online*. He read my name out loud, and a fat young Somali at a neighboring table glanced over.

"You are Michael Scott Moore?"

"Yes."

"I have seen you on the internet," he said. "You are famous."

I wrinkled my forehead.

"No, I'm not."

Alarm bells should have been ringing in my head—whispers had swept the rumor kitchen. I felt a mild wash of dread from this weird conversation; but by now it was far too late.

Ashwin's plane landed, after a long delay, and we shook hands with him on a square of tarmac beside the airstrip. We started back to our hotel in President Alin's car. It was midday, and the sun glared on the rocky graves. Other cars wound behind us. But soon our driver slowed and made a careful remark in Somali.

"Technical," Gerlach translated. "We don't know what kind."

I didn't see it at first. The battlewagon stood to the left of the road, loaded with drowsy-looking men.

"Can we just drive on?" I said.

Gerlach said, "It is one of ours."

I saw the words KIBIR JABIYE on the technical and felt a moment of relief. A car honked. The technical jerked to life. I had not flown to Somalia to test my nerve against the worst fears of a foreign correspondent—I didn't want to tempt death—but I had broken one of the cardinal rules of anyone who pokes around in troublesome parts of the world, which is to keep your family's lives unaffected. The horror of crossing that line wasn't evident to me when the technical approached the car, with its cannon aimed through our windshield. It wasn't even clear when a dozen or so men jumped off, holding weapons. It wasn't clear, because my brain recoiled in denial. I told myself it was a traffic stop. These armed clan soldiers just wanted to see my passport. No problem! My German passport was here in my bag. I had never witnessed denial working in my own head with so much specific clarity, but it moved like a gyroscope compensating for a drastic blow that hadn't even arrived, to maintain some balance, and when the gunmen swarmed to my side of the car and fired into the air, the balance wobbled and my bowels twisted and I understood very well what the fuck was going on. I leaned against Gerlach to cover my face with one arm, as if that would help. When I turned out to be alive in spite of the thunder of gunfire I held the door closed with my right hand. They wrenched it open and pounded my wrist with their Kalashnikovs. I had never felt so much violent malice at such close range, and I kept pulling at the door, hoping to buy time while our guard in the front seat performed his job. I was confused by the number of men who kept pounding my wrist with their gun barrels. I felt bones crack, I let go of the door, and they pulled me into the dust outside and beat me on the head.

Maybe death arrives with the same sudden malice, the same transformative shock. I noticed a lack of gunfire from our guard. He must have quailed at the sight of the cannon. "Somebody help me!" I shouted while the men slugged my face and broke my glasses in the dust. "Somebody *help* me." Of course nobody did. Somalis in the cars behind us, respectful of the violence, just watched. Gunmen pulled at my arms and ripped my shirt. I heard Gerlach shout. I couldn't tell whether kidnappers had subdued him in the car or pulled him into the road, whether this abduction was about to spark a clan war—I was only aware of gunmen, shouted Somali, and white dust. I struggled. The kidnappers pulled my backpack away, and I noticed blood on my clothes from the gun muzzles clobbering my scalp. My wrist ached, and I tried to see faces, to recognize any of the kidnappers from our Hobyo guards, but in the blur of kicks and rifle blows nobody looked familiar.

The horror of crossing that bright, clear line drenched me like a cloudburst, like blood and sweat, and I wanted to rewind everything. While they dragged me away, I felt a reflexive horror for my family and the burden I was about to become.

The men bundled me into a waiting Land Cruiser and drove me to a house on the edge of Galkayo. One of them handed my backpack to a tall and furious-looking man in the driveway. He took the bag but waved us off. We sped away to the east, and I sat with ripped clothes and a bleeding scalp, squeezed by three gunmen, bouncing across the bush, for several hours.

"Okay, okay," the pirates in the front seat said. "No problem."

The car bounced brutally over a ledge, so my head hit the roof and left a bloodstain on the fabric.

"Fuck!" I said, and pointed at the blood, cradling the broken wrist in my lap.

At first I spoke mainly in obscenities.

"Okay, okay," they said.

Part 2

UNDERWORLD

Near sundown we arrived at an outdoor camp in a reddish, sandy part of the bush. The pirates walked me to a foam mattress waiting at the foot of a squat and crumbling cliff. My torn shirt dangled from me like a scarecrow's. I was half-blind and still delirious, but I could make out other Somali gunmen, and other hostages.

The sun sank behind us. We had driven from that direction, which meant Galkayo lay to the west. We hadn't shifted very far north or south, from what I could tell in the car. So, by a rough guess, we were in northeastern Galmudug. Sa'ad territory.

"Okay, Michael?" one guard said.

This earnest young Somali wore a turban around his head and stood on a rise, with his Kalashnikov, and the marbled sky behind him had thin swirls of reddish cloud.

"No," I said after a while.

I squinted at each guard to see if I recognized anyone from our hired team. They weren't the same men. But if they were Sa'ad pirates, it didn't matter. My hosts had betrayed me. Sa'ads had promised to protect me; a Sa'ad, somewhere, had turned.

The men from the Land Cruiser mingled with the other guards. One sloped around with an ammunition vest dangling from his shoulders. His face looked half-melted with anger; he had rotten teeth and stained-looking eyes. The others called him "Ahmed Dirie."*

---

* Pronounced *Ach-med Dir-i-ye.*

Another name I heard over and over was "Abdinuur," normally pronounced with an exclamation point: *Abdinuur!*

My body felt battered and tense, but for some reason I thought about my backpack. I was still fresh enough as a hostage to care about my things, like a man who'd lost his head and wanted to put it back on.

"They took my bag," I told the young guard. "Can you ask someone for my bag? It's a maroon backpack. With a camera in it."

"They steal your camera?"

"Yes."

"Thieves!" he blurted.

I looked at him curiously.

One very dark, very thin Somali came to squat near me with a bottle of water, a can of tuna, and two narrow loaves of bread. I tried to eat. I noticed dried blood on my hands and shirt; there must have been blood in my hair. My wrist throbbed, and when I inspected it, tenderly, I felt pieces of bone moving around.

The watchful silence in the camp made an eerie counterpoint to my ferocious instinct to be free. My still-intact sense of self— the energetic part that identified with possessions, habits, achievements, needs—protested in panic. *You can't do this,* it wanted to say. But of course they could.

The sun set. Everything blurred without my glasses, and after an hour we all sat around in the pitch black, wholly blind, at the base of our sandstone cliff, which sometimes dropped bits of sand on our shoulders. I continued to sit straight up on my mattress, blinking. The pirates wanted me to sleep. One of them, on my left, lanced a flashlight beam into my eyes. He expected me to lie back so he could have a conversation with Ahmed Dirie, on my right.

"Sleeping! Sleeping!" he said, and in the dark I offered him a middle finger.

If I'm in the way, I thought, *you can damn well set me free.*

This part of the bush was arid savanna, a parching transition zone between the ocean and the Ogaden Desert, which stretched north and west into Ethiopia. The landscape had a blanket of hush. But the deep peace of the countryside felt as harrowing as my capture: the pure distance from my family, the stir of commotion this crime would cause at home—in Los Angeles and among my friends in Berlin—set up a quiet, drumming dread. Now I belonged to an underworld of captives who radiated rumors, like the whispers of ghosts, into the more ordinary world. I wondered if Ashwin had called anyone. If Gerlach was free and alive, he would have called Ashwin by now in Mogadishu, and Ashwin had my mother's number in California.

Had Gerlach been captured? Or Hamid?

Was there some kind of war now between subclans of Sa'ads?

Or had my fixers sold me out?

Somehow I must have slept. After the sun rose in the morning, the pirates stuffed me into the rear seat of a car next to a pair of other hostages, both in their sixties. One looked African, but the other was hard to make out. He had cocoa-colored skin and twin furzes of gray hair sticking out over his ears, like a Pacific Islander. This was Rolly Tambara. We were about to become excellent friends.

Armed pirates crammed in beside us and tied our arms together. Ahmed Dirie gave orders from the passenger seat. His melted-seeming face and rotten teeth were heavy with melancholic rage. The car was the same as yesterday's, I noticed. It had the bloodstain from my scalp.

After half an hour of cruising and swaying along the Pirate Road, a second car overtook us. We stopped in the soft white sand. The pirates said, "Go, go, go, go," expecting us to cram into the second car. The orders confused us. A tall Somali from the other car, who had an authoritative squint and wore a half-buttoned dress shirt, hollered, "Come on, come on," as if we weren't moving fast enough. While I ducked into the other car he hit me hard alongside the head.

"No!" he said, as if I had misbehaved. "No, no!"

"Fucking hell," I said.

This man appeared at our window and said to me, in clear English, "We know about your activities as a journalist, but it is okay, if you can pay the ransom, you will go free."

Then he climbed into the first Land Cruiser and sped off.

We continued south for almost an hour but finally steered into the walled compound of some filthy, decrepit house, where the pirates led the two hostages through a doorway and hustled me into the neighboring room. Bare, blue-painted concrete; shuttered windows.

I sat on the floor. Hard to tell where we were. This house lay on the edge of the first town we had met coming south along the Pirate Road, either Hobyo or Harardhere. (Some of the guards had yelled, "Harardhere!" into their phones.) I squinted and tried to bring the yard into focus. At least twenty Somalis lazed on the sunlit concrete with their Kalashnikov rifles and tripoded machine guns, chewing khat.

Flies flurried near my doorway.

Judging by the flies, I thought, we were in Hobyo.

Ahmed Dirie dumped my mattress on the floor. Other Somalis carried in a tall thermos of tea and a few cans of tuna. One handed me a packet of instant coffee and a small plastic strainer. "*Caffè!*" he said with a smile. His enthusiasm was infectious—I love coffee— but he mimed pouring the tea through the strainer, which made no sense. At home, I had a cheap espresso machine that coughed and gasped and filled my kitchen with the smell of steam-pressed coffee

every morning. I was a snob about it. Otherwise I led an unostenta-
tious life—no car, simple furniture, no TV—and, of course, when
I traveled, I could tolerate all kinds of thin and miserable, warmed-
over *jus de chaussette*.* But at home I drank good coffee. I missed it in
Somalia, not from my first day in the country, but from my first day
as a hostage.

Another pirate slid a bowl of cooked brown beans onto the floor
of my room. I was hungry but still nauseated by the new conditions.
Someone handed me a spoon. I ate in silence, flicking away flies.

The yard outside my door included a round concrete well and a
number of dusty tires. The steam rising from my pot of food seemed
to distill an odor of shit or stagnant water that permeated the compound. The beans must have been cooked with well water. This idea
churned my stomach, and after a few bites I retched and puked on
the steps.

"Problem!" the pirates said.

They had trouble finding a rag to clean the mess; they shouted
and scowled. Flashlight Man gaped at me from the yard, the way a
zoo visitor might watch a dromedary. I hoped he understood that
the vomit had been a commentary on my new status as a hostage as
well as a criticism of the food.

After an hour, a smooth-looking man came in, wearing slacks.
He introduced himself as a translator. I learned later that his name
was Boodiin, but he never said so. Instead he offered warnings and
condescending wisdom. I had made a mistake, he said. Mistakes
were human. I should not open the windows. An armed guard waited
outside every wall. "If you open a window," he said, "you will die."

"Hmm."

---

* Sock juice.

"You must eat," he advised me. "If you don't eat, you will die."

"The food is disgusting."

"What would you like to eat for breakfast?"

"I don't know," I said. "Maybe oatmeal."

"You must eat."

He had a lean face with busy eyes. His loose Western clothes gave him status compared with the guards, who wore a slouching, half-traditional uniform of sleeveless T-shirts and skirtlike sarongs. Boodiin was about thirty but hard to pin down. He seemed nervous and twitchy.

By now I had tied a sling around my wrist made from a piece of cloth, which he noticed with some concern.

"What is wrong with your hand?"

"It's broken," I said. "The wrist is broken. I need a doctor."

"You mean it was broken in this operation?" he said, gesturing vaguely out the door.

No, motherfucker, I'm in the habit of walking around Somalia with a broken wrist.

"Yes" is how I chose to phrase it.

"I will submit your request."

II

It was an interesting sentiment to hear from a man who stood to grow rich on my ransom. *You have made a mistake*, he said. *Mistakes are human.*

Clearly I had fucked up, but from Boodiin's point of view, what could have been my mistake? He must have meant journalism, nosing around in a pirate gang's business. But Sa'ad pirates had little to do with the *Taipan*. Most of the pirates in Hamburg were Darod, from Puntland, rivals to my supposed hosts. I hadn't even made it to North Galkayo to research that part of the story. So, I thought—squinting out at the shadows of Somalis chewing khat in the yard—what had I done to threaten these men?

Boodiin referred to a "bad group," meaning the men who'd kidnapped me. He insisted that the guards holding me now were the "good group," as if I ought to be nice to them. In spite of my blurred eyesight, I could spot at least one of my captors lazing in the yard. The slouching, rage-addled Somali called Ahmed Dirie relaxed in a yellow sarong next to a tripoded machine gun.

I scowled at Boodiin. He wasn't even a good liar.

"What's your name?" I said.

"Ali."

But the real Ali, the Ali who mattered, was Ali Duulaay,* who'd slugged me on the Pirate Road. I learned his name later. He paid two visits to the house, and at first I recognized him only as a tall and menacing figure who stood, like a taciturn soldier, in the bright doorway and came in to ask questions in slow and broken English. He was middle aged and well built. He wore khakis and collared shirts as well as his Kalashnikov. He squatted in front of my mattress on the first visit and inspected my swollen wrist.

His mind moved to other things. "You are German?"

"My German passport was in my bag," I said. "You have my bag."

I thought he might be the man who'd received my backpack in front of the house in Galkayo. If I wanted my things, maybe he was the man to ask. I copped a sudden attitude with Ali Duulaay, an air of ownership and expectation at odds with my new role.

---

* Pronounced *Du-LYE*.

"You took my backpack," I babbled. "Someone has my backpack. Bring it here. It has phone numbers. I need to make a telephone call. Someone should bring my backpack here, with all my notebooks. They have phone numbers, that kind of thing."

He stared at me with hard, unblinking eyes.

"You are also American."

"I'm a *German citizen*," I insisted.

He stood up to leave.

"I will send a doctor."

I'd left my U.S. passport in Nairobi, along with a laptop and other important things. I had not wanted to alarm Galmudug officials with an American passport when I landed in Galkayo—I'd wanted to pass as European. But Duulaay could have googled my name, and if news outlets had reported my kidnapping, he could have read every word.

You have made a mistake, Boodiin had said. *Mistakes are human.*

The guards handed me toothpaste, a towel, shampoo, and an assortment of mango drinks, as well as some plastic-wrapped shirts and shorts. They ordered me to change out of my bloodied clothes, the old long-sleeved shirt and cotton slacks, which were torn but still comfortable, so tossing them into a pile for the pirates to dispose of raised feelings of panic and loss. There was nothing *wrong* with my previous clothes. There was nothing *wrong* with my previous life. The sense of waste was sickening. The new clothes felt too tight.

I changed awkwardly, gingerly, without the benefit of a button-down shirt. I stuffed my wrist through a tight polyester sleeve. The guards watched me dress. Then one of them ordered me out to the shower.

"Now? I just put this on."

"Now, now. Come on."

"Can't it wait?"

"Go, go, go, go."

So, at gunpoint, holding a new bottle of shampoo, I picked my way across the filthy compound yard. The pirates watched me with curious loathing. The shower was just a walled-off corner, open to the sky, with a pit toilet. One gunman handed a jerry can full of water past the sagging metal door.

While he waited, I undressed and threw the fresh clothes across the top of the dusty wall, which had ornamented breeze-blocks I could squint through. I saw the blur of an unpaved road and a few distant, impressionistic white houses. (Beyond a couple of yards, without my glasses, everything looked like Monet.) Also bushes and a seaside horizon. Robed women and goats wandered along the road.

None of it helped orient me; none of it told me where to run.

I used my left arm to lift the jerry can and dump water on my head. Probably well water—I tried to avoid my face. I lathered everything with shampoo and rinsed myself in careful slops. It was a nice evening, I noticed. The sun was going down, and in the distance I heard Somali children sing.

III

From such a remote corner of the world, I found it hard to imagine what my mom in California had learned, or how she'd learned it. But the chain of information was swift. Gerlach had called Ashwin, who had called U.S. and German authorities from Mogadishu, and FBI headquarters in Washington had mustered five agents in southwestern L.A. County within twelve hours of my capture.

My mother was seventy-two at the time, spry, with glasses and a sweet, beaming smile, and her retirement was less than relaxing, as far as I could tell from Berlin. She kept up a bruising schedule of tennis and golf. Her first name, Marlis, was a German contraction of "Maria Elisabeth," and her last name, Saunders, had changed with her second marriage. Her husband, Lou, had retired from an aerospace firm called TRW (later absorbed by Northrop Grumman). They lived in a town house in a suburban grid built in the fifties and sixties to shelter TRW engineers and middle managers. The sprawling, sun-beaten beach cities of Los Angeles had grown rich since the seventies; but my mother's condominium was stuck in time.

She had been sitting and reading a newspaper at home when five people in suits climbed out of a nondescript American sedan by the curb. The strangers roused her curiosity. It was about noon on a winter Saturday, and on Saturdays, in Redondo Beach, people didn't walk around in suits.

Family friends were due at the door any minute. She was looking forward to lunch at a Mexican restaurant. Through a window she saw the five suits clustered on the porch, and she opened up. One of them flashed a badge.

"Mrs. Saunders?"

"Yes?"

"When I saw their badges," she said later, "my heart just dropped. It was the worst day of my life."

The FBI investigates any major crime against an American, at home or overseas. The German Bundeskriminalamt, or BKA, also investigates crimes against Germans. So agents from the BKA appeared at my uncle's door in Cologne. More BKA agents went to the *Spiegel* office in Berlin. FBI agents also visited the Pulitzer Center, in Washington, D.C., and in every case they gave instructions on how to react. "Basically they told us how to keep calm in case a pirate put you on the phone and threatened to cut your fingers off," said Charles Hawley, a colleague and friend at *Spiegel Online*.

Mom's town house became a hive of federal activity. The agents wanted to know about my trip, about Ashwin and Gerlach, about my acquaintances and friends. They wanted to tap the landline. They told Mom what to say in case a pirate called. They tried to ease her mind by saying my kidnappers just wanted cash, not a dead hostage. Mom spent the afternoon in a blurred state of shock. "Their Black-Berrys were going like crazy," she remembered. "I had no idea so many federal agents lived around here."

Meanwhile, her friends arrived for lunch. A crowd of Germans and Americans from my parents' distant past descended on the condominium from various parts of L.A. "Denis and Sylvia and Hilde arrived, and they were all shocked," my mother said. "They didn't even come in the house."

Hilde was a friend of the family; Denis Lyon was the bearded and gravel-voiced man who'd been on my mind in Idaan. It surprised his wife, Sylvia, to see Mom at the door with a tear-strained face. "Your mother came to the door and told us what happened," she said. "Then two FBI agents came to the door and said, 'We'd prefer if you didn't come in right now.'

"And Denis said, 'We better go outside.'"

I hadn't seen Denis or Sylvia, or any of our old friends, in years. They belonged to my earliest memories. Nevertheless, it strikes me as a weird coincidence that Denis had a peripheral presence around my kidnapping in both parts of the world, not just on my mind in Somalia but in front of my mother's door. "My dad was extremely concerned about you and devoured every piece of information he could find," said his daughter, Sonja, much later. "We talked about you often, and one of the many times when I asked him what could be done to get you out, he simply said, 'I don't have an answer for that, kid. Michael is stuck between a rock and a hard place.'"

IV

The next morning, at the filthy house, I noticed a difference in my inventory of things. Someone had delivered a case of bottled water and a tub of dry oatmeal. But a bottle of mango juice was missing. While I sat up on my mattress and thought about how to eat the oatmeal, a furtive pirate squinted into my room.

"*Wuuriyaa!*" he said. "Mango!"

"Hmm?"

"Give me mango."

"Why?"

"Mango, mango."

One of the drinks was an oversweet mango soda, which looked unpleasant, so I handed it over. The man disappeared without a word. I felt affronted: Why would a pirate bum a drink? The pirates *gave* me drinks. I had no source for food or drink besides pirates.

Another hostage came out of the next-door room and went to the toilet. I caught him speaking a broken, maritime-sounding English. He still had twin furzes of hair over his ears; the guards found him comical and called him "Lorry." He asked for a haircut, and when I caught a glimpse of him again, he had short-clipped hair and looked almost dapper.

The maritime sound of his English made me think he was a merchant sailor, or else raised on some island with a British colonial past, or both. He ducked into his room without glancing at me. I sat on my mattress and started to crave both coffee and oatmeal. But when I bothered a pirate for boiled water, he didn't seem to understand.

"*Caffè!*" he said with enthusiasm and pointed at my thermos.

I shook my head. The thermos was full of tea.

Evidently I was a stupid hostage. The guard stalked over to open a packet of instant coffee and dump the black dust into my plastic strainer. He motioned for me to hold it over my cup, then poured hot tea through. The resulting liquid was muddy, cloying, molasses-like, but heavily caffeinated.

"That is disgusting," I declared.

"*Caffè!*" insisted the Somali.

"It is not."

I sat there with my weird beverage and reflected on the continuing problem of oatmeal. I didn't want it cooked with water from the well, but if I could coax a guard to boil some bottled water, we might get somewhere.

Flashlight Man strolled into my room and opened the rusted shutters on the window Boodiin had ordered me not to open. I cringed and waited for gunfire. Instead, a lively conversation developed between the pirate and the guard outside.

The window itself had no glass, I noticed, but a fixed, florid-looking metal screen. Inconvenient for escapes.

When the conversation ended, Flashlight Man left the shutters open, as if he'd never heard of Boodiin's order to keep them closed, and on his way out the door he stooped to pick up my canister of oatmeal.

"Hey!" I said, and my raised voice upset the Somalis.

"What is the problem?" one of them said.

Sudden outrage stiffened the hairs on my neck. "That guy stole my oatmeal."

The Somali smiled sympathetically, as if I had again failed to understand.

"Oatmeal should be in the kitchen," he said. "Is better that way."

"Why?"

No one could answer my question. I thought the paradox was clear. The pirates *gave* me the fucking oatmeal. Why would one of them steal it? The calamity of my abduction on a remote edge of the world expressed itself in minor irritations, and *A pirate stole my oatmeal* became an obsessive chant in my head.

A pirate stole my oatmeal. A pirate stole my oatmeal.

That evening, Ahmed Dirie came into the room with a plastic-wrapped mosquito tent, which the boss must have ordered, to keep me malaria-free. The net baffled Ahmed Dirie. I had the dubious pleasure of watching him and one other Somali pull out the flexible sectioned tent posts, assemble them, try to stuff the lances through the loops in the net, and fail. Ahmed Dirie and the other guards were too looped on khat by this point in the day, or just too thick, to perform such a delicate operation. They left the net in a pile. One of the rods had broken, and eventually someone cleared it away.

You have made a mistake, Boodiin had said. *Mistakes are human.*

A pirate stole my oatmeal.

I spent three or four days in this anxious and stricken and irritated state before Boodiin escorted a new man in, hours after sundown—an unarmed older Somali with a small, peppery beard and a patient, intelligent manner.

"He is a doctor," Boodiin said.

By the dismal light of a fluorescent lantern, I unwrapped my improvised sling. My wrist had swollen. I could still feel shifting, clacking scraps of bone. The doctor's eyes moved from Boodiin to me to Ahmed Dirie, who stood in the door. He was a different sort of person from the pirates—a man with a conscience, to judge from his harrowed face—and he seemed uncertain, if not afraid.

"It is not broken," he said after a brief examination. "It is only cracked, and it will heal in three weeks."

From a bag of utensils he produced a splint made of bamboo strips and faded purple cloth. He sewed it onto my wrist with a needle, biting the thread to cut it free. I appreciated the handiwork, though it seemed like a lot of painstaking effort for a treatment that would help so little. I was in no position to argue, but my wrist was broken.

I fell asleep with the splinted wrist across my chest. I woke up again in the dark to the clang of the compound door. A car pulled in and rumbled. Much later I would get used to a pattern of switching houses at night, but I understood without being told that an engine idling in darkness was a bad omen. My heart began to pound. Soon the men hustled me into the crowded Land Cruiser, where only one other hostage—"Lorry"—sat watching the young pirates with a grandfatherly look of disgust. Ahmed Dirie sat in the passenger seat and grinned. Other pirates squeezed in around us with their weapons, acting panicky, and before the sun rose, we drove far into the bush, without any clear destination.

When the sun was high, Ahmed Dirie pointed at the sky and spoke to me in rapid Somali. They were upset about a plane, or something in the air.

"Are you a Marine general?" Ahmed Dirie's driver suddenly demanded.

"What? No."

"Colonel?"

"No."

Whatever had happened, they held me accountable. They thought

I was U.S. military. Full of panicked emotion they told me something urgent in Somali, sprinkled with incomprehensible English.

"Helicopters!" Ahmed Dirie said. "American!"

All I understood was that a dozen people had died in some distant place.

"Oh boy," I said. "Boom-boom? Fighting?"

"Yes!"

U.S. forces rarely operated inside Somalia. Ever since the Battle of Mogadishu, the military had kept ground missions here to a minimum. I shrugged and figured the pirates were just repeating a crazy rumor. The excitement subsided, and we drove at random across the desert bush for the rest of the morning, sometimes, for some reason, in circles.

V

Four days after my capture a posse of American helicopters rescued the two kidnapped aid workers, Jessica Buchanan and Poul Thisted, from a bush camp south of Galkayo. They were sleeping in the open, surrounded by Somali foot soldiers. A team of Navy SEALs parachuted some distance from the camp and marched up quietly with rifles. They shot nine sleeping guards and hustled Buchanan and Thisted away to a helicopter.

That evening, my mother watched a State of the Union address on TV. Cameras showed President Obama's entourage entering the House chamber. "Obama marched in," said Mom, "and as usual he shook everybody's hand. He came to Leon Panetta," who was secretary of defense. "The camera was focused on them, and usually they don't record any of the conversations, but when he came to Leon Panetta, he stopped and said, 'Good job tonight.' He kept shaking his hand and said, 'Really good job tonight.' Nobody knew what that was about. But the next morning, it came out that Buchanan was rescued." The leap of hope my mother felt at the news wilted into disappointment that I wasn't among the rescued hostages. Her circle of golf and tennis friends—athletic Republican ladies, dry-humored retirees—wondered out loud whether the SEALs would do it again. "My friends all called," Mom said, "and they told me, 'If anything happens to Michael, it's going to be Obama's fault!'"

The rescue came early in the morning on January 25, 2012. FBI agents assigned to my case discussed it with Mom, but only in general terms. "They never said it, but I think rescuing you was always in their sights," she said. "Of course, it had to go through the White House. No one could orchestrate a rescue without Obama's okay."

Thisted was Danish; Buchanan was American. They'd both worked in the calm northern province of Somaliland for the Danish Demining Group, a European nonprofit dedicated to pulling up live mines. I'd learned little else before I went to Somalia—why they went to Galmudug, exactly who had captured them—and as a hostage I heard nothing about their rescue right away. All I knew in Somalia was that America's military presence on the Horn of Africa had less to do with pirates than with tracking al-Shabaab. The Buchanan rescue was therefore a promising sign. It showed that Obama would send a team to Somalia for a humble pirate hostage, even with European powers involved. It showed leadership. "The United States will not tolerate the abduction of our people," Obama said after his State of the Union address. "We will spare no effort to secure the safety of our citizens, and to bring their captors to justice."

VI

My fellow hostage had small eyes and a bald pate over his trimmed hedge of gray hair. His skin was coffee brown, rather than black, and I still couldn't place his nationality, although I learned his full name, Rolly Tambara. Every time I asked where he came from, he lifted a knotty, twisted finger to his lips. I gathered that he and his now-missing friend were seafarers, but the vessel he named, the *Aride*, left me clueless.

Around sundown that evening, we found an empty spot on the savanna to meet a second car, which delivered piles of khat and plastic bags full of cooked pasta. The pirates laid a mat in the dust beside our Land Cruiser. We were supposed to relax. But my wrist hurt, and I had no idea where we were headed. All I wanted to do was get there. I still lived in a world of logic and purpose and resolve, and I hadn't figured out how much pointlessness a hostage has to put up with.

The hard and dusty savanna stretched in every direction—we saw nothing taller than white thornbushes and windswept acacias— but the sun went down in magnificent silence, infesting the whole lunar landscape with a soft red glow.

"Where's your friend?" I mumbled to Rolly.

He shrugged. "I not know. They leave him behind."

"In the house?"

"Yah."

Now his accent sounded French. I asked another question, but Rolly raised his finger. Wrong time to talk.

After sunset, we piled into the Land Cruiser again and set off into wooded highlands. The car pounded and rocked on the trail— for several hours—and we had to listen to Somali folk music blaring on the stereo. It had a stark, twanging, mournful sound I might have enjoyed in different circumstances. For now it was the sound of oppression.

In the dark wooded hills, we sometimes came to a steel bar blocking the road, a gate of some kind, so the driver had to lean on the horn until a group of graceful women in robes emerged to open the gate and sweep away dust in front of us with hand brooms. It felt dreamlike and strange, since women were already so rare; this world of khat-chewing pirates was almost entirely male.

At last we came to a ridge road overlooking a valley. Gunfire flashed and boomed in the distance. We slowed until a car overtook us, and soon Ali Duulaay leaned in to glare through a window with his flashlight and give terse orders in Somali. Rolly and I had to get out and walk through a nearby thicket of thornbushes. "Where we going?" demanded Rolly, because no one seemed to have the slightest idea. Ahmed Dirie just muttered, "Go, go, go, go," and later I would refer to these bushes as "the Garden of Pointless Torture."

At the exit to the Garden, our car waited for us. We climbed in, bleeding slightly. Duulaay appeared with two gunmen to deal some more abuse. He ordered Ahmed Dirie to step out, and between the vehicles he hollered and beat Ahmed Dirie with a stick. His henchmen blasted two deafening, flashing rounds into the air, and we saw Ahmed Dirie's form buckle between the cars. He panted in pain while Duulaay ordered us to step outside. He examined our faces using the flashlight. He must not have liked the look on mine, because with no explanation he clubbed the side of my head with his fist and my eyes bloomed with floating light.

"Motherfucker," I hissed.

Duulaay, satisfied, climbed into our car with his men and drove off.

The pirates forced us to march down a bluff along a cliffside trail. Pale moonlight revealed some kind of wooded valley, but we stopped at a shallow cave in the cliff wall, where two men dropped our foam mattresses. My ear still rang from the blow, and I must have shivered from the damp, or from raw nerves, because a skinny, gentle Somali said, "Michael. No sleep?"

"No blanket," I explained.

He happened to be wearing a leather bomber jacket. He slipped out of it in the dark and let me sleep in it. I don't know how I lost consciousness that night, after such a long and evil day; but I didn't open my eyes again until a warm light had started to creep across the valley.

VII

Rolly, flat on his back, was awake. When I sat up he said, "What's the matter."

"I have to go to the bathroom."

"Piss?" he said kindly. "Or shit?"

"Piss."

"Is called '*kadi*.'" He addressed the guards. "Hey!" He pointed at me. "*Kadi, kadi.*"

One of the guards led me up a narrow trail to a pile of trash, gestured at it, and wandered a little farther to post himself with his Kalashnikov and gaze across the valley. We stood on a crumbling bluff that overlooked a gorge in the dry savanna, filled with dusty trees.

Two pirates carried our mattresses down the hill and we followed, picking our way through green bushes and white thorn branches. We settled under a bower of trees at the bottom of the valley, and the pirates made a production of filling in gaps around us with white thorn brambles. "*Qorrax!*" they said, and pointed at the sun, as if they wanted us to be comfortable and cool. But no sun streamed in from that direction. It crossed my mind that the obsession with shade—as well as all the hysterical driving around—owed itself to a fear of drones.

The skinny pirate didn't ask for his coat back. I fingered the sleeve. Not bad quality. The leather was soft, the elastic cuffs were thick and firm.

"Ah, Angelo give you this jacket?" said Rolly.

"Who?"

"That Somali, An-*gel*-o," he said, pronouncing the name for me.* "I see he give you this jacket last night. He give you food that day you arrive," he added. "In the desert." I must have looked confused. "We send over the tuna and bread. Angelo bring it for you."

"Oh."

"He's a good man, eh?"

Pirates had captured Rolly and his friend Marc Songoire three months earlier, in November 2011, about fifty miles from Mahé, the main island of the Seychelles. They were cleaning fish in Rolly's boat by night when a skiff approached under a crackle of gunfire. The Seychelles are African islands, scattered around the Indian Ocean north of Madagascar, and Mahé lies more than eight hundred miles from Somalia. (Their trip to Hobyo, at gunpoint, took seven days.) But the pirates thought Rolly was too light skinned to be African. "Seychelles, you know, is many islands," he said. "We are mixed, mixed, mixed. Me, I am part Chinese."

The looniness of the pirates still astounded him. They had read the rear of his little boat—ARIDE, PORT VICTORIA—and put the letters together in some dyslexic way that led them to accuse Rolly

---

* Angelo isn't a Somali name, but Rolly called him that, and it seemed to work.

of being Australian. Maybe they thought an Australian hostage could bring higher ransom. One pirate liked this idea so much that he aimed a rifle at Marc's chest on the boat and ordered him to make an out-loud declaration, demanding to hear that Rolly was indeed Australian. But Marc spoke only Seychellois Creole. He said nothing. The pirate took it for insolence and pulled the trigger. The detonation of a blank charge in his AK-47 left the old fisherman quivering for the rest of the day.

"After," said Rolly, "when they bring us to Somalia, you know, they torture him."

"What?"

"Yah! Marc, when they ask him to call his family, he not understand. The pirates, they take the battery cables from my boat. They use generator. They put cables"—he patted each arm to show where they had clamped the cables—"and they electrocute him like that."

I winced.

"At first he cannot eat." Marc had lost the use of his arms.

"So I have to take his fork and feed him, like a child."

A dread settled on my chest and wouldn't move. "Jesus," I said.

"These men are crazy," he said with a shrug. "We are like the devil, they are like God, Michael. You can't tell them nothing."

VIII

Our dusty valley, with its proliferation of bushes and trees, was unusual in the blasted landscape of central Somalia because it had leaf and shade. It sustained thousands of little creatures, and I could spend a diverting hour defending my mattress from lines of ants, persistent spiders, and curious black-and-red beetles. Wasplike insects the size of a fist went motoring on dry wings between the sun-shot trees. And I noticed a weird shimmering call on the brushy slopes that seemed indistinguishable from a horse's whinny. It moved here and there in absolute silence, without the violent rustle a horse would make.

"Is that some kind of bird?" I asked Rolly.

He listened.

"Is a *corbeau*," he said.

"It sounded like a disembodied horse."

I started to imagine these equine-voiced vultures flapping in silence, like spirits, from tree to tree.

Somalis came down a slope of the valley on the second morning with cases of bottled water and mango juice, boxes of spaghetti, canned tuna, powdered milk, three brands of cookies, a sack of rice, a sack of beans, a sack of flour, and—crucially—toilet paper.

"A truck arrive, eh?" said Rolly.

"Up on the bluff." I nodded.

For lunch we ate tuna with bread rolls called "roti." The rolls were short loaves, like soft baguettes, not like Indian roti, which is a flatbread. But it was interesting that Somalis had borrowed an Indian word. The word *shaah*,* for their all-important tea, also pointed across the water, toward Urdu or Arabic. The country was Muslim because of old trade links to Arab cultures to the north (across the Gulf of Aden), to Sudan in the west (beyond Ethiopia), and to the Mughal Empire, far across the sea. Gerlach liked to say Somalia wasn't African but "oriental." Of course it was both. On our way to Hobyo we had seen squat and ragged pyramids in the bush, uncovered by the Indian Ocean tsunami eight years before: Gerlach had

---

* Pronounced *sheh*.

said they were ancient remains of colonization by Egyptian pharaohs.

A large, blustery pirate named Abdinasser, with broad sloping shoulders and an eager smile, started to use the word "sahib" with me in the first few days of my captivity. "*Aniga, adiga,*" he said, pointing at himself and me in turn, "*SAHIB!*"

To me *sahib* also sounded Indian, and in South Asia it implied a colonial relationship, but Somalis used it to refer to a relationship of equals. That meaning was closer to the original Arabic—the first sahibs were companions of Mohammed—and pirates used the word among themselves.

Abdinasser's voice was chesty and high, not booming as you'd expect from such a barrel-shaped man. Unlike the other pirates he never said bitter or sarcastic things. For my shower that afternoon he brought us two heavy, one-and-a-half-liter bottles of clean water. Afterward he handed us freshening products like skin moisturizer and purple cologne. I thought they were effeminate things to see in a bush camp, so I pointed to a female model on Abdinasser's moisturizer bottle and teased him.

"For women only, sahib," I said. "Not for men."

"*Haa*, yes," he said with an enormous smile, "SAHIB!"

Abdinasser proved hard to embarrass. Most pirates were touchy and proud, but he harbored none of their grim suspicion. From then on we called each other nothing but sahib.

The next morning at breakfast, he saved us from an awkward impasse when I complained about the coffee, the vile tea-and-Nescafé mixture, which Rolly didn't like, either. "*Shaah-caffè,*" I said to the pirates, trying out my grasp of the language. "No good."

My noncaptive self was still intact, and I asked for simple boiled water to mix with our satchels of instant coffee, as if decent coffee were a basic necessity, some kind of human right. The guards listened in bewilderment. The atmosphere grew tense. ("Not make them angry, Michael," muttered Rolly.) At last Abdinasser said, "*Haa*, yes!" and boiled a kettle of fresh bottled water.

The pirates watched us make instant coffee with hot water and powdered milk, then gave our innovative beverage a name:

"Water-*caffè*!"

"*Haa*, water-*caffè*," I said.

We were learning to communicate.

IX

Rolly and I talked in short bursts under the canopy of leaves, and during our silences my mind seemed to flip through pages of memory like a film. The impulse to study the past reminded me of those supposed moments before you die—"life passing before your eyes"—except that my sense of urgency just went on and on. During my first week of captivity I was tense and afraid for my life, so I called up the past like a man dying in slow motion.

First I remembered Berlin. At breakfast I liked to sit in the kitchen window of my apartment and look at the massive, waving trees at the corner of Helmholtzplatz, a park where a nineteenth-century streetlamp stood next to an odd, Space Age plastic street clock. I missed having a soft-boiled egg with my coffee and listening to the BBC. I'd never been rich, but in the Somali wilderness the coffee, the radio, and the egg felt like impossible luxuries.

I thought about the words on the rear of the technical, KIBIR JABIYE—"To bring down the arrogant"—and wondered if the same technical had accompanied us out to the coast. Most likely. I had not acted arrogant or overweening in Galkayo, but to the Somalis

I was a white man, a symbol of colonialism and latter-day wars. It had been arrogant to think I could come to Somalia and expect to be treated as anything else.

You have made a mistake, Boodiin had said. *Mistakes are human.*

I started to think back years, rather than weeks or months, to find out where I'd gone wrong. Maybe it was normal to gnash my teeth and rake the past for answers; it certainly wasn't rational. But camping in the woods like this reminded me of a summer when my parents and I drove up Pacific Coast Highway and stopped at Big Sur, by a freshwater stream, close enough to the ocean to smell salt among the redwoods and pines. In those days the name Big Sur had a countercultural flair; my only experience of it was trout fishing with Dad and burning some roasted marshmallows. Now I missed the whole thing with every fiber of my heart: the salty Pacific and the campground dust and the rich, vanilla-tinged odor of the California forest.

During that road trip, Dad was drinking hard. Mom exiled him on some nights to sleep outside. I noticed the friction only when I stepped out in the morning to use the campground toilets and saw Dad wrapped in a dark-blue sleeping bag, covered in dew, beside the wheels of the van. It always happened in silence—this tension between them smoldered but never flared into the open. Somehow Mom kept in good humor and excellent maternal form throughout this shambling trip, as if the family weren't under threat.

I had no brothers or sisters, so the hopes of my parents had settled on my unsuspecting head like a heap of wet hay. Growing up means leaving certain expectations behind, along with received ideas from your childhood; on the other hand, they stick to you. Back then I wanted to be an astronaut or a doctor. I could have *been* a doctor—I could have trained for any profession at all. Instead I had to be a writer.

"Michael," said Abdinasser, my sahib, holding out a handful of khat. "Sahib."

"No."

"Cigarette?" said another pirate.

It was a game for the pirates to find out what the hostages would consume. Out of boredom I took a cigarette. The pirate handed me a lighter. Oddly enough it had a cheap photo of the Lorelei, a rock formation on the Rhine River near Koblenz. My parents had met in that part of the world.

"Thanks," I said.

I remembered photos of my father from that era showing a more suave and self-controlled man than the one I remembered. A snapshot from the early sixties showed him wearing a trim black suit, with polished shoes, next to a new white Volkswagen, pinching a slim cigarette. In those days he worked with Denis Lyon. They might have traveled together to the Koblenz office. I had time to imagine them seeing the Rhine Valley for the first time, on a smoke-filled train. "That's the Lorelei," Denis might have said, gazing out the window at some cliffs beside the river, and he would have explained the legend of a beautiful siren singing river navigators to their doom.

Dad was smart but indifferently educated; he'd spent a semester at MIT in the fifties and finished his training in the Navy. "I guess I thought the sirens were Greek," I imagined him saying, and Denis would have coughed out a dry, sarcastic laugh.

"Well, I think this one's a blonde, Bert."

They had belonged to the hard-drinking culture of aerospace in the sixties, practical but hell-raising men who remembered childhoods during World War II. The global reach of the United States, with its satellites and fighter planes, was a project they supported. For them it belonged to the natural order after 1945: America's newfound significance after Hitler's defeat was a sensible counterweight to Communism. Mom in those days had a generous, marquee-worthy smile, and my parents were sleek and fashionable, annoyed and bewildered by sixties counterculture. If drugs and alcohol infected our household in Northridge, misgivings about the American imperium never did.

I spent hours, eventually days, rebuilding chapters of my family's past. Everything flowed like an underground stream. The strange association with Nuur, the gap-toothed security chief, cast me back to scenes I could remember with Denis and scenes I had to invent. Aerospace used to infuse life in Southern California, and I remembered the tone of that world, the banalities and the international glamour, and I remembered Denis and Sylvia sitting on our concrete patio in Northridge, after family dinners, smoking cigarettes and speaking German. The women spoke it with uncommon grace; the men sounded more like drill sergeants from *Gomer Pyle*. They sat for hours on dry Los Angeles evenings with glasses of wine and flickering citronella candles. It was easy to reject the American suburbs, easy to disregard the whole military-industrial complex for its weapons and its habits of war, but the keenest emotion I felt now was a profound sense of failure, not just for the catastrophe of getting kidnapped but for a sense of spiritual waste: for *not having loved everyone enough.*

I was at the rough edge of what I thought would be a foreshortened life, and the memories amounted to a frenetic and subconscious groping around for the person I had been, since I couldn't accept the label "hostage" and didn't yet know what it meant.

X

The next morning we woke up to find a pirate squatting near our beds, his head wrapped in a turban. He was tall and fine featured, and he watched us in the gray dawn with a long mistrustful stare. No one prepared food, not even a thermos of tea. For breakfast Rolly and I shared a packet of cookies.

"Who is that man?" I mumbled to Rolly, nodding at the lean, unsmiling guard. "I don't think I've seen him before."

Rolly had. "Angelo say he Ali's brother," he said.

He'd replaced Ahmed Dirie, who had disappeared after his beating. Too injured by the boss to continue as group leader, apparently.

Khat arrived in the early afternoon, and Rolly made fun of it. Every day, he put on a grinning, grandfatherly act for the ritual arrival of the drug. "Tchat!" he said to Angelo. "Tchat!" he said to a guard named Hersi. "Tchat!" he said to Abdinasser the Sahib.

They all lifted their thumbs.

"Why do you say 'tchat' instead of 'khat'?" I said.

"Is their word, Michael. Is what the Somalis say."

That was true. Our pirates all softened the first consonant and said "tchat." A regional difference. But Rolly had never heard it pronounced another way.

"Do you have 'tchat' in the Seychelles?" I teased him.

"Oh no, Michael."

Rolly watched them unwrap their bundles of leaf.

"They no feed us," he observed, "but they buy this fucking tchat."

Ali's Brother ordered Rolly to his feet in the midafternoon and marched him across the valley and up the hill. I didn't know what was going on, but Abdinasser, my sahib, made a telephone gesture with his hand.

Rolly returned after half an hour, seeming despondent. The pirates' demand was still outrageous, he said, and his family in the Seychelles held out little hope. "The pirates say if they do not get money in twenty-four hours, I will starve," he said in a hoarse and quiet voice. "My son-in-law not know what to say. He tell me, 'Papa, God will take you up to him. God will accept you.'"

Ali's Brother stood in front of us.

"Come on," he said to me.

We climbed the hill. On the grass-grown bluff I saw a Land Cruiser, a fire pit, and several more armed Somalis. A pair of men sat cross-legged under an acacia, and I recognized one as Ali Duulaay, holding a pistol in his lap. The other was a plump and fleshy man with a high voice, who called himself Omar. He spoke decent English.

"We will have to call your family," he said, fingering a mobile phone.

"I don't have much family," I said.

"Your wife?"

"I am divorced."

"Your father?"

"My father died when I was young."

"What about your mother? You will need to ask for a ransom of twenty million dollars."

My heart sank like a bag of sand. A demand of twenty million was pathological. I must have given a desolate smirk.

"Do not laugh!" shouted Omar, and Ali Duulaay raised his pistol, threatening to beat me. "It is not a joke! We have information that you are a spy!"

"I am not a spy."

"Tell them not to listen for your voice!" Omar pointed at the clouds and added, as if to clarify this mysterious demand, "Tell them not to listen with planes! Tell them we need twenty million!"

"My mother doesn't have twenty million dollars," I said. "Nobody has that."

"If she does not send the money in twenty-four hours, we will stop giving you food and water! You must tell her that. Your treatment until now has been good. Tell her that! But if she does not pay in twenty-four hours, you will starve."

I said nothing.

"And tell her to deliver a message to President Obama: If someone tries to rescue you, you will be shot! Tell President Obama!"

"We don't know President Obama."

"Your mother will tell him! It is not a joke! Many Somalis were killed last week in a rescue. This man lost his brother!"

Duulaay, looking crazed, aimed his pistol at my face and shook it. I'd never stared down the borehole of a firearm before. My heart vibrated, and the dark notion that he might pull the trigger—that I might just see a muzzle flash and flop over in the dust—infected me with a heavy, unusual calm. I wanted to leap and run, but that would have been stupid. I had to sit and accept the prospect of a sudden death. Omar held out his hand to quell Duulaay, and I blinked, half-surprised in a rush of adrenaline that I hadn't been shot dead.

"What happened in the raid?" I managed to ask.

"Thirteen people were killed."

"Including hostages?"

"Yes."

Nausea rose in me. Omar handed me his phone, but I choked on the idea of tapping my mother's number into it. The proper place to call was the Pulitzer Center on Crisis Reporting.

"Can't you bring my backpack?" I said. "The pirates took it. A maroon backpack, with my camera. All my phone numbers—"

"We don't have it."

"You must have it. Who else would have it?"

"We must make a phone call."

I squinted around the bluff. Half a dozen Somalis paced here and there with rifles. The angle of the Land Cruiser indicated the direction of the road. But escape was impossible for now.

I sighed and dialed the number.

Omar took the phone, and when somebody answered, he said, "Hold on please for the hostage." I said, "Hello?" and heard my mother ask, in a sane and sensible voice, for the name of my childhood cat.

Someone had prepared her for the call. I repeated what Omar had said about the president. "The men here say I'll be shot if there's a rescue attempt. They mentioned something about a rescue the other day?"

"Oh, yes, the rescue!" she said, and from her tone I thought something had gone right. There must have been headlines, TV reports. But I decided not to upset the pirates by asking for details.

"Mom, they want twenty million dollars."

She seemed short of breath. "Where are we going to get twenty million dollars?"

Good question. I had no kidnapping insurance. My application for coverage had been rejected in the weeks before we left. Independent journalists were often turned down; but now I was boiling in hell for my decision not to call off the entire trip.

I delivered a veiled message to Suzy, my ex-girlfriend in Berlin and an author. "Tell her, 'Three books to Judith.'"

"Which books?" Mom said.

"Suzy will understand."

I wanted Suzy to send two manuscripts and a book proposal to her agent in London. *Sell the books*, I thought—*let me help raise the money*. Of course, raising millions of dollars with a book, even three books, was a joke. But the prospect of tangling up my family with these nasty criminals made my stomach swim.

"I'm also supposed to tell you that I won't get any food if you don't send money now," I said. "They'll stop my water and food in twenty-four hours."

The apparent high stakes of this call summoned so much adrenaline that knowing what to say was impossible. She had handwritten notes beside the bed, a list of things to ask; but notes were flimsy preparation for a conversation with pirates. "Whenever a phone call came in like that, my brain just went in circles," she said later. To me, her questions sounded cool minded and calm—the FBI had coached her well—but her thinking blurred on the phone, and so did mine. Later she couldn't even remember the pirates' promise to let me starve. "I was probably in shock," she said.

After the call, I clambered down the slope again with Ali's Brother. The silence on the camp, in the slanting late-afternoon light, felt eerie. Rolly had nothing to eat. He lay on his mattress and sipped bottled water.

"How much they want for you?" he asked.

"Twenty million."

"Yah, me too."

I couldn't believe that. "Really?"

"Yah! Twenty million! For me and Marc."

"Ten million each. Jesus."

"Your family can pay?" he said.

"Not even close, Rolly."

"Is too much," he agreed, with a grave expression. "You know how much is twenty million in my country?"

"I can take a guess," I said.

He creased his forehead while he made the calculations. "Is a *lot* of money. You can buy house, you can buy car . . ."

I chuckled. "A pretty nice car."

We wondered if the pirates would feed us. We felt taut with hunger. I thought about my phone call, about the shock of mortality in front of Duulaay's weapon and the ranting of Omar. *We have information that you are a spy.* Was that what Boodiin had meant by "mistake," back in town? Did he consider me a spy? Had a rumor burned through the savanna that I worked for NATO, or Atalanta, and could this misunderstanding be corrected? Or was I giving the laws of this underworld too much credit for logic?

In the distance we heard the sound of a tool, of metal and earth, like a spade slicing the ground. A breeze stirred the branches, and the horselike vultures whinnied somewhere on the slope.

Rolly rubbed his face with one hand.

"Ah, Michael," he mumbled. "Why you come to this bad place?"

"I can't remember," I said.

Part 3

LIVING IN CIVILIZATION
KEEPS US CIVILIZED

I

Two nights after the phone call I drifted half-awake in the moon-light because the Somalis were shuffling and gathering up clothes and guns. I tried to sleep again, but Ali's Brother ordered us up. "*Go, go, go, go.* Come on."

I stood and settled my wrist in the sling. Pirates picked up our mattresses and wandered down the valley. "Where are we going?" I said, and when I missed my cue to walk, Ali's Brother hit me in the face.

"What the fuck was that for?"

The Somalis said, "*Shhhhh,*" and someone shoved me. "Go, go, go."

We pushed through switch-like tree branches and thornbushes until somebody discovered a high shelf of dirt overhung by low trees. One pirate climbed up a face of rock and soil and ordered us to follow.

"You want me to climb that?" I said.

"*Haa.*" Yes.

"My wrist is broken."

"Go, go, go, go."

The wall stood eight or ten feet high. We clambered up on roots and rocks to a natural, hollowed-out thicket. Our mattresses were handed up, and someone folded them into this hollow and spread them on the ground.

"Okay, Michael?" one of the pirates said, pointing into our new home through the thorns.

"No."

The pirates bedded down outside the thicket. It was like a slumber party. For a while we heard no other noise besides a strange, trilling chorus of nighttime creatures in the valley, a million unseen insects and birds offering thin rills of song to the desert sky.

I couldn't sleep. My face still stung from the blow, and soon we had to listen to a handful of our captors whispering *"Allahu akbar"* and genuflecting in their cotton sarongs. Until then I had never seen a pirate pray. I had believed the conventional wisdom that pirates were un-Islamic, irreligious, so listening to the prayer boiled my blood.

Rationally, of course, I knew that wondering how a pirate could justify himself to God was as ridiculous as asking a Mafia hit man why he went to church. But imagining these contradictions in a stranger is different from experiencing them as a captive. The idea that a pirate could pretend to holiness, would even pray at the site of such a naked crime, opened a ferocious channel of rage.

I remembered what Gerlach had said in the car when we drove past the mosque in Hobyo: "Pirates are not real Muslims." I also remembered my visit to Djibouti in 2009, when I spent four days on the frigate *Gediz*, where an officer had said the same thing. The *Gediz* was a Turkish warship in the NATO fleet, charged with capturing stray pirates in the Gulf of Aden, and during our brief September voyage, the high-wind summer monsoon had just ended, so "pirate season" was about to start. "But it's Ramadan now," our minder, Yaşar, had said. "It might be quieter for this reason."

Yaşar had moody eyes and an appealingly awkward, earnest manner. Another journalist on board asked if Ramadan would be a motivation for pirates. "I've heard they like to go out during Ramadan," he said, "because if they die, the rewards for jihad are double."

Yaşar shook his head. Pirates were infidels, in his opinion as an observant Muslim: "They are thieves." He gave us his line of argument by quoting a story from the hadith, a body of traditional stories about Mohammed. "When he was coming from a war, Mohammed told his followers, 'We have just come from the lesser jihad. Now it is time for the greater jihad.' That means the inner struggle—the struggle against yourself, your feelings," said Yaşar. Theft was a selfish temptation for every true Muslim to resist. "So I don't think the pirates can do this for jihad. If they say they do, they have misused the word."

I liked Yaşar immensely, and most Muslims I knew held the same commonsense ideas. What he'd said about Ramadan, though, implied that pirates observed it. I had this epiphany rather late, lying in the dark next to Rolly. I'd been so quick to agree with Yaşar on the *Gediz* that I had missed the more important idea. Pirates—who rode diesel-powered skiffs to hijack massive cargo vessels, who didn't mind notoriety as thieves in the international press—fasted for Ramadan.

Understanding this required some background. Yaşar couldn't represent Islam as a whole, because nobody could; the religion has never had a pope.* By saying pirates weren't religious, Yaşar and Gerlach had both engaged in *takfir*, the rejection of one Muslim by another.

Like most Somalis, though, my guards were Sufi. They were also Sunni as opposed to Shiite.† (Sufism coexists with either denomination.) Many orthodox Muslims rejected the old, sometimes quirky, highly mutable traditions of Sufism, but Sufism had followers around

---

* Caliphs had similar authority as territorial religious monarchs, but there were too many of them—and each had less influence than a single pope.

† Later I noticed that my pirates hated Shiites almost as much as they hated Jews, never having met members of either group.

the world, even in places—like Somalia—where people often didn't bother with the word. In many regions Islam had expanded precisely because Sufis could tolerate the absorption of odd, provincial, non-Islamic beliefs. Ryszard Kapuscinski's neat distinction between two kinds of Islam would have categorized average Somalis as "people of the road and of the bazaar" and lined up Sufism with an Islam of sea travelers and businessmen. Ordinary Somalis listened to music on their phones, smoked cigarettes, and chewed khat. They venerated their ancestors. They had integrated their ancient clan structures into a Sufi cult of genealogies and saints.

For Sunni fundamentalists, though, music and cigarettes were religious infractions, and sainthood and ancestor veneration were deep heresies. A rift between Sufism and fundamentalism partly explained Somalia's ever-shifting civil war. The Wahhabi jihadists in al-Shabaab had declared regular Somalis, like my pirates, impure, and some of our guards would later boast about their battles with Shabaab elsewhere in Galmudug. As a foreign journalist in another setting, I would have wanted Sufis like these gunmen on my side.

But whenever I thought about "pirates," part of my brain wiped the religious dimension away. Until this rage-filled moment in the bush I had thought of Somali pirates as lapsed Sufis by definition, indifferent and godless, not the sort of men who would pray in the wilderness at night.

Of course I knew about Sufi "whirling dervishes" in Turkey, I knew about the Sufism of hippies—I had even read Robert Graves's mysterious assertion that Sufism was older than Islam itself. He'd called Sufism "an ancient spiritual freemasonry whose origins have never been traced or dated. . . . If [some Sufis] call Islam the 'shell' of Sufism, this is because they believe Sufism to be the secret teaching within all religions." It all seemed wonderfully strange and enlightened. The Sufi poet Rumi, in his famous *Masnavi* epic, wrote that "thousands of hidden kings" were exalted by the love of God, and by "kings" he meant the unknown dead as well as King David, Jesus, and Mohammed:

I swear by those made of pure light from Him,
*Such men are fish which in His ocean swim.**

But Rumi's graceful verse was light-years from our camp in that dry and desolate valley, and it would be months before I understood what was going on.

II
_____

In the morning the camp was silent, but I had to pee. We'd slept under a thick, sideways-growing tree with sharp thorns and loose, fibrous bark. A sandstone boulder leaned over our feet. Stiffly, carefully, I arranged my wrist in the sling and crawled through a gap in the thicket of thorns. Outside our rustic prison I saw a half-dozen Somalis cocooned in their own sarongs, lying on dirty mats.

They used the word *ma'awiis* for "sarong," and now I saw that the thin skirts could serve as sleeping bags in the bush as well as traditional dress. They were just long tubes of cloth, imported, usually, from Indonesia. They kept off the damp.

One cocoon stirred. A thin effeminate Somali named Abdul lifted his head.

"*Kadi*," I announced.

_____

* *The Masnavi: Book Two*, translated by Jawid Mojaddedi.

He waved his hand in the direction we had come, down the wall of rock and dirt. We were stuffed in a corner of the wooded valley, which wasn't a single long cleft in the savanna but a system of overgrown crevasses that were probably dry riverbeds, or wadis. Our crevasse had a sloping gravel bottom and some tall outcroppings of sandstone. The whole valley, I thought, might flood in a heavy rain.

I found a private place to pee behind an outcropping, beyond Abdul's line of vision, which must have annoyed him. I squinted along the wadi and saw our path from the previous night. A thick fallen log lay across the trail. If I wanted to, I thought, I could run out in that direction—I did have shoes on—but where to? The guards might hear my footsteps, or catch sight of me clambering over the log. They might also be good trackers. A young Somali in Galkayo had told me a story of a girl who ran into the bush to escape her family before they could subject her to the ritual of womanhood referred to as "female circumcision," which is not circumcision but the bloody removal of the clitoris using broken glass or a razor blade. "Her people were nomads," the Somali had said with a shrug. "They can track animals for days. Of course they found her."

I returned to camp. Angelo crawled into our thicket and sat politely on the ground with his rifle. He guarded us in silence for a while, until Rolly thought to ask, "Angelo, why we move last night?"

Angelo pointed at the sky, mimicked the flight of an aircraft with his hand, and used an LED on his cigarette lighter to flash the ground.

"Aeroplane?" I said. "Or helicopter?"

Angelo nodded vaguely.

"Helicopter here? Or out there?" I said, and waved into the uncertain distance.

He imitated the wave.

"Hmm," I said.

Angelo sat with his limbs folded like a wooden marionette's, half shading his eyes with one hand, out of shyness or contrition. I couldn't tell if he meant that someone had attempted a rescue or that surveillance planes had buzzed the camp. But I felt a charge of sudden, irrational hope.

Our first few days in this camp were quiet, though the pirates claimed we were surrounded by al-Shabaab. When a car arrived with provisions, Ahmed Dirie came down the slope looking sweaty and excited from a difficult drive. He chattered, and somebody translated. Al-Shabaab had stopped the car at a roadblock, he said. The gunmen had detained Ahmed Dirie and his driver, tied their hands behind their backs, and shot the driver—a man we'd met, called Muse—in the head. For some reason they hadn't shot Ahmed Dirie.

"Why?" I asked.

"Al-Shabaab!"

There was no other explanation. At first I felt queasy about the death of someone I knew. Then I wondered if the story was meant to frighten us.

Abdinasser the Sahib carried down a load of cooked pasta in plastic shopping bags, shouted, "SAHIB!" and plopped one bag in front of us on the dirt. "*Baasto!*" he added.* The spaghetti was mixed with onion and boiled goat, somehow still warm. Rolly and I had forks, but no bowls. We had to take bites, one at a time, straight from the dusty bag.

Abdinasser also brought us a much-needed nail clipper. After lunch I tried it out, and the first thing I noticed about this item was the dullness of the blades. They chewed, more than clipped. I sat on a boulder near the edge of our dirt platform, aiming the fragments

---

* "Pasta!"

of nail into a trench of bushes and rocks. This process took a while. My position left me exposed to the sky.

Ali's Brother stood outside our thicket and said, "Michael."

I decided to ignore him.

"Michael," he said again, and I started to feel annoyed. Did he really want me to move? Why couldn't I sit on a rock?

I went on chewing at my nails and noticed an odd faint sound, an uneven buzz in the sky. Ali's Brother crawled into our hollow. He gazed with dead eyes and gave me a direct order in Somali. I knew what he wanted; but the mechanical noise was distant enough to ignore.

He snapped a twig from the overhead tree and started to whip my arm, the way a nomad might whip cattle.

"No, don't hit me," I said in a loud voice. He kept at it, so I shouted, *"Don't fucking hit me! What is this man doing?"* and the other Somalis scolded him through the thicket. He shoved me toward the mattress and I yelled another protest. By now the overhead noise was undeniable, and my heart beat with excitement.

"Shhh!" said the pirates.

The plane seemed to move in long, lowering circles over the valley. I listened to the propellers and imagined a fat long-distance Orion,* something like the plane that had filmed the *Taipan* pirates from seven miles off. We'd camped in this valley for almost a week without hearing a passenger plane, so a commercial flight path was out of the question.

I said something out loud to Rolly, but the Somalis hissed, and Rolly held up a knotty finger. "Not make them angry, Michael." The idea that someone knew enough about our location to send an Orion

---

* Built by Lockheed.

gave me a thrill of terror and hope. Angelo's gossip about a plane, like the talk of a rescue during my phone call, was enough to raise the proposition that another raid might target us.

The corkscrew traced by the plane seemed to rise again. We couldn't tell if it had spotted our camp. It never flew straight overhead. A real spy mission could have watched us from several miles off, well out of sight, which meant that if we could hear the plane, someone *wanted* us to hear the plane, unless it had just wandered into range by accident, like a lumbering bear.

At last the sound grew faint again and vanished. Our guards sat around in unmistakable terror.

"They scared, eh?" said Rolly. "They think that plane come for you."

I smiled for the first time in several days.

"I think maybe it did."

III

While Rolly and I tried to sleep that night, we heard a passionate argument among the guards about a *"helikopter"* and a *"telefon,"* and I started to wonder if the hostage rescue Mom had mentioned bore some relation to my capture. The pirates had stolen my smartphone, among other things in my backpack. Ashwin would have provided the number to both Washington and Berlin. The raid had targeted the other hostages, obviously—I couldn't imagine SEALs moving in on a camp that wasn't well known to American surveillance—but suppose they had some reason to think I was there, too? Suppose my phone had found its way to that camp? Suppose a pirate had turned it on?

My heart thumped. If the hostages were dead, I would have their lives on my conscience.

Two days later another car arrived, and a number of new Somalis hiked down to the camp. They brought a watermelon, more vanilla cookies, and a live goat, which Angelo slaughtered on the bluff. Our camp also gained a new boss. Ali's Brother disappeared, and a quirky and gentle new Somali stayed behind. Mohammed Tahliil had a shy, snaggletoothed smile and a furze of almost Ethiopian-looking hair. He seemed at first like a low-ranking man, a cook, because he was so diligent about building a fire and providing us rice and tea. Unlike the others, he seemed to enjoy his work.

"We call this a 'cat' in the Seychelles," said Rolly.

"What do you mean?" I said.

"A man like that, who work in the kitchen."

The next morning, a Somali dropped something rectangular at my knees, a wallet-like case. "Okay, boss," he said and added two packs of batteries. From the furtive way he behaved I knew to keep it quiet from the other pirates. Rolly noticed and said, "Ah, you get a radio?"

"Shhh," I whispered. "We can listen to the news."

Reception was terrible. But I found English lessons in Chinese, news in Somali, something in Arabic, and a keening, lonely call to prayer. With difficulty, I stumbled across a station with officious British voices.

"Holy shit."

"What you got?" mumbled Rolly.

"It's the BBC World Service."

After two weeks in the wilderness, the World Service felt like a miracle. I stood up to ask Tahliil for "water-*caffè*." By the time another news bulletin came around, in half an hour, I could sit on a boulder, in the cold morning sun, with a glass mug of instant coffee in one hand and the murmuring, staticky radio to my ear, feeling almost human. All I needed was a boiled egg.

We listened for news about Somalia; instead we learned about a hurricane off Madagascar, a sinking Italian cruise ship, and Syria's deepening civil war.

"I work on a cruise ship like that," Rolly said after a while.

"Really?" I said. "Where?"

And he was off—Rolly's term of relative silence had ended. Between spurts of news on the BBC, I learned all about his previous life. In the eighties he had worked as a steward on a Greek cruise line, sailing the Mediterranean from Italy to Israel. He mentioned passengers who tipped well, and passengers who didn't. (After two and a half decades, those details remained in his mind.) He also told a good story about a forced-air heater in a hotel room in Greece. "I put this electric heater on. And the stove, you know, it was gas—you can make your tea on this stove. But it leak. And me, I don't smell this gas."

His room had a sliding glass door overlooking an Athens street. When he turned on the heater, it ignited the leaking gas and forced a tremendous plume of flame through the door.

"Mi-*chael!*" said Rolly, squeezing his eyes at the memory. "That glass shatter! Thank God, nobody was in the road. The man there, the manager, he say it cost three thousand drachma to fix. I give him four thousand. Is not a lot of money. But he say, 'Not talk about this to your wife.'"

He acted roosterish about his early career as a fisherman and a laborer in the 1960s, when he went skin diving for sea cucumbers and sea turtles. His job on the cruise line represented an international phase, when he saw the world and earned a good salary. His wife had worked as a housecleaner in the Middle East during the same period, and they traveled back and forth—a season in the Seychelles, a season abroad. But after several years they settled in Mahé for good. Rolly grew out of his life as an employee when a son-in-law, named Dylan, purchased the *Aride*, a yellow fishing cruiser with a sleeping cabin and four fixed drop lines. For the first time in his life, he ran his own show. Long experience of the Seychelles' reefs and shoals made him a good skipper. He sailed out for days at a time. "Other fishermen, they follow me," he boasted. "Because in the harbor, they see I come in with a lotta fish."

"What do you catch?"

"Red snapper, island snapper, like that."

But now the *Aride* was gone. He thought about it every day. They'd neglected to buy insurance. His family was poor.

"Mi-chael—" he concluded. "When you poor, people look at you like this." He gave an evil squint. "But when you rich, people say, 'Look at this rich man!'"

Rolly was a chatterbox by nature, and once he decided to talk, he chattered about anything that came into his head. I never felt bored. His English reminded me of the French-inflected Caribbean patois in Derek Walcott's plays, *Ti-Jean and His Brothers* or *The Sea at Dauphin*—his voice could be dirty, low-down, clever, funny, and sad. He told me a Seychellois legend about a madman in the woods. "We are like the Dodosya under a rock," he said. "We say that in the Seychelles. Dodosya, like a crazy man.* He go to the forest because his wife no good. He sit under a rock and laugh, laugh, laugh. These men got us here in the forest like that."

---

* Or a zombie.

IV

A sandstone rock in the forest, though, was no match for Somalia's weather. Even during the dry season, water could pour like a faucet into the arid savanna. One night we woke up to a wet patter on the leaves. The pirates told us to pack our sparse belongings into plastic bags. They drove us like cattle through a gentle rain—down the crevasse, up a trail, across the thorn-grown bluff—until we piled, wet and exhausted, just before the downpour started, into a waiting car.

We sped through the forest and the bush at top speed, for several hours, until the pirates pulled off to one side of the road and waited on a moonlit expanse. We had outrun the rain, at least for now. Somali folk music pounded and scraped from the stereo. We had no choice but to listen to a stark female voice and a careening, melancholy oud.* In a Somali musician's hands the oud can sound spare and thorny, like the savanna itself, and this song was so strange I started to pay attention. The woman used a glottal stop to keep time. A glottal stop is a consonant sound in Somali—it's written into words as an apostrophe or as a *c*, which is why one common spelling of Galkayo includes a *c*—Galkacyo—and why Sa'ad has two syllables.†

The woman sang whole trills of glottal stops, in perfect time, to drive the rhythm of her song. My resistance melted. The music had a strange beauty, and the bending, frantic oud reminded me of American blues.

I had just started to forget where I was when our driver pulled out his smartphone, flipped through some pictures, and tilted his phone back to show me a photo of my own face in the dark. A chill

---

* A stringed instrument common throughout the Middle East and Muslim Africa.
† Sometimes "Galka'yo" or "Sacad."

washed through my limbs. Pirates laughed. It was my own author photo, ripped from the *New York Times*. The bosses must have sent it around to their foot soldiers' phones.

Soon we drove to a dismal stone ruin with faint light glowing behind colored rags in the windows. Pirates wrapped a blindfold around my head. I stumbled up a broken stone staircase, and when they unwrapped me, I stood in a half-lit honeycomb of crumbling, filthy rooms. Pirates listened to twanging folk music and sat in front of piles of leaf, chewing their narcotic cud and staring up with startled, stoned, urgent expressions, as if we'd interrupted them. Thorn brambles were stuffed in one doorway—tumbleweeds in place of a door. Someone led us down the hall to a tattered cloth hanging in another doorway, and behind it three mattresses lay on the ground. A tall man slept on one.

"It is Marc!" Rolly whispered.

We set down our bags. Marc stirred and spoke from the corner, and Rolly answered him in minor-toned Creole. In the light from a fluorescent lantern I saw Marc was an old man with stiff limbs. I shook his leathery hand.

"He say is getting better," said Rolly. "He feed himself now."

"Better from the electrocution?" I asked.

"Yah."

A man came in wearing a white shirt and dress slacks. I recognized him in the uneven light as Boodiin, the translator from our first house.

"You are safe here now, you are okay," he said. "You can sleep."

I didn't feel safe.

"Are we in Hobyo?" I said.

"Yes."

One or two men in another room began to pray, and their chanting mixed with the clamor of folk music on their phones.

"Can you ask the men to turn their music down?" I said. "It's very loud."

"I will ask," he said. "But these men are soldiers."

So?

"Ask them to be quiet soldiers."

He went out. The volume lowered on one or two phones. Boodiin returned, and I remembered my manners and thanked him. He wondered if it would rain again. He was in a hopped-up, conversational mood, although he'd instructed us to sleep.

"I hope it won't rain, because I want to go fishing tomorrow," he said.

"Really?" I said. "What do you catch?"

Boodiin dressed like a small-time businessman, a hustler putting on airs, more than some kind of fisherman.

"Lobster, I fish for lobster," he said. "I hope tomorrow I will catch . . . five k-g!"

He raised his eyebrows and smiled. "Five k-g," about eleven pounds, was meant to be a lot for a man like him. I remembered thinking before that he was a world-class liar; now his will to disorient me rattled my nerve. Was I expected to believe, on this particular layer of hell, that pirates were just needy fishermen? I remembered Boodiin's admonition from our first meeting in Hobyo—*You have made a mistake*—and wondered if he would repeat it. My real mistake had been coming to Somalia at all. What did I think I would find around here? Pirates who trusted writers? Truth? Some war correspondents come away from the battlefield more disoriented than before, less confident about the facts, and by now I just wanted to be unconscious. I wasn't in the mood to hear Boodiin offer up some pirate public relations line. This trashed and nightmarish stone building stood in a uniquely desolate part of the world, where escape was impractical and even my dreams of freedom had no obvious place to wander; but it was Boodiin's insistent dishonesty that gave me the creeps.

"That man get seasick," Rolly said when he left. "Boodiin, he not a fisherman."

I snorted.

"How do you know?

"When I come to Hobyo on the *Aride*," he said, "he get on with some other bosses. After five minutes, he go to the rail and vomit."

V

At dawn I saw more of the house. We'd slept in a filthy room colored with layers of pastel paint, flaking blue and yellow and dusty green. The thick walls rose twelve feet overhead to reveal a barnlike space crossed by rafters. Birds fluttered among them. The slanted corrugated roof had rust holes that shone bright from the morning sun.

My blood pressure had a way of zinging to a certain level every morning when I woke up from a benign dream to realize I was in Somalia. Angelo now sat folded beside the doorway with a rifle across his thighs, deep in thought, shielding his forehead with one languid hand. He noticed me stir.

I cleared my throat and said, "*Kadi?*"

He leaned through the hanging cloth to give an order. Feet shuffled; Kalashnikovs clacked. The hall was like the room, a pastiche of flaking paint, except that a patterned ceiling that must have once decked the entire building still remained, half broken away. Lengths of wirelike metal suspended the remnants of it. This ruin, in its day, would have been a well-appointed European-style house.

"Toilet?" I asked, since no Somalis were offering guidance.

One of them waved into a room near his end of the hall. There was a toilet inside, but it looked as if someone had assaulted it with a sledgehammer. The floor had a litter of rock, plaster, and dried human shit. The toilet was a broken plinth of porcelain with a hole gaping into a stinking watery sump.

I peed into it.

"Somali bullshit," I whispered to the guards on my way back, making sure to remove my shoes and leave them in the filthy hall. By now Rolly had woken up. "What is this place?" I said when I sat down.

"I not know. I stay here before." He glanced around. "Angelo say is seventy years old."

"Really?"

"Thick walls, eh? And this roof is good iron."

The deep-set windows had broad sills of concrete on either side. The walls were a yard thick and almost twelve feet high. The design felt Fascist monumental, simple but massive, like a farmhouse built by Mussolini.

"Seventy years ago," I said, "the Fascists were in charge here. This place might be Italian."

"Yah?"

The colonies of Italian and British Somaliland had united in 1960 to become modern Somalia; but during World War II, they had fought on behalf of their colonial masters. Gerlach had told me one of his earliest memories was the sight of Somali soldiers marching through Galkayo for the Italians. I remembered an excellent book by Gerald Hanley called *Warriors*, about Somalia during and after World War II. Hanley was an ethnic Irishman, born in England and sent by the British Army to East Africa. He had no passionate loyalty to the British Empire, so his book is an independent-minded snapshot of Somalia during that dramatic span of years when war had weakened Europe's colonial grip on much of the world and Africa was full of hope. "I can remember sitting by the waterhole," he wrote, "wondering how it was that the war I had joined because it was against Fascism had landed me in ragged shorts and shirts in a geography like the moon where Fascism had vanished like a thin mist and the war had rolled far away into distant silences."

Marc stood up, gingerly, to use the toilet. He was shy, almost docile, and he looked older than Rolly, though he was younger by seven years. He had imploring eyes and white-dusted hair, and he held his arms in-curled, like broken wings.

When he returned to lie down, I saw how weak his arms were from the electrocution. But I caught no trace of resentment in his manner. He was gentle and calm. He lit up when Rolly spoke to him in patois, which sounded like mischievous broken street French.*

For lunch that afternoon, the pirates delivered a large, restaurant-prepared platter of rice, yellowish and decorated with wedges of lime. For some reason, they brought a separate bowl for me.

"You get extra?" said Rolly.

"I don't know. I don't want extra."

We shared it equally. Khat arrived at the house while we ate. Strange voices outside began to shout. Our guards gravitated to rooms across the hall to watch the commotion through the windows. Even Angelo stood up to crane his head.

"What's the problem?" I asked.

Angelo patted his hand at me, as if patting an invisible dog. The shouting grew louder. Angelo picked up his gun, and I felt a wash of anxiety.

"Angelo," Rolly whispered. "Problem?"

_____

* Spelled *patwa* in the Seychelles.

Angelo shook his head. "Problem khat."

The noise rose to a near riot. The only word I could make out was not *khat* but *bariis.** That was the word for rice. "*Bariis! Bariis!*" the strangers were shouting. I looked at Rolly and nodded at the platter.

"Someone saw them deliver our lunch," I said.

Either it was a food riot, or the fancy tray had tipped off a rival group to our presence. It occurred to me that members of Gerlach's subclan might want to rescue us. A rescue by SEALs sounded risky enough; I hadn't considered the prospect of a Somali militia battle.

The shouting grew louder. Ahmed Dirie came in to dig through a pile of belongings in the corner for his military vest, an olive-green jacket with pockets for Kalashnikov magazines. He strapped it around his belly.

"No problem," he told us and stepped out.

Rolly grunted. On a normal day as a hostage, the worst condition is uncertainty, a sheer terror of what might happen. This riot made it worse. The ferocity of the shouting altered like the weather but never dissolved. I didn't believe Angelo about the khat. On the other hand, I couldn't imagine pirates growing so passionate about anything else, except maybe a fight over hostages. We heard gunfire—crackling warning gunfire, aimed at the sky—but the noise rolled on and on, rising and subsiding, for most of the afternoon. We felt like trapped animals. *I don't want to die,* I thought. *I don't want to die.*

The riot was a mockery of my fledgling wish for a military raid. I sat on my mattress in a pair of thin cotton shorts and a T-shirt, helpless as a boy, leaning against the yard-thick walls and wondering how to defend myself against death when it came, if it came, in a scatter of ricocheting rifle rounds.

---

* Pronounced *breece*.

Angelo sat down again and mumbled, "No problem."

Rolly tapped me on the elbow. "These men always say 'no problem,' Michael. When they say 'problem,' I think on that day we die."

"We might die right now," I suggested.

"No say that," Rolly answered.

When the riot dissipated, Rolly turned to our guard and said, "Angelo—why?"

"Problem, *bariis*?" I interjected with a crooked smile.

"Problem *khat*," Angelo said.

VI

When we complained about the wretched toilet room, pirates took us elsewhere for piss breaks and showers—out to an expanse of white rocks littered with goat and human shit. Beyond this dead zone stood the crumbling walls of an even older house, which someone had built by mortaring field rocks together. When I took a shower inside this ruin, I noticed that rotting wooden beams were slanting through the tops of the rough white walls. Also European-looking, like something from a spaghetti western.* Below us, to our right, lay the dull ranked houses of modern Hobyo. Beyond them, the vast blue sea.

I wondered if Hanley had seen these buildings after the war. He certainly knew the feelings they evoked. The heat and isolation and dry loneliness of Somalia had carried some British soldiers to

-----

* The first Italian colonial district office in Hobyo went up at this location in 1909.

the edge of suicide, and Hanley tried to make sense of the ones who pulled the trigger. "It does not follow that because all the suicides I knew were very serious, earnest men with little sense of humor, that only the humorless kill themselves when they are in good physical health and still young," he wrote. "We do not know the size and strength of our manias until they fall upon us and drag us down, or the barrenness of our inner deserts until real loneliness, fear, bewilderment and sun-madness have cast us into them."

I wasn't yet in the grip of a mania—not sun-mad, not bewildered—but suicide was more than a literary topic for me. My father had killed himself. Mom had called it a heart attack to protect my impressionable mind, and I could understand the compulsion to shield a twelve-year-old kid from the shattering awareness that his father no longer wanted to live. But the fairy tale had lasted almost thirty years. I'd learned about his suicide only after some research as an adult.

I did remember Dad's drinking bouts—how he yelled when he drank, then forgot what he yelled. He also took Tylenol with codeine. He suffered from arthritis in his back, and before my mother evicted him, I remember Dad standing up from a nap one weekend afternoon to find her watering plants in the yard. "Five hours, no pain!" he said, and he must have meant the codeine, because he said it with the earnest passion of a man who wanted to convince his wife of something questionable.

"That Tylenol is *super*," he said.

"Mm-hmm," Mom said.

Her attitude to his shysterism was to roll her eyes and keep watering the oleanders. Mom was a liberated woman for her time and place: tennis-playing, cigarette-smoking, ironic. But, even from her earliest girlhood she had a conservative understanding of right and wrong. Her first full sentence, as a two-year-old, burst out at a zoo in Frankfurt in the 1940s, when an elephant stole a wooden stick from her young hands by reaching its trunk through the bars of its cage. *"Elephant took my stick,"* she blurted, looking for justice from the adults around her. *"But he's not allowed."*

After seventy years that story surfaced sometimes at family dinners, in L.A. or Cologne, to howls of laughter.

Moving from a small German town to L.A. in the sixties was a long, pioneering step—glamorous from one point of view, dangerous from another—and her father at first refused to fly halfway across the planet just to visit her. The family lived in Europe, either in Catholic parts of the Rhineland in Germany or across the border in southern Holland. But Mom liked the New World. Germans impressed her as kind of stuffy and cold. She was traditional but free-spirited. She liked the weather in California; she liked the wine and the tennis in December.

She kicked Dad out at the start of 1981. He found a bachelor apartment in our neighborhood and checked himself into an alcohol rehab center called Raleigh Hills, a short-term residential hospital with psychologists and counselors, mild and soft-spoken people who, when I visited, made a point of explaining alcoholism as an incurable disease. How it altered the mind, how it could turn a strong man into a raging stranger. A twelve-year-old could understand that. But I didn't understand the pills, and when Dad seemed to master his urge for alcohol in the middle of his year of exile, I thought he'd won. He asked to move home from his apartment. Mom said no.

"He wasn't ready," she said afterward. "He hadn't even quit drinking. He certainly hadn't given up the codeine."

We learned about his death, at the end of the summer, only when he failed to show up for work. The police went to his apartment and opened the door. Mom came home and told me the news. I believed her heart attack version of events because everything Dad liked was bad for his heart—cigarettes, booze, the rim of fat on every barbecued steak—but even at twelve it was a surprise to hear that no one would conduct an autopsy. How could they know it was a heart attack? That discrepancy, along with some others, lingered at the back of my mind long into what I thought of as a well-adjusted adulthood. In 2010 I ordered a copy of his death certificate, on a hunch. I had just read *Legend of a Suicide*, the novel by David Vann, which paints an adolescence lived under the shadow of a father's suicide. It sounded like a grim way to grow up. *I'm glad that didn't happen to me*, I thought, about a week before Dad's death certificate came in the mail.

I opened the envelope standing at my breakfast table in Berlin, which overlooked the cobblestones and the swaying, wavering, massive green trees in the park. I pulled out the colored certificate and saw four strange words in the bureaucratic box labeled CAUSE OF DEATH:

GUNSHOT TO LEFT CHEST

I swayed a little on my feet.

At the time I was happy in Europe, far from the oppressive heat of strip malls and liquor stores in Southern California. But the notion of a gunshot blast in Dad's little apartment brought back all the hot and stifling emotion I associated with L.A. It was jarring, revelatory, alien, bizarre.

Mom and I saw each other every year or so, either in Germany or in L.A. We had suffered a lot together, but we rarely talked about the past. We maintained a warm and cordial relationship. The unspoken idea was to keep from dramatizing our troubles, to keep from wallowing. I saw the drawbacks to this very German arrangement as well as the benefits—I wasn't Californian enough to insist on "talking it out"—but the alternative was a closet-skeleton secrecy, a habit of suppression. In high school I had suspected Mom of "denial," of covering something up with her cheerfulness and her relentless California pleasures, but after a while I realized the white wine and the games of tennis belonged to a conscious method of moving on.

A month after I had ordered the certificate, Mom happened to visit Berlin. I brought up the suicide over dinner at a small restaurant. She said, "Oh—yes," as if she'd been meaning to mention it all this time.

"Was there a note?" I said.

"No note."

And, I guess, we didn't need one. What had happened was clear. Gutting and tragic, unspeakably bleak—but in part of my mind, for decades, perhaps I already knew.

VII

One night Ahmed Dirie came into our room and pointed at me.

"Come on!" he said. "Get up."

He expected me to bolt to attention. I made a point of adjusting my sling, pulling on each sock and shoe, and gathering my spare items for wherever we were headed.

Rolly groaned at my recalcitrance and muttered, "Not make them angry, Michael."

Together with Mohammed Tahliil—the reedy group leader from our forest camp—Ahmed Dirie held my elbow and walked me across a sandy waste of weeds and goat droppings, away from Mussolini's Farmhouse to the newer, more thickly settled area, where

110

slab houses stood in rows. As a free man, I had eaten lunch in this neighborhood with Gerlach and Ashwin. The moon was bright, the air was misted with brine, and to our left I noticed a blinking light on top of Hobyo's cell-phone tower.

We passed a Somali in a collared shirt, sitting on a berm of sand. I recognized Ali Duulaay and moved toward him; but the others steered me away and led me along a compound wall, where they unlocked a clanking door.

The house had raw concrete floors and slab walls painted powder blue. No furniture. A plastic-wrapped mattress and pillow waited for me on the floor of one room. It was a safe house, new looking but barren, half-built, maybe waiting for a spurt of ransom cash to finish construction. By the light of a fluorescent lantern, I unwrapped the mattress and tried to make myself comfortable. A generator grumbled in the distance.

Was this new arrangement a response to the riot outside Mussolini's Farmhouse? A new phase of captivity? Or just softer accommodation for the American? I didn't like one option better than the others, and while I pulled the thin blanket around my shoulders and tried to sleep, the generator stirred up dreams of helicopters and deliverance by gunfire.

I called this place "Mohammed's House," because Tahliil seemed to be in charge. The guards acted mild mannered, less intentionally cruel. They let me sit outdoors in the afternoon. They spread mats on the porch and offered me cigarettes and khat. A "good group." I resisted the khat even when I felt depressed, since I didn't want to pick up a habit, but once in a while, with a bottle of mango juice or a glass of oversweet tea, I allowed myself the pleasure of a cigarette in the prison yard.

One morning on the porch I noticed some useful items scattered on the pirates' mat, not just Kalashnikovs and khat but also cigarette lighters, pens, and grade-school notebooks. The guards used these notebooks to keep track of their shifts.

The young pirate named Hersi offered me a cigarette. When I lit up, I noticed that his lighter had an LED at one end.

"Can I keep this?" I said.

"*Haa*, yes."

Hersi flipped through a menu of songs on his phone. Pirate phones provided several forms of entertainment and distraction, not just songs but also video clips and recorded Sufi sermons.

"K'naan!" he said, and played something by the Somali-Canadian rapper.

The song Hersi had chosen—"Until the Lion Learns to Speak"—resembled a Somali folk song I had noticed in the pirates' SUV. It had the same call-and-response, the same urgent falling rhythm. But the Somali version sounded more traditional.

Hersi and another guard talked about K'naan in excited voices. A translator named Yoonis, who sat with us on the porch, said, "They are his cousins."

"Both of them?" I weighed the likelihood in my mind. "Both Hawiye?"*

"Yes."

"Are you all Sa'ad?" I said.

"Yes," he said.

I didn't care very much.

"This group, the good group, is Sa'ad," he said. "The big group is Hawiye and Darod."

"A mix of clans," I said.

"Yes."

---

* The Sa'ad are a subclan of the Hawiye.

"Can I borrow this notebook?" I said.

"Yes."

I scrounged a pen, too, and retreated to my room, where I started a journal. From the radio I learned the date and made small notes about each day. But I had to restrict the writing to an hour or so at a time, because it bothered my wrist.

One afternoon I took notes on a fascinating BBC report about spy plane flights over Somalia. The correspondent flew with the Royal Australian Air Force "over the pirate-infested waters off the Horn of Africa." Its P-3 Orion amounted to an airborne surveillance station, stuffed with equipment and analysts. Every morning, these enormous planes lumbered out along predetermined paths from Bahrain, in the Persian Gulf, which told me that my guessed-at location on any given day would be one stop on a long, bureaucratic mission.

This gave me an idea. I figured drones were overhead, too, somewhere out of sight, so I started going to the bathroom with Hersi's cigarette lighter in my shorts pocket. The sky at dawn and sunset was dusky enough to make a sharp LED shine like a dim little star—I hoped—so I aimed the light through a toilet-paper tube, to hide the glare from my guards, and flashed *SOS* at the sky in Morse code.

To my surprise it seemed to work. Surveillance planes started cruising low over Hobyo every other day. One afternoon, while I sat on the porch, I became aware of a distant buzz, strengthening over Hobyo like the noise we'd heard over the forest. Hersi's eyes widened.

"Michael! AC!"

They hustled me into my bedroom and closed the dented shutters. The pirates called these aircraft "AC," as shorthand for AC-130. The C-130 Hercules is a workhorse transport plane, similar in size to an Orion, but it can be outfitted for harder jobs, and a variant called the AC-130 gunship had hunted Somali jihadists in a battle for Ras Kamboni, near Kenya, in 2007. The carnage was so notorious, I think the pirates knew no other name.

Each room in Mohammed's House was a cube of concrete. The prospect of a raid sending bullets around in the dark tended to paralyze me. The less confusion, I thought, the better. One morning I drew a map of the compound in my notebook. I wrote in block letters that I slept alone in *this* room, while guards slept in *this* and *that* room: "7 GUARDS TOTAL," I wrote, and slipped the page into my shorts pocket.

"*Kadi*," I said.

The men stood at attention with their rifles and watched me cross the yard. I locked the outhouse door and unfolded my map. No drones or planes were visible. But I knew the rumor that certain spy satellites could read license plates from orbit. It was an antiquated rumor, maybe an urban myth, but my notebook page was almost the size of an American license plate, and I had nothing better to do.

For the next week I unfolded the map on every trip to the bathroom. I made a point of taking a piss at the same time every morning, around six, because my only hope for such a desperate plan would be regular habit. I doubted a drone analyst would just stumble across an image of me flashing vital information from a compromising position; but if the LED signals drew attention to the house, and operators learned when to watch for my toilet runs, well, after a while, I thought, we might get somewhere.

VIII

My guards had a knee-jerk terror of aircraft, matched by a wild and defiant bravado, as you would, too, if you had to worry about a SEAL raid. I tried to imagine what they were thinking. The history of So-malia's bloody relationship to air power stretched back further than Ras Kamboni or the Battle of Mogadishu. It dated to 1920, when a squadron of Royal Air Force planes landed in British Somaliland. In those days, few people on earth had seen flying machines of any kind; but Douglas James Jardine, the military chronicler of Britain's imperial adventure in Somalia, pointed out that the "Z" squadron's arrival in Berbera caused very little stir.

> The average unsophisticated Somali, instead of expressing
> surprise and admiration at such a remarkable invention of
> modern science as the aeroplane, gave but a passing glance
> at the machines and remarked that the Somali would also
> build aeroplanes "if he only knew how."

That's from Jardine's colorful but colonialist 1923 book *The Mad Mullah of Somaliland*. It describes the British war against Sayyid Mohammed Abdullah Hassan, who filled the same role in the Western imagination in the early 1900s that Osama bin Laden occupied a century later. According to Jardine, Sayyid Mohammed "traded upon the avarice and superstitions of his fellow-countrymen to convert them into robbers and cut-throats." Maybe; but a lot of Somalis still consider him a national hero.

Sayyid Mohammed came from the Ogaden, northeast of Galkayo, and his fighters were Somali herdsmen who gave up traditional clan allegiances to become "dervishes," or Sufi devotionalists.* He stirred

---

* Traditional dervishes are mendicant Sufis in distinctive robes who move door-to-door, offering chants or rituals in exchange for money. They still exist, and many regular Somalis—even if they themselves follow Sufi traditions—reserve the name "Sufi" for such men.

his men through fiery sermons to a spiritual-political cause. "With all the corrosive invective of the born agitator and the recklessness of the reformer," wrote Jardine, "he inveighed against the luxury of the age. He proclaimed that the Somalis were wasting their substance on riotous living, especially on tea-drinking. He protested against the immorality of chewing kat, or the gluttony of gorging the fat of sheep's tail."

Sayyid Mohammed's odd strain of Sufism had historic links to Wahhabism,* which means that Sufi mysticism and Salafi fundamentalism aren't mutually exclusive in this part of the world. Somalia has absorbed larger or smaller waves of fundamentalist influence from the Arabian Peninsula for at least two hundred years. The most recent wave started in the eighties, when Somali migrants moved north for Saudi service jobs. (Some came home radicalized.)

The more I thought about the tidy categories Kapuscinski had noticed in North Africa, the more they tended to blur. There was a spectrum of Muslim belief, and a tincture of Wahhabism in Somali Sufism accounted for Sayyid Mohammed's dervish holy war.

His logic toward the British, in any case, was irrefutable. In 1903, Sayyid Mohammed wrote:

> I have no cultivated fields, no silver or gold for you to take. You gained no benefit by killing my men and my country is of no good to you. . . . If you want wood and stone, you can get them in plenty. There are also many ant-heaps. The sun is very hot. All you can get from me is war. . . . If you wish peace, go away from my country to your own.

---

* According to I. M. Lewis, in *Saints and Somalis.*

Sayyid Mohammed wanted to liberate his people from Europe and unify them under Islam, and he gave the British seventeen more years of sporadic war until London decided to solve the "dervish problem" with aircraft. The "Z" squadron's bombing raids in early 1920 were a military experiment, the first Western air assaults in Africa. Sayyid Mohammed and his dervishes were far from prepared. One dervish told him the incoming planes were "chariots of Allah come to take the Mullah up to heaven." Another declared them a Turkish invention from the Great War, bringing tidings of triumph from Istanbul. Sayyid Mohammed believed this man, put on his best clothes, and went out to meet the messengers.

"Then the first bomb fell," wrote Jardine. One adviser "was killed outright, and the Mullah's garments were singed. Thus the first shot all but ended the campaign."

Sayyid Mohammed's dream of a united Somalia ended that afternoon in the desert. He survived until the end of 1920, only to die of the flu.

IX

One day I sat with Yoonis and Hersi on the porch, drinking from a bottle of mango juice and trying to enjoy the sunshine. Hersi handed me a stem of khat. "He wants to know if you are his friend," said Yoonis. "He says he makes sure that you have mango juice and tuna fish every morning. He says you are his sahib."

"Mm-hmm," I said.

"He says we may not get so much payment for protecting you in this house. Not as much as we thought. He wants to know if you will send him ten thousand dollars when you are free."

I cleared my throat and thought about it.

"Of course," I said at last, and Hersi looked surprised.

"Yes?" he said.

"If he gets me out tomorrow, he can have my firstborn."

Yoonis and Hersi conferred.

"He says he would rather have the money," said Yoonis.

I shrugged and sipped my mango juice. Dry tree branches growing over the compound wall wavered in an ocean breeze. I heard cattle groan beyond it, some kind of cow or buffalo.

"Hersi wants to know," said Yoonis finally, "if you have ever had sex with a woman with a clit."

I nearly spat my mango juice across the porch.

"He wants to know if you can bring him one," he added.

"A girlfriend with a clitoris?"

"Yes."

Somehow Yoonis knew the slang word better than the real one. I squinted at him. "You mean because all the girls in Somalia are 'circumcised'?" I said. "Don't men in Somalia support this tradition?"

"I think it is not so much fun," Yoonis confessed.

"Why do Somalis do it?"

"It is in the Koran."

I shook my head. "No, it isn't, Yoonis."

"It is the law in all Muslim lands," Yoonis informed me.

"That's not true," I said. "It's not the law in Indonesia. Some of them do it, but it's not the law."

"You have experienced?" Yoonis said. "Or you have read?"

I smiled. "I have read. But I've been there. Indonesians are Sufis, too, you know. Same as Somalis. Most don't cut their women."

Yoonis shook his head. "I think this is not true," he said.

"Do you have a Koran?"

"No."

"You have to show me the passage where your religion orders Muslims to do this thing." In fact, some parts of the hadith encourage it, but not the Koran. "It's a custom from thousands of years ago, Yoonis, from ancient Egypt. Before Islam." I was agitated now. "If Somalis didn't cut their women, Somalia would be a happier place."

My guards wavered; they weren't sure it wasn't true. But there was no convincing them.

Once, in another lifetime, I had received a nice pair of sandals from an activist in California who had appreciated a column of mine arguing against "female circumcision." But around here—where my clever ideas might have made some difference—I had no clout.

At last I retreated to my room. The whole compound at Mohammed's House had a terrible insect problem. Over my mattress I'd assembled a gauzy mosquito tent, which served as a retreat from all insects, the carnivorous daytime flies as well as mosquitoes at night. The patio conversation about firstborn children made me brood about my bachelor life in Berlin, my own lack of children, and my dad. I sat in the tent and started to scribble.

For thirty years I thought my father had died of a heart attack, and for almost as long I had maintained a wariness of our domestic life in Northridge, our model family, which had not filled him with understanding or joy. Alcohol and pills had eroded both. But before he killed himself, he had started to question why he worked for Lockheed, why he lived in the San Fernando Valley at all. At heart he was a fifties-style dad who liked to camp and fish, an American Romantic about the wilderness, and I remembered sitting with him in his rattling Volkswagen one hot afternoon, waiting for a red light to turn, while he gazed out the windshield through a pair of sunglasses with a look of half-astonished disgust. He took in the vast boulevard, the traffic, maybe the smog in the sky.

At last he looked at me.

"I wonder how much of our lives we waste sitting at stoplights," he said.

This memory startled me in Somalia. His desolation before he died must have been bottomless. I had pursued a different career because of his disenchantment—I had defined myself against my father to dodge the frustrations and disillusionments that had strained his heart. I preferred cities over suburbs, I liked exotic travel, I tried to avoid most addictive drugs and eat low-cholesterol food. I thought these habits would save me from a death like his. When I learned it wasn't a heart attack, of course, I still believed—without thinking too hard—that my career choices might keep me from suicide.

The irony appalled me now. I scribbled and scribbled. I wrote that Dad would have opposed my career. He would have hollered and yelled. And here—in a place where I had a strong and relevant opinion about female circumcision—I had no power to change a goddamn thing. But I also noticed that my notebook was becoming an essential refuge at Mohammed's house. The stress of captivity had turned my mind into a cauldron of contradictory ideas—frustration, self-hatred, surprising impulses to violence—and nothing but the discipline of composition could lead me out of the soup. When I thought about it like that, I could answer the criticisms, in his voice, that rose in my imagination while I sat alone under the mosquito tent, these nightmarish and unanswerable condemnations from beyond the grave. *Writing is impractical, selfish, narcissistic, and soft.* Maybe; but I had found pleasure in it as a young man because it could reframe a scrambled mind. Good writing could be a *release* from narcissism, a declaration of independence, a way to order and furnish the mental prison.

You're not real independent now, are you?

No, Dad, not exactly. Thanks for asking.

X

On a warm night in February, the men at Mohammed's House woke me up by the glare of a fluorescent lantern and crammed me into a Land Rover. They bristled with weapons and ammunition. Tahliil drove us out of Hobyo and across the moonlit waste for more than an hour. A strong beam of light flashed across the bush like a beacon, and Tahliil aimed for it until we pulled beside a pair of unknown cars. Yoonis and Tahliil then grasped my elbows and walked me to a cluster of eight or ten Somalis squatting in the dust.

"Hello, Michael," a plump man said. "My name is Mohamed."

I wore nothing but thin cotton shorts and a T-shirt. I felt vulnerable and terrified. The boss in the middle, sitting cross-legged, had fat cheeks and a peculiar squint, heavy lidded and insolent. He acted groggy, like a man who needed his khat, and he drew a pall of quiet menace around himself, a fear I could sense from his gunmen. He spoke in a high, almost childish voice.

"We will make a phone call," he told me, "to someone who can help with your case. You must tell him that I need a letter from President Obama. It must request that I will be the main negotiator for your case, and it must declare me innocent of your kidnapping. It must have an official seal, from the White House."

"I'll need your full name," I said.

"Just tell them Mohamed; that is enough," he said. "And you must tell them that these pirates want their money right now. It is very important."

"How much is the demand?" I said.

"Twenty million dollars."

I felt sick to my stomach. The outrageous demand was still in place. After a month of captivity, nothing had changed.

The boss dialed a private American negotiator on his orange-glowing Samsung. The number placed the negotiator in Washington, D.C., and the voice on the phone was sane and good-humored. It calmed me to hear clarity in my own language after so many weeks of confusion.

"The gentleman who handed you the phone: Is that the first time you're meeting him?" said the negotiator. "Or you've chatted with him before?"

"No, it's the first time."

"That's the main guy in charge, just so you know. That's Mohamed Garfanji," he said, and my vision swam—my blood felt just like ice water. Until then Garfanji had been a phantom, a figment of a rumor, and it weakened me to think that I was at his mercy.

"Has he made a demand?" the negotiator asked.

"Yes, he wants twenty million dollars and some kind of form letter from the White House."

"Signed by Obama!" Garfanji shouted. "It must say I am innocent!"

"He's asking for twenty million dollars?" the negotiator said, with just a hitch in his professional manner—he sounded surprised.

"Yeah, and a letter from the White House," I said.

"It must say I am innocent!" Garfanji shouted.

To this demand the negotiator gave a quiet, self-assured laugh.

He'd been contacted through the Pulitzer Center on Crisis Reporting, he said. He reassured me that people were trying to help. Then he tried to patch our call through to my mother. "Just bear with me." I heard a phone ring, and my mother said "Hello?" in the tone of someone who was not, at that moment, dreading a call from Somalia. We'd caught her off guard. By then she had a "command center" established in the dining room—she kept a phone on the table, surrounded by notebooks and coffee mugs and lists of questions to ask. The phone had been souped up with caller ID, "so

I would know who was calling me," she said, and this ever shifting mess remained on the table for most of my captivity.

"Hi, Mom, it's Mike."

"Hi, Michael, it's so good to hear your voice!"

"I'm just calling—uh, to say hello," I faltered. "And I miss you."

These phone calls, with their intense pressure and terrible connections, were masterpieces of understatement. Hearing her voice was like hearing music for the first time in weeks. I thought about my family and friends every day, but Mom's voice brought back the dry heat of Los Angeles and all the changing resonance of the word *home*, this old carousel of personal scenery, from Northridge to the beach to the sound of German voices in Berlin. My heart unraveled like a film reel.

"Are you healthy?" she said.

"Uh, yes," I said. "Terrified, but basically in good shape. A little food and a little water every day."

"After we talked last time," she said, "we continued to call that number they gave us, but there was never any answer."

I started to wonder if Garfanji was the same person as Omar, the high-voiced Somali on the bluff. He seemed to be a different man. But in the dark it was hard to tell. After more confused conversation, I worked up my courage to speak German, to test whether Garfanji knew the difference. I babbled about a duffel bag I had left in a Nairobi hotel, containing my U.S. passport and a laptop. "Somebody found the bag," Mom said in German. "It was transferred to the U.S. embassy."

"That's very good," I said.

So government people were taking care of her. It eased my mind. I could also tell, from Garfanji's glazed expression, that he wasn't following our chitchat. I added in German that I had "nothing against" a military raid—"regardless of what the pirates here say."

"Yes," Mom said. "Yes. Exactly."

Most of the time she sounded earnest on the phone, striving to hear my voice or just to understand this freakish situation; but she could also be guarded and veiled. She had a poker hand to play. Now she exposed a tough lack of sentimentality, a seeming indifference to the danger of a rescue. I didn't mind at all. The pirates' erratic behavior had steeled us both against the prospect of a raid.

"Time's off," Garfanji said. "Come on."

I finished up and handed him the phone. The call had accomplished nothing. Twenty million dollars was a ridiculous outrage—Garfanji understood that as well as the rest of us. He started to scroll through some files on the phone menu and said, in an apathetic slur, "Your people have killed nine of my people. If they try it with you, we will shoot you."

"What happened?" I said.

"There was a rescue operation," he said vaguely.

I wanted to know if the hostages were safe, so I repeated my question from the phone call on the bluff.

"What happened to the hostages?"

"They were both killed."

My lungs constricted; my chest seemed to squeeze and bleed. Garfanji tapped his screen to open a sound file and tossed his phone in the dust. I didn't want to hear about dead hostages. But a news clip on Garfanji's phone explained in clear English that two aid workers held captive in Somalia since the fall of 2011 had been flown by U.S. helicopters, alive, to Camp Lemonnier in Djibouti.

My heart thumped with hope.

"I'm very sorry to hear that," I told Garfanji, and I think no one in that circle of pirates could tell how the phone had made a fool of their boss, by revealing his poor command of English.

XI

My mother and the FBI in California ignored Garfanji's demand for a letter, but the way he insisted on a pardon from the president, on embossed letterhead, did suggest he was half-insane. "We wondered if he was the same person as Omar," Mom said later. Garfanji became an inconstant, flickering figure to me. I met Omar in the sunshine on a bluff, Garfanji in the sandy waste under a full moon; and in the panic of a hostage's mind, maybe one person could seem like two people, and two people could seem like one.

"Mohamed Garfanji"—also known as Mohamed Osman Mohamed—invested in real estate, both in Galmudug and outside Somalia. "He likes to drink, he likes women, and he likes to beat the shit out of people," a security contractor told me later. "He's close to the Somali government, and he wants to be *in* the government, so he puts his men to work as if they were the government." That meant patrolling the oceans and cultivating a "coast guard" image off Somalia as well as providing security forces for smaller Galmudug towns. He was a Suleiman, not a Sa'ad, but both clans belonged to a larger clan called the Habar Gidir. They could work together. Garfanji kept a private militia in Hobyo, but his pirates tended to be inland bandits and irregular fighters, closer to the violent highwaymen called *shifta* than to fishermen.

The word *shifta* derived from another clan, the Mshifta, but referred to "any roaming bandit in the great desert that extended from Somalia to Sudan and took in the whole of northern Kenya," according to Paul Theroux, who'd met them in southern Ethiopia. Garfanji hired men like that. A number of central-Somali pirates no doubt were former fishermen who needed jobs, but most of the foot soldiers I met came from Galkayo or landlocked nomadic villages. They were children of the desert bush.

One reason piracy spiked in the early 2000s, in fact, was that security forces in Puntland went unpaid—and so many of the gunmen simply turned to different work.

Garfanji also played a social justice game, a Robin Hood gambit for popular support intended to blunt local opposition to his crimes. He paid doctors' bills in Hobyo. He made generous loans. He offered people jobs. He kept them from starvation. "There are no beggars in Hobyo," Gerlach told me. "Garfanji is very popular there."

So from one point of view, Garfanji was a monster. From another, he was a social-minded capitalist working in tough terrain. I didn't want either manifestation talking on the phone to my mom. But her poise surprised the FBI. Even when a phone call took her by surprise, she snapped to attention. "She amazed all of us," one agent said later. "It didn't seem to matter how much stress or anxiety she had—she could switch it on or off. Once she got on the phone, she was totally on point."

Mom was never aware of Garfanji as an individual boss. The name she heard most often on the phone was "Abdi Yare."* But several bosses used that nickname, and Mom couldn't tell which boss was which. During a conference call with three top-ranking pirates, she tried to distinguish each voice, one at a time, without success. "They didn't want to talk," she said, except through a translator. "And I was shaking inside. But I figured if I burst out in tears, that wouldn't work. They had no compassion. So I tried to just keep

---

* Pronounced *Abdi Yeri*. I never heard this name until late in my captivity.

to the subject, and keep on repeating what I was trying to say. Sometimes I sounded like a broken record."

She dealt with the stress on the tennis court. Golf had become her retirement game, but somehow tennis felt more satisfying while I was in Somalia. Between ransom calls, she reverted to her more strenuous sport. "I needed something to hit with a racket," she told me. "And I thought of the ball as Abdi Yare's head."

XII

Plane visits over Hobyo became more common after the phone call, and for the next two weeks, at Mohammed's House, I made a strict habit of unfolding my hand-drawn map in the outhouse and flashing Morse code at the sky. The sound of aircraft tracing a wide arc overhead could lift my mood for hours. Otherwise Mohammed's prison compound was a tedious and nasty solitary confinement, and in spite of the relative calm I preferred the Italian ruin with Rolly and Marc. I missed Rolly's conversation; I missed the way he said, "We are *prizhonerr*," and explained things to me with one palm open, like an old Frenchman making an appeal.

One afternoon in the first or second week of March, I heard a commotion on the porch and saw a black arm, with a gold wristwatch, point into my room. Ali Duulaay. I sat in the mosquito tent with a notebook and pen. Duulaay wanted to know from the guards why I wasn't ready to leave. With a wash of dread I tossed my radio and notebooks into a plastic bag, and Duulaay lurched in wearing his rifle. He threatened me with it and shook the curved ribs of the tent. There was no time to grab an important bag of clothes, and I left other things hanging or scattered around the room—towel, toothbrush, leather jacket concealing my LED lighter. Since I was barefoot, I stopped to put on my shoes. Duulaay pinched a slab of flesh in my side and twisted.

"*Go, go, go, go,*" he said.

A white car waited in the road. I climbed in front, and Duulaay crammed into the rear. Other pirates glared at me from the back seat while we sped off, as if I were the source of their trouble; Duulaay muttered something bitter and slugged me in the head.

Soon another car caught up to us, churning dust. We bounced through the trackless bush, over ridges and rocks, and my head whanged with adrenaline. We arrived at some kind of gully south of Hobyo, another dry riverbed cut into the sand. Somalis piled out of the second car with equipment—pots, mattresses, weapons—and two other hostages made their way toward the wadi. Even at a distance, with blurry eyes, I recognized Rolly and Marc.

The Somalis flopped our mattresses at the foot of a crumbling six-foot bank. A tree with its root system exposed in the wall of dirt stretched up a canopy of leaves. We had to lie beside the roots. Nervous birds fluttered and chirped overhead.

"Ali come get you?" said Rolly.

"Yeah. I didn't have time to bring my clothes."

"What you got there?" He nodded at my plastic bag.

"Notebooks. A change of shorts."

"Marc, also. Ali come in and say, '*Go, go, go.*' I no listen, I take my time, I duck under Ali's arm," he said. "I got all my bags. But Marc have to go without his things."

"Why do you think we left in such a hurry?" I said.

"I not know."

The open bush struck me as a good staging area for a SEAL raid, less dangerous than a house with concrete walls. I didn't mind the prospect of my friends getting rescued, too. But Rolly's face worked again with nervous anguish, maybe churning through his old, unchanging trenches of thought. At last he made his declaration.

"Now we in the desert," he said.

A pirate came down to attach a blanket to the thorny tree branches over our head. "No blanket," I objected, meaning I didn't want the shade, but he insisted. "Because *qorrax*," he said, meaning sun, but I knew very well it wasn't because of the sun.

Fifteen or twenty minutes later, we saw the glint of an aircraft to the south.

"Is an airplane," said Rolly.

The Somali hadn't dangled a blanket on that side, so I mumbled, "It can see all three of us."

"Is too far, Michael."

"I doubt that."

A nearby pirate lit a cigarette, using an LED-equipped lighter, so I bummed a smoke. When he obliged, I palmed the lighter. It would have been appalling manners anywhere else in the world, but the guard just nodded and smiled. There was no shortage of lighters in the camp. Now I had a flashlight again.

Later the pirates delivered thick, sturdy rubber thongs in a plastic package marked MADE IN THAILAND. These Thai sandals replaced my shoes. We each received a pair, and we quibbled about the colors. Rolly took yellow, Marc took orange, I took light blue.

I explained to the pirates that because of Ali Duulaay, we lacked other important items. Marc had no blanket. I had no coat. "Tonight, cold," I told them. "Desert, cold."

"*Haa.*" Yes.

"Jacket coming?"

"No problem."

An hour later, I stood up to unhook the blanket from thorns

in the tree. The Somalis stared. I handed it to Marc. The guards weren't about to confiscate the blanket from an old man, so, after a while, a pirate came around to hang a new blanket, a pink one with flowers, to protect us from the "sun."

"No blanket," I protested.

"*Haa*, blanket."

"Jacket coming?"

"No problem."

None materialized, so by the end of the day, when sundown had cooled the air, I made the same complaint.

"No jacket. Problem!" I said, and stood up to unhook the pink blanket from the tree. "Tonight, cold!"

Now we had a flashlight, two blankets, and nothing to block the view of another surveillance plane. Rolly found it amusing. But he wiped his anguished face with one hand and said, with as much irony as force of habit, "Not make them angry, Michael . . ."

"Okay, Rolly." I smiled. "I'll try."

XIII

We spent most of March in the desert bush: a week under the bird-infested tree, then more time under an arching white thorn bramble, a cluster of bushes so large that Rolly could stand up inside it. We ate car-delivered pasta from plastic sacks and listened to the radio. The white thorns were supposed to shield us from overhead view, but I made a point of flashing the sky with my cigarette lighter in the morning and evening, away from camp, when I went to relieve myself in the weeds. Large planes cruised near us twice a week.

Meanwhile, I scribbled in my notebook. Whenever a guard noticed, I told him that writing helped my wrist heal. Most of the pirates didn't give a damn, but I felt an instinct to keep the book hidden from Ahmed Dirie.

One afternoon, the fading sunlight in our thorn bramble struck a fat bead of red sap bulging from a branch. I reached up from my mattress to inspect it. I'd never seen such a garnet color seep out of a plant before. These white thornbushes were a source of myrrh resin—they grow across Yemen and Somalia and parts of Ethiopia—so the symbolism was about as subtle as a crucifix on Mexican velvet. But Rolly said, "You know, Michael, in my country, we say when you see thorns, you going to heaven. But when you see flowers, then you going to hell."

I cleared my throat.

"Well, we haven't seen a flower in months," I said. "We must be doing okay."

"Yes, but . . ." He looked deeply troubled. He had just lost a rosary, a charm he'd rescued from the *Aride*. "I not know if I believe that now."

Late one morning, we piled into a pair of cars and drove north for most of the day. Near sundown we found a strange village close to the coast, a near ghost town with widely spaced stone buildings. We parked outside this village, seemingly at random, and Ahmed Dirie climbed out to stand next to our car with his phone in the air, as if to check for signals. He gave me a rotten smile.

"What are you doing?" I said.

"No problem."

The evening sun cast a sulfurous, green-yellow light. The pirates ordered Rolly out and led him to a distant rise overlooking the ocean, just out of sight, where he had to dial his family in the Seychelles. But something went wrong with the connection. There seemed to be no other point to our endless drive, as if we'd come all the way up here to shake aerial surveillance, to make a phone call to Mahé in signal-free air, without interference from international authorities— only the line was busy.

We continued north while the sun disappeared. In the dark we crossed an expanse of desert on a straight highway made of powdery dust. Nothing seemed to exist in the damnable blackness outside, and we spent almost an hour on the same unbending road. We drifted through the darkness on the soft dust, and the only feature I remember was another Land Rover, silver painted but blank as a shipwreck, rearing into view so fast that our driver had to jerk the steering wheel.

Abandoned. Someone else had tried to cross this desert, and failed.

Late the same night we drove into some hills and found a small cluster of huts. A herding family with curious children had prepared a place for us to sleep. In absolute silence they watched us, these ragged foreign strangers, as well as the glamorous pirates with their guns. A young girl climbed out of a squat hut the size of a doghouse, where we were supposed to sleep, and her innocence, her thirsty curious eyes, broke me open like an egg. Her presence was a stark, astonishing exception to the anger and sarcasm I had felt aimed in my direction for more than two months. The night felt cold, windless, and silent like no part of the world I'd ever seen.

"I been here before," mumbled Rolly after we settled into the little hut. "They take us here once before."

"Really?" I said.

"Yah, we come up from Hobyo. While you live in that house."

"How long?" I said.

"Five, six days, like that. We live in this hut. They make Marc pee in a bottle."

"Why?"

"They no let him outside."

We did get to leave the hut for bathroom breaks, but the emptiness of the countryside, whenever I did, alarmed me. The thornbushes grew evenly spaced, brown instead of white, all about three feet high. There were no acacia trees, nothing remarkable besides this single, far-flung breed of vegetation. Dying out here would be like drowning at sea. No one would even notice. We'd ventured beyond any landmarks that could help me orient my mind, and the long detour had frayed my sense of forward motion toward freedom. I just felt whirl and watery fear. I retraced our car trip and tried to fathom how I had arrived at this precise corner of the world, squatting near a thornbush and flashing the sky with my ridiculous LED, through a tube of toilet paper.

On the first evening, I noticed a boy from the nomad family, far off to one side. He'd followed me out here. Was he spying on my Morse-code habits? I put the lighter away, but while I pissed in the weeds, I tried to weigh my ambition to write a unique book about Somalia against the vastation of this place.

You have made a mistake, Boodiin had said. *Mistakes are human.*

On the second night, I went out to pee and noticed Ahmed Dirie and one other pirate pointing at the sky. One of them said "aeroplane," and after an hour they gave us an unexpected order to move. If dodging surveillance was the purpose of this detour, it had failed. Drones, or something, had pursued us. The pirates filled our car with mattresses, provisions, and cooking pots. Before we drove off, they searched my belongings. The LED cigarette lighter was in the pocket of my cotton shorts, which they didn't check. But Ahmed Dirie found my notebook.

"What is this?" he said, flipping through the tightly written pages.

"Practice. For my wrist."

Abdinasser the Sahib backed me up. He argued my case in Somali. Ahmed Dirie gave me a bitter squint, and rolled up the notebook to keep for himself. Weeks of therapeutic note-taking disappeared into his dusty bag.

"You respect me!" he ordered, and lifted his rifle.

"Oh, sure, boss," I said.

"You have a flashlight?" he asked in Somali.

Someone translated, and I said no, hoping they wouldn't search my shorts.

"Do you flash signals at satellites in the sky?" he said.

"No."

"If you flash signals at the sky, you will go down!" said Ahmed Dirie. He clicked the safety off his rifle and aimed the barrel at my chest. "You—like Michael Jackson," he said. "Boom. Dead!"

"I understand."

"You respect me!" he shouted.

"Oh, I respect you, boss."

"Or BOOM—down!"

"That's right."

Reluctantly, to my considerable surprise, he returned the notebook. After nightfall we took off under a fat moon. I recognized some of the silvered landscape and a few turns in the road. We started to speed along the straight, soft highway, and the driver bounced his wheels over stray rocks and jammed them into potholes. At last the abandoned Land Rover loomed up again like a ghost.

Rolly cried, *"Oh!* Jesus," and I grimaced. I thought we might flip the car. Instead we slammed into a pothole, and the left front wheel started to knock like a hammer.

Ahmed Dirie told the driver to stop.

"We're fucked," I mumbled to Rolly.

"Why you say that?"

They hauled out a jack to lift the car. In the glare of a flash-light, they banged and twisted with hammers and wrenches until someone decided the wheel was fixed. The driver started again at a prudent speed. At last—still nervous about aircraft, I think, but convinced the wheel would hold—he stood on the gas.

It was like floating through darkness again, fishtailing along that soft, ethereal highway with almost no feeling of gravity, not even traction, until the left wheel slammed into another hole and we slid to a stop with the front axle leaning into the dust.

"Oh, Jesus," Rolly said again.

"Told you we were fucked," I mumbled.

"What happened?"

"Rolly, we lost a *wheel*."

"Oh, Jesus."

XIV

The sheer alarming stupidity of breaking off a wheel in the middle of the desert while running from a plane, or a drone, or nothing at all, made the blood pound and slosh in my head. There had to be a limit to the volume of absurdity we could suffer. But no nightmare dissipated, no director lowered his jib crane to stop the idiotic film, and no American analyst seemed to recognize this car accident as a wide-open chance to rescue three stranded hostages. "There is nothing like isolation in an atmosphere of electric violence for bringing before one's mind the understanding that the varnish of two thousand years is so thin as to be transparent," wrote Hanley in *Warriors*. "It is living in civilization that keeps us civilized. It is very surprising, and alarming at first, how swiftly it vanishes when one is threatened by other men, men of almost mindless resolve."

The rest of the night was too dumb to explain. But I noticed that living among lunatic people had made me depressed and lunatic, too. Hanley was right: chaos was contagious. Pirates acted like criminals because they belonged to a criminal gang. While we sat in the car and waited for them to solve our asinine situation I considered filching a Kalashnikov and solving it myself. I knew how to fire a weapon, but I wasn't a gunman, and without glasses I was half-blind. Not a good combination. But idiocy, evil, and entropy fed on themselves like a hurricane over warm water.

We returned to Mussolini's Farmhouse the next day in another car, and stayed about a week. One evening, I went out to piss on the white rocks and noticed a line of sharp lights on the dusky water. I didn't mention them afterward to Rolly, because I didn't know what they were, but the next morning, after he and Marc had traded shifts outside, Rolly said from his mattress, "Big ship, eh?"

"What?"

"Big ship in the water. Must be fifty meters, like that."

My heart fluttered. "Did it have a flag?"

"I didn't see no flag."

I went out to the white rocks myself and saw the vessel in broad daylight—a long, rusted, industrial-looking tub with a white bridge tower. Not a warship, not a freighter.

"Angelo say is from this pirate group," Rolly said when I returned. "Is hijacked."

"Oh. Where's it from?"

"He say China."

Our relationship with this vessel developed in quick phases. First, we almost ran out of toilet paper. When we harassed Ahmed

Dirie for more, he brought a Chinese-printed package of coarse, flat, folded stuff that was like paper towels.

A few days later, I went for a shower in the white stone ruin, shadowed by a tall Somali named Issa. He told me to take a "one-minute" shower, and while I tilted a plastic yellow jerry can full of water over my head, we heard the thump of a helicopter. I squatted behind a window of the ruin and watched. The wasplike helo raced across the ocean and circled the ship. Issa waved me over to a wall, where he stood holding his rifle.

"Get down!"

"What's the problem?" I said.

"NATO!" said Issa.

NATO was an all-purpose term for him, but NATO warships in fact worked only in the Gulf of Aden. The central Somali coast was monitored by the EU and a U.S.-led naval group. Either way, it was interesting. I took my time hiding behind the broken front wall.

That night the pirates woke up Rolly and me and hustled us into a car. We slept in the bush again, with Ahmed Dirie's group of guards. Despite the pirates' efforts to keep us out of sight, we were harassed by aircraft for almost a week. In mid-April—after days of playing tag with surveillance planes in the bush, moving camp almost every night—we packed up in the dark, and someone confiscated my notebook and radio. We drove for an hour and swapped vehicles among chaotic promises of freedom. "Make a good telephone call," said one guard, obscurely. "*Adiga*, free!" But there was no phone call. Instead we sped toward the coast, and while I considered how it might feel to see my family and friends again, our driver steered crazily through the quiet houses of Hobyo, past dimly lit businesses and food shacks—where townspeople had gathered for late-night meals—and raced across the curving beach until the Land Rover came to a stop beside the water's edge.

"What are we doing?" I said.

"Go, go, go, go."

A skiff had drawn up under the moon. With our Thai sandals in our hands, we waded into lukewarm surf. Pirates hopped in and told me to keep my pink blanket on my head, while the pilot puttered our skiff over crumbling whitewash, then higher swells, and around the seawall of rock, which Hamid, in a different lifetime, had insisted should be a loading pier.

Then the pilot opened his throttle. He pushed us faster over the swells, up and down, causing the hull to slap. The blanket slipped off my head. We spent more and more time in the air between each wave.

"Slow down!" I shouted into the wind.

One pirate motioned as if he expected me to fix my pink head covering. For that I would have to let go of the rail.

"Slow the fuck *down!*" I shouted.

The guards sat on a relatively stable bulkhead at the rear of the boat. We sat in the bouncing front. As we picked up speed, Rolly shifted his weight off our bulkhead and squatted in the hull, holding the rail with one tight-knuckled hand. He used his knees to absorb the motion of the waves, and I tried to do the same, but we flew over another swell and the boat dropped away from my butt. Our bulkhead floated downward, leaving me in the air. When we came together again, the bulkhead hammered my spine, and pain shot from my tailbone to the base of my skull. I collapsed into the bottom of the skiff. ("I see you go down," Rolly said later. "You go down like a leaf.")

The pilot brought his speed under control. I managed to sit up, but my back throbbed. We pulled alongside the ship, and someone hurled a rope. The motion of the rolling hull, together with the waves, bounced our boat like an elevator, and a pirate showed us how to climb up. Rolly did it first, standing on the skiff's prow until a cutaway section of the gunwale lurched into range. Someone lifted him, he grabbed the gunwale, and a group of Somalis on the ship leaned over to grasp his shoulders and pull him aboard.

I went up the same way. My back hurt, but the feeling of four men lifting me helpfully by the shoulders was a strange distraction. We found ourselves on a square deck lit with sharp white lamps, where dozens of Chinese-looking hostages lay on mats, arranged like dominoes. We had woken them up. The Somalis led us up a set of metal stairs and around to a forward section of the ship, where our two mattresses waited on the upper deck.

"Sleeping, sleeping," they said.

I certainly wanted to be unconscious. But my sore spine kept me aware of the ocean wind and a large number of spidery, unknown pirate guards. My notebooks and radio were gone. I wondered if the Somalis had moved us here to dodge a raid on land. If so, everything had to reset. Drones would have to find us again. Military plans, if any, would be redrawn. Three wasted months in filthy prison houses and the desert bush had themselves gone to waste. My breathing came fast. I still wanted forward momentum, progress, logic, but instead I felt the edge of an emotional hurricane, the whistle of a gathering panic. Several hours earlier I had indulged fantasies of freedom; now I was injured and stuck on a ship. For the first time in Somalia, but not the last, I considered suicide.

One common story about the trauma of gunfire is that you feel the bullets at first like a spatter of rain. The body registers a brush of metal but recoils from the rest of the damage in a merciful cloud of shock. The burning horror comes later. On the deck of this wind-blown vessel I think my captivity first started to feel really hopeless. I couldn't see well in the dark, my back radiated pain, and, with my notebook gone, I wondered how to sort out the confusion in my head.

The notes also represented a small pile of work, so my time on land seemed triply wasted. And the confusion of ocean elements didn't help. I thought our vessel had started to move. Seagulls flapped into the wind under the strong deck lamps, not flying forward but scouting for fish in the artificial light; they seemed to glide and flap next to a sailing ship. I didn't realize the vessel was straining against its anchor chain in a stiff current. It wavered back and forth in the water, so the moon changed position in the sky, and the flapping of the birds, with the shifting of the moon, gave me the false impression that we were motoring north. This wrong idea infested me with a ferocious despair, and after a long sail to some forsaken part of the Somali coast, I thought, the pirates would no doubt assemble armies of men to defend this vessel of the damned; and it was time, at last, to check out.

Part 4

THE AMBIGUOUS ASIAN FISHING BOAT

I

The illusion of sailing north persisted through the night. But I must have slept, because the pirates had to wake us up in the morning under a bright sun. They said an American warship was standing two or three miles off. "Aeroplane!" they added mysteriously, and ordered us down to the lower deck.

The ship tilted back and forth on gentle swells. I moved gingerly for the staircase. But I wasn't fast enough for Abdinuur, who shoved my shoulder, causing the pain in my spine to flare.

Abdinuur carried a machine gun with a heavy band of .30-caliber rounds,* and we stood near a railing. I snapped, "Abdinuur, if you do that again, I'll throw you over the side of this fucking ship," and I meant it with all my heart. Lucky for both of us Abdinuur spoke no English.

Downstairs, the pirates tossed our mattresses under a workbench-size conveyor belt installed along the forward edge of the deck. Stuffed under this metal-and-rubber contraption, we would be harder for a drone to find.

The Asian crew sat around the deck, watching us with young, gentle, curious faces. Some looked Southeast Asian, not Chinese. They seemed pleasant enough, but the back injury put me in a snappish and fatalistic mood. I squinted around the deck for the best place to jump. I did not want to be on the ship.

---

* A Kalashnikov "PKM," with its heavy ribbons of ammunition, is the machine gun commonly seen lugged across the shoulders in photos of Somali pirates. The rounds are 7.62 millimeters wide, equal to about .30 caliber.

White and aquamarine paint seemed to flake off the walls of the bridge tower, across from us. The whole steel vessel thrummed with noise from a generator. My vision blurred the faces of the sailors, the sunlit rubber deck, and the rail of the ship, so escape was hard to assess. But I thought the cutaway section of the gunwale might work just fine. Maybe not now, not in front of everyone. Right now my spine throbbed. I understood why back pain had driven my father to pills.

A Filipino said, "Would you like some coffee?"

"What? Oh, sure," I said.

We received tin mugs of milky Nescafé. The Filipinos also handed around wads of fried dough, which had been sizzling in an electric wok.

"Coffee and doughnuts," I muttered with approval.

"Is good!" Rolly said.

The more I squinted, the more the ship impressed me. It had no flies. It had working electrical outlets and trickling water pumps. An old Honda motor loomed next to our conveyor belt, with curved metallic-green surfaces like an antique fridge. Behind us, under a steel ceiling, in what English sailors would call the forecastle, many more hostages were crammed. Caged lightbulbs burned on the steel ceiling inside; clotheslines had been laced between the metal cages. I saw T-shirts, flowered surf shorts, peaked straw hats dangling by their strings. Everything swayed with the listing ship. The Pacific tone of the crew's belongings salved my homesick brain.

The ship was a tuna vessel called the *Naham 3*, and it had sailed from Mauritius, an African island nation south of the Seychelles. The owners were Taiwanese. The crew came from China, Taiwan, Cambodia, Indonesia, the Philippines, Vietnam. The captain had been Taiwanese, but the captain was gone. Pirates had shot him.

One Filipino, Ferdinand, had a calm face with pooling brown

eyes. He seemed quiet and circumspect. His friend Arnel was lean and tall, with a brilliant smile. When he told us his name, he rolled the r—*Arrrnel*—so I could tell he was used to people from various parts of the world misunderstanding him. The Filipinos introduced us to a wiry Chinese man called Li Bo Hai—severe-looking, lean, with white flecks in his hair—who seemed to be in charge. Through Ferdinand's translation, he gave us a few basic facts. We were anchored near Hobyo, he said, in eighteen meters of water, a little over a mile from shore—

"Oh," I said. "Didn't we sail all night?"

"What do you mean?" said Ferdinand.

"Where are we now?"

"Yes, near Hobyo. We have been here since the end of March."

Ferdinand pointed, and in the distance I could just make out dirt-colored buildings clustered on the sand, spangled with bright reflections from the hot zinc roofs. In time, I learned to see the spindly shape of a cell-phone tower and the stranded fishing boat Hamid had pointed out from the beach, the *Shiuh Fu 1*, with the Chinese hostage who had committed suicide. It was a gray, distant, tilted wreck.

"Interesting," I said.

"That ship is just like this one," Ferdinand told us.

"Really? Run by the same company?"

"No. But also from Taiwan."

"I see."

A cry went up from the men behind us in the forecastle— "*Suban, suban!*"* is what I heard—and everyone sprang up to grab a bowl and chopsticks. Two crewmen came down the steps with

* "*Chi-fan, chi-fan!*"—Chinese for "eat."

fresh-cooked pots of rice, and a Chinese man handed us each a green plastic bowl and a pair of chopsticks. Another took our bowls away again but returned with breakfast, which involved Szechuan-spiced goat, soy-cooked vegetables, and green spinach noodles on a hot pile of rice.

This meal pulled me out of my funk. My spine still throbbed, but I hadn't seen such a wealth of food in almost three months. I dug in with my chopsticks.

Rolly said, "Michael, how you do this?"

"You never used chopsticks at home? I thought you were part Chinese."

"My mother!" he said. "Me, only one-quarter."

The *Naham 3* had no silverware. I stopped to give him a chopsticks lesson.

"This is good food," I said.

We ate squatting like peasants on the deck. Mixed with the spinach noodles was a twisted, chewy mushroom, or maybe a meat, which tasted delicious compared with the slop we'd been fed on land. When Rolly got the hang of the chopsticks, he cried out in recognition.

"Ah, I know this!" he said. "We call it *pans ton*."*

"What does that mean?"

"You no speak French?" he said.

"Only a little."

"Is the stomach from the tuna."

"Oh."

It was my turn to stop eating.

"Is good!" Rolly said.

---

* From *panse de thon* in French.

II

After breakfast, a cherubic young Filipino cook named Tony Libres introduced himself, using good English, and we spent the next hour dispelling false impressions.

"When you came on board last night," he said, "I thought you were a boss of the pirates."

"Why?"

He was bashful. "Because you are white."

Tony had briefly entertained the idea that Somali pirates took orders from white overlords. A few Chinese crewmen plied him with other questions. They wanted to know if Rolly and I were related. Americans, they understood, could be black or white. They also hadn't understood our names, so Tony found a glossy magazine, turned it to a color foldout of Michael Jackson, and held it up for everyone to see.

"You are Michael?" he prompted me, pointing at the picture.

"Yes," I said.

"Ahhh," said most of the crew.

We faced backward on the ship, toward the tall white bridge tower, which loomed out of sight. A few Somalis sat in front of it with Kalashnikovs in their languid hands, gazing down from an upper deck. A row of lozenge windows over their heads made up the ship's forward eyes, and two panes had been spiderwebbed by gunfire. Rolly pointed them out.

"Look like a bullet go in," he said.

The crew's astonishing story came together in fragments and shards, like a mosaic, throughout the rest of the morning. The *Naham 3* had left Mauritius in late 2011 to range off the African coast, chasing schools of tuna for several months, until the captain steered too close to Somalia in March. One night after twelve, two skiffloads of pirates fired sudden, scattered shots at the bridge. Three Chinese men scrambled from their cabins to find a flare gun. Flares and bullets flew on the high port side of the vessel until the pirates clambered up, using hooked ladders. The Chinese men ran out of flares and retreated. Chen Lui Te, the sixty-three-year-old captain, had picked up a stool to defend the ship's controls, but pirates appeared at the bridge's entrance, firing wildly. Chen Lui Te took two bullets in the neck and another in the chest. The panicked Somalis ran off, but blood spurted from the captain's neck.

"He didn't even sway a bit," one of the Chinese flare gunners said later. "He simply put down the stool and walked to the back of the ship."

He survived long enough to reach the engine room, where he sat down and died.

Arnel and the other men who slept in the cabins behind the bridge tried to lock their hollow doors. But pirates charging through the corridor shot out the knobs. Eventually the gunmen rounded up the twenty-eight crew and forced them to kneel in the bridge, blindfolded, hands behind their backs. For three days they sat like prisoners of war. Twice a day they went free to eat rice at the small captain's table.

A pair of Chinese engineers, Li Bo Hai and one other man, were excused from rough treatment—they had to steer. The Somalis gave them GPS coordinates. The ship trundled steadily for almost seventy-two hours, at ten knots, to reach Hobyo.

While we listened to these details, I saw a naked crewman take a shower across the work deck. Water burbled from a large hose tied at the height of his shoulders. Right next to him, another crewman opened a steel freezer door set into the wall, without regard for the naked man's comfort, and vapor from the freezer tumbled around his ankles.

"The captain is in the back," said Arnel.

"In the freezer?"

"All the way back, in the deep freeze," he said. "It has different rooms."

"I see."

"Most of this ship is a freezer."

Late in the morning, Ali Tuure, the pirate boss, came to sit next to us under the conveyor belt. He resembled a happy skeleton, haggard and stoop shouldered,* with a rictus of horrible teeth. He spoke in wheezy Somali and pinched his cigarette between his thumb and index finger. Worst of all, he acted happy to see me. He patted my bare leg the way a farmer would pat fine livestock. My back still hurt, and I didn't like being patted. I explained my injury on the skiff. Tuure summoned Li Bo Hai, who went to fetch a bottle of ginger oil. I still felt snappish, fatalistic, and slightly unhinged. My first experience with Chinese medicine didn't cure me of suicidal thinking or the sharp anguish I felt over the loss of my notebooks, but it did ease my back pain. The whole Asian crew watched me lie on my belly to let Li Bo Hai pound hand-warmed oil into my spine.

Captain Tuure acted like a sarcastic gentleman: he wanted his new guests to feel at home. He gave us permission to use his private toilet and shower—upstairs in the captain's cabin. We had a dim notion of the privilege he was offering, since the ordinary crew toilets consisted of two square grilles, which functioned as all-purpose drains, in the corners of the work deck. Saltwater pumping from a hose, like the one by the freezer door, would flow into a cubic space beneath each grille, where it washed everything into the ocean.

---

* "Tuure" is a Somali nickname for a hunchback.

That was the whole system. A tarp could be pulled across the front of the toilet area for (not much) privacy.

Before he went upstairs, Tuure said, "Whiskey?"

"What?"

Did I want whiskey? What a strange question.

"Sure," I said, though in this case I didn't understand the morbid extent of the privilege he was offering. Tuure stood up and disappeared.

The crew on the *Naham 3* carved out blocks of time for meals, coffee, TV, and showers. They took most of their showers around dusk, after dinner. They lined up near each corner grille to wait their turn at the hoses of saltwater. For half an hour, Rolly and I watched all twenty-eight men strip naked and wash. They made rude jokes in Cambodian or Chinese and snapped one another with towels. One Cambodian had bowl-cut hair and Buddhist tattoos across his muscled back. Arnel pointed at him.

"When I go free," he said, "I will marry his sister."

The Cambodian had a strong, square ass and a brilliant smile. I laughed out loud.

"Have you met his sister?"

"I don't know if he has one," Arnel said in a lilting, comical voice. "But I will marry her."

After showers, the men smoked cigarettes. Bluish-white deck lamps snapped on as the sun set behind Hobyo. In a rush, the crew laid out sleeping mats on the conveyor belt, on deck—on any flat surface of the ship. Meanwhile, Captain Tuure came downstairs and surprised me with a bottle of Taiwanese malted whiskey.

"Whiskey, okay!" he said with a wheezy flourish, and returned upstairs.

I turned the brown bottle in my hand.

"This belonged to the captain," Tony said.

I wasn't about to drink a dead man's whiskey in front of his captive crew. I wasn't about to hoard it, either. At last I twisted open the cap and passed it around. The efficient Chinese used some empty plastic water bottles to divide up the precious liquid. Western whiskies are clear and sharp, but this tasted closer to thick brown beer, sweet and lightly carbonated. No one got drunk that night. But the weight of thirst behind me, the sheer mass of silent and frustrated desire, was my first lingering impression of the crew.

III

The *Naham 3* belonged to the vast international fleet of rusted boats that deliver sushi to the developed world. It was an old vessel, commissioned in 1982, registered in Oman but owned by a family in Taiwan. Asian ships like the *Naham 3* and the *Shiuh Fu 1* were common off Somalia. They caught tons of bigeye and yellowfin tuna near Africa and hauled the meat back to the Seychelles or Mauritius, flash-frozen, to be transferred to large freighters for the final trip to market. The fish could wind up anywhere in the world, depending on quality—from cans in American convenience stores to elegant markets in Europe—but the *Naham 3*, with its legitimate registration papers, caught fresh tuna for sushi bars in Japan and Taiwan.

Long-lining is factory fishing, but it's not the same as trawling. A tuna trawler can shred coral reefs. A longline uses baited hooks on an industrial scale. Tony and the other men explained how the *Naham 3* worked. The line itself was a kilometer-long rope spun out by the moss-green Honda motor standing next to us. It had three wheels, like bare car rims. While the rope wheeled out, the men had to attach sink lines to it, using stiff clamps. These lines were called snoods. They had weights as well as a number of hooks, and each hook bore a single six-inch mackerel for bait.

In the water, the baited snoods hung from the longline at ten-foot intervals, suspended on the surface by round yellow floats. The ship, in effect, laid a kilometer-long curtain of bait in the water. Then it moved off some distance to do it again. At the end of the day, it made another round to collect each curtain, and then the men's work started in earnest. The rope wheeling back through the Honda motor would drag the snoods over the gunwale, heavy with fish. It was somebody's job to cut each tuna free and slide it down a fiberglass tray to let other men carve out the hook, gills, and guts. "See that bench?" Tony said, pointing at a fiberglass bench against the wall where a half-dozen hostages sat. "That is a tuna tray." Every day they fished, the men had to assemble sections of this tray system, and each massive tuna would slide from the conveyor belt into the fiberglass maze, losing its gills and its insides, acquiring a loop of rope through the tail, until someone dangled it from the hooked fish scale to record its weight. Then it went into the freezer.

Each tuna weighed between 50 and 80 kilograms,* and the ship, at the time of capture, was carrying around 100 metric tons of fish.

It was half-full.

---

* 110 to 180 pounds.

The economics of tuna were brutal, and some business owners could be little more than slave drivers. The *Naham 3* had valid labor contracts, but some crewmen still felt hoodwinked by their terms of employment. A Singaporean staffing agency called Step Up Marine Enterprise had recruited the Filipinos. "When I signed up, I didn't know I would have to fish near Africa," Tony said. He thought it would be a boat in the South China Sea. His recruiter had offered a good wage and an impressive plane ticket to Singapore to finalize the contract. The Step Up office, though, turned out to be a cramped room in a flashing Chinatown mall known as the People's Park Centre. The agents there said Tony would have to fly to Mauritius, an island off Africa that he had never heard of, to board a long-distance industrial vessel and fish the Indian Ocean. If he wanted the job.

"What if you said no?" I asked.

"Then I could go home." His eyes rounded. "But pay my own ticket!"

The hourly wage disappointed him. Some days there was nothing to do, of course, and while they sailed from one fishing spot to another, the crew found time to read, watch TV, or weave thick white hammocks. (Two swinging hammocks near the tuna bench were Arnel's handiwork.) But when they had to fish, which was often, they worked twenty hours a day. They ate fifteen-minute meals. Tony shook his head at the deceit. Four hours of sleep a night! The Step Up people hadn't mentioned that. "We make two hundred and fifty dollars a month," said Arnel, still using the present tense, because, even as hostages, the men expected to be paid through the end of their contracts. He added, in a sweet, ironic-dolorous tone, "Small money!"

Step Up Marine Enterprise later changed its name on the shop at the mall, and its owner, Victor Lim, was charged with trafficking Filipino sailors in another case. Other *Naham 3* crewmen would tell similar recruitment stories. And now they were hostages in Somalia, where pirates were happy to treat them like thieves.

A number of pirate bosses had boarded the *Naham 3* when it anchored in Hobyo, and they beat the Chinese crew with broom handles. They interrogated the Filipinos, who spoke English. "One man aimed a rifle at me from behind," said Ferdinand. "Another asked how long we had been in the Somali area. He said, 'Since December, right?' I said no—it was only a few days. But they didn't like this answer." So the interrogator ordered his gunman to blow off Ferdinand's head. "I make my prayer to God," Ferdinand told me, "and the man pulled his trigger."

There was an explosion, and a flash, but the rifle was loaded with blanks.

Asian and European ships have exploited Somalia's rich fisheries for decades. They've exploited the ill-defended waters of almost every African nation, up and down both coasts of the continent, and this foreign heist of live fish represents a disgusting crime against people who can hardly feed themselves. The crime is exacerbated by trawlers, which rake heavy nets behind them and essentially bulldoze the bottom of the sea. Illegal industrial fishing can make refugees of traditional fishermen in places like Madagascar, Kenya, São Tomé, and Senegal, where seafood matters to the culture.

Seafood plays a less important role in Somalia, where the culture is nomadic more than seafaring; but the crime is real, even if pirates tried to extend their sense of grievance. Most pirates I met, for example, seemed vaguely aware of a two-hundred-mile "exclusive economic zone." International law tends to draw two borders off the coast of any nation—twelve nautical miles from shore, and two hundred. The twelve-mile limit represents territorial waters, and foreign fishing within that margin is a crime, outright theft of food. The U.N. also recognizes a two-hundred-mile "exclusive economic zone" for most countries, where it would break treaties for foreign interests to fish or, say, drill for oil. The legal hitch for Somalia was that no government in Mogadishu had ever claimed the two-hundred-mile zone under the 1982 United Nations Convention on the Law of the Sea. "Somalia doesn't have an EEZ because it's never claimed an EEZ," a U.N. expert told me in early 2012.* Some foreign vessels therefore came in to exploit this stretch of water, and some pirates claimed to defend it.

The Hobyo pirates, in any case, had captured the *Naham 3* hundreds of miles off Somalia. The nearest landmass was the Seychelles' Bird Island, more than seven hundred miles from Hobyo. The Taiwanese owners and captain had made the dicey but not illegal decision to fish near pirate-infested waters. They may have overfished—the owners were later fined in South Africa for landing too much tuna with a similar vessel in their fleet—but the *Naham 3* had not been stealing Somali fish. It was innocent, as far as any industrial vessel could be innocent.

The crew felt these tensions keenly. Later in the afternoon, three pirates came down to the work deck, and Abdinuur, the machine gunner, wanted to try some recreational fishing. The crew fell silent. Someone baited the line. We watched him hurl it out. Abdinuur wore a gold-colored watch high on his wrist; he could be flashy and arrogant, but he had no patience, no feeling for a meaningful tug. Soon, in a panic, he tried to reel in the line. His thin arms flailed; the gold watch glinted in the sun.

---

* A new president, Hassan Sheikh Mohamud, finally did claim a Somali EEZ in 2014.

All the hostages laughed.

"Why are you laughing?" I asked Tony.

"Pirates can't fish," he said.

IV

Later, from our mattresses under the conveyor belt, Rolly and I watched a Vietnamese man toss out the same fishing line and pull up a fat, fire-red snapper. He wore a round straw hat in the mounting sun. We saw him clobber the fish with a knife.

Rolly frowned. "You must not kill a fish like this," he said.

"How do you kill them?"

"You must cut their necks," he said, and drew a finger across his own. "Is better."

I shuddered. Rolly went on watching with professional interest.

"We anchored over a reef," he said.

A pirate upstairs pointed at a crewman and yelled, "Fish, Somali!"—a direct order, meaning "Prepare fish for Somalis." Three hostages cleared tools from the top of a dark box built in to the deck, which resembled a workbench. They lifted off the metal top; vapor rose from below. With gloves and a hand hook they wrestled out a massive tuna and thumped it onto the rubber deck mat. It was iron-colored, with snowy eyes, four or five feet long and plump as a sow. D-shaped holes were carved where its gills had been. Someone produced a circular saw, and two men leaned on the fish to steady it with gloved hands while the other started a lateral cut through the side. The blade whined and tossed an arc of pink dust.

The strips of meat and silver skin went clattering like metal bars into a pan filled with seawater. The tuna carcass went back into the freezer hold. When the meat had defrosted, a small team hacked the strips into smaller pieces. Tony then disappeared to cook them in the kitchen for the pirates' lunch.

"That's slave labor," I said from under the conveyor belt.

"Yah. I want to say this, too." Rolly nodded. "Is slavery."

On our second morning aboard the *Naham 3*, the guards upstairs grew agitated and shuffled around with brandished guns. One came down to yell, "Michael! Helicopter!" and ordered me to sit deep in the work area. I moved into the prow and sat near a sunwarmed steel wall, where I made friends with two Cambodians and an Indonesian. The sound of rotor blades descended and circled us more than once; from our stowage I watched Somalis on the bridge deck aim rifles at the sky. I never saw the helicopter, but I could imagine what it was doing.

When I had sailed on the *Gediz*, with Captain Özyurt and Yaşar, I had also flown on the ship's helicopter. We'd ridden out to inspect a mysterious dhow. I sat near an open side door, next to a sniper, who held a high-powered rifle in his lap. We circled close to the dhow but saw only lumps of unidentifiable cargo covered in blue tarps. The vessel had a wooden bridge, painted white and yellow and blue. The crew looked Indian or Pakistani. They stared up from the deck while the Turkish sniper took aim through our open door.

"Why did you aim your gun?" I asked after our first pass.

"Force protection." He smiled. "This is the rule."

Pirates often hijacked dhows to use as mother ships, trailing skiffs across the Gulf of Aden or hundreds of miles into the Indian Ocean. This one had no visible weapons, ladders, or fuel tanks, no skiffs or outboard motors. "Force protection" was a euphemism for *We make sure we don't get popped.*

When the helicopter came around the *Naham 3* again, the chop of its rotors vibrated the steel hull. All the fishermen hunched. Every pass, in their minds, carried the threat of a raid. I didn't think the helicopter would attack in broad daylight, but I didn't mind being watched, and I had no doubt that a uniformed sniper was aiming out the side, making sure our pirates could see him.

The helicopter left, and Somalis quit pacing the bridge deck. The mood of the fishermen relaxed. I returned to my spot under the conveyor belt.

"How often do these helicopters come?" I asked Tony.

"We have been here three weeks," he said. "There have been three helicopters."

V

A supply skiff buzzed out from Hobyo twice a day, as a rule, and the first skiff on our second morning delivered a load of new clothes. I got a red Manchester United jersey wrapped in plastic and cardboard. A label on the package had sultry underwear models and cheap slogans in Chinese, and where exactly the Somalis had acquired this merchandise was a glaring question. One crewman, a kid named Jie, with full lips and a dark swoop of hair—who could have been a Chinese underwear model himself—took the package, studied it, gave an impenetrable smile, shrugged, and handed it back.

"Cargo," he quipped.

On the third morning, pirates on a bouncing skiff handed up a live goat and a tall, awkward-looking Somali who carried no weapon but wore a lethal Hawaiian-print shirt. He disappeared up to the bridge. Another Somali tied the goat to the staircase. The goat watched him sharpen a rusted fish knife and bleated in the wind. Soon four men wrestled it to the rubber mat and held its kicking legs while the Somali sawed open its neck. The goat protested by trying to leap off the boat, but the men held its legs, and blood spread across one corner of the deck. I noticed the nervous tail wag even after the rest of its body had fallen still.

They strung the hind legs from an upper railing and let the gash bleed out. Chinese and Cambodian men made expert cuts at the heel of each leg and flayed the skin. What swung from the upper rail was soon no different from the meat suspended in any Muslim butcher shop—I had seen ribbed sections of goat like that in Morocco, Gaza, and northern Iraq—but with a staring, swinging head.

Someone washed away the blood with a seawater hose. Parts of the goat went straight to the kitchen. The rest went into the freezer.

The Hawaiian-shirted man came down to sit on the tuna bench. He had work to do, apparently, involving his mobile phone and a notebook. He used a plastic chair for a makeshift desk. He ordered Tony to fry him a fish. After a while he asked me a question.

"How do you like the food on this ship?"

It felt strange to be addressed like that, with no preliminaries, from about twelve feet off.

"An improvement," I said.

"Yeah, it's because they got dedicated cooks on board here."

That was not the only reason, but I decided not to mention the relative sophistication of Chinese versus Somali cuisine.

This man's name was Abdul. He had clear, American-accented English. Ferdinand whispered to us that he was the pirate who had questioned him about the ship's whereabouts in December and ordered his mock execution. The crew seemed afraid of him. They thought he was a pirate boss.

At last Tony served up a whole deep-fried wrasse, and Abdul asked for ketchup.

"Okay, I want all the Vietnamese over here," he announced.

Three fishermen crawled out from the crowded work area to squat around him. Abdul explained, through Arnel, that he would call the Vietnamese embassy in Kenya. "Then we're gonna talk to your families," he said. He dialed a number and we listened to him give a glib spiel to an English-speaking embassy worker: "Yeah, I'm calling about your guys who are hostages on a fishing boat here in Somalia? Yeah. The *Naham 3*. What? I'm calling from Somalia. I just came from talkin' to these guys, and I gotta say, they're really, really suffering a lot . . ."

When the conversation ended, he dialed each Vietnamese man's home, one at a time. When the calls went through, we heard quiet discussions in Vietnamese. The negotiator then summoned the Cambodians and went through the same cycle. It lasted all morning.

Arnel translated because he understood English, not because he spoke other languages on the boat. The *Naham 3* had no common language. Arnel spoke to the other men in an improvised pidgin of English and Chinese and several other languages. They used the Chinese *hai dao** for "pirate." *Saitei* was "the worst" or "no good," from Japanese, and *loco-loco* meant "crazy."† Doubling any simple word could turn it into pidgin, so "laundry" was *washy-wash*, "a little" was *small-small*, and "eating," as well as "food," was *chum-chum*.

---

* We pronounced it *hai-tau*.

† I have no idea where they learned the Spanish word.

"Talking" was *bow-wow*. "Too much" or "plenty" of anything was *sa-sa*, and it could apply to water, food, or insanity among the pirates. I learned quickly that if you wanted to express how pirates flapped their mouths with little or no consequence—an idea that came up more than once—you said, *"Hai dao bow-wow sa-sa."*

One man called Nguyen Van Ha sat with us after his phone call and showed us notes written on a scrap of cigarette carton. He was the Vietnamese man who liked to fish in a peaked straw hat. The pirates wanted three hundred thousand dollars per Vietnamese sailor—a total of nine hundred thousand dollars from the Hanoi government—but they had also demanded three hundred thousand from each family. So they were demanding the same ransom twice.[*] Nguyen Van Ha tapped his head.

"Loco-loco," he said.

Ransom demands were different for every national group. A Chinese man cost three hundred fifty thousand dollars, a Cambodian one hundred fifty thousand. The twenty-eight ransoms were supposed to total about twenty million dollars, but what each figure had in common was the impression it made on the hostage and his family at home: *That's fucking crazy.* (*"Hai dao loco-loco."*)

During a pause between phone calls, the negotiator came over to chat. Like Boodiin, he had deeply dishonest habits of speech, mixing his chummy American slang with a Somali talent for insult. It harmed my blood pressure to talk to him.

"I heard about your case," he said to me. "You got arrested in January."

"'Arrested' is a funny word for what happened to me," I said.

---

[*] Three times, it later turned out—they wanted equivalent sums from the shipowners.

"The commander just now said you got something wrong with your back."

By "commander" he meant Tuure. I told him about the skiff accident.

"Well, maybe you don't know how to ride in these boats," he chided me.

"No one advised me to take boating lessons before I came to Somalia," I said. "But your pilot was a madman."

Abdul tried to act worldly and smooth, but when he smiled, he looked smug as well as depraved. His upper teeth flared in a neat fan. "We will get you some antibiotics," he promised.

"No, hang on," I said. "I don't have an infection in my gut, I have a bone-and-muscle problem. Antibiotics won't do any good."

"What do you need?"

"Pain relief."

Abdul nodded and turned to Rolly. "We've met before." He held out his hand to shake, but Rolly, God bless him, answered:

"Yah, we meet in Hobyo! You tell me you a doctor."

I laughed out loud.

"No, I didn't," said Abdul.

"Yah!" Rolly protested. "When I come to Hobyo, you ask if I need medicine—because me, I'm an old man. You say, you can get any kind of medicine."

"Oh." He gave us the fan-toothed smile. "But I wouldn't have said I was a doctor."

"Yes, you told me that!"

Rolly wasn't doing this for my sake—he didn't even look at me. He just wanted the truth to be known. He was full of outraged justice, and in these moods he was wonderful to watch.

"Okay, okay," said Abdul, routed, and he returned to his position on the bench.

VI

Rolly and I slept under the conveyor belt for five nights. We got used to the rhythm of the other twenty-eight men unrolling their mats and arranging themselves for sleep while sharp floodlights glared from the upper deck, swells rolled under the ship, and Somalis upstairs played music on a tinny radio. But I woke up in the middle of each night with my heart trotting. If the worst condition for an untortured hostage is uncertainty, the rocking of the ocean deepened my disorientation. I thought about jumping into the dark water and wondered if I had steered myself into a psychological trap, similar to my father's, a situation with no clear way out but self-destruction. *You have made a mistake. Mistakes are human.* Like any human I preferred to be proud of myself, not ashamed. Like any writer I wanted to be right. Now I was wrong—worse than wrong: I'd taken a spectacular risk in coming to this dangerous place, and the evil that continued to flow from my mistake was impossible to square or defend.

Late on the fifth night, around ten, Abdul came out to wake everyone up. "Come on, we're going upstairs," he said. "Let's go, come on."

The dutiful Asian crew took their mats and lined up for the stairs.

"What's the matter?" I said.

"We are under attack," said the negotiator. "We got helicopters comin' in."

"Oh, boy."

"Yeah, you gotta get upstairs."

The crew was groggily obedient. No one moved very fast. We filed up the narrow bridge stairs, but the line of hostages stalled, and we had to rock with the ship about three stories over the dark, floodlit sea. Abdul lost his patience. "Come on, motherfuckers, get inside!" he yelled. The Asians shifted on their feet. They seemed willing to help, but they couldn't move. "Come on, motherfuckers!" Abdul hollered again, and in a frustrated rage he rounded on me, as if my presence were the source of his trouble. "Make yourself small!" he shouted. "Cover your head with your blanket! It is you they will be looking for!"

I gave him a cold stare. If helicopters were coming, I wanted to be seen, and he had no weapon, no authority beyond his frantic tantrum. I was not about to "make myself small" for Abdul.

In the tiny captain's cabin, several of us had to lie on the floor while a pirate sat in the corridor and aimed a rifle at my head. He sat at a small table where the late captain used to eat his meals. This pirate was crazy. "Do not even open your eyes!" he warned me. "If you open your eyes, you will be shot!"

Behind the bridge and down a set of stairs, the fluorescent-lit corridor led to a line of cabins where the others had to cram themselves. Abdul's panic accelerated during this organizational mess. He said pirates had noticed "signals" on the ship's radar. "Maybe they will attack, maybe they won't!" he said as he passed our cabin door, his bloodshot eyes widening. "Maybe we will all get killed! We don't know."

"Mm-hmm."

Four of us had to lie on the floor, with two others on the bed, in a room intended for one. The thin hollow door to the cabin had a ragged hole where the knob had been. It swung open and closed all night with the listing ship.

I slept in fits and woke from a doze around six thirty. Sun streamed into the corridor from the bridge. My guard looked sleepy and resentful, but when he saw me open my eyes, instead of shooting, he said, "Okay, come on," and a few of us filed down the steps.

We milled on the work deck before breakfast, trying to understand what had happened. Arnel told me the radar had malfunctioned. When the pirates couldn't fix it, they forced us upstairs for safekeeping.

"So, all fake?" I asked.

"I don't know!"

Captain Tuure came to sit with us before breakfast and said, "Five helicopters! NATO!" Abdul came down, too, and I asked him for an explanation.

"We saw it on the radar, and some of our guys, they got the phone number for NATO," Abdul said. "So when we saw them coming, we called 'em up and said, 'We got some hostages here, and we're gonna kill 'em all if the commandos try to come on board.'"

"I see."

"So they turned back."

"You saved our lives," I said.

"Yeah!" Abdul smiled. He liked that one. "It coulda been bad, man."

Captain Tuure pulled up his shirt and showed me a twisted-looking scar in his side. "NATO," he said.

"He's been shot by NATO?" I said.

"You know *Black Hawk Down*?" said Abdul.

"Yes. That was the U.N."

"Captain Tuure fought in that. He got hit by a helicopter. So he don't like to hear about helicopters."

"I guess not."

"He don't like Americans, either."

Captain Tuure started to speak in rapid Somali.

"He says, 'Why do we gotta deal with American planes all the time? These ACs, these fucking drones?'" Abdul said with equal feeling. "He says, 'Is this America, or is this Somalia?'"

I chuckled and said dryly, "Maybe if you didn't take Americans hostage you wouldn't see so many American planes."

Tuure spoke with more heat. "He says in Mogadishu that day, the American pilots got dragged through the streets," Abdul interpreted.

"*Black Hawk Down.* I know."

Tuure made hacking gestures with his hands, at his shoulders and knees. "You know what the people in Mogadishu did?" Abdul interpreted. "They chopped up the Americans and made a barbecue."

"Horseshit," I said.

"He was there. Tuure was there, man. He says the people were so mad, they chopped up the soldiers and had 'em for dinner."

"Are you going to stick to that story?" I asked Tuure.

"Were you there?" Abdul said.

"I'm a writer, Abdul. You want me to write that Somalis are cannibals?"

"American!" said Captain Tuure, and made his hacking gestures.

"Oh, for God's sake."

VII

After the Night of the Five-Helicopter Raid, the pirates chose ten of us to sleep every night on bunks in the cramped, humid cabins behind the bridge. Rolly and I had to line up with Arnel, six Chinese men, and Nguyen Van Ha, the Vietnamese fisherman, at the base of the stairs every evening to file up to our beds. Nguyen's black hair held the shape of a once stylish pompadour, and the more we talked, the more I understood that the *Naham 3* crew was a cross section of hip young Asian youth. Ha* liked to play guitar. He sometimes smoked opium. One night in my cabin, using a scrap of cigarette cardboard, he wrote out the economics of his decision to fish on a tuna boat. As a rice farmer in Vietnam he used to earn six dollars a day. His recruiter had offered him ten. He realized, too late, that "ten dollars a day" would be traded for hard, nearly unlimited hours of work. The recruiter in his case wasn't Step Up, but a Vietnam-based firm, and Ha, when pushed, was too polite to accuse them of trickery. But he divided ten dollars by twenty work-hours on the scrap of cardboard and showed me how the hourly wage for a day of fishing—fifty cents!—was smaller than the wage for farming rice.

He shook his head and batted it with his flat hand, as if to blame himself for the failed logic.

"*Loco-loco,*" he said.

Different nationalities on the *Naham 3* earned different wages for the exact same work, because different agencies had hired them. "The Chinese earn the most—three-fifty a month," said Tony. The Chinese recruiting firm seemed to have a relationship with the Taiwanese shipowners, which made the non-Chinese-speaking men second-class, almost by definition.

The pirates picked out one Cambodian, called Hen, for physical work. He was a squat, strong man with bulking shoulders, panda-faced and mischievous, maybe twenty-five years old. I call him "Hen" because that was his name, Kim Koem Hen, but the crew and the Somalis called him by a nickname that's hard to render in English. It sounded like "Hayle," but when I asked the Filipinos how to spell it, they said it was "Gel," short for the Spanish name Angel. The Filipinos had told him what *hen* meant in English and made

---

* As with many Southeast Asians, his given name came last.

fun of him for it. He protested, so they found a more affectionate nickname.

Hen attracted abuse from the Chinese. They would sock him just for walking by. Squeezing through a cluster of the wrong men in the work area would bring down a gauntlet of punches on his shoulders, half-joking, half-admiring, a direct function of his strength. From a Chinese point of view, Cambodians were lower-class, but Hen possessed a natural cool. He ignored the punches and took most of his saltwater showers with a burning cigarette in his mouth.

Rolly referred to the crew as "children," since most of them were under thirty. They referred to him as "grandfather." These Asian kids were unencumbered about bisexuality, and it flustered Rolly at first. While we sat under the conveyor belt, Tony would come over to share his mattress, sometimes embracing the old fisherman like a big teddy bear.

"Grandfather," he would say.

"Tony, stop that. You know I no like."

I didn't care one way or another. My libido had flagged. Somalia was unarousing, and ignoring my emotions was one powerful strategy to navigate an average day. So, among other sad developments, I had started to feel like a depressed old man. Rolly and I cultivated this role together, under the conveyor belt.

"We are like the Dodosya under a rock," he would say.

I think Rolly would have preferred to tell all his stories to his five-year-old granddaughter, since adults asked too many questions. He described his granddaughter often and seemed to miss her uncomplicated trust as much as he missed his island home. He painted a picture for me of rain on ragged palms, churches with sea-softened wooden floors, sea turtles and sea cucumbers and shoals of red snapper. He said the Seychelles in the 1940s were so poor that it was the privilege of a rich man to own a bike. Regular people walked. Almost no one owned a car. He remembered playing soccer in the road with a ball made of banana leaves. "We tied it with a rope," he said. "Sometimes you see one piece go over here, and one piece go over there."

The French had run the Seychelles before Britain took over in 1811, and the British didn't leave until 1976. "In 1977, coup d'état!" said Rolly. He'd learned to write English in school, not Creole, because the British in those days had considered Creole a low street slang. So he'd never learned to spell in his own language.

"Michael, you know in my neighborhood we got a big mango tree. Is near the store, where we buy our beer. When we not fishing, Marc and I sit under this tree."

"Under a mango tree?" I said.

"Yah."

It sounded nice compared with this rusted ship. And I wanted a beer, come to think of it.

"If you and I ever get out of here," I said, "I want to have a beer with you under the mango tree."

He gave a sad and elderly smile. "Okay, we do that, Michael."

Some time later, he asked me if I "knew about the ground turtle" in the Seychelles, meaning giant land tortoises that live wild on the islands, even in the capital, Victoria.

"With turtle," he explained, "you got ground turtle and sea turtle."

"Okay. Yes," I said.

"You know about the ground turtle?"

"No."

"Michael, why you just tell me yes, when you don't know about the ground turtle?"

"I just want to hear the story."

"But—the ground turtle, you know what he do?"

"I have no idea."

Rolly gave a twinkling smile. "He yell, eh?"

"What does he yell?" I said.

"When he do that."

"When he does what?"

Rolly lowered his voice. "When he fuck."

"Oh!"

"Yah!" said Rolly.

And he gave me a vision of giant, frowning tortoises crawling across the island of Mahé in the spring, females lying still while enormous males climbed on top of their shells to yell and holler and grunt.

"They get happy about the rain. That's true, eh? They make a *lot* of noise."

VIII

One morning, Tony handed us a thick, gold-bound Bible. "I don't know if it will help you to read this, but it helps some of us," he said.

I was starved for a book; I'd gone three months with nothing to read but food labels.

"Thanks," I said.

"Yah, thank you, Tony," said Rolly.

The Filipinos had three or four Bibles. When Tony noticed us trading the large book back and forth, he handed Rolly a small abridgment, with fraying pages. Rolly read it easily. He remembered verses in English from grammar school. He liked the Psalms in particular.

I hadn't studied the Bible in years. I would reread it twice. At first I browsed the Song of Songs for the racy bits, and this passage brought me up short:

My beloved spake, and said unto me, Rise up, my love, my
    fair one, and come away.
For, lo, the winter is past, the rain is over and gone;
The flowers appear on the earth; the time of the singing of
    birds is come, and the voice of the turtle is heard in our
    land.*

"Rolly," I said.

"Eh?"

"Your ground turtle's in the Bible."

"What you mean?"

"You just told me about the ground turtle. It's right here in the
Song of Solomon."

Rolly squinted at the page. He didn't understand.

"There's a line about the 'voice of the turtle' in the spring. It's
just like you said about the turtles yelling."

"In Seychelles?"

"No, in ancient Israel."

"Ahh."

I read the Bible urgently, critically, like a man starved for good
ideas. As a young Catholic I had never read it literally: I had thought
that the value of the Gospels wasn't their promise of a literal afterlife
but the gesture toward something durable in the human soul. *Something* could outlast death. Right? I'd written a novel about a dead
suburban teenager that investigated the ancient Jewish notions of
the soul—*nefesh, ruach,* and *neshamah*—underlying the language
in the Bible, and it had helped me refine my own coarse childhood
ideas about death and the hereafter. Of course none of it had pre-

---

* Song of Solomon 2:10–12.

pared me for that stark moment before my first phone call home, on the bluff with Ali Duulaay, staring down the barrel of a gun.

God, to the ancient Jews, was the sum and source of life, and "going back to God" was not just an idiom for death but the goal of spiritual pursuit. I wanted to firm up these ideas in Somalia, but most references to rebirth in the New Testament were realistic and therefore strange. The Gospels promised an unpoetic resurrection of the dead, and after rereading them, I could see why fundamentalists believe in a mass resurrection, almost a zombie apocalypse, when the corpses of believers would awake to the Second Coming.

I wanted to train my mind for actual nonexistence, and my Catholic-shaped mind still preferred my own death to be useful if possible, transcendent, selfless, not driven by panic. The first thing I noticed was that parts of the Old Testament pushed a gritty ethic of survival. Ecclesiastes, for example, is the record of late and pessimistic reflections by King Solomon—wise judge, chief rabbi, fantastic womanizer, and enlightened monarch during an unparalleled era of prosperity in Israel—who placed no stock in a transcendent afterlife.

> For that which befalleth the sons of man befalleth beasts;
> even one thing befalleth them: as the one dieth, so dieth
> the other; yea, they have all one breath;* so that a man
> hath no preeminence above a beast: for all is vanity.
>
> (ECCLESIASTES 3:19)

I thought about the goat kicking when a pirate sawed open its throat, the way its tail wagged while it bled.

---

* *Ruach* in Hebrew.

All go unto one place; all are of the dust, and all turn to dust
again.

(ECCLESIASTES 3:20)

I thought about the snapper flapping on the deck after a flat
knife to the skull.

For to him who is joined to all the living there is hope: for a
living dog is better than a dead lion.

(ECCLESIASTES 9:4)

King Solomon wasn't helping.

IX

A new pirate leader named Bakayle came aboard in late April. He
was large and loping, fleshy-faced, with ears like Mickey Mouse and a
cruel gangsterish smile. His teeth had metal crowns as well as a gap
in front. When he noticed us reading the Bible, he mocked us by fold-
ing his hands in prayer. He straightened his posture and gathered
himself to look very pious, then recommended, in a mild but pater-
nal voice, my swift conversion to Islam. He uttered the name *Allah*
with an overscrupulous Arabic pronunciation, careful to scratch his
throat; he pretended to care very much for our moral improvement.
But he was khat-addled and stupid.

Tony told me in private that Bakayle had boarded the ship after
they first anchored near Hobyo. Bakayle had personally beaten the
Chinese men with a broom.

"Michael," he asked on his first day, with a clever smile. "Ham?"

"What?"

Abdul the translator happened to be lingering on the work deck, too, so Bakayle waved him over.

"He wants to know if you want ham," Abdul translated.

"Why would I want ham?"

The pirates conferred and snickered like schoolboys.

"When you go back to Germany," Abdul translated, "you can have all the ham you want."

I nodded. "Great, thanks."

Ever since my capture I had dreamed about steak, beer, greasy quesadillas, great bowls of fresh berries and melon, spareribs, grilled vegetables, and pumpkin pie. I didn't miss ham. But the pirates mentioned it again a few days later. During dinner, at sunset, we ate oily strips of pork belly on our piles of rice, and the Somalis whiffed the pork fat. They gazed down from the upper deck in disgust and condescension. Soon we heard jokes about "ham," and I squinted at Bakayle, who was standing on the upper deck.

"Do you mean pork?" I said. "Eating pig?"

"*Haa*, yes," Bakayle said.

That was how he understood us. Hostages were eaters of pig.

Bakayle means "rabbit" in Somali—a reference to his gapped teeth and oversize ears. I made a serious face and tried to explain something to him.

"Christian, ham—no problem," I said in a deadpan voice. "*Yehud*, no ham." Jews don't eat ham. "Muslim, no ham," I went on and bumped my fingers together in a way that meant equal or equivalent.

"Muslim, *Yehud*, same-same!" I concluded, with a big sarcastic smile.

Arnel, sitting near us, giggled. Bakayle's face darkened. A direct hit. If a comparison to Jews insulted him, I thought, he could boil in his own hate.

I passed as Christian in Somalia because I was white and not Muslim, and the whole *Naham 3* crew looked Christian to the guards because we traded a handful of Bibles. Pirates were just clannish enough to consider themselves at war with most of the world. Which made enemies easy to find.

Another pirate, a friend of Bakayle's named Chorr, liked to wear rings and a fancy watch.* He had no clear status as a boss, but he imitated Bakayle by trying to humiliate hostages. One afternoon he sat on the work deck while I stood in front of a bucket of fresh water, at a table beside the conveyor belt, cleaning my tin mug. A group of hostages who sat behind the Honda motor glanced up and past me. I turned around, and there was Chorr, flashing a sheepish smile.

"Okay, Michael," he said.

"Problem?" I asked.

"No problem."

I noticed him drop a fish knife on the freezer portal and scurry up the stairs. I went back to sit next to Rolly.

"That man pretend to stab your back," he said.

"What?"

"Yah! He take that knife and pretend to kill you."

Chorr had mimed my murder in silence while I cleaned my cup. Charming. He turned out to be just a nuisance, but much later he kicked the frayed paper Bible out of Rolly's hands and found himself punished by Captain Tuure. When Rolly told Tuure the story, the old pirate lost his temper, and in a show of justice he hauled two or three guards downstairs, by the ear, to stand in front of us. Rolly shook his head each time—always the wrong man. But after a day or two, he saw Chorr upstairs and fingered him.

---

* The watches signified a certain rank within the pirate gang.

Tuure marched him away, but we never saw the punishment. A rumor circulated that Chorr had spent all night on the filthy floor of a cabin with his wrists and ankles trussed, like a pig.

"That make you feel better?" I asked Rolly when the story came around.

"No, Michael," he said in his grandfatherly voice, unwilling to take pleasure in the pirate's misery. "Nothing make me feel better in Somalia."

X

The *Naham 3* crew had a sack of DVDs, all "pirated." A player was fixed to the green Honda motor, and a black TV set dangled from the ceiling by four strong, ribbonlike tethers. The tethers let the TV rock with the ship. Since the Chinese made up the largest bloc— ten men[*]—they set the programming, and it started in the morning with Chinese karaoke. Keening, syrupy ballads rang out like strange birdsong over the deck after breakfast, and the Chinese would sing along.

The most popular DVD was a collection of *Tom and Jerry* cartoons. We all sat rapt and silent whenever Tom prepared fancy traps for the mouse, who scampered around outsmarting him. I hadn't seen *Tom and Jerry* in years. At first it reminded me of cheap and boring things from my childhood—fluorescent lights, mouthwash,

---

[*] Plus one Taiwanese engineer, so eleven Chinese speakers. There were five men each from Indonesia and the Philippines, four from Cambodia, and three from Vietnam.

Doritos—but after one or two cartoons I learned a deep appreciation for the MGM Studio Orchestra. Out here in the Indian Ocean, floating near Hobyo, I noticed the qualities of an L.A. big band that could play smooth jazz or evoke the flight of bowling balls, or crashing garbage cans, with kettle drums and prepared pianos and kazoos. There were hot, flaring trumpets and scurrying violins. Some of the music wasn't just clean stuff for kids. I tried to imagine the musicians who daylighted in Burbank to finance nightclub careers in L.A.; and I felt grateful for every one.

On Saturday mornings in Northridge, Dad would sometimes pause between chores in the garage to stare at *Tom and Jerry* with his bifocals on, smiling. He loved those cartoons. I tried to imagine what he thought of the jazz. Maybe the garbage-can mayhem reminded him of Spike Jones, who was on the radio during his childhood, or Betty Boop singing "Hell's Bells"—but come to think of it, he never collected jazz, and when he returned home to drink in the evenings, he would slump in one of the living room chairs with the stereo tuned to easy listening. *Coastin' with you here on the coast. K-O-S-T, Los Angeles.*

After Mom kicked him out, Dad tried to sober up. His formal appeal to come home, after six months at Raleigh Hills, took place in the living room, where he used to listen to the radio, and I think he followed some formula of apology. Mom wasn't convinced. Our house had been quieter since he'd left—no arguments or fights— and she knew he wasn't free of pills. Some addicts try to manipulate people, and Mom had a delicate instinct for Dad's deceptions and tricks. She understood herself as a protector of house and child; she acted flinty and strong, and when she shook her head, I was quietly on her side.

What neither of us knew, of course, was that this living room apology was a Hail Mary shot, Dad's last-minute bid for redemption.

XI

Helicopters and surveillance planes paid occasional visits during our first three weeks on the water, and one afternoon in early May, while I sat on the tuna bench, a black, open-sided helicopter came within two hundred yards of the ship and circled us. Pirates readied their rifles. They growled at me to drape the pink blanket over my head, to sit still, and when the machine passed into view, it felt like a taunt. The little machine crossed the clear air between us and Hobyo in smooth, wasplike flight, daring the pirates to shoot. Even without my glasses I could pick out the helmeted sniper aiming his weapon. For the first time I considered a leap off the ship. But the Somalis were hopped-up, agitated. Suppose I snapped the uneasy ceasefire? Would there be a gun battle? I wanted to end this vile situation for my family; on the other hand hostages might die; on the other hand, I could just dart across the deck; on the other hand, I liked to plan things a little more carefully; on the other hand, the helicopter was *right there*—

It made a single pass around the ship, without waiting for me to make up my mind. I hadn't even unclenched my teeth before its rotors chopped into the distance.

This brief but nerve-charging visit left me excited and depressed, and it must have rattled the pirates, because Ali Duulaay came aboard the next day in a blue, half-unbuttoned shirt and paced the ship with a handgun. He conferred with the guards before disappearing up to the bridge. Late in the morning, he squatted in front of us, with the translator Abdul, and they presented an ultimatum to Rolly.

"These guys talked to your family," said Abdul, referring to Duulaay and other bosses on shore. "If your family can't pay the money in three days, you will be killed."

"Three days," Ali Duulaay emphasized, holding up three thick fingers.

Rolly squinted and tried to understand. It was never smart to take a pirate at face value, also not wise to disregard him. But they didn't elaborate. Duulaay turned to me and said something acidic and grave. "He says the planes and helicopters gotta stop coming," Abdul translated. "If there's any trouble from America, you will be shot."

"I know."

Duulaay's well-formed face had a pattern of pockmarks, like acne scars, and there was a violent undercurrent of strain in his eyes.

He must have changed the guards' standing orders not to fire at aircraft, because later in the afternoon an Orion cruised high over the *Naham 3*, and the pirates loosed a thundering volley of rounds. Hostages scattered. Abdul cackled at the uproar. The fear in the crew was involuntary—it must have been the first moment of sustained gunfire their eardrums had endured since the hijacking—and Abdul found it hilarious. "Don't worry, you guys!" he shouted, but fear had seized us all, and I stood up, too, as quietly as possible, because of Duulaay's threat, and hid in the work area, just in case, until the spy plane disappeared.

XII

"In three days, I going to die," Rolly said later in the afternoon. "I say hi to God for you."

"Yup," I said. "Thanks."

"What you do without me?" he chided.

"I don't know."

I really didn't.

Rolly couldn't ignore the threat from Duulaay, but he also couldn't believe it. His mind returned to the problem in trenchlike cycles, the way it returned to his daily anxieties. He fidgeted for a while.

"*Twenty* million dollars, Michael."

"I know."

"They trying to kill me."

"I doubt they will," I said.

"You know how much twenty million dollars is in my money?"

"It's twenty million dollars."

"Yes, but—in Seychelles rupees."

"I have no idea."

"Is one hundred—wait, two hundred . . ." He shook his head and came back to his usual refrain. "Is a *lot* of money. You can buy house. . . . You can buy car. . . ."

"Rolly, with twenty million dollars you can buy a corporation."

"Heh, heh."

The next day, he admired his yellow Thai sandals and said, "Michael, not to worry. Soon you have my shoes."

"How come?"

"Because in two days, I going to die."

But the third day passed quietly. The pirates ordered us upstairs at sundown while a storm approached. The *Naham 3*, in the fading light, rocked in high waves like an enormous cradle, and I went to sleep in my cabin thinking Ali Duulaay had been full of thuggish nonsense.

Later that night, Abdinasser shook me awake.

"Sahib," he whispered.

"What's going on?"

"Hobyo," he said, and held a flat hand, jovially, up to his ear. "Telephone, telephone."

He wore his rifle and a turban. I had a feeling of dread.

"No, sahib."

"Telephone!" he said. "No problem!"

I hesitated, because a move to Hobyo seemed decisive. I thought we would never see the *Naham 3* again. The pirates were too frightened of helicopters. The prospect of returning to Somali soil also filled me with foreboding and fear. The muscles around my spine hadn't fully recovered from the skiff accident on our first night, about three weeks before, so I didn't relish a boat ride; and I wondered what would happen to Rolly.

The ship rocked hard, in a mild rainstorm. The fluorescent-lit cabin swung and tilted like a lantern in a farmer's hand. I packed up, and when I walked down the narrow corridor the walls knocked my shoulders and almost unbalanced Abdinasser, with his rifle. A warm drizzle fell on the deck outside. We saw how Rolly and a handful of pirates, including Bakayle, had already boarded the skiff, which heaved up and down beside the ship while Hen struggled with the rope.

I looked down at the moiling, floodlit sea. It hurt my back just to watch it.

"No," I said. "Not in this weather."

I started back upstairs.

"Michael!" Captain Tuure and a bearded translator named Abdiwali caught up with me on the upper deck. "You must go ashore," the translator said.

"Why? No."

I had no authority, no particular plan, just the courage of my own recalcitrance, and I had a true instinct to fear whatever waited for us on land. I headed back to my cabin. More Somalis closed ranks around me. I told Captain Tuure through Abdiwali, "The last time I rode in that skiff, the pilot hurt my back. That was a calm night." I shook my head. "I won't go in this weather."

"But you must go."

"Why must I?"

One large pirate grabbed my shirt and pulled me toward the lower deck. "You have no choice," he said. "It is an order."

"I will tell the pilot to drive slowly over the waves," Tuure promised.

Of course it was a hopeless cause. The men were armed. I returned downstairs and handed my bag to one pirate. Soft rain pattered everywhere, and the skiff knocked against the hull. It lurched up and down in slow, twenty-foot intervals. The trick was to ride the boat down to the bottom of the swell, like an elevator. "Do not jump while the boat comes up," said one of the Somalis. After the peak of the next swell, which carried the boat to within a yard of the cutaway rail, the men shouted, and I jumped. The landing was surprisingly soft—easier than jumping the same distance onto hard ground—and Abdinasser grabbed my jersey. I sat on the bulkhead, next to Rolly, who looked frustrated with my reluctance. "Ah, Michael," he said in his rueful voice. "Not make them angry."

The pilot moved with gentle speed over the spitting waves. Our ride through the wind and drizzle had an almost sinister softness, and instead of running like devils we chugged and slopped along until a wave caught us, the propeller whined, and we stranded, suddenly, on the beach.

Bakayle, Abdinasser, and a few other pirates crammed us into a Land Rover. The moon-tinged clouds were marbled and heavy. We drove along familiar paths to Mussolini's Farmhouse and parked beside another vehicle, but we had to wait while two Somalis climbed onto the roof of the other car and held their phones up, as if to sniff the air for drones.

This tactic baffled me; I'd never seen it before Ahmed Dirie's mysterious effort a few weeks earlier. (Drones could pick up cell-phone signals, but could it work the other way around?) While my brain spun for an answer, Bakayle grinned at us from the front seat. His whole presence felt unquiet and cruel. His character lacked a moral brake, any glint of compassion. He said something in Somali and made a flying gesture with his hand. The pirates in the Land Rover laughed.

"Tomorrow you will get your plane ticket home," one of them translated.

XIII

In the morning Rōlly and I found ourselves crammed into another car, with more gunmen, driving through the dusty bush to the west of Hobyo. A pirate named Dag sat next to me, ruminating on stems of khat, sometimes allowing his mouth to hang open. Dag could brood for ages with an occasional dreamy smile, like a wistful girl, only to come up with some foul remark.

"Michael," he said, "you must ask your family to send money. Otherwise the pirates will sell you to al-Shabaab."

"Well," I told him, "you have to lower your demand."

"How much are they asking?"

They, as if Dag were not a pirate.

"Twenty million."

"I think they will accept ten million," Dag said.

"How sensible."

Camels gazed in the scrub outside. Their rear ankles had been fettered by nomad owners, and when we zoomed past, they would lift their noses and make awkward hops away from the car. Furry wild hogs also scurried through the dust.

"*Michael, Rolly!*" cried Bakayle from the front seat, pointing at the black-and-white bush pigs, which to my poor eyes looked like undergrown dogs.

"HAM!" cried Bakayle.

"Oh, Jesus," Rolly muttered.

The cars wound toward a sloping, wooded area where other cars, and other Somalis, waited under the trees. I'd never seen this place before. Rolly mumbled that he and Marc had lived here once, in a shady washout, which later flooded.

"We call it the River," he said.

We parked under some trees, and the guards marched Rolly away behind a thicket, where unknown Somalis had gathered.

"Don't worry," Dag told me. "It is not al-Shabaab."

I squinted at him.

Something weird was going on. They moved me to a more luxurious SUV, outfitted with video screens in the headrests. We sat around while Somali pop videos played like entertainment in a waiting plane—stiff dancers, awful processed synthesizers—and I had time to think that bush pigs were ugly animals, that I might not eat pig, either, if I lived in this part of the world. Then a phone rang. A guard rolled down his window and we heard a harsh voice cry out. "Rolly!" said Abdinasser the Sahib, and the pirates led me to a cluster of tangled trees where a group of men stood or squatted in the dust. Some wore turbans and keffiyehs, all held long weapons, and I spotted Bakayle, Ali Duulaay, Ahmed Dirie. A gathering of pirate bosses? Or a convention of bosses, clan leaders, and investors. They watched me for a reaction with wary eyes, like predatory cats. I didn't understand at first. They were waiting. On the other hand, something worse waited, something more malevolent that they wanted me to observe.

Rolly dangled upside down from a tree.

"Oh, fuck," I said.

He swung free in a pair of cotton shorts; his arms flopped like a rag doll's. They'd tied him by the ankles to a heavy bough. A plump, deep-black man with a high voice whacked him on the chest and feet with a bamboo cane. It was a torture scene from old Islamic memory, when Ottoman officials used to tie the feet of criminals and subject them to bastinado, or public foot whipping. Two teen-agers filmed it. Other Somalis ran up to kick Rolly in the ribs with their dusty feet; they seemed to enjoy it. Rolly didn't scream again. He closed his eyes and let it happen, and I wondered if he was in shock.

The plump man—Garfanji—handed his cane to another Somali and came up the slope. He squatted some distance away from me and glanced up with his peculiar squint.

"Hello, Michael, do you remember me?"

"Yes, Mohamed."

"Your friend Rolly is being punished."

"What for?" I said.

"He will not say he is Israeli."

The idiocy hurt my head.

"Well," I said, "he *isn't* Israeli."

"I have found proof on the internet!" Garfanji answered.

The man with the cane slid it through the cotton knot at Rolly's feet and used it to turn his whole body this way and that while other men kicked. I was about to point out that Rolly spoke no Hebrew. But that could have led to an awkward line of questioning—"Have you been to Israel?" (I had)—so I decided to say, "He speaks like a man from the Seychelles."

This answer was no use to Garfanji; he said nothing. I had to wait while Duulaay harassed my friend with a lit cigarette. He held the filter end to Rolly's upside-down face and spoke with a mocking smile. He tried to slip the cigarette between Rolly's lips.

"No, Ali, you know I no like cigarettes," Rolly said. But Duulaay was grinning.

The other Somalis went on with their torture in a bizarre and listless way, running up to kick him, or trading blows with the cane, as if they could think of nothing else to do. The Somalis were like boys who'd found something to engage their casual cruelty on a weekend afternoon. I marveled at how thin an excuse any man needed to treat another like a piece of meat. Duulaay took the cane and whacked Rolly in swift, sharp blows on his exposed chest, his stomach, his thighs. The cane left fading marks on his light-brown skin; Rolly winced but kept silent. Even when Bakayle made taunts about his ransom—"We will get fifty million dollars from your family!"—he pretended not to hear. But from that day on, he would refer to Bakayle as "Fifty Million."

At last the pirates lowered him to the dirt. Rolly lay on his side, propped on one elbow, to gain his breath. "I want you to counsel him!" Garfanji shouted at me. "Explain to him that it will be better if he admits that he is from Israel." I went to sit near him and asked two Somalis for food and water. Abdinasser brought a bottle and a box of biscuits. I welled up with pity and fear; I had no idea what to do. "Are you hungry?" I said, and Rolly nodded. "These men have gone crazy, Rolly; they think you're from Israel." He shrugged. One of the teenagers photographed us. "Try to relax for a while," I said. "I think it's over."

The fear and helplessness were so extreme, and so contradictory, that I sank into a dark and peculiar calm. It was like the moment when Duulaay shook his pistol in my face. After the mortal shock I found a strange, ice-cold balance. I returned to where Garfanji squatted, and he said that "these men"—the turbaned bosses—wanted to know why no one had wired my ransom. The demand for my hide was still twenty million dollars.

"I want my money!" Garfanji blustered.

"You're asking too much," I said quietly. "Even you know that."

He bellowed my answer to the assembled pirates, who hollered their dissatisfaction and shook their weapons. They held machine guns, grenade-mounted rifles, and AK-47s. One looked like Mustaf Mohammed Sheikh, the pirate Ashwin and I had interviewed in Hobyo. He kept a keffiyeh wrapped around his face, so it was hard to tell, but the resemblance chilled my blood.

Garfanji said I would be sold to al-Shabaab in one hour if the money wasn't sent immediately. "They are coming here now!" he said.

He was lying, but he was in command: I felt a mixture of fear and ashen contempt.

"We don't have the money," I said. "There just isn't that much money available."

"You're lying!" he shouted. "I have looked into your bank account! I know how much money you have."

It was true that his men had stolen a bank card. I didn't know if someone had hacked the account. But I said: "So you know I don't even have one million, Mohamed," and that tripped him up. Garfanji had an image to maintain. Any answer he gave would upset his projection as an all-seeing, all-demanding crime lord. Either he knew we weren't rich or he didn't. He couldn't be all-seeing as well as honest. I watched him carefully, and from the way he dissembled, I gathered he had not cracked my account.

"The American government hasn't given us any answer," he said. "How can we find more money?"

"You have my German passport," I said. "Maybe the German government can help."

I didn't think it could, but I was surrounded by armed men and had to say something. Garfanji hollered my answer to the others. They shook their weapons in approval. Garfanji suggested a video. The whole episode, from start to finish, was pirate theater—Garfanji's Theater of Cruelty in the woods—and while the teenage cameramen adjusted their tripod, a few pirates stepped behind me, quietly, holding heavy weapons. I didn't notice them at first.[*] Other pirates insisted I wear a blanket over my head, to disguise me from aerial surveillance.

"This blanket?"

"*Haa*, yes."

It was the pink flowered blanket I carried everywhere. I also wore a pink tank top and bright-green soccer silks. I hadn't shaved in weeks. I was grimly aware that in the video I would look not just wretched but ridiculous. I draped the blanket over my head, and soon Garfanji played the inquiring journalist, shouting from behind the camera.

"What are you requesting from the government?" he said.

"I have to request, from the American or the German government, the full ransom," I answered, as rehearsed.

"Which government, especially, will pay?"

"The German government?"

"And how do you want it to pay?"

"They need to give an answer within three days," I said.

---

[*] But on the video they're hard to miss.

"Is there any problem if they do not pay?"

"Yes. If there's no answer . . . the kidnappers here will sell me to al-Shabaab."

Afterward, I sat on the ground and watched Garfanji mount a rise of alluvial soil to address the men. He'd pretended to mediate between the hostages and this wild gang of bosses; now he rose to his true role as their chief. He swung the bamboo cane and pontificated. He reminded me of Jack from *Lord of the Flies*—"tyrant" was too big a word. He was a play-tyrant, a sadistic bully removed from any government or power to contradict his nasty will, and he introduced me to the real meaning of *anarchy*, where justice and reason, the conceits of civilization, just evaporated like a fog. I watched Garfanji rave. I strained to understand his speech, and in the afternoon light streaming through the trees I noticed for the first time how this pirate lord—this high-voiced, overweight child—had flecks of gray in his hair.

The young cameramen packed their equipment. After Garfanji's speech, they paused in front of me to apologize. One had small wire-frame glasses; he looked idealistic and spry and spoke decent English.

"We can't do anything here," he said. "We are only journalists. We will put these videos on the internet."

"What for?" I said.

"We will tell people about your plight."

"This wasn't journalism," I said, with a gesture at Rolly. "It was humiliation."

The young Somali adjusted his glasses and said, "Humanitarian, yes."

I squinted at him. There was no way either boy could have reached this corner of the bush without a clan connection to the pirates. I didn't believe their story. *Humanitarian* was also a special word in places like Somalia; it stood for the U.N. and the Red Cross, for Médecins Sans Frontières, for all the organizations that provided a link to the greater, more merciful world.

"That's not what I said," I told him.

XIV

The pirates loaded Rolly into a car and led me up a dusty incline, away from the trees. Garfanji said it was time for a phone call. He tapped my chest with his bamboo cane and swore that if my family didn't send twenty million dollars in three days, I would be sold like chattel to the jihadist beasts. Other bosses, including Duulaay and Ahmed Dirie, sat in the dust around a big thornbush, aiming their rifles at my head.

"Mohamed, I'm cooperating," I said. "Why are you acting like this?"

That tripped him up, too—he had no response when I acted reasonable. He scrolled through the list of contacts on his phone and found my mother's number, pressed "call," and handed it to me. Her contact name on the screen was "Habar Galo." *Mother of the Infidel.*

"Hello?" said the infidel's mother.

"Mom," I said, "the men here are threatening to sell me to al-Shabaab within three days if they don't get their money."

"Okay," she said, playing it quite cool.

Garfanji repeated his demand for a letter of absolution from the president. "It must be signed by Obama! It must have a White House seal!"

"How should she send it?" I asked.

"She can send it by email," said the pirate boss.

"You can just mock something up in Word," I mumbled into the phone.

"Oh," said my mother, who would have been coached on this question by the FBI, "I don't know if we can do that, Michael. That would be forgery."

"Tell her the demand is still twenty million," Garfanji said. "What is her counteroffer?"

Mom answered: "Eight thousand? Maybe we could go up to ten."

The distance between the two offers made me dizzy, but I felt proud of my mom. It was the only serious response.

"She says ten thousand."

"Oh, now she is joking," said the pirate.

"She thinks *you're* joking," I blurted.

"Can I call him back at this number?" Mom said.

I hesitated. The question implied caller ID. It didn't seem wise to tip off Garfanji to the fact that she could see his number. He bellowed again about "twenty million," so I skipped her question and said, "He says the whole amount has to be wired to Somalia in three days. All twenty million."

"Can we call him back at this number?" she repeated.

I glanced up. "She wants to know if she can call you back at this number."

"What does that mean?" Garfanji hollered and began to lose his mind. "Is she tracing this call? How does she see my number?" He took the phone and roared that I would be sold to terrorists. "Three days!" he cried. "Not three months! THREE DAYS." He ended the call, dismantled his phone, and flicked out the SIM card. It was a small and fiddling gesture that proved tricky for a pirate lord to accomplish with real diabolical finesse. The card fell into the dust, and he used his sandaled foot to stamp it, over and over, to ensure that the Mother of the Infidel would not be calling him back.

A sale to al-Shabaab was on the dark edge of my mind before and after this call; but as long as the groups were at war, I thought it would remain theoretical. Garfanji had assembled a private militia around Hobyo in part to protect his business interests from al-Shabaab, and I was one of those interests. The jihadists also claimed to oppose piracy for religious reasons. But that was like saying Somali pirates were just poor fishermen—al-Shabaab probably did profit from pirate ransoms by taxing the gangs in regions where they coexisted. Would they reverse the flow of money, and strengthen the pirates, to nab an American? An asset sale like that was hard to imagine. But not impossible.

We returned to Mussolini's Farmhouse in the late afternoon. Marc was there, and around dusk the pirates served us a large platter of rice. We weren't allowed to talk. My fork trembled in my fingers; I felt enraged and confused. I expected to be driven far into the wilderness that night, maybe back to the wooded valley with the horse-voiced vultures.

Around sunset, while storm clouds massed like dark cliffs over the sea, Duulaay appeared in our doorway with a rifle on his shoulder. "How are you, Rolly? Fine?" he said, and smiled like a hyena, hoping to joke away the bitterness of the horrible afternoon. "'I am fine'?" he added, and I think this odd phrase came from Somali English primers, an answer parroted from grammar class, which Rolly was supposed to parrot back. (Q: How are you? A: I am fine.) I wanted to shoot Duulaay with his own Kalashnikov. Rolly gave a feeble, ironic, grandfatherly chuckle.

But when the pirate left, we prepared our beds for the night on the floor, and in the fading light Rolly gave his own interpretation of the grammar lesson.

"Me, I want to die," he said.

Part 5

FLIGHT

My mother's professional cool on the phone was deceptive. "Of course, I was freaking out," she would say later. The call from Garfanji woke her up before dawn, and she knew little about al-Shabaab; she had no way to assess the pirate's threats. FBI agents arrived at her town house later the same morning with a laptop. They sat around the mess on the dinner table and reviewed the conversation. "The FBI told me, 'Don't get all stressed. . . . First of all, the pirates and al-Shabaab hate each other. So the terrorists are not about to pay the pirates any money.'"

Whenever the FBI paid a visit, she served coffee and bagels, and whenever a meeting or a phone call had been scheduled in advance, she ordered sandwiches. Later she baked banana bread and cookies. She'd started to think of the agents as surrogate family. One of them, named Steve, said, "She was so incredibly generous in spite of what was going on, we had to tell her, just, to stop. Because she would have done that every time we came over."

Steve lived about a mile away in Redondo Beach. "There were times," he said, "when there was nothing going on, and I would go over there to check in, and just talk about other things. To keep her somewhat focused on trying to take care of herself, and make sure she was keeping busy."

Mom had made an agonizing decision to keep my case quiet in the news. At her instigation, *Der Spiegel* asked for an embargo on the story from American and European outlets, and the result was a near-total news blackout on stories about my case. The logic went that hostages made famous by coverage became more expensive.

Whenever negotiations faltered, though, so did Mom's faith in the tactic, and sometimes she warned negotiators and officials around her that she wanted to tell the world. "I'd call up and say, 'Steve, I'm gonna go national!' . . . And then he would come over and we would discuss the possible outcomes."

The point of big publicity in a hostage case is to exert pressure on a sluggish or recalcitrant government. Since the U.S. and German governments had both mobilized, Mom decided to keep quiet. The final decision was always hers, so I don't question it.* But the embargo failed to shorten my stay in Somalia. As long as I had a radio, I listened for clues about my case, and it seemed curious that the World Service never mentioned it even during reports about Somalia. Part of me felt isolated and forgotten; I had no idea what was going on. But I also knew that publicity would give leverage and comfort to my kidnappers. My guards even listened to the radio like eager kids whenever we made a video. They wanted to hear my name; they looked forward to a media circus, and it frustrated them to hear nothing.

While Mom reviewed the first video in the first week of May, Steve and the other agents pointed out that I looked alert and decently fed. I wasn't starving. I had to speak under duress, but the bristle of machine guns and grenade launchers made the agents laugh. "I mean, it looked so horrible, and so scary, but it was meant to intimidate," Mom said. "They would say, 'Look at how they're pointing their weapons. This is all staged for optimum effect on the family.'

---

* A blackout imposed by the FBI, or any government agency, would be immoral.

"That's how we watched every film."

I made five proof-of-life videos in Somalia. This first one came up for sale in mid-May. A Somali sent an email to Ashwin in Germany, offering the footage for two thousand dollars. Ashwin declined. Instead it wound up, later the same month, on Somalia Report, a news site, which broke the embargo. It became the single well-known clip from my time as a hostage.

II

Rolly and I drifted to sleep in Mussolini's Farmhouse while a storm broke outside. Through the window we could see lightning flash over the ship in piled banks of blackening cloud. Around nine o'clock, the pirates woke us up. "Come on," they said, but I balked at the idea of driving off in a storm.

"You've got to be kidding."

"Go, go, go, go."

Rain pattered the tin roof of the gloomy Italian ruin. I climbed into the Land Rover feeling depressed and convinced the pirates would drive us to some distant corner of the bush, to make us miserable in the storm, if not to sell me to al-Shabaab. Instead we went speeding through the damp white sand on the Hobyo waterfront and stopped in front of a skiff. We boarded like before, in warm, slapping waves; lightning flashed over the *Naham 3*; but our pilot didn't rush. He still had standing orders to keep his speed down, so we chugged gently through rocking swells in the rain.

Returning to the ship quelled my terror of starting a new chapter as a hostage, I suppose because the familiar scenery was reassuring, but I also had a strange optimism about escaping, somehow, at sea. I liked the ocean. I felt halfway to freedom out there. And I would be easy for surveillance planes to track.

No one on the ship had expected to see us again. There was a flurry of excitement on the work deck before we retired to our cabins. When I woke in the morning, around six, the Filipinos had made coffee and some wads of celebratory fried dough. I sat on the fiberglass bench and noticed the creak of a cricket under the damp floorboards. A gray dawn light had spread across the ocean, and I was just wondering whether the cricket had sailed from Mauritius with the *Naham 3* or somehow hopped its way from the Somali mainland when Tony said:

"Helicopter this morning, Michael."

"Really?"

"Half an hour ago," he said.

"What did it do?"

"It circled the ship, only."

I told him what Garfanji had done on land. The story spread among the Filipinos, and by the time Rolly came down the steps before breakfast to sit in our corner, it was like the advent of a wounded king. He found his tin mug and accepted coffee from Ferdinand.

"How do you feel?" I said.

He shook his head. "Me, I hurt, Michael."

The other men woke up and stowed their bedrolls. We spread our mattresses under the conveyor belt, and Rolly rested for a while. When he told the story himself that morning, he seemed to relive each humiliation with the stick. "*BAP! BAP!*" he said and showed them blue marks from the cane on his coffee-colored skin. "They think I Israeli. This fat man! He think he find something with his computer." Rolly's face looked wooden. "Me, Israeli?"

We spent the rest of the day in a state of relief, sitting under the conveyor belt and watching the crew toss out fishing lines. Rolly gave me the Creole names of the fish that came over the side. Some were exotic to me—including groupers, spangled emperors, hump-head snappers, and rainbow runners—but the most common fish were the karang, a small yellowspotted trevally, and the inedible scavenging remora, which clung to the sides of the ship and cleaned up scraps of anything.

Rolly watched with such a yearning professional interest that I said, "Don't you want to fish?"

"Oh, me, I like to fish," he said. "At home I go to fishing because it make me happy. You understand? But I no like to remember that here."

I understood very well. We'd learned to hood ourselves in So-malia, to starve and blunt our pleasures, to protect ourselves from madness.

Under the rising heat on the ship I remembered my dad's passion for fishing, his motorboat on a trailer in the driveway, and his eagerness to drive it up to a reservoir in the mountains north of L.A., where he could waste an afternoon in the hot sun, with a beer, waiting for trout. Mom and I went with him, nor-mally, but we couldn't appreciate the solemn need to keep silent on the boat, which seemed as important for my father's nerves as it was for the fishing project. Mom would chitchat, impishly. Dad would say, "*Shhhh*. You're scaring the trout," and Mom and I would giggle.

Good Christ I missed my family.

But I no like to remember that here.

"Now we on the ship again," Rolly remarked after a while.

"You feeling better?"

"Ahh," he said, and gave a dismissive wave.

III

After the early helicopter visit, I made a point of waking up around five every morning, because the prospect of jumping for a helicopter at that hour, when the pirates were drowsy and the sun cast blue shadows on the landward side of the ship, gave me hope. I would be harder to see in the half dark—harder to shoot—and I looked forward to taking the pirates by surprise.

The Filipinos kept a plastic alarm clock near their wok and electric kettle. I asked Tony if I could take it to my cabin at night. He said yes, but after I had done it twice, one of the Chinese-speaking crew objected. He was an older man with a potbelly and melancholy eyes, an alternate engineer, actually from Taiwan. The crew called him Taso.* He didn't seem to get along with the Filipinos or with Li Bo Hai, the first engineer, who had pounded my back into shape when I first came onto the ship.

I tried to explain why I wanted the clock, but Taso didn't understand. When I continued to borrow the clock, he stopped the generous favor of taking our bowls before each mealtime to serve us food. At last I quit using the clock. But Taso's objection signaled something more important. We were no longer guests aboard the *Naham 3*. After our return from land, we had joined the hostage crew.

Our rights to the captain's cabin also disintegrated. When Tuure left on shore leave, a Somali we called "Big Jacket" shut down our bathroom privileges. Big Jacket was a skinny guard-lieutenant who wore an oversize blue blazer in every kind of weather. He didn't like

---

* A corruption of *dàchē*, a Chinese nautical word for "engineer." His real name is Shen Jui-chang.

having to muster his men to attention whenever we climbed the stairs. But it bothered me to lose even a small and petty freedom to such a low-ranking guard. "They're just making up rules," I grumbled to Rolly.

"I not care," said Rolly. "I shower with salt water, like the children."

"He didn't say no shower; he said no toilet upstairs." I glanced at Rolly. "You're giving up too easily. These guys are just lazy."

"This man, Big Jacket," he said.

"Yeah, Big Jacket." I smiled at the name. "He thinks he runs the ship."

"But he got the gun."

After lunch that day, Rolly undressed near the front of the deck and took a cold saltwater shower. It made an impression on the crew. I still resented the pirates' arbitrariness, so I copped an American attitude of protest. When Big Jacket disappeared to another part of the deck, I took my bright-yellow towel and went up the stairs to demand a shower. The baffled guards let me go. As a team, they didn't know their own rules.

"There, see?" I said when I came back down to the work deck, toweling off my hair. "Completely arbitrary."

"Yes, Michael. Now you go up there alone," Rolly said, and looked away.

"Oh, come on! You could go up there, too. I'm just saying we can challenge the pirates' rules."

"Me, I take saltwater shower," he said with a kind of bitter pride.

He had a point. An American attitude of protest was also an attitude of privilege, looked at from the right angle, and marching upstairs with a bright-yellow towel sent the wrong message to the non-English-speaking crew, who might have wondered why the American still got to use their murdered captain's facilities. So I started using the saltwater hose the next day. The steady, urgent flow of lukewarm brine didn't clean your hair and skin, exactly, but stripping naked for a few minutes, and getting wet, broke up the boredom of a standard afternoon.

IV

Without a clock in my cabin, I learned to tell time by the color of the sky. Somalia is near-equatorial, so the sun rises and sets around six all year round. I fell asleep by eight. The ship would rock and I would doze, in nervous catnaps, until four thirty or five, when the dark sky turned blue outside my window. By five thirty an orange stain had spread on the horizon, and I got up. A Somali gunman sat in the bridge to watch for movement in the corridor, and with his permission, holding my foam mattress and my pink patterned blanket, awkwardly, I picked my way down the hall, outside to the steel stairs, down to the deck. The swaying boat and narrow stairs were tricky with the mattress. I sometimes lost my balance, and sometimes the big thing caught the wind like a sail. I didn't care. It was conscious and deliberate. I moved the mattress back and forth like an idiot to flag the attention of drones. I thought a man lugging his foam mattress up and down the stairs of a tuna boat, wearing a flowered pink blanket on his head, at a predictable hour, twice a day, might become easy to track from the sky.*

Before 6:00 a.m., the air felt quiet and damp. I heated up water

---

* Rolly went back and forth without a bed on his shoulders because we had somehow ended up with three foam mattresses. He left one in his cabin, and one outdoors.

for coffee in an electric kettle and took a spoonful of Nescafé from a can. I mixed it with sugar and powdered milk while the crew snored. And I waited. Around six, the nighttime guard shift changed over to more alert Somalis, and every morning before it happened I hoped for the distant chop of a helicopter. I would have been off the deck like a cannonball.

Rolly came down from the cabins by six thirty, followed, normally, by Ha, who was comical in the morning, because he never tried to spruce up. He just looked like crap until he had his coffee and cigarette. He also made an amusing game of bumming the cigarette by leaning against one of the Chinese men and holding his hand like a beggar, as if to admit to himself that his desire for nicotine was degrading.

I don't know why he never had his own pack. The ship had a vast supply of cigarettes. Every couple of days a man came out of the freezer, brushing frost off a new carton, and passed out hinge-topped packs like candy. No one seemed to bother about running out, although everyone knew the ship's provisions had a limit, like the ship itself—we understood the omen of the *Shiuh Fu 1* on the shore.

Another cabin sleeper who came early down the stairs was a Chinese officer, Qiong Kuan. We nodded at each other as he settled on the fiberglass bench, still wrapped in a thin blanket, and we taught each other to say "Good morning" in English and Chinese. The crew had an English-Chinese dictionary, a fat little cube of important information, which became a subject of contemplation for me, like the Bible.

"Good—morning," Qiong Kuan had learned to say in clear but halting English.

"*Zaoshang hao*," he had taught me to say, and then he would correct my intonation.

"*Zaoshang hao*," I would repeat.

Again a correction.

"*Zaoshang hao*," I would say, and Kuan would hold up his thumb.

Kuan had a paunch and a growing bald patch on his round head, which made him look middle aged. In fact he was thirty-seven. He smoked with a stony, comical, phlegmatic gaze, as if nothing surprised him. He was first mate, a rank higher than Li Bo Hai, but he rarely asserted himself. Li Bo Hai had assumed everyday leadership, maybe because the pirates preferred to deal with him. No one cared. The hijacking was too absurd. Kuan had quit. He smoked cigarettes with Li Bo Hai and with another engineer named Cao Yong. Those three were the leading cadre, the most experienced men.

From our halting conversations I learned that Kuan came from a rice-farming province of China, and no one in his family—not his wife and kids, not his parents—understood the problem in Somalia. The crazy demands by pirates on the phone were like noises from a distant star.

The Chinese kept a paper calendar, and each wide sheet gave a Western and a Chinese date. Taso and Jian Zui maintained it. By June there were near-daily arguments about the actual date, which led to scuffles in the corner by the Honda motor. Accurate or not, a page from the calendar drifted around the deck as a ritual, from one man to another, while we gathered for morning coffee on the bench. Sometimes I kept it to scribble on, since I missed my notebook. Sometimes Ha, with his hair in a messy pompadour, cigarette dangling from his lips and curling smoke in his eyes, folded the sheet into a tight paper plane. He moved to the edge of the boat to launch it over the sea, and we watched it loop around, caught by an air current, and glide over the morning glass, which at the right hour was touched with bronze patches of wavering light. The plane would fall and stick to the surface of the water, like a flying insect newly captured in sap. We might or might not stand up to watch it sink.

V

One morning in May I used the Chinese dictionary to converse with Cao Yong, the wiry second engineer. He had the angriest energy of all the *Naham 3* crew and seemed the least beaten down. He hated the pirates, but he did his work, which sometimes included repair trips to the engine room. Part of the ship's engine ran as a generator, day and night, and I'd learned to appreciate the steady thrum as an indicator of our comforts on the ocean. It had started to spit and falter. The freezer hold, the kitchen, the filtration system for drinking water—nothing ran without the cycling generator, and if it gave out, we would have to move ashore.

Along with my fantasies of escape, I dreamed up a collective mutiny. The story of a suicidal hostage from the *Shiuh Fu 1* haunted me every day. "Fifteen months," Hamid had said. Maybe that was some kind of limit. I'd been a hostage for almost four, Rolly about seven. The crew had been captive for two and a half.

We had free use of steel fish knives on the work deck, as well as whetting stones, marlinspikes, and a sharp fishing gaff (a hook mounted at the end of a twelve-foot bamboo pole). I brooded about these weapons and tried to guess the number of pirates. Thirty, at most? One for each hostage? Of course, we lived on this forward deck by design—the pirates could be anywhere on the ship, and we weren't supposed to count them.

"Cao Yong," I said, and flipped through the dictionary. When I found a word in English, I pointed to the Chinese character, and he nodded. We built up phrases that way.

Life on land no good, I suggested.

Cao Yong nodded. I came to the point:

Should the crew attack the pirates?

It was a dangerous idea, but not out of the question. It needed Chinese leadership. The Somalis were superfluous on the *Naham 3*; Cao Yong, Li Bo Hai, and Qiong Kuan were not.

Then again, none of us had military training, and the ship was possibly hobbled. Cao Yong took the dictionary.

Very dangerous was his reply. I nodded.

He flipped through and showed me further English words:

Pirates do not kill. Eventually they release.

I worried about death or suicide on land. But that was too elaborate, too conjectural to explain.

Cao Yong flipped through the pages again and found the Chinese character for a single, conclusive phrase:

Not worthwhile.

I nodded and shrugged.

VI

Every afternoon, when "tchat" arrived in a skiff, the Somalis would shuffle back and forth upstairs like cats about to receive a treat. They lined up to receive their rations, and Big Jacket came to the upper rail to summon Taso, because Taso and several other hostages had developed fledgling habits—out of stress or boredom, or both—and the pirates donated half a bundle every day to their corner of the deck. Taso hustled out in nothing but a pair of red shorts and returned, clutching his bundle, with a comical, mournful, baffled expression of need.

"Is happy hour," said Rolly.

One Cambodian who chewed with Taso was intense and reedy, and he mouthed off in a way that inspired abuse from the Chinese, who punched him in the arm when they grew tired of his comments. His name was Ngem Sosan. He and Taso had been close friends of the dead captain's. They had enjoyed certain privileges while the *Naham 3* was in regular operation, and now Sosan complained in a braying voice about the pirates and refused to do much work. After a while I realized he raised his voice during shower time to make loud, sarcastic appraisals of the size of each man's cock. That was one reason they slugged him.

These stress fractures in the muted, quiet society of hostages on the *Naham 3* came slowly into focus. The hijacking had shifted a balance of power on the ship. It was a Chinese-dominant vessel, so the Chinese speakers and their friends were used to feeling privileged. But English became more important after the hijacking. "The Somalis think I am the crew chief," Arnel said. "I'm not—I'm just a crewman—but I speak English, so I became the translator."

"You got a promotion," I said.

Arnel laughed brightly. "Yes!"

Rolly and I had gravitated toward the Filipinos because of their English. Skiff deliveries of mango juice and vanilla cookies* came only for me, the expensive hostage, and I tried to distribute them fairly, but side benefits tended to pile up in the Filipino corner. So the Chinese and their allies gained the impression that extra bottles weren't for them.

One hot morning Sosan protested his maltreatment in a reedy-voiced, sarcastic, but also comical diatribe complaining about the Filipinos and the Chinese and the Somalis and the food on the ship and the American and the lack of mango juice for Sosan. I handed him my last bottle, but he shook his head, electrically aware that I wanted

---

* Abu Walad–brand *"biskit"* in Somali.

him to shut up. Instead he made fun of my pale skin and my pointy nose.* The rest of the crew grumbled with uneasy laughter—no one knew what to say—and Sosan continued in a mixture of ship's pidgin and Cambodian until I shouted, "Cambodia, *saitei*! Cambodia, *loco-loco*!" *That Cambodian's crazy!*

Everyone laughed, including Sosan. Of course. Insults blew off steam. Later Sosan and I would be friends.

Several days after this tirade, we heard Taso complain in Chinese. He sat in his corner by the Honda motor, while Li Bo Hai sat near us on the bench and listened over a smoldering cigarette. Li Bo Hai was an arbiter of justice on board; he tried not to take sides among national cliques. After a while he brayed back in Chinese.

"What's the matter?" I asked Tony.

"They are arguing about coffee."

"What about it?"

The whole crew acted chastised. Taso complained a little more. Tony said the main complaint was that coffee in the Filipino corner had disappeared too quickly.

"Well, that's because of us," I said.

"Shhh."

Taso stood up, as if he wanted to fight. Li Bo Hai stood up in response. Instead of climbing over to grapple with Taso, though, the chief engineer darted to a closet in the work area. "Heh!" he shouted and tossed out a packet of tea. "Heh!" he shouted and tossed out a box of Abu Walad biscuits. "Heh!" he shouted and returned to the sunlit deck to empty a plastic jar of tea packets and other hoarded food. Taso fell silent, like the rest of the crew. Li Bo Hai sat down again on the bench.

---

* I had never thought of my nose as pointy before.

"Those are Taso's things," said Tony. "He says Taso should not complain so much about the coffee."

VII

Apart from these outbursts, it was hard to tell how everyone coped with the constant strain. Our anger should have been directed upward, at the pirates, but it tended to slop sideways, back and forth, like acid in a vat. Most of us no doubt fell back on religious training; but our ship's pidgin kept us from indulging in sustained philosophical conversation.

Four Indonesians were Muslim, a fifth was Christian. The Cambodians and Vietnamese were Buddhist, and sometimes I saw Phumanny, the tattooed man with bowl-cut hair, chant rapid Buddhist prayers at the back of the work area. The Chinese might have been Buddhist or Taoist or Confucian. When I thought about the man from the *Shiuh Fu 1* who'd killed himself, I wondered how Buddhists regarded suicide, and this question reminded me of Thich Quang Duc, the Buddhist monk who'd famously doused himself with gasoline on a Saigon street corner in 1963. He had wanted to protest religious inequality in South Vietnam. The most striking aspect of the photo of his fiery death was his erect posture, his look of evident calm. A student at the University of California, San Diego, imitated Quang Duc in 1970 to protest the Vietnam War, but instead of remaining on the pavement in monkish serenity, George Winne Jr. jumped up to run, flaming, across a wide plaza. Before he died in the hospital, several hours later, he said to his mom, "I believe in God and the hereafter and I will see you there."

I didn't want to die like that. The promise of a hereafter didn't spark my imagination. Quang Duc had shown a deeper religious instinct: Buddhism promises no personal afterlife, no survival of individual consciousness,* and I figured any man who could sit un-flinching, without the prospect of heaven, while his robes and body burned, had learned to loosen the bonds of selfishness and desire. There was no other yardstick for philosophy or religion, from my point of view. I lined up with Albert Einstein: "The true value of a human being is determined by the measure and the sense in which they have obtained liberation from the self," he wrote in a letter in 1934, and by this brilliant, simple formulation even our devoutest pirates were imbeciles.

Rolly put it another way while we sat under the conveyor belt one morning. He watched the pirates bumble around on the deck while they unloaded a supply skiff, refusing to help one another out, like clowns.

Rolly was the closest thing to a philosopher we had on the swel-tering work deck, and, knowingly or not, he paraphrased Socrates.

"They not evil, Michael," he said after a while. "They just not *know.*"

VIII

One day in June, Abdul the translator came aboard wearing a Hawaiian-print shirt over his printed Indonesian sarong, with a pair of sunglasses, maybe to shield his eyes from the confusion of pat-terned cloth. He disappeared upstairs for a while. In the late morn-

---

* Reincarnation doesn't count.

ing, he came down to sit on the bench and ordered Tony to fry him a fish. He also loaded a few wads of tobacco-like dry tea straight into our electric kettle, where it would stain the plastic (instead of parceling it out into mugs, as we did), and before everything boiled he used a hammer and a piece of cloth to crush two plump cardamom pods he had carried in the pocket of his shirt.

"This is how you're supposed to drink it—with a little spice," he told me. "It's how my mother made tea when I was young."

He poured out a fragrant cup and handed it to me with one of his flare-toothed smiles. "For the boss," he said.

"No, no."

The whole crew watched. Some of them resented what he had done to the electric kettle. There was also not enough spiced tea to go around.

"Just take it, man. It's good."

"What for?" I said.

"Just taste it, then; I'll drink the rest. It ain't poisoned."

I took a sip and handed it back. Not bad.

"Okay," I said. Why was he buttering me up?

"We gonna do a phone call tonight, to your mother," Abdul said at last. "The bosses on shore, they gave me permission to handle your case." He found a scrap of cardboard. "Do me a favor and write down your phone number and your mother's name."

I did so.

"I think we gonna get somewhere," he said.

I'd never made a phone call with Abdul before. My mind began to churn. Would he recognize German? His English was better than Garfanji's. The pirate master spoke an orotund, almost Kenyan-colonial English, but Abdul's had an edge of American slang.

Which was odd.

"Where'd you learn to speak English?" I asked him.

"Right here, in Somalia."

"Have you ever been abroad?"

"No, man, I haven't been outta the country."

"Hmm."

Later, a Somali guard came down to distribute supplies. He handed out shampoo, detergent,* and cigarette lighters. When the lighters appeared, the work deck pounded with bare feet—every man from behind the conveyor belt rushed the unsuspecting, unarmed pirate. Tony returned from the scrum with a new LED lighter. He knew I wanted one, since my last LED had burned out, so I dug through my stash of things and produced the old lighter, with less fuel, and traded it, along with two bottles of mango juice, for Tony's high-end equipment.

That evening Abdul came to sit next to me and said, "Okay, tonight we gonna call this guy in Norway. He's gonna wrap up your case. Somali guy. Just answer his questions. Don't say anything else."

"Sure." I waited for more. "Why's he in Norway?"

"I don't really know."

At sundown, the hostages assigned to cabins filed upstairs for bed. I spent an hour wide awake on my bunk, wondering what to say on the phone. I wanted to request a helicopter in German. We hadn't seen a helicopter since before our video shoot with Garfanji. The sky in the meantime had been suspiciously, perhaps deliberately, quiet.

We sat in the dining booth in the hallway, across from the captain's cabin, to make the call. Pirates manning the bridge used this table for lunch and dinner. They ate with their hands, without nap-

---

* A brand called Top-O-Mol.

kins, so there were dried formations of scraped-off pasta and rice on the table's edge.

"These guys are disgusting," Abdul said.

He dialed a number and hesitated. "If he asks about your location, tell him you're in the bush." I nodded. He connected the call and spoke rapid-fire Somali, with the volume up loud enough for me to hear the other man. His Somali sounded as rapid and strong as Abdul's, so it surprised me, when I took the phone, to hear a Scandinavian speaking fluid English. I'll call him Anders.

He asked a few basic questions, and I gathered that he was a private negotiator, just opening a file. "When we finish here," he said, "I will talk to your mother. Do you have any message for your mother?"

The false hope Abdul had sparked by lying about Anders incensed me. I blurted in German that I was on a ship. Abdul grabbed the phone and hung up.

"Who was that guy?" he asked, and my eyes must have widened in astonishment.

"He's a mediator! I thought you said he was going to settle my case."

"He's from the media?" Abdul said.

Astonishing. I was ready to smash furniture. Abdul was a complete idiot.

"A *mediator*, Abdul. Jesus. He's a negotiator, just like you. He's in your fucking line of work."

The general ignorance that had me stuck out here on the water made me want to punch him. My kidnappers weren't even good kidnappers.

"Did he ask your location?" he said.

"No."

Which was true.

I returned to my cabin but couldn't sleep. The generator thrummed, and the *Naham 3* rocked like a duck in a tub. I thought about Abdul's concern over our location. He'd ordered me to mention the bush most likely because he wanted American planes to look for me inland from the Hobyo cell-phone tower—which would be traceable from Abdul's number, but might have many miles of range—rather than out at sea. In German I had said "*Schiff*," not "*Naham 3*" or "Hobyo." But no other ships lay nearby.

I'd said enough. Somebody could figure it out.

Before I fell asleep I remembered my lighter from Tony. My porthole stared east, across the open ocean, so pulsing signals through it wouldn't alarm Somalis in Hobyo. I rooted in my bag for a roll of toilet paper to shield and direct the light, as I had done on land, and started flashing *SOS* into the black intractable sky.

IX

A monsoon started to rock the ship in mid-June, a constant wind, which raised heavy chop on the water as well as storms of reddish dust over Hobyo. The sun set every evening like a white puck in a smudged ocher painting. "We call it the southeast," Rolly said, which hinted at the mutability of the season across the Indian Ocean.* Trade winds shifted direction over the Seychelles during a summer monsoon, bringing drier weather; they dumped warm

---

* The Indian Ocean has two monsoon seasons, a strong and a weak. In the Seychelles, they're called the southeast and the northwest. Somalis refer to the stronger monsoon, during their summer, as *hagar*.

rain on Mumbai; they delivered cold nights and squalls of rain to Somalia. They also changed the ocean temperature. Until the monsoon our saltwater showers on the ship were almost luxuriously warm, but in the first days of summer, the stream pouring from the pump felt like snowmelt. My skin twitched, and I tried to imagine how it would feel to jump off the ship. The notion of escape was always there, and on some days during the monsoon I worried about hypothermia.

"Is like South Africa," said Rolly. "Summer is winter."

"But for a different reason," I said.

"Yes, but we got June now," said Rolly. "In Somalia, is cold."

"Right, but it really is summer in Somalia. South Africa's below the equator."

"Yes, but in summer, Michael, South Africa is also cold."

"Because it's really winter."

"Is like winter now!" Rolly said.

The Seychelles lay below the equator, too, but that didn't matter—we enjoyed bickering. It passed the time. The Filipinos referred to us as "Tom and Jerry."

These petty, confrontational exchanges were also a way to ignore our situation, and in the afternoon I read in the Bible about the Unforgiving Servant, a man who found himself released by his king from a great debt. He walked from the palace to the street and collared another servant for not paying a much smaller debt. The king summoned him back to revoke his act of mercy. "So likewise shall my heavenly Father do unto you, if ye from your hearts forgive not every one his brother their trespasses."*

It was a chastening, awful thing to read in captivity.

---

* Matthew 18:34–35.

That day, or the next, a delegation of pirates came down to discuss a construction project with Li Bo Hai. Arnel translated while an old and damaged-looking Somali inquired about building a platform across the tuna tray from the middle of some unused stairs, at about chest height, like a bunk bed. Somali guards had complained about the cold at night. The idea was to let them sit halfway downstairs, out of the monsoon wind.

I objected in passionate silence. The platform would take precious bench space away from the hostage crew.

The damaged-looking man had ragged hair and a stoop. He acted mean and ruthless, and he looked near sixty, as old as Captain Tuure. I thought of him as a rough old soldier, because he seemed to have military training, but otherwise I knew nothing about him. He noticed my silent protest and gave me a filthy look.

"That man not like you," Rolly said.

"The feeling's mutual."

I objected to the wooden platform for another reason. I still wanted to jump. On the phone with Anders, I had missed my chance to request a helicopter, but I still hoped for the sound of chopper blades on some quiet morning. I felt guilt ridden and restless every day. I wanted to *do* something to make up for the grief and horror at home—I wanted to restore the lost harmony of my old life, of all the pleasures I had time to recall—and I knew that if Somalis sat down here on a new platform, they might shoot a leaping hostage even before he left the ship.

The Chinese also saw this construction project as a threat to our seating arrangements. They responded with an act of passive-aggressive arts and crafts. They ripped up some pulp novels from their luggage and folded Mandarin-printed pages into little origami cranes. They tied the cranes to lengths of fishing line, which they strung along the steel wall and the overhead deck. Every Chinese man knew how to fold an origami crane, somehow, but it still took three days of diligent effort before the port wall of the deck bloomed with six rows of paper birds, all cream-colored and fluttering in the wind, like blossoms on a garden bower.

"I see the Chinese make *déco*" was how Rolly put it.

"I think it's a protest," I told him.

He stared for a while at the strange and delicate creation.

"Look like somebody gonna have a wedding," he said.

X

Living on the *Naham 3* made me weird in the head. Along with a quick temper, I developed a strange lassitude. The salt wind, the persistent rocking, the elements—the damp and the cold and the blazing sun—seemed to soften my hold on reality, and I fell under the hypnotic influence of the open sea. The idea of jumping to freedom was half-crazy. But was it crazier than staying *on* a pirate ship? I felt restless but salt eaten, and my reflexes had slowed, which could be dangerous, because as a hostage I sometimes had to think about enormous and sudden piles of vague information.

Abdul returned to the *Naham 3* at the end of June, and I asked how negotiations were going.

"I haven't heard anything new."

"Last time you said the man in Norway was going to wrap up my case."

"These guys on shore," he said, nodding toward Hobyo and referring to the pirate bosses, "they're not hearin' what they wanna hear."

Money was on offer, in other words, but they had refused.

"I see."

Abdul and I had to lie to each other with strategy and persistence. He was like a diabolical tax inspector who probed for hidden income. It's a mistake to mention any amount of money to a kidnapper, so I dodged his questions, but I nodded along with his cover story that he was "not a pirate." He painted a picture of his role as a freelance negotiator, a man in business for himself, who drifted among gangs and tried to free hostages around Somalia. He provided a service. He did have more freedom than the pirate guards, possibly more disengagement from a single gang; but I believed Ferdinand's story about the mock execution, and I knew very well that Abdul was a pirate.

The same evening—a Saturday—after we retired to our cabins, I used the captain's bathroom to brush my teeth. Abdul had slumped on the captain's bunk to watch TV. When I came out of the tiny room, he said, "Sit down here. I wanna talk to you."

I leaned on the edge of the bunk while he snapped off the television.

"We're gonna do a phone call in a couple of hours," he said. "I just wanted to explain. Every time I get an offer from your side, I gotta bring it to this committee of bosses on land. They're crazy, you know. They're mean guys. And they're not gettin' any offer that's even close to what they want."

It sounded as if negotiations had nudged forward, so I said, "Well, how much is their demand right now?"

"Twenty million."

"That's completely insane."

"If I want 'em to come down," he said, "I gotta hear something a little more in line with what they want."

"You haven't done any work, have you? It's been a month."

"Write down your email addresses for me," he said. "And your passwords."

"What for?"

"Aw, don't be suspicious. I won't give the passwords to anyone else."

"You *are* anyone else," I pointed out.

"I'm trying to help you."

I took the pen and made a show of trying to remember my details. "I don't know everything by heart," I said, and wrote down a fake address. "But the password's obsolete. You guys've held me too long; it won't work anymore."

Abdul glanced at the paper. The pretended friendliness vanished. "So you won't give me your passwords," he said ponderously. "Okay. When we talk on the phone later, you gotta beg for the money. Pour on the emotion, right? Because we're not gettin' the offers we need."

I went back to my cabin and rehearsed a clear description of my location at sea in German, as well as a request for a helicopter. I decided that whoever might listen to the call—military intelligence, the FBI—would need time to translate my German and work out a plan, so tomorrow morning might be too early; on the other hand we couldn't wait too long, since Abdul might record the call. He might notice the German and have it translated. I tried to imagine the consequences. My panicked, sea-softened mind raced but came to no conclusion.

I decided to request a helicopter for Monday morning. Abdul summoned me after an hour, and we dialed the number to Norway. The negotiator Anders asked about my health and my diet. I told him nothing had changed.

"Okay, I'm going to connect you with your mother. We'll all be on the phone together."

"Fine."

My mother answered the phone sounding deeply concerned for my welfare. "Michael, how *are* you?" By now she would have seen the Garfanji video, and I wondered if she'd seen pictures of Rolly hanging from a tree.

"Are you eating enough?" she said.

"Nothing has changed," I said.

This refrain, repeated with feeling, meant *I'm still on the ship.* "Can we send you a care package?" Mom said, and I almost lost my composure. Abdul made a rolling hand gesture, as if to say I should crank up the rhetoric, and I expressed alarm that no one had talked the figure down from twenty million. I grew emotional; I raised my voice and started to holler in German. Abdul grabbed the phone and clicked off.

"No, you can't do that," he said. "I don't know what you're saying."

"I was telling them I needed help."

"Say it in English."

He dialed Anders again and made the move-it-along gesture. I yelled about negotiations and money and my own desperation "on land" in Somalia. I added a quick line in German about the ship and glanced at Abdul. No response. The way to speak German, I realized, was to weave it into English. He couldn't recognize short fragments. So I blew some more smoke in English and blurted: *"Ich bitte um einen Hubschrauber, Montag morgen um halb sechs." I'd like to request a helicopter for five thirty this Monday morning.*

"What was that? I didn't understand," my mother said.

"I heard it, Marlis. I will tell you," said Anders.

"This line isn't very good," she complained.

I'd poured my frustration into the role, all my nervous fear. I'd made passionate calls for help. I'd hollered like a murder victim, and in the middle of my yelling I had done a dangerous thing that I hoped would set me free. I couldn't tell whether Abdul had noticed.

"How was that?" I asked him.

"That was much better."

XI

Mom knew I was living on a ship even before I mentioned it to her. An FBI agent had visited one afternoon in the spring or early summer of 2012 with a blurry printed photo taken from high above the *Naham 3* that showed me standing on deck in a red shirt not unlike my Manchester United jersey. "It was hard to make out, but I thought, from the stature, that it was you," she said. "They said it was a satellite picture."

When she mentioned a "care package" on the phone, I felt grief as well as filial guilt, and the knot of feeling that formed in me whenever I thought about my family and friends was not just grief but desperation; I felt the ridiculous insufficiency of my own love for the people who loved me best. A long kidnapping resembles a death, for the family of the hostage above all; but "resembles" can be worse than "equals" for relatives who have to wonder every day whether a wrong move might kill the hostage outright. I didn't see this dynamic well in Somalia. On the *Naham 3* I grew restless and impatient and strange enough in the head to regard suicide and escape as near-equal opportunities. I wanted my helicopter scheme to work because I could tell my mother was suffering. I wanted to redeem myself, to wrench myself out of this nightmare and ease her mind.

I also thought the care-package idea was delusional. It wasn't, exactly. Mom had found the phone numbers of NGOs in Kenya, including the International Committee of the Red Cross (ICRC) and Médecins Sans Frontières, to ask whether their missions to Somalia could deliver a box to relief workers in Galmudug, who could hand it off to middlemen, who might hand it off to pirates, until the package reached me. She knew I was half-blind. So, with the help of friends in Berlin, she had found my optometrist, who had found my prescription on file. She wanted to send a pair of glasses. "A few NGOs thought they could reach you," Mom said later. "But nothing ever happened. Most of them said it was too dangerous for their teams. I was just sitting there thinking, *What can I do?* So that was one thing I tried."

Ashwin, meanwhile, helped her correspond with people in Europe, including Anders, and he unearthed an eccentric side offer for my freedom. "It may sound a bit comical, but a serious contact from Galkayo has written to me saying the pirates are willing to release Mike in exchange for 400 camels!" he wrote. The cost of holding me for seven months apparently was equal to four hundred head of prime livestock. "I am forwarding this info because everything is possible in Somalia," he continued. "Please forgive me if this sounds too silly. I also don't know what a camel costs."

XII

The morning after my phone call I sat with Rolly under the bower of fluttering cranes. To my right, on the tuna bench, sat Abdul and Li Bo Hai, with Tony between them, interpreting. Tony's boyish face squinted with the seriousness of the conversation.

"Ask him how much oil is left," mumbled Abdul.

Tony and Li Bo Hai conferred.

"He says about thirty days," Tony reported.

"And how much diesel?"

"About sixty days," Tony said.

Abdul smoked a cigarette and rubbed his forehead with his thumb. "Okay, tell him we might have to start alternating days without the generator," he said, and I had nightmare visions of a hobbled ship, with tuna starting to stink in the freezer while thirty of us waited for pirate-skiff rides to Hobyo. I also thought: *My helicopter appointment's well timed.*

Then again I was nervous to near panic about a leap from the rail. The notion of diving away from the *Naham 3*—exposing my back to a curtain of gunfire from pirate PKMs while I tried to swim for one of those helicopters—set my heart thumping through a swamp of adrenaline. The only consolation was the time I'd selected. In the half-dark around dawn, there would be more Somali grogginess, more confusion, and (I hoped) less gunfire.

For most of Sunday, I watched the ocean chop and wondered how well I could swim. I'd started to do yoga in my room to keep in shape. But I still felt underweight, frightened, and skinny. From the cutaway rail I watched the fish, mainly trevallies and remoras, patrol the water where we threw baited lines as well as uneaten food. The current was strong: ocean swells rocking the boat moved at a consistent angle toward the shore. The fish struggled against it with sluggish, almost lazy swerves, then turned and shot twice as fast downstream.

I kept washing my hands at the saltwater hose, to test the temperature. (It was cold, but not snowmelt cold.) During the afternoon, I saw a pod of dolphins move in glistening arcs to the north, and I admired the way they could disappear for whole minutes under the surface of the waves.

After lunch, we sat under the conveyor belt, and I edged around the topic with Rolly. I didn't ask for a straight opinion, because I knew what he would say, but I wanted to vent my anxieties.

"Rolly, didn't you go skin diving for sea cucumbers in the Seychelles?"

"Long time ago, yah."

"How long could you hold your breath?" I said.

"'Bout four minutes, like that."

I nodded. "I think I can hold my breath for about two."

"Why you asking?" he said.

"No reason."

"You want to jump at sea?"

"I never said that."

"Ah, Michael. You crazy. I know how you think."

For a while we watched the wind blowing laundry on the ropes. The *Naham 3* had four or five clotheslines and a constant cycle of newly cleaned hostage clothes flapping in the wind.

At last Rolly said, "You know, Michael. Me, I am a skipper. Is my job. I never say to another man, 'Jump at sea.'"

"I know."

"Never, never. Is not safe."

"Unless a helicopter can scoop you," I said.

He gave me a dark look. "What helicopter?"

"Unless a helicopter could come and rescue the man who jumped off the ship."

Rolly was quiet for a long time.

"But, Michael, they will shoot you," he said.

After some careful thought, he added, "Only—if you can tell the helicopter when it must come."

"Like an appointment for the jump," I said.

"Yah."

After dinner I borrowed the plastic alarm clock. I agonized about telling Rolly more; I didn't want to leave him behind. But earlier in the summer I had asked him, "Would you come with me, if we found a way off this ship?" and he had shaken his head: "I no want to leave Marc." Which was a strong point—I didn't want to leave anyone behind, and I would have preferred a military rescue of the entire *Naham 3*. But I'd already blurted my request.

We filed up the stairs at sundown. Under the bunk in my cabin I did push-ups on my few square feet of dirty floor. I also did leg stretches, to avoid cramping in the water. I went to sleep wondering whether I should jump first, at an unguarded spot along the upper rail, in anticipation of my appointment, or keep moving down to the work deck, as usual, wait for the sound of a helicopter, and then sprint.

When the clock rang at 5:00 a.m., the sea looked calm. The breeze through my porthole window felt not too cold. By 5:25 I had assembled the pink flowered blanket over my head and tied up my mattress instead of lugging it outside. For several days I had alternated lugging the mattress with leaving it behind. But whenever I left it in my cabin, I noticed that night-shift pirates would sleep on it during the day, smudging it with dirt and grease. I'd learned to tie the mattress with a rope and stash it under the bunk.

I walked out to the corridor in a state of nerves. The bearded translator named Abdiwali lounged with his rifle on the floor of the bridge. He waved me out, but I must have looked suspicious, because the damaged-looking pirate gave a fierce and wary glare and followed me to the stairs with his pistol raised. My head whanged with alarm. I went down the first set of stairs and listened for any sound of rotor blades on the wind. I glanced back and up at the old Somali, who waved his pistol from the door as if to say, *Keep moving.*

I scowled at him—*What's your problem?*—and trotted down the deck stairs as usual.

The damp morning silence was heartbreaking. The clearing sky looked iron blue. Bleary pirates watched me like huddled scarecrows, and my whole body seemed to vibrate from nervous anticipation. I forced myself to sit still. It was less easy to listen for rotor blades from the origami-bowered bench, but soon enough I could tell that my helicopter, imaginary or real, was about to miss its appointment.

XIII

After breakfast, Big Jacket and some other Somalis attached a cardboard flag to a pole on the upper deck and moved through some patriotic military drills. The damaged-looking man stood with his rifle and shouted orders while two other pirates marched in formal, quasi-fascist style. Most pirates had, or wanted to have, real training, and I wondered how much antiquated Italian discipline had clung to the national army while the older pirate had served in it.

Their powder-blue flag hung on its head. "We are celebrating independence!" Big Jacket told me. "Today is our liberation day! Fuck Europe, fuck America, fuck South Africa!" He meant all the racist colonialists of the world. "We are free!"

I gave him a thumbs-up.

"But your flag's upside down," I said.

"Hah?"

"Look at the star on your flag. It's upside down."

He waved me away, angrily.

The guards strutted through these maneuvers all afternoon, in shifts. Their pride in "Somalia" fascinated me. The federal government was a shambles, the state hardly existed, but the nation lived on as a passionate idea. Loyalties to any of Somalia's bickering clans ranked below a feeling of Somaliness, and all the warring sides on every front of the desultory civil war considered themselves Somali. That was unique in Africa. Most modern countries on the continent were postcolonial constructions, and European-drawn boundaries had lumped together different religions and tribes, which led to civil strife. But modern Somalia was a natural nation-state. European boundaries aggravated it in a different way, by carving three regions away from the heartland, leaving ethnic Somalis stranded across the borders of Ethiopia, Kenya, and Djibouti. This exile became a founding wound. The national flag raised in 1960 had a five-pointed "star of unity" to show the dream of Greater Somalia, the hoped-for unification of people who had lived under five separate colonial systems.* So the flag itself was a land claim, a vision of the future, a refusal to accept postcolonial lines.

Despite this patriotic fervor, clan warfare had trashed the state. The most obvious unifier was Islam. By 2006 a religious movement called the Islamic Courts Union had expanded throughout large parts of Somalia to replace local clan justice, which often sparked clan wars, with sharia law. The ICU brought relative stability. But it also had links to al-Qaeda, and it threatened the weak transitional government in Mogadishu. The Bush administration helped Ethiopian troops defeat it, and the success of this remote front in the war on terror by Christian soldiers inflamed Islamist hard-liners in Somalia and left the bloody ground fertile for an even worse group:

---

* British and Italian Somaliland had fused in 1960; the other three points of the star represented Somalis in Kenya, Ethiopia, and Djibouti (French Somaliland before 1977).

al-Shabaab. American meddling had backfired, and suddenly the complicated civil war had a religious front.

Strict religious rules never sat well with Somalis, though, and "Islam" proved as useful a unifier as "Somalia." Nationalism and religion relied on such powerful emotions of selfhood that civil war had been hard to avoid. Now I found it hard to think of Somalia as anything but splintered. The entropy on land that drove piracy at sea was no longer mysterious. Entropy wasn't nation-specific, of course, and Somalia wasn't a *traditional* mess—which meant there was no reason the same chaos couldn't wander to other parts of the world. Somalia had once been peaceable and calm, and Mogadishu had been a jewel of the East African coast. But the current clannish violence had spun up fast in the final years of Siad Barre's rule and the first years of civil war, and the pirates who arrived now on skiffs alongside the *Naham 3* couldn't cooperate long enough to carry a bag of khat up the stairs, or a case of pasta, or jerry cans of World Food Program–labeled cooking oil, foreign donations which had found their way into Somalia's cash economy. The chaos made me think of Naipaul's *Guerrillas*, a novel about a corrupt black Muslim leader in the Caribbean named Jimmy Ahmed. His sour, self-ironic remark at the core of the story could apply all over the world: "When everybody wants to fight," the fictional Jimmy says, "there's nothing to fight for. Everybody wants to fight his own little war, everybody is a guerrilla."

Somalis looked gaunt and poor to a TV audience, but they were proud as cowboys, and their culture had a tradition of independence that would have rung bells in America. They viewed neighboring Swahili and Bantu cultures as complacent, comfortable, and lazy. They saw themselves as restless, lean, and self-reliant. They were nomads instead of farmers, Muslim slave traders (as a rule) rather than Bantu slaves. One Somali folktale has a sheep explaining to a gazelle that following humans will bring him to some top-notch grass. The gazelle grows impatient. "A sheep cannot understand," he says. "My family and yours are not alike. We are the children of liberty and open space. . . . My heart is not the heart of a sheep."

I watched the cardboard flag quiver upside down in the wind.

XIV

July moved along in a sluggish series of cold, bright weeks. One Cambodian fisherman landed four or five "sawara,"* enormous black fish with silver bellies, every night, and their powerful tails thumped the rubber mat until somebody clocked them with a crowbar. Because of the drop in water temperature these fish became harder to find. So the Cambodian worked in the afternoon. His name was Korn Vanthy. He seemed to have no status on the crew, but he was deft at hurling out hooks and bait by swinging the whole line sideways, like a weighted net. The twirling hooks could sometimes catch a hand or an arm, and one afternoon a hook went straight through the flesh between Korn Vanthy's thumb and his forefinger. He gave a little cry; the line clattered against the side of the ship. Some of us ran over to help. Pirates came down, too. The hook was a four-inch length of steel, bent into a question mark. The barbed end had raised only a small bead of blood, but removing it would have ripped the muscle. Jian Zui suggested cutting the hook with a pair of pliers.

I had a bottle of iodine among my stash of things in the cabin.

---

* Either Spanish or king mackerel.

I asked permission to go upstairs. When I came back, Jian Zui had clipped the hook, and Korn Vanthy was bleeding into a rag. Captain Tuure guided him back to the tuna bench. The old pirate was solic- itous toward the injured man, and while I doused the wound with iodine, he told Korn Vanthy about his own wounds from the Battle of Mogadishu. "*Helikopter!* American!" he told anyone who would listen, lifting his shirt to show Korn Vanthy the scar. But none of the Asians knew about *Black Hawk Down*.

Korn Vanthy was goofy and young. His ears stuck out; he had a broad, silly smile. When I asked his name, he seemed pleased by the attention and sat with me for the rest of the afternoon. Some- times he said something in ship's pidgin, with extra commentary in Khmer, so I hardly understood. He made these remarks with either a grin or a narrow, philosophical stare across the water.

"You have a new friend," Arnel commented.

"Looks like it."

When I opened a pack of cookies, Korn Vanthy was happy to eat one. When I made tea, Korn Vanthy didn't mind a cup. He had so little status on the ship—and I was so disengaged from crew politics—that our friendship became important. After a few days, whenever I sat under the conveyor belt next to Rolly, Korn Vanthy found a reason to join me for a couple of hours. He relaxed on part of my mattress and fell asleep.

He had been a truck driver before he signed up to fish, and he enjoyed it, judging from the way he mimed bouncing through the Cambodian countryside. In his own language, Korn Vanthy must have been good humored and funny, and I wanted to talk to him through a Khmer interpreter—I wanted to know about his fam- ily, his fears, and his path to the *Naham 3*. Again I felt like an ig- noramus, living next to marvelous stories without the equipment to listen. He asked for vocabulary words in English, including the name of the origami birds. "Swan," I said, since the word *crane* had escaped me at the moment; but when I corrected myself, Korn Vanthy had latched on to the word "swan."

The pirates had contributed an avian creation of their own to the fluttering bower, a dinosaur-like thing made from cardboard and patched together with duct tape. It had a terrifying beak and long airplane wings. Also a pair of gray wheels.

"Michael," Korn Vanthy said, and pointed at the monster. "Name?"

"I don't know."

"'I don't know.'"

"No—sorry." I was confusing him. "Dinosaur," I ventured.

"'Dinosaur.'"

It was just a guess. "Or helicopter."

"*Helikopter?*"

"Yes."

He pointed off the ship to indicate the metal birds we'd seen over the water, the helicopters that, in my lonesome opinion, had grown too scarce.

"*Helikopter!*" he said.

"Yes."

But it was hard to tell. The pirates' weird art project may have expressed a fear of helicopters, or sarcasm toward the Chinese, or general cussedness, or all three. Maybe I was projecting my own wishes onto the wrinkled gray tape.

"I don't know," I admitted.

"'I don't know,'" Korn Vanthy repeated.

Later, while fishing over the rail, he pulled up a chunk of soft reddish coral and hung it up to dry. In a fit of hilarity, he told me it was for a rare Cambodian recipe, "coral soup," which he would cook for me with onions.

"Okay, Korn Vanthy," I said.

We were both full of amiable bullshit, which helped pass the time.

XV

Somebody unearthed an antique meat grinder from the bowels of the ship, and Sosan set to work on a three-day project to clean and reassemble it. He let the parts soak in salt water and cleaning fluid. He scrubbed everything with steel wool. He cleaned it, again, in fresh water, but couldn't decide where to use it. The bottom formed a vise clamp, for the edge of a table, so Taso found a beam of wood. Someone else found a wooden dowel for a handle, and soon the men were feeding carefully filleted sides of grouper into the greenish-copper machine.

The final result was a bowl of mashed fish, which Taso kneaded with flour. We formed the mixture into little rounds. The Cambodians cooked them in a sizzling wok. Then they were salted and left to dry, and soon everyone had fish cakes.

The strangest meal on the *Naham 3*, however, was also the simplest. Whenever the crew hauled a new tuna from the freezer and carved it up with the buzz saw, Tony made sure to keep aside a small brick of red meat. Before dinner the brick would be washed and defrosted, and by dinnertime Tony would carry out a tin platter of cold, sliced sashimi.

"Sashimi, okay!" said Korn Vanthy.

"Psycho-psycho," said Sosan, meaning *crazy good*.

The Chinese had a bag of powdered wasabi mix, and they stirred up a batch of watery green sauce in a plastic bowl. The men were used to helping themselves to sashimi this way, now and then, from the frozen stock, as an indulgent treat from the captain. ("The captain ate raw fish a lot," said Tony. "He was over sixty years old, but very strong!") Everyone ate five or six slices on a hot pile of rice. Some slices were still half-frozen, but the fish tasted surprisingly fresh. Without thinking about it, I suppose, I had lived under the impression that "sushi grade" tuna in the West was somehow fresh—once frozen, maybe, but recently caught, within weeks or days. But sushi-grade fish may sit flash-frozen on a ship like the *Naham 3* for many months. A "sushi grade" designation in the United States, in fact, requires a week of freezing to kill parasites.

One afternoon, a number of rainbow runners were lying on the deck, and I took a filleting lesson from Em Phumanny, the bowl-cut Cambodian with Buddhist tattoos. We planned to make kinilaw, a kind of Filipino ceviche made of cold, chopped, vinegary whitefish. "The fish is not cooked, you know?" said Tony. "It is cured in the vinegar."

I squatted in the sun near the cutaway rail while the pirates watched us drowsily. Phumanny showed me how to start the cut. It was late morning. There would be no fresh khat for hours, and when I pulled the first fillet free and walked over to lay it on a plate, I heard an unnatural buzz from the north, to the rear of the ship. A light wind blew the sound away. It didn't rouse the Somalis. I listened. By now I knew the difference between helicopter rotors and airplane propellers, and I was still anxious to jump.

Two quick steps over the cutaway section, a twenty-foot dive to the rocking surface of the water . . . I was tempted. But the sound didn't chop like a helicopter. I heard a steady, rising buzz. A helicopter could have dropped a safety line, but no plane could have scooped me from the sea.

My mind raced.

I stood still and listened.

It was spectacular: a twin-engine plane with numbers on its flank roared up the shore-facing side of the *Naham 3* and roused all the Somalis. I hollered my delight and made sure whoever it was had a clear view of me on deck. The plane banked away and buzzed into the sky. The startled pirates reached for their guns. Before one of them could order me back to the work area, I retreated on my own, to make tea, but the plane returned while my water boiled, and this time the pirates opened fire. The thunder of their machine guns sent a group of five Chinese men tumbling into the work area. They knocked me over while I scooped sugar into my cup, and my brain went black. I didn't faint, but I must have gone into shock, because in the confusion and panic I didn't even feel my knee knock against the conveyor belt. Adrenaline from the gunfire swamped my senses, and afterward I had a mysteriously painful bruised kneecap and a surprising mess of sugar on the floor.

Nothing worse—and no one got shot. Ferdinand said the plane had opened a side door on its second pass, revealing a man with a camera.

"Spy purposes only," he said. "No weapons."

"Okay."

I had no idea what the plane meant; I had no idea what any of it meant. But the work area rang with chatter. Rumors came around from the Somalis that it was an American plane. When a young pirate named Hamed ventured downstairs to beg for powdered milk, Taso pointed at him with a smile on his melancholy face and mimed snapping a camera. *Busted!* (Pirates hated to be photographed.)

Later, a pirate who'd been watching us from a plastic chair on the upper deck, right beside the steps, wanted to talk about the plane. "Michael!" he said. I shaded my eyes to look up. "Aeroplane!"

he said, and gestured with his hand to remind me of how it had buzzed the ship.

"Yes."

He wore a colored turban against the sun and gave me a bright, ironic smile. His name was Bashir—"Bashko" for short—and he thought the whole thing was funny. "Now—finished," he said. "No more aeroplane. Because Somalis—" and he aimed his rifle out to sea to demonstrate their terrifying resistance.

"Scared off?"

"Yah!"

I doubted that. But whoever had sent the plane had wanted us to feel observed. I wondered if it was also a vague response to my (two-week-old) request for a helicopter. Maybe I should have jumped? My charging, unsteady mind tilted into a swamp of speculation. I could imagine several creative ways for the Navy to coax a surfer off a pirate ship. But a twin-engine without pontoons was not a rescue craft. It couldn't hover. It couldn't land on water. It couldn't even impose a ceasefire—it had just drawn a hail of bullets—but it stirred my hope, and I think it raised every hostage's morale to believe that a superpower had eyes on our ship.

XVI

Around this time, Big Jacket came downstairs to make a pot of tea. Pirates had been using our electric kettles for tea ever since Abdul set the precedent. Previously, they could choose from half a dozen electric kettles upstairs for their own tea, but somehow, by late July, they had all broken. So they came downstairs to use ours.

Big Jacket was thin as a corpse, with a sarcastic and contemptuous turn of mind, and while he waited for his tea to boil, he told us we were sitting here in Somalia to help pay for khat. He mimed chewing khat, then pointed at the sky and said "money-money-money-coming"; then he mimed eating more khat. "Okay!" he said, and held up his thumb.

The cycle of life, for a pirate.

"Mm-hmm," I said.

"Tomorrow Ramadan," he went on. "No *chum-chum.*"

I squinted at Big Jacket. "*Adiga* Muslim?" *You are Muslim?*

"*Haa,* yes."

His kettle boiled. He pulled our can of powdered milk from under the conveyor belt, said, "*Ano,* okay," and helped himself, spooning it straight into the kettle. *Ano* was powdered milk. We happened to be running low on *ano.* Rolly protested, "Big Jacket, this *ano* belong to us. Is not for pirates."

Big Jacket poured his milky tea into a thermos and handed Tony the kettle to wash.

"*Adiga*, Jacketweyne," I taunted him. *You are "Big Jacket."*

"Aha—no!" he said.

It startled him to hear his nickname in Somali, and I think it made him self-conscious, because a few days later he took to wearing a different coat.

Another Somali came down the same afternoon with his mug, this time to cadge *ano* and coffee. He hassled Sosan and Taso, in the opposite corner. The guards knew it was against the rules to take advantage of our supplies; they even explained the rules whenever they set down powdered milk or mango juice, or even bottled water. "Somali, no!" they would say, meaning "just for hostages." But a few days later the same guard would come begging. It was the simplest explanation for the pirate who had stolen my oatmeal in Hobyo. Pirate bosses short-provisioned the guards, so when stuff ran out, we had to defend our milk and coffee and juice.

Rolly and I watched the pirate mix everything in his mug, taste it, and make a face. Not up to his standards, apparently. He poured it over the rail.

"Hey!" Rolly shouted, standing up to appeal to the other pirates upstairs. He pointed his finger and hollered. I loved to watch Rolly lose his temper. He made a holy fuss until the Somalis had to respond. The coffee-thieving pirate retreated, intending to disappear toward the rear of the ship before Captain Tuure could punish him.

"Rolly! *Adiga!* Fucking!" he said.

"What that mean?" Rolly asked when he sat down again.

"I think it's Somali for 'Fuck you,'" I said.

Rolly grumbled and shook his head. At last he summed it up:

"They bring you here to their country, and they say you, 'Fuck.'"

I chuckled.

"There is no *ano* among thieves," I said.

XVII

The start of Ramadan, the next day, changed the mood of the guards, in the sense that most of them tried to fast. They lazed around upstairs in quiet misery, seeming to doze in the sun. Somehow it was redemptive in this world of thieves to observe a holy month. It still made no sense to me. Islam, for the pirates, remained a wellspring of respect and renewal, a sacred idea conveniently removed from their own behavior.

Four Indonesian men on the *Naham 3* were Muslim, too, including a lanky kid with a mullet and a bashful smile, named Sudirman. He'd worked as a wedding DJ in Sumatra before joining this crew. I loved Indonesia, and I wanted to talk about the lush forests of Java, the banana plantations, the mosques, and the red-dust trails. But Sudirman—the most talkative of all the Indonesians—was extremely shy.

"Have the pirates given you any special treatment," I asked him, "because you're Muslim?"

He grinned—wide, ironic, bashful. "No!" he said.

The only special treatment came during Ramadan. The four Muslim hostages joined our daytime scrums for meals but saved their bowls of rice and meat in a little fridge, for after sundown. They fasted quietly in a corner of the sweltering work area. At the end of the day—to show enthusiastic solidarity with his captive Muslim brothers—Abdinasser the Sahib would come downstairs with bowls of pasta and fried tuna left over from the pirates' fast-breaking *iftar* meals.

Abdinasser, alone among the pirates I met, had a deep-seated good nature. He was blustery and passionate, eager to pray and praise the Koran, but he didn't mind the sight of Bibles. In his high, chesty voice he would fiercely defend our right to read what we wanted, the way he had defended my right to keep a journal on land. He also became our connection on the *Naham 3* for a pain tablet called "Relief." These vital tablets helped us sleep. I think Abdinasser bought cheap packets of them in Hobyo with his own spare change—in sharp contrast to the pirates who filched our provisions—and sometimes, when he approached the *Naham 3* on a supply boat from town, Abdinasser would spot me on deck and yell, "SAHIB!" across the water, and I would squint and see him waving a tiny red cardboard package while the skiff bounced across the waves. "RELIEF!"

Meanwhile the twin-engine plane, which I very much wanted to be a helicopter, returned to the *Naham 3* every week or so, unpredictably and at different altitudes. I almost never saw it. Whenever we heard its distinctive engines in the distance, our guards would jerk to attention and brandish their guns, long before I could assemble some unrealistic plan to leave the ship. Their twitchy nervous energy during plane visits was terrifying.

One afternoon, while I took a saltwater shower, Big Jacket leaned over the top rail to give me an order. "Michael! Sit down!" he said, and pointed at the tuna bench. From the panic in his eyes I could tell some kind of aircraft was on its way. I still had shampoo in my hair. I considered the water temperature—cold—and wondered how it would be to jump, stark naked, off the ship.

"Sit down!" Big Jacket repeated.

I took my time removing my towel from the laundry line and drying off.

"You mean don't get dressed?"

"SIT DOWN." He pointed again. "Go!"

I listened again. For a helicopter I would have jumped naked. But it sounded like a plane. I slipped on my shorts and soccer jersey and sat on the bench.

"Be quiet!" he ordered, unnecessarily.

"*Jacketweyne*," I taunted him.

"Fucking!"

The plane flew about four hundred feet overhead, at an awkward angle, somewhere out of sight. I watched the Somalis track it with their guns. It seemed to move in a slow, tight circle behind the bridge. At last—still about four hundred feet up—it crossed a visible patch of cloud-marbled sky.

"Is a small plane," said Rolly, who was in a better position. "It look like a drone."

"It's the same plane as before," I said.

Most of the crew had retreated to the work area. They stared up in silence, maybe worried about gunfire. The plane didn't cross again. It never came near the ship.

"How you know is the same?" Rolly said, and I shrugged.

"Just a hunch."

XVIII

The *Naham 3* kept a stash of bright orange parkas, overalls, and moon boots for deep excursions into the freezer hold. The freezer consisted of different levels and rooms, and although crewmen liked to dart in and out of the shallowest part in just sandals and shorts (using the latched door by the shower), moving further inside needed heavy gear. One morning in August a group of pirates came downstairs and started pulling on parkas and boots. I had never seen anything like it. Bakayle, Big Jacket, Abdul the translator, and Abdinasser the Sahib spent half an hour in the Somali sunshine, suiting up like Arctic explorers.

"What do you think's going on?" I asked Rolly.

"Look like a visit to the captain."

The Taiwanese captain lay dead in a room near the stern, wrapped in sheets and plastic, according to Tony.

"Or they gonna count the fish," Rolly said.

Arnel had to suit up, too. He would guide the Somalis through the frozen maze.

"Arnel," I whispered, "what are they doing?"

He just shook his head.

They disappeared through the door, which stood open, leaking fog. Akes,* a Filipino, sat on the tuna bench with a slight grin. He had straight hair in a mullet shape, wide-set eyes, and a quiet manner. The other men protected him from doing too much work, because his contract had ended a week after the hijacking. Everyone else, technically, was still on the job—some hoped to get paid through the end of their contracts if they survived—but Akes should have been home in the Philippines.

"What are they looking for in the freezer?" I asked him. "The captain's body? Or are they doing a fish inventory?"

"Gold and jewels," he said calmly.

"What?"

"Gold and jewels," he repeated.

"You're kidding."

Akes finally laughed. "The pirates think we hid our valuables in the fish. They think they will find treasure in there."

"In the freezer," I said.

"In the *fish*."

"Good God."

The Somalis had stolen everyone's phones and valuables, but now they wanted more, and for some reason they believed enough jewels would be stashed in the tuna carcasses to make a spelunking expedition worthwhile. I watched in mild amazement. The pirates were nuts; that was long established. But it got worse. The parka-suited Somalis returned after half an hour and gave some kind of order. We had to take our laundry down from the ropes. Two men opened the freezer portal, and more crew set to work moving a small crane arm from its retracted position near the bridge. Ferdinand and Taso guided a hook from the crane down into the hold,

---

* Pronounced *Arkis*.

where someone attached it to the loop of rope in the tail of a frozen tuna.

The crane raised fish, one at a time, until a number of fat, iron-colored tuna lay defrosting in the tropical sun. To me it looked like an obscure omen of the ship's demise, a stocktaking before the pirates moved us ashore. Rolly felt the same way.

"You think they gonna sell this tuna?" Rolly said.

"I don't know," I said.

"Why they counting it?"

I told him what Akes had said about "gold and jewels," and Rolly was incredulous.

"But—is crazy, Michael."

"I know."

"I not believe you."

We kept watching. It seemed a tedious way to unload a hundred tons of anything—one piece at a time, on a swinging rope.

Ferdinand came to join us and lit a cigarette. He looked at the growing school of steaming, startled-looking fish, which would lie there pointlessly for an hour, only to move back before they defrosted.

"If they are really looking for treasure," he said, "it is lying right here."

"All the tuna," I said.

"Yes."

"How much is it worth?"

"Is a *lot* of money," Rolly mumbled.

Ferdinand squinted. "Market rate, last year? When we leave Mauritius?"

"Yeah," I said.

"Biggest fish here, might be two thousand dollars."

"I think the pirates got to sell it somehow," said Rolly.

We wondered how a tuna-packing firm could buy the fish from

pirates. It seemed impossible at first glance, not worth the risk, because anyone with a ship outfitted to accept so much frozen meat would have to sail it too close to Somalia. But I knew the story of an industrial fishing company from Thailand that had paid for peace and protection on the water off Puntland in exchange for fishing rights.* The Thai company anchored a canning vessel near Bosaso, a port town, and a Somali "coast guard" offered the foreigners Mafia-style protection, even shooting at small-time Somali fishermen who competed for fish within the twelve-mile limit. (Corruption, in some parts of Somalia, was total.)

"I think it's complicated," I said.

"I not understand," Rolly said.

"It depends," I said, "on whether Ali Duulaay knows anyone in the tuna industry."

The crew piled two dozen tuna, like boulders, in a shaded corner of the deck, where they wouldn't defrost so fast. They pulled more unofficial catch out of the walk-in freezer. Soon a whole ecosystem of frozen seafood lay on the deck, including clusters of little trevallies, dark and glistening sawara, silvery moonfish—which were flat and round, the size of manhole covers—and two or three blue sharks, nine feet long and magnificent with their jagged grins. Someone also hauled out a collection of roped shark fins, like an enormous set of clattering keys.

"Why so many fins?" I asked Akes.

He said that some of the crew had sliced the fins off accidentally caught sharks in the hope of supplementing their income when the ship returned to port.

"Side business," he said.

---

* According to U.N. reports and *Deadly Waters*, by Jay Bahadur.

"I see."

Low wages and an appetite in China for shark-fin soup drove the destruction of sharks by vessels like the *Naham 3*. The crew wasn't innocent. None of us were innocent. But innocence was no longer the point.

XIX

In August, the generator sputtered. A team of Chinese mechanics made near-daily trips to the rear of the vessel to keep it running, but the *Naham 3* was a dwindling resource.

When the ship ran out of rice in August, the pirates delivered new twenty-pound sacks from Hobyo, which the crew regarded as a deep misfortune. They were chauvinists about rice and preferred fluffy, short-grained white stuff grown in Southeast Asia. Now they had to eat brownish basmati imported from Pakistan. Nguyen Van Ha pulled a face when he tried his first bowl and shook his head in disgust.

Near the end of August, water flowing from our shower hoses felt warmer, which meant the monsoon season had started to turn. Abdul the translator came aboard to question Li Bo Hai, again, on behalf of the pirate bosses, and again I overheard the conversation. How much life was in the generator? How much oil, how much fuel? Answer, about a month. Somehow we had a reprieve. But Abdul acted vague about whether the bosses would preserve the ship.

Later the same day, Abdul carried a round-screened instrument down from the bridge, trailing electric wire. "I want this working again," he ordered. "If you need parts from that ship over there"—he pointed out at the *Shiuh Fu 1*—"we can get 'em. But we can't stay on this boat without a radar."

One by one the men squatted to inspect the colorful soldered guts of the radar monitor. Taso and Cao Yong fiddled the longest, with an air of resignation, under the warm shade near our conveyor belt. For the first time, Abdul had mentioned the ship on the beach. He'd named our worst nightmare. Our mood plummeted, but the radar wouldn't come on again. Arnel explained the problem to Abdul. Finally someone piled the parts into a box and shelved it in a closet.

Word went around the next day that the generator would have to shut down to save fuel. We ate breakfast in morbid silence. Afterward we rushed the electric kettles to brew coffee and tea and save it all in thermoses. Around 8:00 a.m. the motor quit, with a long and terrifying shudder that vibrated the hull and left us alone with ourselves. For the first time we noticed the desertlike silence on the water. The generator had not only powered a surprising number of instruments, including the TV, the kettles, the trickling seawater hoses, and the sizzling woks—it had muffled Somali voices, meaning it had sheltered us from an unbroken awareness of living at their mercy. We tried to play cards, but during the long afternoon the tropical heat mounted, and we had little to keep us from remembering our status as prisoners, or the tons of rigid fish, or the captain. We wondered if he would decompose. A smell rose from the corner grate we used for a latrine.

Abdul ended this day without power by four in the afternoon, I think because he wanted tea. But the threat had not been lost on the crew. The pirates had wanted to warn us about living on shore, and the shock of the silent ship was linked to a fierce rumor of freedom that had circulated for several days.

The source of the rumor was hard to locate, but a few days earlier Ferdinand had said, "I feel it in my heart. I think we're gonna go free by the end of the month."

"You mean August?" I said.

Which was almost over.

"Maybe September. I think the owners have started to negotiate."

Then a friend of Ha's—another Vietnamese man called Nguyen Van Xuan—told me that one pirate had told him the whole ship would go free "in five days."

"Everyone?" I said. "Including Rolly and Michael?"

I wanted reassurance as much as everyone else. Xuan was a modest man who wore old tasseled loafers and had smiling, wide-set eyes. He looked troubled for a moment, then beamed with joy. In broken ship's pidgin he answered:

"*Hai dao* speak, all ship. Michael and Rolly, okay!" *The pirate said the whole ship, so Michael and Rolly, too!*

I felt better for about three hours. But this gossip was pure sentimentality, nothing but junk food for the starving. I started to recognize the scam. In the scheme of the Five-Day Rumor, our day without power was Day Four. On the next morning, no one went free—the generator shutdown had been a scare tactic. Instead, Abdul presided over a long series of phone calls to Asia. Every crewman climbed the stairs to the bridge, to use the ship's telephone, on a warm tide of hope. They were shocked to hear protests of helplessness from their bewildered families. On their way down they endured sarcasm from the pirates, who saw it as the families' stubborn fault that the men would not go free.

Korn Vanthy returned from his call and flopped on my mattress. He covered his face with one arm. In ship's pidgin he said, "My parents can't send the money. I will die."

"Who said you would die?"

"The translator. Abdul."

"Korn Vanthy—"

"He said the pirates will shoot me."

"Korn Vanthy, listen. *Hai dao bow-wow sa-sa.*" *The pirates gab a lot.* "They won't shoot you. Don't worry."

I didn't believe it myself, or not entirely. Evidence against my position was lying in the freezer. But I kept up my line of argument until Korn Vanthy appeared to relax.

XX

After the day of failed telephone calls, the rumor of freedom dissipated. Everyone's apprehension focused on a new rumor about a massive fish feeding near the *Naham 3*. The hull of our ship had grown into a rich colony of barnacles and algae, which attracted grazing fish and predators of increasing size. I remembered a line in *Der Spiegel* about the sharks trailing a hijacked German freighter while it limped to freedom after a four-month anchorage off Somalia. "The large numbers of mussels attached to its hull slowed its progress, allowing an entire food chain to follow behind, with sharks bringing up the rear."

The next day, we spotted the fish. It was a lumbering shadow in the waves—not a shark, according to Ha, but maybe a fat ocean sunfish or even a little whale. The crew rushed over to look. The shadow vanished, and the ship lurched. I can't say now whether the lurching caused by the sudden movement of men stretched our rusted anchor chain, or whether the bulbous monster somehow swam into it and snapped it. The crew, afterward, would blame the fish. But when I sat down again with Rolly on the fiberglass bench, a sickening thunk vibrated through the hull.

"What happen?" Rolly said. "The anchor break?"

Hobyo and the *Shiuh Fu 1* started to roll away toward the south. We were moving with a fast, shoreward-angling current. The ship began to turn.

"Yes," I said.

Our view of the shore gave way to a view of rough open water. Half a dozen Chinese men hurried toward the engine room. The rest of the crew pulled on gloves and went upstairs to haul in what was left of the anchor chain. Rolly and I stayed downstairs on the work deck with Tony, who, as a cook, had no heavier duties.

The ship spun in the water because of the way the heavy current caught the hull. The *Naham 3* had a deep keel, and the current must have caught it and turned us like a crank. We spun in long, lurching circles. I wanted to jump before things got worse, but Somalis had swarmed the upper deck with their weapons to yell at the laboring men. The shore twirled in and out of view. I wasn't sure whether to feel dizzy, sick, or terrified. Sooner or later we would beach. I didn't want to lose my last chance to jump, but I also didn't want to screw up. Any jump would have to be timed for the turning ship as well as the current.

While I thought about that, the twin-engine plane reappeared, flying in an aggressive circle. Rolly said, "Look!" and my blood seethed with adrenaline. Big Jacket appeared right away with his rifle, ordering us to cover our heads and hurry upstairs. Other Somalis bristled upstairs with their guns.

It seemed smarter to follow orders than to jump, so I went up the stairs with Rolly and hurried along the gangway. I had to lie on the bunk in my cabin and watch the horizon spin. I felt depressed and a little seasick. *I missed my chance. I missed my chance.* But an escape attempt would have been crazy. I'd never seen the Somalis so panicked and ready to shoot.

My own understanding of the problem, and my own resolve, were as straight and stable as the anchorless *Naham 3*, and together we turned like a merry-go-round on the edge of the Indian Ocean, moving northward for almost an hour, which wasn't long enough to wash the heavy vessel ashore. The engineers got the motor started. It rumbled twice as loud as the generator, with a rough dirty voice. The ship was soon puttering south in a line against the powerful current. At sundown the pirates ordered us back outside for dinner, under a monsoon sky, and everyone sat around the deck looking morose.

"What's going to happen?" I asked Hen, who sat by himself with his bowl of rice. "Are we going to Hobyo?"

"Hobyo!" he spluttered, with dark humor and frustration in his eyes, as if he couldn't believe the anchor chain was about to cause such a stupid shift in everyone's fate.

I felt no different. The sun sank in a gray-orange haze. I thought this would be our last night at sea. I didn't want to see Hobyo again, and I returned to my room feeling nervous and wired. Drones *had* to be in the air. Someone with the power to launch a twin-engine aircraft had noticed the accident and reacted, quickly, so it was possible that even an aircraft carrier stood not far off. This ship was moving an American hostage to an unknown destination. The Navy *had* to be watching.

XXI

Maybe the sea-craziness and lassitude had loosened my brain; maybe I'd lost some portion of sanity in five months on the water. I decided not to go to Hobyo. Instead I rolled the LED lighter into a plastic bag, sealed it as well as I could, using a tight elastic string, and lay in the fluorescent light of the cabin, running through what I hoped would be the order of events. Whoever had sent that airplane could send a rescue helicopter just as fast, I thought. I could leap with the LED lighter in my pocket and use it to identify myself in the water to any watching drone. Our engine was in such wobbly condition that the *Naham 3* would have to keep chugging forward.

There could be a rescue, even in the dark, as soon as I swam out of range of the pirates' guns.

No, hang on, that's crazy.

If it failed, I would probably die. If I did nothing, I might go ashore.

I felt moody, depressed, and afraid. Ready to end the whole ordeal.

I lay flat on my bunk and wondered how it would feel to do nothing. I imagined Abdinasser waking me around midnight, and a series of skiffs shuttling us to a darkened beach. Then it would be goat liver and canned tuna for breakfast, and no more chances to escape.

I climbed down from my bed at about 8:00 p.m. to ask permission to use the bathroom. Abdiwali, the translator with a grizzled black-and-white beard, came into view on the bridge.

"What's the matter?" he said.

"I need toilet paper."

"We don't have any."

I approached the bridge. "I have some downstairs, by the work area," I said. "Rolly and I have a bag in the closet."

"You can't go out there now."

"I need some," I said. "It's a problem."

Abdiwali turned to discuss the problem with another Somali, the damaged-looking man who spoke no English.

"We will get you more tomorrow," Abdiwali said.

"That doesn't help me now."

Abdiwali looked annoyed. They exchanged a few more words.

"Okay. Come on."

The crew had rolled out sleeping mats; in the glare of white deck lamps they smoked cigarettes and watched TV. Abdiwali carried no rifle: that was good. He waited for me, unarmed, near the foot of the steps.

I smiled at the other hostages and found a random plastic bag in the closet. I rustled it and pretended to stuff something into my shorts pocket. When I returned to the open deck, Abdiwali started upstairs. There was no better chance. I kicked off my sandals so they skittered across the deck and ran for the cutaway section, launched myself off the gunwale with one bare foot, and dove, fingertips first, about twenty feet into the wavering, black, surprisingly warm water. ("Michael!" Abdiwali's voice hollered behind me.) The culmination of a dream that had percolated in me for more than five months at sea gave me a quick thrill of hope. But when I came up for air I noticed how buoyant I was, and how afraid.

I dove again, waiting for bullets. My only consolation was that pirates would have terrible aim. The *Naham 3* churned forward, and I swam with the slanting current, toward the rear, keeping just under the waves like a dolphin. I raised my head to breathe. For days I'd calculated how long it might take to swim out of that margin of water where shooting me from the ship would have been all too easy for a pirate on an upper deck, like sniping a fish in a bucket. But the vessel's industrial hulk seemed to pass in a minute. Its forward speed, and the swift shoreward current, worked in my favor. Excited Somalis ran around on the upper decks of the ship to maneuver two searchlights across the water.

Nobody fired a shot.

Soon I was a ship's length away, about fifty yards. The swells were long and gentle. The water tasted brinier than other oceans I knew, and I floated easily because of the salt. I also wasn't cold. But my body felt electrified with fear. Before I jumped, I knew the chances of success were low, and the notion of escape was deliriously insane, half-suicidal, so I had left the ship with self-destruction at the front of my mind. I would go free or die trying. It took fear and desperation to urge me off the ship, but fear and desperation are forms of energy, which convert to something powerful if you express them well. Emotionally I had made no mistake: I felt fantastic. I no longer wanted to die.

I dove and swam again. The warm, pulsing swells were like black dunes. I stopped more than two hundred yards from the ship, and while the searchlights lanced across the water I decided to try the LED. I wanted to flash a signal up to whatever might be watching. It should have been clear to a drone that a hostage had jumped, and I thought an SOS pattern would help identify me. (I was also, by this point, quite out of my mind.) I rooted in my cotton shorts and came up with the plastic-wrapped lighter, waited for a large swell to shelter me—as if a black wave could hide what I was about to do— then aimed my plastic lighter at the sky. I clicked.

Nothing.

Of course not.

"Fuck!" I hollered and hurled the thing away.

Now I had several choices. I could swim around, evade the searchlights, tread water, and hope for a helicopter. I could swim for the beach. Or I could drown myself.

The ship slowed. Searchlights traced the water. I wondered whether to tread here awhile or swim for the beach. The mile of ocean didn't bother me; what I feared was machine-gun fire. If a Somali caught a glimpse of my shoulder moving away in the searchlight, he could shatter the waves with a PKM.

I leaned back to keep my head low on the surface of the gentle swells and found a way to float on my back. It was easier than expected because of the salt. When a searchlight swept near me, I ducked, and it was blissful to submerge in the thick warm sea.

I blinked and squinted and listened for a helicopter. I watched the *Naham 3* move on. Part of me still believed in the omniscience and desperation of a bureaucratic force like the Navy, a desperation as strong as my own, to recognize my poor figure in the water and glean my intentions and seize the slim chance to scoop me out as soon as I was free of the ship. I thought we'd have time. I thought it would take the pirates an hour or more to organize a skiff from land, since we weren't near Hobyo. And I thought I could still drown myself if necessary.

But the ship made an unexpected move. Instead of chugging away, it stalled and started to list. One searchlight beam found me but moved up and down, unsteadily, across the surface. I managed to duck and swim away. But the ship was leaning *toward* me on the swells. It was astonishing to watch. Everything—searchlights, running lights, water tanks, the still-turning radar antenna, all three decks and all the men at the rail—tilted like an oil platform in heavy weather. All two hundred tons of the *Naham 3* were lurching in my direction.

I cleared my eyes and searched the sky for any artificial light. I listened for a helicopter. My buzzing blood was ecstatic, but the *Naham 3* tilted and gathered speed on the waves. I wondered whether to swim around the stern, evade, and try to vanish into deep water, or turn and swim for the beach. I'd been floating for almost half an hour. I could comfortably survive the exertion, but I realized with dread that the massive ship would outpace me. It was a principle from surfing: a larger craft on any swell has more momentum. Whether I stayed put or swam for shore, I risked getting keelhauled by the barnacle-crusted hull.

The searchlight found me again while the ship listed. I could imagine a slow-motion chase, back and forth, if I swam around for deeper water.

And I could imagine drowning myself.

I could see the hollering crew.

Fuck.

The ship lumbered close, lights blazing. Someone tossed a life preserver attached to a rope. I had to decide whether to swim around the hull—now—or grab the preserver.

I swam and grabbed the rope. I held the ring close to my chest; the men pulled. It was only while I scaled the hull that I thought of a decent alibi.

"What were you thinking, man?" said Abdul frantically, his eyes manic and wide. "Why the fuck did you jump?"

Four men led me to the tuna bench, where somebody draped me with a blanket. Taso handed me a bowl of warm water to drink, in case I had hypothermia. Hen gave me disinfectant for my toes, which for some reason had started to bleed, and Tony handed me the sandals I had kicked away. I asked for bandages and tape.

My alibi was obvious. "Garfanji," I said to Abdul. "Al-Shabaab."

I said I didn't want to move ashore to be sold to terrorists; I didn't want to hang from a tree. Those threats had been half-serious in May, and now, almost four months on, they were like rotten fish. But Garfanji had made them, so he could damn well hear them again.

"Who told you that?" said Abdul.

"Everyone," I said. "Garfanji himself."

Bakayle—Fifty Million—sat further down the bench. I pointed to him.

"That man did."

"Okay," said Abdul.

When the excitement subsided, two pirates escorted me back to my cabin. My blood still thrummed. I didn't sleep well, and in the morning I wasn't allowed outside with the rest of the crew. I would be condemned to three weeks of solitary confinement in my cabin. Meanwhile the *Naham 3* would be tethered to a hijacked cargo ship called the MV *Orna*, which had a sturdy anchor.

My mind felt wild and strange, like a caged animal's. I wondered how much ferocity and gnashing regret a human heart could stand. But the swim had been fabulous, invigorating, the very opposite of suicide. It had reminded me of freedom.

Part 6

NO GOD BUT GOD

Three weeks later I found myself in a high-ceilinged room with a dim and dirty fluorescent light and a mosquito tent on the bed. There was an almost urban finish to the blue-painted walls, and the air felt different from the air on the coast—it had the stifling, malarial warmth I remembered from Galkayo. I slept inside the mosquito tent, a little awkwardly, and woke up around sunrise when an airplane roared low over the rooftops.

The other piece of furniture here, besides my bed, was a mirrored vanity table crowded with skin creams and beauty products. It reminded me of Digsi's sister's house in Budbud. Thinking of that now distant visit recalled Ashwin's droll question, delivered to Hamid with straight-faced irony: "What goes on, in this room?"

My new prison was like a bordello crossed with a utility closet.

Four pirates dozed on a mat on the floor. When another plane landed, two of them glanced up at me for a reaction. We'd spent the night near an airport. One pirate, Issa, was a tall, loping Somali who had guarded me on the *Naham 3* and in Mussolini's Farmhouse. Judging from the way he sometimes laughed with the other men, he had a silly sense of humor; but he stared at me now with a cold face.

A dingy pink curtain hung in the doorway, lit by the climbing sun. The humid heat of morning mounted quickly, so Issa plugged in a dusty fan. He moved it to the doorway and aimed it at my bed, and I started to cough.

"Okay, Michael?" he said.

"Not really."

The other pirates woke up. I squinted at a new man who was

shaking hands with Issa. He looked familiar; the guards pointed and smiled. "Yoonis!" they said, and I remembered the translator from Mohammed Tahliil's safe house in Hobyo. My mosquito tent was from Mohammed's house, too, come to think of it.

"Hi, Yoonis," I said, but he adopted a haughty sarcasm I hadn't remembered in him.

"From today," he said, "we will be using Arabic names. I am no longer called Yoonis. You should now call me Faisal."

"Really?"

"You must call me Faisal. It is my real name, my Muslim name."

"That seems complicated."

"You must do it," he insisted.

I did remember a rumor on board the *Naham 3* that someone had shot Yoonis dead.

"I didn't think you were alive," I told him.

"Why?"

"I don't know; a pirate on the ship said you'd been killed by al-Shabaab."

He laughed. "It is not true."

"So I see."

After a long while, a new man unlocked the front gate to the compound and parted the curtain. He was smiling, handsome, young, and urbane. He handed us two thermoses of hot fresh tea, and he carried a plastic bag packed with tinfoil trays full of seasoned rice and meat from a restaurant. The food smelled delicious. The pirates handed me a tray and I opened it on the vanity table, noticing, on the plastic lid, a sticker with the name of the restaurant as well as our current town: GALKACYO—SOMALIA.

Good to know.

Three nights earlier, on a skiff, the guard called Bashko had predicted we would come to Galkayo. We'd pulled away from the

Naham 3 in the dark, and I had stared up at our long, rust-streaked prison ship for the last time. It was dwarfed by the *Orna*, which glowed like an industrial neighborhood on the water, lifting its brownish hull and stacks of sodium-lit cargo containers high into the marine mist. Ten pirates had crammed around me in the boat, and as we motored off, Bashko leaned forward to whisper, "Michael," over the slap of water and the rumble of the outboard motor. "No problem—tomorrow, Galkayo!"

"Oh, yeah?"

He made an airplane motion with his hand. "*Adiga*, free!"

The skiff pilot moved at a slow, deliberate speed, still under orders, perhaps, from Tuure. By my own reckoning we were south of Hobyo, maybe near Harardhere, and I thought I saw something blink in the sky far ahead, either a drone or the top of a cell-phone tower. I wanted to jump. (Certain instincts die hard.) The pirates were tense and quiet. They maintained a tactical-seeming silence along the whole black and placid stretch of water, as if they wanted to avoid detection.

We came to a skidding halt on the beach, and the guards hustled me across the sand to a pair of waiting cars. We drove north along unlit roads for two hours. When we settled, at last, in a shambling house, I breathed the dry odors of Somalia again—the dust, the ocean breeze, the wild sour smell of certain insects—with the openhearted gusto of a man who was about to go free.

Untangling truth from pirate fabrications, never mind my own self-deceptions, could be tricky work. From the shambling house near the ocean we had driven hours inland to reach this Broom-Closet Bordello. The urbane-looking runner, who called himself Mustaf, stood beside me while I ate my breakfast on the wooden dresser. He rummaged through a drawer. When another plane shook the building on its way to what I took to be Galkayo's airport,

Issa watched me again for a reaction. He giggled and whispered to another guard.

Something odd was going on.

I said to Mustaf, "Excuse me, what's going to happen? Am I going free?"

"*Inshallah,*" he said politely. *If Allah wills it.*

"Where are we now?" I asked.

"You know Harardhere?" he said.

"Yes."

"We are in Harardhere."

I blinked.

Bashko listened with a bright, alert face and seemed to hope I wouldn't remember our chat in the skiff. Had the pirates not even noticed the stickers on our meals?

"Really?" I said.

"Yes. There is much danger here from al-Shabaab in Harardhere," said Mustaf. "You must be quiet."

"I see!" I raised an obedient finger to my lips. "*Shhhh.*"

"Yes, yes."

"Harardhere, okay!" I said.

"Yes."

II

The Broom-Closet Bordello was not much larger than my cabin on the *Naham 3*, where I had spent three weeks in solitary confinement. My brain moved back to the ship in sudden jerks, like someone punching "rewind" on a cassette recorder.

You have made a mistake. Mistakes are human.

To distract myself in the cabin I had done push-ups on the floor, as well as a yoga routine on the bed. Li Bo Hai had excavated a spiral-bound notebook from somewhere on the ship so I could write, which may have been all that stood between my feverish mind and an aura of madness after my failed escape.

You have made a mistake. Mistakes are human.

On the first morning after my jump, the *Naham 3* stood somewhere along the coast, farther from the beach, and through a shoreward window across the hall I could see the distant shape of a cargo ship moving in and out of view. We wavered on our moorings, in a strong current, like a flag moving in the wind. From my own porthole window, if I looked forward, I saw the rusted stern of the *Orna*. The salt-streaked wall of greenish steel tilted back and forth about fifty yards ahead, and if I craned my neck I could see the long cables tethering us together. Now and then they tugged with the strain.

We hadn't moved ashore. We were floating in a field of hijacked ships.

Ali Duulaay came to my door on this first morning and said, "Eh?" as if he deserved an explanation. He stood beside my bunk and thumped me in the chest with his fist. My muscles were loose and thin, and I felt a chest ligament snap. (It would hurt for several weeks.) He also clubbed me several times along my body with a filled bottle of water and said, "*No! No! No!*" and thrust his salt-chapped fingers in front of my eyes to rub them together. His eyes burned with incoherent rage. "Money, money, money!" he added, and stomped out.

In the evening, now and then, Rolly or Ha came in to chat. Rolly said Duulaay had beat him on the feet, with the flat blade of a knife, in front of the whole *Naham 3* crew, as punishment for my escape attempt. My head swam with guilt and sorrow. I should have realized Rolly might also be punished, and thinking about it was a worse punishment, for me, than the beating I took.

I couldn't tell what to expect during my three weeks of solitary confinement, but there was a sense that I would leave the ship, so I showed Ha the stack of folded clothes I had borrowed from certain crewmen. We exchanged addresses on a scrap of cardboard.

Food arrived twice a day, on a plate. Tony or Big Jacket brought it. Big Jacket gave me a crooked smile of personal resignation, as if my leap had threatened his role as a guard leader. He disappeared, in fact, after a few days, and I never saw him again.

Tony was more cheerful. "If you need anything, just ask," he said. The plates of food included a lot of defrosted tuna from the hold, either boiled or deep-fried. There was less fresh fish. We no longer floated near a reef.

Bashko came in one afternoon with fresh soap and shampoo, acting friendly—good humored, with a polite manner but a lively, sarcastic smile—and when I explained my escape attempt by mentioning Garfanji and al-Shabaab, he nodded. "No al-Shabaab. No more Garfanji. Finished!" he said and made a grand sweep with his hand, as if he had personally banished these threats from my future.

I stored the shampoo and soap in a closet that was cluttered with spare clothing and trash. The pirates had broken the closet knob. The door swung open and closed whenever the ship swayed.

You have made a mistake. Mistakes are human.

One afternoon the guard called Dag appeared in the sunshine outside my window. "Michael," he said, and I shoved my notebook under a pillow to hide it.

"You remember me?" he said. "It is Dag."

"Yes, Dag."

He seemed groggy rather than hyperalert, possibly also drunk, a vision of simple pirate greed. I could tell he'd been chewing khat from the ooze of green mash in one corner of his mouth. If I gave him a good shove through the window, I thought, he would lose his balance and topple over the rail.

"We want your money," he said.

"I know, Dag. I don't have any."

"You are a writer."

I laughed. "Yes, and writers don't make money."

"But your mother—"

The rocking boat challenged his feet.

"Yes?"

"Your *mother*—"

"She doesn't have enough money, either," I said.

He swayed like a drunken sailor, wearing a heavy Kalashnikov.

"Michael," he said at last, in a tone of personal confession. "I want the Good Life."

He was too far gone to maintain the mask of an honorable fisherman. He didn't even try to pretend. He was just a stoned bush soldier who wanted what he saw on TV.

"I don't have the Good Life, Dag," I told him. "You guys kidnapped the wrong man."

III

The pirates in the Broom-Closet Bordello made an excitable show of standing in formation with their guns whenever I had to shower, guarding the short outdoor path to the toilet. The barren courtyard had a separate small, unattached building made of crumbling stone, which I took for a storage room. I had to pick my way around it, past some automotive junk—wheel rims, electrical wire—to a tin-sided outhouse door.

My first shower happened at night. I half closed the outhouse door and stripped naked in the dark. I was told, mysteriously, not to look up. While I lathered my hair with shampoo and thought no one was watching, of course, I did look up—the outhouse was open to the sky. Nothing to see except blurry stars and the top of a stone-and-mortar wall. A guard noticed me break the rules, though, and the uproar and hysteria didn't subside until they had pushed me back into the bordello room, wrapped a brand-new chain around my ankles, and fixed it with a small brass lock.

"Why?" I said.

"Boss speak—Michael, chains!" said Bashko.

Someone had called the boss to rat me out, apparently. Now I had to be punished. I heard Rolly's voice in my head: *Not make them angry, Michael.* But I had done nothing else but make them angry ever since my leap from the ship.

"Bashko—notebook?" I said after a while.

"Shut up."

Before we left the *Naham 3*, the guards had searched my bag and discovered my spiral-bound notebook. "No, no!" Issa had said, as if I'd committed a crime. He rolled up the notebook, and I felt an ache of frustration. For the second time in my captivity my notes had been confiscated.[*]

Now I had nothing to write with and no way to move, and a cold bicycle chain gritted the skin around my ankles.

Late one night in the Broom-Closet Bordello, in early October, they loaded me into a Toyota Surf. We met another SUV on the outskirts of Galkayo, beside a lonely tree, and for two hours both cars moved like a caravan deep into the lunar wilderness. The driv-

---

[*] The third time if you count notes in my backpack on the day of the kidnapping.

ers knew how to avoid boulders as well as acacia trees and thickets of thorn. Sometimes camels trotted into our headlight glare, and I was thinking about stories from the Old Testament—the elders and patriarchs, the armed brethren caught up in cycles of murder and revenge—when, somewhere along the way, we passed an actual burning bush, far to the right of our car. Most likely set by a nomad. No one even mentioned it.

The story of the burning bush occurs in the Koran, too. The desert landscape of snakes and clans and prophets, with its traditions of the Tower of Babel and the Garden of Eden, is common to the Jewish, Christian, and Muslim holy books; and all three monotheisms share an even older set of myths from Mesopotamia, where the stories of Moses and Adam and Noah had moved like spirits, for centuries, under more ancient names. "We are the same!" Rolly had told the pirates months ago in the bush, when they inspected his crucifix. "We all got the same God." But the Somalis were unconvinced.

The cars stopped, and my guards led me to a patch of sand where a fat man sat on a blanket. He spoke decent English, in a high, feminine voice and a correct manner. But it wasn't Garfanji. We shook hands and he introduced himself as Fuad.

"Nice meeting," he said. "You are not in very much danger, unless your family will be uncooperative. You are now being held by the family that captured you."

"Okay."

"I belong to their subclan. I have lived in Europe before. Now I have come to mediate for you. I will live in Galkayo. I do not wish to remain more than thirty days, and I wish to have your case concluded in that time."

Fuad held a small packet of nuts, which he fed into his plump mouth.

"You are Sa'ad ?" I said.

"Yes."

"My captors are demanding too much money," I told him. "It's still at twenty million, isn't it?"

"I believe so, yes."

"Please explain to my captors that I am not a cargo ship."

Fuad broke his grave, correct demeanor to titter out a laugh. He produced his phone—another elegant, orange-glowing Samsung. One purpose of the long drive was no doubt to use a distant cell tower, to locate the call outside Galkayo.

"Hello?" said my mother.

"Mom, it's me."

"Yes, hi, Michael, how are you?"

Her voice was clear and strong. The phone had beautiful reception. I couldn't tell how much she knew about my circumstances, but Mom seemed more self-assured than before.

She asked, "Are you still on the ship?"

"No," I muttered, and my stomach swirled. For the second time in my captivity, I worried that the horror, the hunger, the months of yearning—all the wasted time itself—had simply gone to waste. For nine months Abdul and Garfanji had fucked with us. Now negotiations would simply restart. (If they had ever, in any sense, started.) My head spun on the dark savanna, and I wasn't sure what to say. I wanted to tip my location, but I didn't know if we would return to Galkayo, and uttering that name would have invited punishment. So I said, *"Ich bin da geblieben, wo ich gefangen worden bin." I've been staying in the place where I was captured.*

"Yes," said my mother, and Fuad didn't notice the German.

When the phone call ended I was piled into the car, and we steered through the savanna again, without headlights, for several hours. This time we arrived at a pastel-painted villa, one of the pirate mansions I had read about as a journalist. A plastic-wrapped foam mattress lay on a concrete floor, along with a fresh mosquito net. I unwrapped the mattress, and the pirates came in with heavy sacks of beans and sugar, cases of pasta, cigarettes, and mango juice.

The place was barren, unlit except for some dim fluorescent bulbs. One or two pirates remained visible through a doorway, on a ragged mat. The light flickered over their heads, so the rectangle of the door seemed to flash on and off.

When Bashko settled in the doorway, I asked him, "This house—who?" *Who owns this house?*

"Bur'ad!" he said.

A pirate!

"Right, thanks." I glanced around. "Are we still in 'Harardhere'?"

"*Haa.*"

"Okay."

Galkayo, then.

It mattered for several reasons. As long as they maintained the "Harardhere" story, I had secret information to reveal on the phone. Our location also indicated which pirates were in charge. In Galkayo, assuming it was South Galkayo, they were Sa'ad, "the family that captured you," as Fuad had said.

A few nights earlier, in the Broom-Closet Bordello, a new boss had waddled in to sit on a plastic chair by the foot of my bed. He was shapeless and squat, with wide-set eyes, and he smoked a cigarette while he listened to long explanations from my guards. He glanced at me through the mosquito tent now and then, sidelong, to nod. I sensed he was learning about my time on the ship. I found him ugly and sinister, and I wondered if he belonged to a whole new gang. Now I decided Fuad had told the truth: the gang was Sa'ad, maybe Gerlach and Digsi's family, as opposed to the Hobyo crowd; we were back in Galkayo; and Fuad, just possibly, had meant it when he said "thirty days."

IV

The hollow house grew bright in the morning, but cold weather kept it from warming up. The pastel colors of the walls—solid blue, pink, or green, depending on the room—seemed to glow in the African sun. I saw that my room had plenty of open, dusty space. Several weeks had passed since I last exercised, so I wanted a yoga mat.

"Bashko," I said, since he sat in the doorway again. "Bashko, I need a mat."

"Eh?"

"*Salli*," I said, using the Somali word for a mat, which sounded like "sully." "*Aniga*." I pointed at myself, then at the open floor. "Exercise."

Bashko gathered my meaning.

"Okay!" he said, and lifted his thumb.

The morning was so cold that he and Issa had wrapped themselves in blankets and built a coal fire. Bashko had dropped two or three hot coals from the kitchen into an empty powdered-milk tin and set it in the entry hall. In the late morning, for laughs—or to ward off flies—he also threw rocks of incense into the tin and sent a small cloud of white smoke wandering through the doorway.

The pirate villa started to smell like a Catholic church.

"Bashko, what is that?"

He came in to show me, carrying the hot tin with a rag. He made an exaggerated show of sniffing the smoke, which burned off in fierce, thick gouts and had a sharp odor somewhere between soap and spice. He set down the can and held out a spare rock of unburned incense resin, dried sap from the Somali bush.

"Somalia, full!" he said.

Somalia had more than one source of incense, including a

gnarled tree that produced frankincense and a white thornbush that gave up myrrh.* Both grew throughout Yemen, Oman, and the Horn of Africa. The dried-out bushes and trees used to mean real money. The Horn of Africa and the Arabian Peninsula had once belonged to a swerve of the Spice Route, and some traditions maintained that the "Wise Men of the East" were traders known to ancient Jews and early Christians from these pre-Muslim places.

"You could sell this to churches around the world," I told him, rubbing my fingers together. "Business, business."

"Okay!" Bashko laughed.

A limited trade in both myrrh and frankincense resins existed in Somalia, and Bashko had a wiry intelligence that might have made him a good businessman. Part of me hoped that his share of my ransom, if any, would go toward funding an incense business. But I couldn't be too optimistic. Bashko was also a khat addict, with a habit costing six hundred dollars a month. That was rent in some Western cities.

He returned the censer to the hall doorway and waved at the smoke with a paper exercise booklet. The Somalis used this booklet to learn English.

I pointed at it. *"Aniga*, okay?" I said. *Can I read that?*

"Haa."

Bashko brought it over. I had left the *Naham 3* without a Bible or a book of any kind. I devoured the pamphlet like a novel. It contained some poignant exercise questions.

What is the purpose of human life?
The purpose of life is to worship Allah.

---

* *Boswellia carterii* and *Commiphora myrrha*, respectively.

Who destroyed Somalia?

Somalia was destroyed by Somalis, but most of all by the warlords.

The other thing I noticed was a line at the bottom of each page indicating that the booklet belonged to an English class at a Galkayo private school, taught by a man named Abdurrahman. I'd heard the name Abdurrahman whenever Mustaf, the urbane young runner, delivered food.

"Bashko," I said, and described Mustaf. "*Maga'iid?*" I said, using a new vocabulary word from the book, meaning "name."

"Abdurrahman," he answered carefully.

"Abdurrahman the translator?"

"Yes," Bashko said.

Interesting.

I had gathered that Abdurrahman and Fuad were both in charge of negotiations. They worked together. The presence of Fuad in particular seemed to give everyone hope. The guards figured he was a pro because he spoke understandable English, and he claimed to be an educated member of the Somali diaspora in Europe. I found out later that the FBI in California considered him a rational middleman, at least compared with previous negotiators. But his written English fluctuated between excellent and poor, and his ideas seemed to waver between sanity and nonsense. One possible reason for this divide was that Abdurrahman and Fuad traded email and telephone duties, and Abdurrahman had smoother English. "Gunmen are winners here," one of them wrote in an email to my mother, "while educated ones are losers in life. . . . I must assure you that kidnappers holding your son are the most ignorant and not like civilized pirates we used to see.* . . . For the release of your innocent

---

* I don't know what he meant by this.

son who has been wrongly abducted, we fully cooperate with you by any means that can quicken his rescue."

After a week or two of making hopeful signs, in patchy correspondence, following my phone call in the bush, in mid-October "Fuad" announced a reduction in the ransom demand.

"At last," he wrote, "the bosses decreased to nineteen million and eight hundred thousand dollars US."

The fact that this bumbling criminal tag team woke up a glimmer of hope in California shows how desperate things had looked for most of 2012. My mother, in response, asked for a direct phone number to a pirate boss.

"Fuad" wrote back:

Hi marlis I am also glad for our contact and as human I much feel pitty for your problem, dear I can give you their number but, none of them speaks english . . . If you can understand somali language or get one who can speak somali in amerika with you I can provide you their contact addresses. You have the choice. thanks byeeeeeeeeee.

V

Abdinasser the Sahib came in one morning in October with a new, green, woven-plastic mat, still wrapped in a clear plastic bag. He flopped it on the floor, tapped his chest with his fist in a gesture of brotherhood, and said, in his barrel-chested voice:

"SAHIB! *Salli, adiga.*"

"Thank you, sahib."

"Okay!"

I asked for a broom and swept the concrete. I spread out the mat in front of a window and used it, first, to do push-ups. When I finished, three guards from the hall were staring into the room.

"Exercise!" I told them.

I figured the pirates would find yoga kind of strange, so I tried to wait for a gap in the afternoon when no guard sat by the door. But I was under close observation. The men seemed to have orders to watch me day and night.

I started by standing on the mat and lowering my pulse with a series of deep breaths. I had done yoga in Berlin to keep myself in shape to surf, and I liked a tough regimen that made my heart beat and my skin sweat. Meditation was never the point. But in Somalia I was so used to feeling wild with nerves that half an hour of mental concentration had a powerful effect; it calmed me for hours at a time.

I moved through a few postures and noticed all the guards laughing and smiling at the door.

"Exercise!" I said again.

"Exercise!" said Abdinasser.

"Exercise!" repeated Bashko, and he lifted his thumb.

The next day, when I did it again, both men came into my room and spread flattened cardboard boxes on the unclean floor and imitated my postures, with enthusiastic smiles. At first I thought they were goofing around. Soon they picked up their boxes, laughed, and went out. But it happened again the next day, and the next. To my intense surprise, they wanted to learn yoga.

"No, put your feet there," I said. "Like that. Twist your back like this."

"Okay, sahib!"

These lessons embarrassed the other pirates, but Bashko and Abdinasser, and sometimes Issa, came in for yoga class because they never got "exercise" of their own. They were locked in this Pirate Villa, too.

I tried to imagine a yoga studio in Galkayo, or the intrepid teacher who would venture to Somalia to spread this bizarre but calming discipline, which, since it came from India, might be viewed with derision and hate. Though, come to think of it, either Indians or Pakistanis did seem to live in town. Sometimes the pirates ordered batches of samosas for me, the greasy Indian snack East Africans call sambusi, and they arrived from a local shop in scraps of newspaper printed in Urdu, Arabic, Sinhalese, or (occasionally) English.

"Sahib—exercise!" said Bashko when he needed help with a pose.

"Like this," I said. "Don't forget to breathe."

They never held a pose long enough to accomplish very much, and sometimes out of boredom they shifted from yoga to quasi-military calisthenics. I saw stiff and comical marching drills as well as wild, flailing backbends. I said, *"Askari* exercise?"—using the word for "soldier"—and Bashko lit up with pride.

"Askari, yes," he said.

"But you are *shifta,*" I teased him. *Thieves.*

"Haa, yes," he added in a rare moment of bashful candor.

When I quizzed him for biographical details, Bashko described himself as a Sa'ad from Mogadishu who had never worked as a pirate on the water. He'd trained, instead, as a soldier in Somalia and a commando in Russia. I had to weigh everything he said. Bashko's name did sound like a Slavic diminutive of Bashir, and Somalia had maintained political links to Russia under Siad Barre; but Bashko spoke no Russian. He was also vague about the weather in Moscow. (He never mentioned snow.) He boasted about commando training in Pakistan, too, and that seemed more plausible. He might have learned some English there.

In any case, he was handy with a weapon, which suggested training, and he liked the word *askari*, which elevated his self-esteem. The word had an odd resonance, because in East African countries once under the colonial heel of the Italians or the British or the Germans, *askari* used to refer to local soldiers trained by a European colonial power. Gerlach had used it as an epithet, something like "Uncle Tom." But for Bashko it just meant "soldier," which sounded better than "thief."

Bashko and Abdinasser both mimicked my yoga poses like housewives watching a weight-loss video. Through these improvised classes they became my "sahibs" in the Pirate Villa. Whenever I needed something, they were the guys to ask. Bashko, in particular, kept my hope alive with rumors of negotiations. He made it sound as if I would go free in a matter of days. Of course I was happy to believe him. But then hope is like heroin for a hostage, and it can be just as destructive.

VI

"This afternoon we must make a video for the U.N.," said Yoonis in early November. "They will mediate your release."

"Really?"

I sat up on my mattress. Yoonis loomed over me and seemed to sway with the uncertainty of his words.

"What kind of message?" I said.

"They want to know what you need. For your health."

Yoonis had a high forehead, round earnest eyes, and a light patch of hair on the end of his chin. In Hobyo, at least, his face had seemed friendly enough. Now he cultivated the deep, thuggish tones of a gang leader.

"In the video," he ordered, "you must say three things: You must give your name. You must talk about your health. And you must give a message to the United Nations."

I nodded.

"And you must not give your location," he warned me.

"Don't mention Harardhere?"

"Yah!" he said with a grin.

After lunch, Abdurrahman appeared, still calling himself "Mustaf," and wearing a white robe with a turban attached—an obvious costume, unless he moonlighted as a sheikh. He also carried a digital camera. He hung the robe on a door and worked with several guards for a while in another room. I heard Bashko having an excited conversation in the hall. At last he leaned into my doorway.

"Michael—news!" he said, using his hand to indicate the motion of a flying plane. "Rolly and Marc! Seychelles!"

I sat up.

"Really?"

"Free!" said Bashko.

"How much?"

"Four million!"

It was an exorbitant price, probably inflated by the rumor kitchen—the guards were encouraged by their bosses to believe that if two poor fishermen could be ransomed for a total of four million dollars, Michael might fetch eight or ten. How exciting! They talked about what to do with their cash. Most wanted to leave Somalia for Nairobi, Dubai, or even Europe. Bashko, with another flying-plane gesture, said, "Ahmed Dirie. London."

"Really?" I said.

"*Haa!*"

"How?"

But there was no time. I had to put on a *ma'awiis*, a sarong, instead of long pants. Yoonis led me to the other room. The men had converted it to a movie set by suspending an orange tarp from lines tied to metal shutters. Inside this tent lay a torn and dusty mat, a bag with clothes spilling out, and a fire-blackened field kettle. All of it faced a window to let in natural light.

"I see. We're in the bush now?" I said.

"Yah!" said Yoonis.

More pirate theater. He ordered me to kneel on the mat. Someone wrapped the chains from the Broom-Closet Bordello around my wrists and looped them over my neck. Bashko and Issa and two other guards wrapped their faces in keffiyehs and surrounded me, aiming their weapons.

Yoonis asked questions while Abdurrahman pointed the camera.

"What are the names of your parents?"

"Marlis Saunders and Bert Moore," I said. "He's deceased," I added, in case they wanted to call him for money.

"Your father is dead?" said Yoonis, who'd never heard this before.

"Yes."

"Do you have any diseases?"

"Not right now."

We ran through the date and circumstances of my capture, and Yoonis asked, "Do you have any message for the U.N.?"

"These men tell me I'm about to go free," I said. "I hope that's true. I've been in Somalia for too long, and I don't have any glasses or lenses—I'm half-blind—so, uh, I'd like to request a pair of glasses."

Strange interview. Afterward, I returned to my mattress, and for some reason I felt optimistic. It was early November, and the day felt bright and warm. The bustle of excitement over the video and the gossip about "the U.N." suggested real momentum toward my freedom. The only hitch in the stride of Yoonis's questions was that my father was gone, and I wondered if it shocked him to hear I had only one parent left to rob.

VII

I remembered a bargain "emerald" my father had once bought for $24.95, in a hinged plastic box, squirreled away in a drawer. The gem was faded green plastic. Dad went in for get-rich-quick schemes, and he'd ordered this one from the back pages of the *L.A. Times*. As a hostage I could imagine three reasons for Dad to jump at such a gimcrack idea. It might have been (a) drunken misjudgment, (b) common panic about the family budget, or (c) plain curiosity. But he never talked about the emerald, and he kept it in the desk in our study, where I sat with him sometimes to build model planes and ships. We glued plastic wings and tail sections together and painted them from little cube-shaped bottles of enamel paint that clacked in the drawer like thick glass dice.

The father I remembered from my distant boyhood was enthusiastic and strong; but the older man, from my preadolescence, wore a troubled, clenched expression behind a pair of plastic sunglasses and seemed to take the world too seriously. I imagined the difference as a disturbance in psychic weather, a shift in the chemical patterns of his brain, and these perhaps heritable mysteries felt awful to contemplate in Somalia, where changes in psychic weather were so probable and sudden. For a twelve-year-old boy, they would have been impossible to understand. At that age you took everything personally. An adult who removed himself from your life did not obviously love you. In that sense I was grateful for Mom's protection, since knowing details at that age would have left a permanent and baffling scar.

But I couldn't submit to these memories in Somalia and cling to the notion of my dad as a rival. We would have locked horns when I grew up, but who cares? Fathers and sons did that. The lack of a father to struggle against was the unnatural part. I hated his drunken binges, but I didn't hate the man himself. I missed the man himself.

Daniel Pearl, the *Wall Street Journal* reporter beheaded by al-Qaeda after a wrong turn in Pakistan, had grown up in Encino. Not far from Northridge. While I stretched on my mattress in Galkayo I wondered if there was something about the dreariness of the L.A. suburbs that sent writers out to dangerous parts of the world, or something about white writers in particular, who thought the world was theirs to explore. Travel itself was a privilege. Package tours from the United States or Europe to the developing world were vestiges of colonialism, in the sense that tourism rarely operated in the other direction. Overseas journalism, and travel writing in the British or American vein—Gerald Hanley, Graham Greene, Paul Theroux—involved similar privileges. Then again, doing it well required no specific background, and it offended every instinct in my body to think that any writer of any shade of skin "should not" cover a certain story or travel to a certain place.

Then again, I'd pushed the edges of privilege by chasing a book in Somalia. I'd taken a ridiculous risk.

Then again—empires had always sent out travelers. Ibn Battuta, during an era of rising Ottoman power in the 1300s, had published an early and lasting description of Somalia, which he called Barbara, after a visit to the royal city of Maqdashaw (Mogadishu). The sultan of Maqdashaw welcomed Ibn Battuta with a meal of rice and pickled mango. "A single person of the people of Maqdashaw eats as much as a whole company of us would eat," wrote Ibn Battuta, "and they are corpulent and fat in the extreme."

Writers always went wrong, but it was miserable now to think that I had such a bleak story to tell—a story about captivity, assuming I got out at all—when I'd wanted to write something more rich and detached, more original, more humanizing. I also loathed the parochial idea that writers should just "write what they know."

Then again, then again.

My brain had time to waver over this question, back and forth.

You have made a mistake. Mistakes are human.

VIII

A day or two after our video, I asked to use the bathroom while a guard named Madobe sat watch in the doorway.

"*Kadi*," I said.

Madobe was the most pious-acting pirate in the group. All the men scraped and bowed toward Mecca in the hall, five times a day, but no one prayed with more punctiliousness or care. Madobe was long and precise, with a young handsome face, but he seemed to be illiterate, and he could be tediously sarcastic and cruel. When he wasn't at his prayers, he chuckled and joked like a delinquent. He teased me about wanting "ham." His skin was darker than the others', which made a difference in Somalia—the nickname Madobe* meant "black" and referred to his color. He also belonged to a

---

* Real name: Abdisalaan Ma'alin Abdullahi.

different clan, so even within the pirate gang, he may have felt like an outsider.

"*Kadi*," I said.

He didn't even glance over. I said "*kadi*" again and held up an empty water bottle containing my toothbrush, to show that I wanted to brush my teeth.

No answer. He wasn't doing much in particular.

"*Kadi*," I repeated, and stood up.

Now he sprang to attention with his rifle and shouted in Somali. The other men rushed into my room. When I raised my voice in protest, they all shouted as if I had tried to jump over the compound wall. Even Bashko pulled a pistol and shook it in my face, like Ali Duulaay on the bluff. I had to sit down. But that wasn't good enough for Madobe, who strode into my room and kicked the plastic bottle out of my hand.

"Bullshit," I muttered, which was a word they all understood. "Somali bullshit."

"Shut up," said Bashko.

Violence and fury were ecstatic states for these men, and the anger might simmer all day long until someone found an excuse to erupt. I remembered a line from Hanley: "When the violence came, one hated it, and one came to know how it damaged one's slightly phony ideals about how Man longed only for goodness and peace, whereas, actually, he loved fighting and knew he shouldn't. Hypocrisy is the keystone of civilization and should be cherished."

I warmed to this idea in Galkayo. Before leaving Berlin I had cherished the notion that civilized hypocrisy ought to be laid bare and corrected. The comforts of Western cities were just upholstery sewn over the violence and injustice at the heart of the civilized world, and I was against all that. I thought a writer should face unpleasantness, violence, entropy, and horror with unflinching eyes and an understanding heart. Right? Well, then. This broken hostage-world was all entropy and violence, and I was lying in it as punishment for my curiosity.

I lacerated myself for believing I could learn something trenchant and real by coming to Somalia. An uncertainty principle follows writers into conflict zones, and I had noticed it even on the placid Turkish frigate in Djibouti. While we spent four days in the Gulf of Aden, another NATO vessel had captured a pirate mother ship, a dhow full of kidnapped fishermen, used by the pirates as slaves. These interesting people were rescued in the *Gediz*'s usual sector. I said to our minder, Yaşar, "You didn't have your sector changed just because of us, did you?"

"Yes," he said.

"You did?"

"Yes." He smiled. "It is nice to have some quiet days."

So the presence of journalists had shifted the ship's position. The uncertainty principle holds for writers and for anthropologists, quantum physicists, field researchers, even parents—anyone in any role where the fact of observation can change the thing observed. What the fuck did I expect in Somalia? A tall white man, hoping to make friends with pirates? Even during my first days in Galkayo, I was aware of my extreme whiteness, and I knew very well that I was observing Africa through the eyes of a privileged stranger. The Horn of Africa had been hermetic and violent to outsiders since long before Richard Burton's nineteenth-century excursions there; and people in Galkayo had seemed electrically aware of our presence in town. I also lacked Gerald Hanley's matter-of-fact reason to be in Somalia. His flights of lyricism and sense of drama as a white writer in Africa now rubbed me the wrong way. His ideas were good, but the romance of his style gave off too much perfume; the high sound of his prose contradicted his disillusionment about civilization and violence, and the supposed drama of writing about Africa left me feeling bitter and dull.

Now I missed the upholstery of life in the West; the annoying banalities, the traffic, and the fluorescent-lit stores were intimate elements of my childhood. I couldn't reject them without rejecting my family, and I missed my family. I missed everyone I could remember. The end of my romance with Hanley's eloquence brought on a sharpened desire for the people I loved. There was no contradiction, because love isn't a question of dramatic demonstration or lyrical words. It's a question of attention, presence, and time.

Which was going to waste.

IX

Yoonis came and went, making gaseous promises about the U.N. and the ICRC, as if our video would lead to a tense handoff between the pirates and these international groups. He disappeared a day before my deadline. When I asked Bashko for news, he said, "No news," and when I asked if I could speak with Yoonis, he said, "Yoonis, coming."

But Yoonis didn't. His vague promises, along with the supposed U.N. video and Fuad's hint of "thirty days," had swaddled my brain for six weeks in a soft narcotic hope. During the afternoon of Yoonis's fictional deadline this hope burned off like mist.

Evening arrived. The cool sunset over Galkayo brought mosquitoes, and even before dark I could hear their high thin chorus in the courtyard. I had quit worrying about insects and disease on the *Naham 3*. Now they were a problem again. To fend off disease, I had to rely on my own immune system and the gauzy blue net that I unbundled every evening to dangle over my mattress, like a lampshade.

The food on the *Naham 3* must have propped up my immune system, and maybe an unlikely optimism had stilted my health during my first month and a half in Galkayo. But when the sun vanished that evening in a whining haze of mosquitoes, a fever lit up my skeleton; I went to sleep feeling swollen and strange. I overslept in the morning and woke up dizzy. I ate about half my beans. I walked heavily to the bathroom.

"Michael! Problem?" said Bashko when I returned.

"*Aniga* sick."

Malaria feels like a heat in the bones and a leaden weight in the blood. I napped and woke up in a pool of sweat.

I thought about Marie Dedieu, a Frenchwoman who'd been captured by Somalis from her second home, on a northern Kenyan island, in 2011. Pirate gangs as well as factions of al-Shabaab had learned that skiffs could rush the sea boundary between Somalia and Kenya to kidnap vacationing Europeans. Madame Dedieu was a retired journalist and a quadriplegic who relied on drugs for a heart condition. The gunmen had failed to understand her difficulties, and she died within a month.

I asked for goat broth instead of spaghetti for lunch. This special order, with the rumor of illness, brought Yoonis to the house, carrying a massive shoulder of meat. The guards cooked it while Yoonis dodged my questions about going free. At last he served me a plate of goat.

"I can't eat all that," I said when he set it on the floor. "Soup only." I pushed away the plate, and Yoonis made a show of thuggish surprise.

"You refuse?" he said.

"I don't refuse, Yoonis. I'm sick. I can't eat it."

"I don't believe you are sick."

"Believe what you want."

The illness may have been related to stress over the promise of going free, but I was, in fact, sick, and Madame Dedieu's fate scared the hell out of me.

"It is psychological," he said.

"It is not fucking psychological. I need to see a doctor."

"What for?"

"I need a real doctor. Didn't you mention the ICRC?"

"Hah." He smiled, as if he'd caught me out. "You see, it is because of what I said to you. It is all in your head."

"Fuck off," I said.

The next morning, I couldn't hold down water. When I returned from the bathroom, I thought a swig from the water bottle might stabilize my swimming head. Instead, with nothing else in my belly, I puked.

"Problem!" said Bashko.

"Yeah, problem," I agreed.

Abdinasser the Sahib came in with an old shirt to help me clean the water and stomach acid from the floor. *"Kiniin?"* he said, and I thought he meant "quinine." Bashko handed me a scrap of paper and a pen, and at last I understood. *Kiniin* meant "medicine," and he wanted me to diagnose myself so they could order drugs on the phone.

"No," I said. "I need a doctor."

A runner brought a malaria drug, chloroquine, which failed to do much good. I puked again in the morning. I felt sluggish and hot, like a radioactive log.

The same runner turned up the next evening with Yoonis, bearing a blood-test kit, intending to draw blood. I hadn't showered in two days, and the entire house was filthy. Without real hygiene, I didn't want to come near a needle.

"Do you have disinfectant?" I said.

"We do not need."

"Oh, yes, we do. I need to see a doctor, Yoonis. Bring a real doctor here. Someone from the ICRC."

Hearing "ICRC" again upset him. Yoonis had taken lessons somewhere in bully-boy manners. Any reasonable argument now impressed him as a threat.

"If you do not take this test," he said, "you will not receive any treatment."

He and the runner, a mild-faced man who came and went with a pistol tucked into his sarong, squatted in front of my mattress. I insisted on washing my hand with shampoo (since we had no soap). The runner turned out to be conscientious and careful. He drew a small vial of blood and went out. I spent the next day in a near stupor, misted with fever, but Yoonis and the runner returned in the evening with a surprise. A local doctor had tested the blood and found both typhoid and malaria. Yoonis now had a whole bagful of pharmaceuticals. He explained how to take the drugs, in what order, for how many days—everything the pharmacist had told him—and I was impressed. They had visited a real clinic in Galkayo. The hostage was an investment, after all, and he had to be kept alive.

X

I shivered under my blanket for seven days and leaked sweat into my foam mattress. One drug, Cotecxin, seemed to lift me out of my feverish muddle. But there was nothing like disease in a prison house to strip off your mental defenses. On a normal day as a hostage, I had enough cussedness to resist the pirates' nonsense with a critical mind and hope for freedom in the not-too-distant future. With malaria in my blood, I wanted to die.

My appetite returned, slowly, and I harassed the guards for better food. The runner brought bananas and limes for a week. Goat shoulder and soup came every two days. After I appeared healthy again, my diet regressed to a bowl of beans dusted with sugar in the morning, a bowl of almost dry spaghetti for lunch, and another bowl of beans when the sky deepened and the mosquitoes started to whine.

Malaria can kill, so the ordeal humbled me. I had to reorder my head to move myself through an average day. I missed Rolly and Marc, and I tried to imagine them in the Seychelles—their families, the mango tree, the yelling turtles—but I hedged any enthusiasm about their freedom, the way I hedged everything I heard from the pirates.

On the *Naham 3*, I'd compiled a list of crew names on a slab of cigarette cardboard, so I could learn to spell them, along with a list of Creole fish names I'd learned from Rolly. I had reproduced these lists on a few folded scraps of paper in my shorts pocket. One evening, while I scribbled on these scraps, Madobe crept up to my mosquito tent and hissed. I jumped and almost shouted. He confiscated my notes, and I threw a tantrum and compared Madobe to Somalia's last dictator. "*Bur'ad*, Siad Barre—same-same!" I shouted. (These men loathed the memory of Siad Barre as much as they loved their self-image as freedom fighters.)

I was clearly on edge; I had to find another way to manage the inarticulate stress. Without my notepaper I learned to recite the lists of crewman and fish names in my head, every morning, to keep them memorized. I had also left two unfinished books behind in

Berlin, so, to keep my brain busy, I thought about the passages I wanted to change. Every morning I ran through what I could remember of the manuscripts and composed new paragraphs. Once I had a new section "written," I started to rehearse it, the way an actor memorizes lines. Soon I had a two-hour drill.

This mental strategy worked. It was not completely original: the idea came from the Indonesian novelist Pramoedya Ananta Toer, who had spent fourteen years in prison after a military coup in the sixties. I had interviewed him in Jakarta in 2004, not long before his death—a sweet, smiling old man with bifocals who chain-smoked clove cigarettes. Ten of his years in captivity had consisted of hard labor on the jungle island of Buru, where convicts had to clear dense foliage and build their own barracks and roads. "Usually, during a break in forced labor," Pramoedya told me, "the inmates and I were gathered and they would listen to my stories. When they worked somewhere else, they retold the stories to their friends." The other prisoners arranged for him to be excused from work for a few hours every day so he could sit at a desk. Imagining these stories, first for inmates, then on paper, had kept his mind in order. So it occurred to me that story composition, even in silence, might keep me from losing mine.

When I finished my recitations, I stood up to do yoga. Early sun shot through the windows every morning to light the painted concrete room, and while I faced the window on my feet, I could watch guards work in the yellowish courtyard, watering potted trees or washing saucepans from the kitchen. Running from this house was impossible, since the pirates lazed in the hallways leading to both doors, but I studied the courtyard every morning anyhow, with my blurred, still-optimistic eyes, looking for ways to escape.

Sometimes the pirates paused at the front gate to peek through a gap at the road. They were locked in, too.

Around midday a phone would ring and a runner would open a smaller gate with his keys. He handed the pirates a bag of khat, which they carried into my room. The men surrounded the bag like sharks, and when each pirate had his share he would thumb through the stems, looking for a reddish tinge that meant ripe khat and a high afternoon.

For me these afternoons were long and terrifying. The heat mounted; the flies lost their minds. On the worst days I took to lying on my mattress with one arm across my face to shield myself from the torture of their twitchy, intolerable legs. They tried to land on my lips, in my nostrils, on my eyeballs. The flies I knew from home had a near-magnetic evasion instinct for an oncoming hand, but hunger had taught these creatures a stubborn headlong aggression. They didn't care if you hit them. Instead they tried to land on the same patch of skin, over and over, to wear down a victim's will. Trying to kill them turned into a game, and I could fall into a delirious, zombielike afternoon rut:

Smack.

I did that already.

Smack.

I did that already.

Smack.

I did that already.

Smack.

A fly would drop to the floor.

Gunfire punctuated these passages of time like a savage cuckoo clock. People just fired their guns in the street. I was never sure whether someone had been wounded or killed. ("They are happy," said Bashko.) But I understood through these long hours that my sweaty idleness and indiscriminate fear profited no one but some distant investors. "The only real tragedy in life is the being used by personally minded men for purposes which you recognize to be base," wrote George Bernard Shaw, in a very different context. "All the rest is at worst mere misfortune or mortality: this alone is misery, slavery, hell on earth."

Smack.

I did that already.

Five times a day I heard distant muezzins. Five times a day, the pirates swept khat leaves off their mats in the hall to spread thin cloths or sarongs at their feet. They faced north, crossed their arms, murmured *"Allahu akbar,"* and started to kneel and scrape in a flowing, unchanging rhythm.

XI

Somali bananas had an intense, tangy-sweet flavor, and in December I hassled the guards to bring a supply of bananas and limes to eat instead of my second, rather disgusting bowl of sugared beans. Otherwise I ate no fruit. I wanted a better diet.

"Banana, too much," said Bashko.

"Banana good," I argued. "Banana, *liin—vitamin.* Good!"

Liin was the word for "lime." I felt a lack of vitamin C. For a pirate gang demanding millions from my family, it wasn't a crazy demand. Bashko ordered one more bunch of bananas from the runner, but nothing else, and once they ran out we had a simmering debate. I couldn't believe my guards found it easier to cook beans for me twice a day than to provide a cheap dose of fruit. So I borrowed a pen and drew an obsessive little diagram on a scrap of cardboard.

First, there was my regimen of half-nutritious stodge:

DIGIR [beans in the morning]
BAASTO [dry spaghetti in the afternoon]
DIGIR [beans at sundown]

"Somali, no problem!" I added, with an angry flourish in ball-point ink.

Then I gave them my idea of a more balanced prisoner's diet, which was still inadequate but should have been easier to prepare:

DIGIR [beans]
BAASTO [pasta]
BANANA–LIIN [banana–lime]

"Somali PROBLEM FULL!" I wrote.

Bashko took the scrap of cardboard and laughed. He handed it around to his friends, who all had a good chuckle.

"Somali no money," Bashko complained.

"Somali bullshit," I said.

The next day, Bashko sat in the hall in a white plastic chair, which he'd found in another room and placed in the middle of a khat-littered mat. Two other guards, Issa and Abdul, curled around him like dogs. It was the sluggish hour before khat arrived. Bashko wanted to banter again.

"Michael," he said with a grin. "Somalia, money full?"

I sat up and smiled.

"No, no," I clarified. "*Bur'ad*, money full."

Somalia wasn't rich, but its pirates were. Bashko repeated my phrase and grinned. "*Bur'ad*, money full."

"Yes," I insisted. "Issa said he had a house in Galkayo. I don't own a house."

"*Adiga* no house?" he said, surprised.

"No."

Issa sat up from his doze. He remembered that my father, like his, was gone.

"But—your father's house," he said.

"No, that's gone, too." I stared at them. "I don't own a car. Issa says he has a car."

They were both surprised. "*Adiga* no car?"

"No." In Berlin I didn't need one.

"But, before . . ." said Issa.

"I've owned a car in my lifetime," I said.

"Ah, okay."

Bashko adjusted himself in the chair. "Okay—*adiga, aniga*, no problem," he said. *You and I are cool.* "But America, money full. Europe, money full. In Somalia," he added, "hungry-problem."

"That's true," I said and held his eyes. "No good."

A brutal famine had killed thousands of people in other parts of Somalia in 2011 and 2012; but I couldn't tell whether Bashko was also claiming starvation. Refugees from within Somalia had fled to Galmudug because of the relative prosperity there.

"America was not always rich," I said. "Europe was not always rich. You have to build up, slow-slow," I said, and made a stepwise motion with my hand.

We were limited by our failures of language to some pretty crude arguments. We left out the ravages of colonialism; we left out the Somali climate and a hundred other complications.

"Indonesia isn't rich," I went on. "It's poor and Muslim, with many Sufis, like Somalia. They don't shoot each other." By and large.*
"They have roads and decent shops. A lot of people don't have cars,

---

* A Sumatran province, Aceh, had turned to piracy.

but they ride scooters. You can raise a family in peace." I shrugged. "Indonesia's nice."

"Muslim?" said Bashko.

"Yes."

"Muslim good!"

"Sure."

Bashko was surprised to hear such a thing from me. So far I'd been treated like a prisoner of a vague but global war, a captive from a distant subclan that, by definition, hated Muslims. I did not hate Muslims. But now I had a chance to ask a question that had baffled me for most of the year.

"Bashko, you are a Muslim."

"Yes!"

"But you are also a thief." I bumped my fingers together, which by now was a comprehensible gesture for us. *These things don't fit together.* "No same-same."

A smile crept over his face as my intention dawned. He laughed and rattled a translation to his friends. "Hmm," said Issa. Bashko straightened up in his chair and tapped his chest.

"I am a Muslim," he said. "But I am also a thief. Why? Because in Somalia, hungry-problem."

As if Allah could outlaw thievery but make exceptions for pirates. *It's okay, guys, you're poor. Once you steal enough money, you can be good Muslims.*

"I don't think Islam works like that," I said.

Bashko had a spry, combative mind, so the theological problem bothered him for the next two weeks. We returned to it one morning while I ate my dawn ration of beans. He'd been lazy about cooking them, and I had threatened a hunger strike. He'd lost our little showdown and delivered the bowl with ill grace, like a man feeding a dog.

He watched me eat with fervid, resentful eyes.

"Michael."

"What."

"Muslim," he said, and smiled wickedly. "No *chum-chum*, no problem!"

"Oh?"

"Christian, no *chum-chum*—problem full!"

A Muslim could tolerate hunger, in other words, unlike a certain Christian in the room.

I wiped my fingers clean with a scrap of toilet paper. I had great stoic reserves, but I was not about to go hungry just to make life easier for a bunch of lazy pirates.

"Bashko," I said in our mutual language. "Last week you said a Muslim could be a pirate because of the hunger problem."

He nodded.

"Now you say a good Muslim has to bear up under hunger." (In pidgin: *Muslim no chum-chum, Muslim no problem—because, Islam?*)

He nodded.

I bounced my fingers again. "No same-same."

Bashko laughed, then laughed a bit more and held up his thumb. I'd gotten him. "Good!" he said, and translated my response to the other guards. This time it sparked a discussion. I had criticized a faith I saw in action five times a day. Abdul, the effeminate guard, gave the most fervent defense. He'd signed on to watch me when he learned that a foreigner had been kidnapped, he said. He wasn't a pirate—he was just doing the good Muslim work of protecting an infidel in a hostile place. He went on: Did I think Garfanji was a Muslim? Ali Tuure? Ali Duulaay? Had I ever seen them read the Koran? "Uh-uh," he answered himself with a wag of his finger. Those men, he said, were the real *kuffar*, the real infidels.

I'd gleaned this argument already. It was possible that some of my guards had never hijacked a ship. But they'd guarded me since the start of the year, so they had the trust of those infidel bosses.

Bashko came around to his real justification later the same day. He acted sober and earnest while we sat alone in the hot room. The Koran, he said, called for "struggle against the infidel." Thieving from non-Muslims, therefore, wasn't theft.

"What?"

"Jews, Christians, Buddhists"—okay to steal from them, he implied. "Muslim, no."

"But there were four Muslims on the *Naham 3*," I said.

"Yes." He sat cross-legged, upright, trying to seem very correct. "We must not take from their families."

Taking from shipowners or a foreign government—that was different. But if the bosses took ransom from a Muslim family, that would be theft, according to his reading of the Koran.

"What about the captain?" I said. "He was shot dead."

"Christian!" Bashko blurted.

"Buddhist, I imagine." I held his eyes. "But does the Koran say you can kill non-Muslims?"

Again I wanted a long, detailed interview with Bashko—I wished intensely for a translator—but in our pidgin mix of English and Somali, we could speak only in broad terms.

"No," he said, and turned pious again. "Allah speak, *All life good.*"

This idea that all life was sacred under Allah separated pirates from al-Shabaab, said Bashko. Wahhabists in Somalia had interpreted the relevant Koranic verses as a call to lethal jihad. Sufi pirates had a different idea.

"But under Allah," I said, "it's okay to steal from other faiths?"

"Koran speak," he answered, and smiled to imply that there was nothing he could do; the book said so, and the book outranked us both.

One Koranic verse, 9:5, a so-called Verse of the Sword,* does mention abduction. "When the sacred months are over," it reads, "slay the idolaters† wherever you find them. Arrest them, besiege them, and lie in ambush everywhere for them. If they repent and take to prayer and render the alms levy, allow them to go their way. God is forgiving and merciful."

The "alms levy" is a tax for the poor. I could see how a pirate from one of the world's most destitute countries might consider a ransom from the outside world an "alms levy." And in the sealed-off deserts of Somalia, the spiritual notion that a total stranger might have aspects of the sacred was no use whatsoever.

I remembered a Somali phrase from the trial in Hamburg: *Qof aan loo ooyin*, meaning "Those for whom we don't cry." It referred to minorities or strangers within Somalia, but from outside a traditional alliance of clans. For the world of infidels sliding past the country's beaches on freighters full of expensive cargo there was little room for compassion, and no transcendent love. The glories of Sufism had failed to lift these men out of tribalism. In that sense they were no better than fundamentalists; they knew the letter of their religion and little else. But Bashko would have taken it as a mortal insult to hear he was no Muslim. He belonged to a vast pool of undereducated believers with a xenophobia made sharper, not milder, by the Koran.

"It's a funny religion, Bashko," I said after a while.

---

* Verse 9:5 is often called *the* Verse of the Sword, but the term can cover many verses invoked by imams in time of war.

† Polytheists, infidels.

Part 7

THE HOSTAGE COOKBOOK

I
_____

In late December I was fast asleep in the Pirate Villa when the urbane translator, Abdurrahman, woke me up by turning on the querulous fluorescent light. He had a note from his boss:

Dear Michael. My name is Fuad. For the cause of your freedom we must understand the name of your grandmother. Please write it for Mustaf.

"What's this about?" I said.

"You are going free. We need to prove to your side that you are here."

"To my 'side'?" I rubbed my face. "Is your name really Mustaf?"

"Yes, of course."

I stared at him.

"Why do you need my grandmother's name?"

"Michael, it is for your mother." He laid a soothing hand on my shoulder. "So she will know you are alive."

He was quick smiling, unctuous, with pale-brown skin and a small groomed patch of beard. He wore dark slacks and a collared shirt. I almost believed I was "going free." But it was too late at night for such a sudden decision.

"Are you telling the truth?" I said.

He nodded. "If Allah speaks, you will go free," he said.

"What does that mean?"

"If Allah says yes, you will go free. In Arabic we say, *Inshallah*."

More Muslim correctitude. *Inshallah* meant "If Allah wills it," but my pirates often used the term sarcastically.

"Oh, fuck off, I know what *inshallah* means." I was too groggy not to cuss. "You know, Allah hears everything you say. He knows if you're lying."

"Yes, he is watching us now," Abdurrahman purred. "He will know if you lie, too."

"Your name is Abdurrahman, by the way, not Mustaf."

This annoyed him. "No, it is Mustaf," he said.

"It is not."

"Please write the name of your grandmother."

"What if I don't?"

"You will not go free."

My sluggish mind wandered through the possibilities. Maybe negotiators in the United States or Europe were trying to contact me. But it was also plausible that pirate bosses wanted to crack a bank account. On the other hand—I had to strain to remember—did I use my grandmother's name on any account?

I did not.

I blinked and scratched my neck.

"All right, here's her name." I took his pen and wrote LENY YNTEMA on the scrap of paper. Abdurrahman tried to pronounce it. Bringing a name as private and intimate as my grandmother's into this filthy room disgusted me. But I corrected his pronunciation; he looked satisfied; he stood up.

"Thank you, Michael."

"You said I was going free. I won't forget."

"*Inshallah*," he repeated.

The fluorescent light went off again and I lay back on the sweat-dampened mattress. The night was humid, and I couldn't sleep.

My grandmother lived in a pastoral brick house in a Dutch village called Linne, not far from the German border. She was a mischievous lady with the bearing of a character from Proust or Flaubert, a small-town bourgeoise who remembered the Allied invasion of Northern Europe during World War II. Her face, in her eighties, had the mild wrinkles of a softened plum, and she used a scarf to cover her hair on excursions to the store. Time moved like molasses in Linne, and when email started to replace letter writing in the nineties, I used to get occasional, comical messages from her cousin, Rhinny, who sent them on my grandmother's behalf. Oma would write her message on a piece of letter paper, wrap her hair in a scarf, and drive a quarter-mile to Rhinny's, who would serve coffee or schnapps and switch on her computer. The ladies would gossip until it was time to type the email. Oma would read the letter while Rhinny took dictation, happy to use her computer as a village telegraph machine.

I shifted on my mattress and tried to sleep. These memories were hard to stop. Oma cooked heavy European meals of boiled vegetables, pork or beef in great slabs, creamy cucumber salads, and potatoes and asparagus with rich sauces. Remembering this old-fashioned food made my mouth water. The meals seemed traditional and stuck in time, but Oma had surprised me one afternoon, in her lace-curtained dining room, by calling it a Catholic style of cooking. The recipes held purpose and pride. "We don't cook like other people in Holland," she said. "Here in the south we cook like the Belgians, or the French, with more alcohol and cream." The Thirty Years' War had been settled for centuries, but Catholics in Holland maintained old feelings of pride and persecution, and Oma maintained strong parochial links to the past. Even her culinary choices were a bulwark against Protestant austerities.

One of my favorite meals as a kid at Oma's house was Indonesian satay, spears of chicken simmered in peanut sauce. She cooked it first when I was eight or nine. Until then, I had never imagined that peanuts could be anything besides a salty snack at a ball game. The idea of turning them into *dinner* was fantastic and strange. Later, when I understood the relationship between Indonesia and the Netherlands—when I had read about the violent Dutch East India Company and seen rebuilt colonial ships in the Port of Amsterdam, when I had finally walked the sweltering streets of Jakarta myself and bought satay from a char-blackened grill—I knew how sheltered and privileged I had been; but that first moment of surprise was still fresh and bright.

Before my kidnapping I had lived in a twilight between privilege and poverty, the bohemian twilight of a novelist and travel writer. Travel was an escape from definitions and hierarchies at home, and, done properly, it was a discipline of erasing preconceptions, a way to approach the world with intelligence and attention. Travel writing had fallen out of fashion in America, but I still believed in a good travel book as a way to crumble barriers. The medium was imperfect, but so was language itself—so was most human understanding. The effort to step outside your narrow mind-set was important. I happened to like the sense of slipping through a foreign place as a near-invisible stranger, and I liked the lessons of friction during those inevitable moments when you were no longer invisible. But Somalia was another story. In Somalia I had to be Californian and European whether I liked it or not. This crimped self-consciousness was excruciating, worse than useless, because whether you flaunted it or cringed from it such barren labelizing had little to do with self-knowledge.

II
_____

A few nights later, Bashko woke me up and said it was time to leave. "Telephone," he whispered. "No problem."

We piled into a Land Rover and drove to the Broom-Closet Bordello, where they told me to "sleep." After a few hours in this way station, I gathered, we would make another dead-of-night journey to meet Fuad. I didn't know whether to feel hope or dread. But when I drifted awake at around two, most of the guards sat chattering in the darkened courtyard, high on khat, while one man, Issa, had stayed in the room, slumped on a plastic chair, listening to white noise on his phone.

"Telephone?" I said. _Are we going out for a call?_

"_Maya_," he said. _No._

His phone played a high, oscillating signal. The men had started to listen to some open frequency through their phones at night—sometimes they heard pings, like electronic raindrops, and sometimes there was a watery signal, like high-pitched radio interference.

"Problem?" I said.

Issa pointed up and waved his finger around.

Drones? Aircraft were circling Galkayo? To watch for our vehicles? Or had I misunderstood? Pirates obviously tried to detect drone signals on their phones, but I didn't believe these techniques could be fail-safe, or unknown to the U.S. military. So why would a drone circle the house, at close enough range to startle my kidnappers—and prevent us from leaving—if the request for my grandmother's name had been an earnest attempt to put me on the phone? Why would a military force try to shut down proof of life?

Or did the phone technique really work?

I puzzled my situation down to a pair of possibilities. Either the pirates had lied about my imminent release, and the phone-call appointment was another pointless exercise, which the military wanted to squelch, for some reason connected to ransom talks (because my pirates considered a phone call to be a major event, loaded with expectation); or the request for Oma's name was an American ruse, and planes were trying to locate us.

Then again, then again.

At last I fell asleep, exhausted by my own thinking. In the hot morning we returned to the Pirate Villa. For the next two weeks the pirates raised my hopes with rumors of another imminent phone call—a climactic summit conversation that would settle my case and set the whole house free—while Orion-size aircraft swooped low over Galkayo almost every day. I had a weird feeling that the pirates wanted to wait out the planes, but also that the planes wanted to rattle the pirates, as if someone in the American hierarchy knew our approximate location, and wanted to spot us leaving the house. Or else force us to stay put.

At last Yoonis came to the Pirate Villa one morning in mid-January of the new year to ask if I wanted to talk to my mother.

"What, today?" I said.

"If you say yes, they will come to this house."

"Who will?"

"The bad group. The pirates."

Pirate bosses tried to separate their sprawling gangs into job-specific cells, and one cell did set up phone calls—as a rule, we drove out to the bush to meet those men—but my brain cycled through a fog of half-understood facts and came to no conclusion. Was a phone call good or bad? If our trip to the bush had been squelched by military planes, on purpose, was there some reason to say *no* to Yoonis? Or should I say yes, because pirate phones could be traced to the Pirate Villa?

"Yes or no?" said Yoonis.

"Let me think about it."

"I will tell the pirates no, you do not want."

"Don't tell them that."

"So you say yes?"

"I don't know, Yoonis. Give me five minutes."

"I will tell them you do not want."

The strong-arming was bizarre. But he wouldn't elaborate, and I saw little difference between yes and no. I liked the idea of surveillance, and maybe Abdurrahman had told the truth. Maybe I was about to go home.

"All right. Tell them yes."

"Good."

I had the rest of the morning to wonder and think, which was long enough for my hopes to swell like a party balloon. I decided that the elaborate planning and the aerial surveillance pointed to a plan to set me free.

In the afternoon, the steel door to the compound swung open and a rumbling SUV pulled inside. Three or four new Somalis came in and shook hands with my guards. Yoonis came to my mattress and coached me on the call—"Tell them you are sick; do not give your location"—and we moved to another room, where Bashko stood with a pistol.

We sat on somebody's comfortable double mattress. A Somali fiddled with a SIM card and dialed a number. Soon Fuad came on the line, from Mogadishu, and Yoonis leaned beside me to listen.

"I will connect you now with your mother," said Fuad, and my heart pounded.

Mom started the call with a question about my health. She asked whether I needed "medicines." I said something loud and simple about malaria, to please Yoonis. I was no longer sick, and didn't say I was, but he wanted to hear me complain. I added in German that I still wore the same clothes I had used on the *Naham 3*, bright clothes photographed by drones on the ship's laundry lines. I said they were hanging in the courtyard of this very house. I tried to describe the house. Mom just listened.

At last I mumbled, in English, "Are negotiations close?" and waited with anxious and delicate apprehension while my mother said, "We've talked to some clan leaders, some leaders of the community. We're making progress, Michael. But we're not very close. We're still in the millions. Another couple of months!"

My eyesight blackened. I saw pinpricks of swirling light.

"*Nicht aufgeben!*" she said. *Don't give up!*

"I've been here too long," I blurted. "These people aren't negotiating." I made sure the next sentence in German was clear: "A rescue would still be welcome."

Then I started to yammer in English about my health and my poor eyesight, to distract Yoonis from the drift of our conversation. What Mom had just said terrified me. What *I* had just said terrified me. The real stakes of the phone call were obscure to me still, and I had no clue what the pirates would understand, no sense of what I had done or what I had failed to do. But the hopes I had inflated for most of the afternoon just popped like soap bubbles. Fuad said something in Somali, and the line went dead.

III

I'd lived in Somalia for almost a year. My irrational heart had settled on some kind of anniversary release. Now those feelings panicked and flapped—all my sinews, every fiber of atrophied muscle, wanted to soar away from this villa, but every morning brought the flyblown realization that I would stay mired there for an unforeseeable stretch of time.

I started to have specific fantasies of suicide. The greed and contempt of the bosses needed some kind of answer. Greed was the reason I was still in Somalia—greed, not just poverty; greed, not some ringing justification of Somali fishing rights. So I imagined using the sharp lid of a tuna can, or dismantling a Bic razor, to open a vein in my arm, and I would dip toilet paper in the blood and paint GREED on the wall and hope to die under that garish banner of protest while some pirate took a picture and posted it on Facebook or something.

My heart beat through a deep sludge of emotion during these desolate afternoons. The only antidote to so much visceral anguish seemed to be yoga. Nothing else could settle the panic and straighten out my brain. The sweaty routine also gave me an excuse to wash my clothes in a bucket with Top-O-Mol and send my laundry out to dry. I wanted every fresh load to serve as a flag for drones. One guard or another had to carry my freshly rinsed yellow towel, my bright-green soccer shorts, and my red Manchester United jersey to hang in the sun-beaten yard, often with a look of disgust. (The infidel's clothes were considered unclean, even after I'd cleaned them.)

The guards had to serve my breakfast, clean my dishes, tote my laundry, and boil my tea. It put them in an awkward position. They expected a massive payout for watching an American, so guarding the Pirate Villa was in some sense a top-notch job. But the dynamic was hard to ignore. The foreigner lay on his bed and made requests; the Somalis served him. They enforced this cartoon-colonial arrangement with Kalashnikovs. The parents and grandparents of these pirates had resisted Italian occupation as well as

Siad Barre; they had struggled for independence to keep their children free. They would have been appalled by the self-degradation. The men had long afternoons in our concrete villa to understand that piracy was little more than begging with guns, and after several months, I think, this indignity reversed the gangster romance in their minds—although Bashko tried to wield the humiliation to his advantage by claiming that he was a prisoner, too.

"*Adiga, aniga*—same-same!" he would say, meaning we were both locked inside the compound. We certainly were. But I looked Bashko in the eye and answered,

"Same-same—okay, sahib. *Aniga*, Kalashnikov?"

And I lurched, jokingly, for his gun.

"No!" he said. "Fucking."

For about three weeks in February we heard lumbering overflights every handful of days. A circling Orion would rouse us in the cool hours around midnight, and the guards whispered like fugitives while I came straight up from sleep in a charge of confusion and hope. (Had my laundry trick worked? Would SEALs come blasting in?) One of the bosses—in response, I think, to the flights—ordered the men to lock my feet in chains, and from then on we lived by a grim unchanging schedule. When the light faded in the room, when the mosquitoes started to whine, when I had dropped the net around my mattress and eaten a bowl of dull brown beans, when the evening muezzin had called from the nearest mosque and I had gone to the bathroom, I had to submit to a Somali guard squatting in front of me, sometimes with a flashlight, to wrap my ankles in a bicycle chain and snap on a pair of locks. I remained locked up for about eleven hours, until the first muezzin sang over the rooftops at five the next morning when I was allowed to sit up and say, "*Kadi?*" and the guard watching me from the dim hall would root around for a set of tinkling keys.

IV

The padlocks flopping on my ankles changed my state of mind. I had flown to Somalia with curiosity and compassion; I had wanted to show, as far as I could, how Somalis lived and what pirates thought. But with the chains on I struggled every night with hatred and debilitating rage. The men treated me like a herd animal. Around me they smoked, giggled, bowed toward Mecca, and whispered passionate prayers the way nomads in the desert might pass their time around livestock.

While I lay in the dark one night, I realized that Bashko's logic about infidels echoed the reasoning of Barbary pirates. Ottoman leaders on the coast of North Africa used to send out pirates as a form of slow-burning jihad. In those days, the most obvious tension along the southern borders of Europe was between Christians and Muslims, and catching Christian prisoners was just a halal way to raise cash. The ships hunted in both directions. "By the end of the sixteenth century, slave-hunting corsair galleys, both Christian and Muslim, roamed throughout the Mediterranean," wrote Robert C. Davis in *Christian Slaves, Muslim Masters*, "seeking their human booty from Catalonia to Egypt."

Miguel de Cervantes spent five years as an Algerian hostage after pirates attacked his galley in 1575. They caught his brother Rodrigo, too. Both men were soldiers on their way home to Spain; Miguel had lost the use of his left hand in the Battle of Lepanto. The Moors demanded a steep ransom from the Cervantes family, because Miguel had letters of recommendation from powerful-sounding noblemen. But the family struggled to pay. Miguel tried to escape five times. The jailers kept both men chained in the bagnios—royal Moorish baths converted to dungeons underneath Algiers—until the family ransomed each brother, one at a time, with help from an order of Spanish friars.

European captives who couldn't be ransomed were auctioned by pirates into the great Arab-run market for slaves, the trans-African network of bazaars and caravan routes running from Mombasa to Marrakech. Since Ottoman slave owners delighted in converting infidels, the whole saga of Mediterranean kidnapping—captivity under "the Turk," suffering and slavery, then release to a Christian home—became a commonplace in European church services. Whenever freed Italian slaves came home from North Africa, for example, their towns held parades and sang songs of liberation. "The processions usually set out in the late morning," wrote Davis, "often led by soldiers, but sometimes by 'trumpeters [and] drummers, with a chorus' (who sang such appropriate psalms as '*In exitu Israel de Aegypto*' or '*Super flumine Babylonis*')."

Lying on my mattress, I could gnash my teeth and curse this old tradition of Muslim kidnapping; I could remember how the U.S. Navy and Marines had squelched Barbary pirates in 1815 and I could wonder where the hell they were now. But a hundred years before the Barbary missions, American colonists had also sailed as pirates, because it was an accepted way for *them* to raise cash. People who lived in Atlantic seaboard towns in the 1600s were almost as secluded and peculiar as modern Somalis in Hobyo or Eyl, and if the locals had to resort to piracy, well, that was nobody's business but their own. Underemployed sailors did it. Sea captains did it. Before the African slave trade took off in the New World, a white underclass of European servants figured out fast that regular life in the colonies wasn't for them. "Prisoners of war, poor debtors, criminals from the gaols and young men and boys kidnapped in the streets of English towns" were shipped across the Atlantic and sold into colonial servitude, wrote George Francis Dow in *The Pirates of the New England Coast, 1630–1730*. "A roving disposition was soon awakened and runaway servants were almost as common as blackbirds," and some of these rovers became "pirates of the usual type."

When Americans think of colonial piracy, they might imagine
British or Spanish swashbucklers roving the Caribbean, or Black-
beard in Carolina, lighting firecrackers in his hair. But the real money
came from a different part of the world—from long-distance raids on
treasure-heavy ships in the Red Sea. Colonial captains like Henry
Every, Thomas Tew, and William Kidd* sailed from the American
coast to Africa and sacked East Indiamen en route from England, to
annoy the Crown, or hijacked Mughal vessels laden with gold. These
pirates often traveled under contract from northeastern governors,†
and their hunting ground was the watery lane between India and the
Red Sea. They set up year-round camp on Madagascar. The whole
enterprise was a middle finger aimed at the Navigation Acts, the
English laws restricting colonial trade. Supply lines to these distant
Madagascar settlements became a lucrative commerce for American
colonists, and during the hajj the most adventurous captains in Madagascar sailed around the Horn of Africa to attack Muslim-crewed
ships trundling through the Gulf of Aden, and then the Red Sea, toward Mecca. "It is known that Eastern people travel with the utmost
magnificence," wrote Captain Charles Johnson‡ at the time, describ-
ing one raid on an imperial Mughal vessel called the *Ganj-i-Sawai*:

---

* Captain Kidd was hanged as a pirate, but historians have disagreed about his
business in Madagascar.

† "The place that receives them is chiefly Madagascar, where they must touch both
coming and going," wrote New York governor Richard Coote, earl of Bellomont, in
1697. "All the ships that are now out are from New England, except Tew from New
York and Want from Carolina. They build their ships in New England, but come
out under pretense of trading from island to island.... When they come back they
have no place to go but Providence [in the Bahamas], Carolina, New York, New England and Rhode Island, where they have all along been kindly received."

‡ Maybe a pen name for Daniel Defoe; in any case, the author of *A General History
of the Pyrates*.

"They had with them all their slaves and attendants, their rich habits and jewels, with vessels of gold and silver, and great sums of money to defray the charges of their journey by land."

In 1700, William Penn was so impressed by the role pirate treasure had played in colonial finance that he wrote to London, with a baroque flair for sentence construction:

> As for Piracy, I must needs say that if Jamaica had not been the Seminary, where pirates have commenced Masters of Art after having practiced upon the Spaniard, and then launched for the Red & Arabian Sea, and at Madagascar have found a yearly supply of flour, bread, ammunition and arms from some of our neighboring colonies, that perhaps in 10 years' time got a million by it, and then have returned these fellows upon us and our Coasts, we had never had a spot upon our Garment.

Three hundred years before Somali pirates, in other words, the scourges of the Indian Ocean were rebel subjects of the British Empire—American colonial pirates. So I could lie in the dark and curse my kidnappers, but I had done this research and I knew better than to think of myself, or my heritage, as innocent.

V

My guards took orders from pirate bosses because they had little choice—they'd joined the gang out of poverty, and the bosses ruled by violence—but they still had a weird notion of their own moral agency. For them the criminal violence of extortion, hijackings at sea, chains on a hostage's ankles, or even torture in the woods were just things that happened. Pirates did them, sure, but the average pirate considered these evils to be over his head, out of his personal control. Bashko told me I was a hostage because of "Allah's will"—as if Allah could somehow bring Bashko fortune, and me misfortune, without the strenuous intervention of pirates.

One morning in February, Bashko lost the keys, and his carelessness upset me so much that I refused to eat breakfast.

"No problem," he mumbled, by way of encouragement.

"Somali bullshit," I declared.

The keys turned up in another man's bag of clothes. Bashko spent a few minutes tongue-lashing him before he unlocked my chains.

A few days later, he came in to unchain me in the morning gloom and left the keys beside my mattress on the floor. More carelessness; but my heart trotted. I took a strip of toilet paper and waited two hours before my sentry, Madobe, was distracted. Then I swept up the keys and stashed them in an empty biscuit box.

Before a trip to the bathroom, I stuffed this wad of toilet paper into my shorts pocket. The bathroom was a high stall of cracked white plaster, with a vent near the ceiling crafted from filigreed concrete. The porcelain toilet had to be flushed with water from a jerry can. I tossed in the wad of toilet paper, keys and all, and peed onto it. I flushed with a sense of mounting joy, over and over, and left the jerry can where it belonged, beside the bathroom door.

"*Mahadsanid*,"* I said to Madobe, who was guarding the door with his rifle.

---

* "Thank you."

It was a measure of my emotional destitution that something so petty could brighten me up. I felt elated for the rest of the day. When the evening muezzin called and I noticed Bashko rooting for the keys, I felt even better. He came in to ask about them.

"*Aniga*, no," I said, and shrugged. *Wasn't me, boss.*

He stared with a mixture of derision and disbelief. But he had no proof. The memory of missing keys from a few days before worked in my favor. He returned to scold the other men, and they picked up their mat in the hall and scoured the floor.

"Michael!" Bashko said again. "Keys!"

I shrugged. "I dunno."

"Stand up!"

He searched under my mattress, around my mattress, and through the biscuit box. He took the clothes out of a faux-leather bag I used as luggage. He let out a stream of well-chosen Somali.

"*Aniga*, no," I kept repeating.

It felt wonderful to go to bed that night with no chains, but I lay awake while the guards inspected the house and Bashko made a frantic phone call. He shuffled and muttered until a runner arrived with new padlocks, and I had to be roused. Bashko strapped the chains around my ankles himself.

When the first muezzin called in the morning, I sat up, swung my ankles out of the mosquito tent, and let the chains clank on the floor. "*Kadi*," I said, but no one came in with keys. The Somalis took their time standing up to guard my way to the toilet.

I held up the chain.

"No. Fucking," said Bashko. "Come on."

The chains gave me a six-inch stride. I lifted the excess length off the dirty floor and started to shuffle. The links rubbed my ankles raw, and the guards watched with hard satisfaction, as if I had bought and paid for this treatment myself. Maybe I had. But I returned to bed in a flush of rage at the prospect of spending all day fettered like a goat. My heart knocked against my sternum and I lay rigid, one arm over my face, just trying to keep the floor-grimed chains off my mattress, while in my head I recited the capitals of all fifty American states.

When that was done, I tried to name all of Saul Bellow's novels in order.

Then Dylan albums.

Then Faulkner.

I still had an arm over my face when breakfast arrived. The steel bowl made a gritty, ringing noise on the floor.

I didn't stir, and Bashko hadn't been out of the room longer than a minute when he put his head through the doorway again.

"Michael," he said. *"Digir!"*

"No," I said.

"No *digir?*"

I shook my head and waved him off. He returned to take the bowl.

"Fucking!" he said.

I didn't even watch him leave. But he moved with such electric anger I couldn't tell who was in charge. Would I get beaten, or punished in some other way? Were the pirates starving the hostage, or was the hostage refusing to eat? I had no clue how to end a hunger strike, but I knew my terms had to be straight and clear in my head. I was, for one thing, really hungry. Hunger rubbed a hole in my gut on a normal morning in Somalia, but now my body's reaction to a single missed meal was a vivid, unexpected, deep-organ panic: *WHERE'S THE FOOD?* I lay on the mattress all morning with one arm over my face and sirens blaring in my head.

VI

I decided to eat again when the men took off my chains. How long would that take? Two days, maybe three? How long could I last? How long could anyone last without food or water? I must have known, once upon a time, but captivity had softened my brain and I had no way to research these things.

Had I even sworn off water?

In the dry heat of Somalia it would have meant a quick death to drink nothing. I didn't know the rules of a hunger strike, or what the pirates assumed. I reached furtively for a water bottle, and took a gulp. It calmed and refreshed me. I took two more gulps and covered my face with my arm and pretended not to care what the pirates thought. I expected them to make a fuss. They didn't. I ventured a cup of tea. It was delicious, and I realized the treacly hot liquid would become an important source of calories.

Before noon, I heard busywork in the kitchen. Bashko finally carried in a heaping bowl of pasta, drenched in boiled potato and onion.

"Michael—*baasto*, okay!" he said.

Interesting. So they weren't starving the hostage.

"No," I said.

"Fucking!" Bashko said, and carried the bowl away.

I heard an argument in the hall. Bashko used his phone. For lunch, a runner brought heavy plastic bags of restaurant food, including greasy seasoned rice and slabs of camel meat. It smelled like a holiday feast. Someone arranged it in heaps on a round tin tray the men used for communal meals, and they squatted in the hall where I could see them, scooping lunch into their mouths with their hands. It reminded me of our dinner in Budbud, the piles of pasta and Digsi's ceremonial shoulder of goat.

Soon Issa turned, with a deliberately pleasant look on his face, and raised his lanky arm to wave me in. "Michael, come on! *Chum-chum.*"

"No," I said.

"*Gil! Adiga!*" they said. *Camel for you!*

"No."

"Why not?" said Issa.

I shook my head.

The whole team ate; even the night-watch pirates woke up for camel and rice. Afterward Bashko and Issa came in with a small bowl of leftovers and squatted next to my bed.

"Michael, why no *chum-chum?*" said Issa.

"Because chains."

They conferred.

"Chains finished, Michael *chum-chum?*" said Issa.

I had to think about that.

"Yes," I said finally.

Bashko found the keys and opened the padlocks. My stomach thanked me, and the simple holy relief of chain link falling from my skin gave me a rush of joy.

"Okay, Michael?"

I shrugged, still startled by my quick success. What if I'd held out for some greater goal? Better food, or freedom itself?

I didn't look the men in the eyes; I just nodded and searched for my fork.

VII

In the spring of 2013, we moved to a different house in Galkayo, belonging to Dhuxul, an almost bald, almost obese man with deadened eyes and a tuneless voice. He walked with a limp, on a calf-shaped prosthetic—a pirate captain with a wooden leg. He told me his lower right leg had been shot off by American helicopters during the Battle of Mogadishu. That wasn't impossible. He looked old enough—in his forties—to have fought Black Hawks in 1993; but then every pirate with a scar claimed to have memories of that disastrous battle.

Dhuxul—pronounced *Duhul*, a dull and shapeless noise, not so different from the man—looked familiar to me in a way that flipped my stomach. He spent part of his time in the prison house, which was odd for a pirate boss. He kept booze and a TV in his bedroom. Every morning he started his Toyota Surf and let it idle in the court-yard until the house filled with diesel fumes. Then he drove off to some sort of job.

At this house, my mattress lay just inside an open door, facing east. I could see planes land at the Galkayo airport and watch the dawn sky lighten every morning through an arabesque patio arch. When I asked Bashko why we'd moved, he said the other house had "too many drones."

"But here, not so many?"

"Here, okay."

The houses weren't far apart. The men had blindfolded me during our nighttime drive, and we'd taken a detour, but I could tell from the sound of muezzins around Galkayo that we hadn't left the neighborhood.

Two new Somalis joined the group at Dhuxul's. One was lanky and mild-seeming, named Farrah, with a sharp chin and shy, hooded eyes. The other was a young man who called himself Hashi. He had innocent-looking round eyes and a wispy mustache. He approached me, at first, with a round-shouldered meekness, and he left thin little notebooks lying around on the patio. I hadn't seen a notebook in months.

Hashi never tried to do me harm. He never made jokes at my expense. Bashko's loyalty to my welfare depended on his mood, but Hashi was low-key and kind. He and Farrah became friends. These allegiances were significant, because at least half of the ever-shifting team treated me with the same indifference and contempt as Madobe.

One afternoon, while I sat on the edge of my mattress and ate from a bowl of potatoes, I spotted a notebook near Hashi's cross-legged knees. The men used them to record not just shifts but wages, khat debts, and pocket money. They received an allowance, I think as an advance on their expected windfall, and sometimes, after a visit from a boss, I saw them with stacks of Somali shillings. Bundled, rotten stacks of devalued shillings were still traded on the street in Somalia, even though the nation had no central bank and hadn't printed new money since 1991.

Hashi seemed to have extra notebooks. I asked for one.

"Okay!" he said.

I had an old pen stashed in my bag, so after my meal I took the thin stapled notebook—blue, with a UNICEF logo—and sat in a far corner of the room, to hide from the Somalis' unblinking attention.

Recipe ideas came out first:

<u>GREEN SALSA</u>

Green tomatoes, cilantro, lime, poblano, onions, garlic

<u>BAKED HAM WITH SQUASH AND CILANTRO PESTO MASH</u>

<u>RED SNAPPER WITH SHALLOTS, LIME, POBLANO, REFRIED BEANS</u>

FAT WHITE BEANS

Fry garlic in sesame oil, cut tomatoes, let juice mix with oil,
& pour over warm beans. Serve with whatever.

These cravings surprised me. They were sharp and specific. I'd
never cooked any of this stuff before. I rarely cooked ham,* and I
never made recipes up. I was an eager but not an original cook. Now
clear ideas arrived, whole and uninvited, like shimmering poetic
visions.

When the pirates made a stew with mutton kidney, instead of
liver, I remembered a rich brown kidney stew I had tasted in Britain
and scribbled a recipe in my notebook that improved on the pirates'
mess with mushrooms, garlic, salsify, chestnuts, Worcestershire
sauce, and Guinness. The ingredients were pure guesswork. Aston-
ishingly, at least to me, I got most of them right. I had no experience
cooking kidneys, but my body needed protein and iron, and it drove
my brain to compose a recipe from the memory of a single meal
eaten five years before.

Jotting down recipes reintroduced me to the incredible pleasure of composing by hand. Soon I drafted a short story that had
occurred to me during those long, blank afternoons in the Pirate
Villa. I sat cross-legged, with the book on the floor, and because of
my weak eyes I had to bend forward in a way that started to hurt
my shoulders and spine after an hour or two. I structured my day
around these short bursts of writing. No one seemed to care. Something had changed, in me as well as my guards. It felt unnatural

---

* So possibly a joke from my subconscious.

to live in the same house and remain filthy-minded toward someone for twenty-four hours a day. Most people couldn't maintain that
level of enmity, so my attitude tempered, and the guards allowed
themselves to forget the evening, last autumn, when Madobe had
confiscated my scraps of notepaper, when writing was still against
the rules.

VIII

One night at Dhuxul's, I had to urinate before the morning prayer.
The guards sat on the patio, watching me sleep, and when I stirred
too much, they objected. I wasn't supposed to be awake. But my
bladder felt like a balloon. I raised the mosquito net.

Madobe said, "*Wuuriyaa!*" and shone a flashlight at my face. *Hey!*

"*Kadi,*" I said.

"Sleeping!" he said.

I sat still and held up my chains.

"*Kadi,*" I repeated calmly.

I couldn't make out faces in the dark, but I heard Hashi's voice
and Farrah's. Madobe leaned in close to threaten me. Making any
disturbance at this hour was against the rules.

"*Kadi,*" I insisted.

Madobe lurched and flicked his hand, so one knuckle flattened
my eyeball.

"Jesus!" I shouted, and the noise angered Hashi and Farrah.
They argued with Madobe. Hitting hostages was also against the
rules. They hissed in whispers until one of them tossed me the keys.

Madobe had thwacked me this way before, when it was his job,
one evening, to chain my feet. He was adept with his knuckle, and

I knew the eye would hurt for a day or two. It throbbed now with every heartbeat, and I returned to the mattress pulsing with anger. I lay awake until the sun rose. Hashi came in to remove the chains, and after some time Bashko delivered my bowl of beans.

I shook my head and pushed it away.

"No *chum-chum*?" he said.

"No."

"Why?"

"Madobe hit me."

When the boss came out for a shower, Bashko translated my complaint. Hashi and Farrah corroborated the story. Dhuxul listened to everything with dead and quiet eyes, gave his men a phlegmatic order, and went out.

A thermos of tea helped me through the morning. I still felt drawn with hunger, but I knew what to expect, appetite-wise, and while the minutes ticked by without breakfast, I could manage the animal panic.

Dhuxul returned for lunch with a hot restaurant delivery of spiced rice and boiled goat. The men unpacked it from foam trays and feasted. I lay still, and Dhuxul limped in to set a plate of food on the floor, near my pillow. The room filled with the smell of seasoned meat. I stared at Dhuxul, thinking he was the same person I had seen on my first night in Galkayo, the sinister, fat boss who had settled in our room and smoked a cigarette while the guards told him about the *Naham 3*. He seemed familiar in another way, too, but I couldn't place why.

Dhuxul made an offer. He would punish Madobe "tonight." Madobe is sleeping right now, Bashko said.

Would I eat?

Prickly question. Refusing this overture risked punishment, but agreeing would have made it easy for Dhuxul to forget our terms.

Yes, I told Bashko. After Dhuxul punished Madobe, I would eat. Not before.

I pushed away the plate.

Dhuxul picked up my chains from a corner and moved to a room next door. I heard the chains clink. Hashi and Farrah sat on the patio, with worried faces. When I saw Dhuxul again, he held Madobe in the posture of a slave, bent forward, with his chained hands yanked behind his back. He smacked the young guard across the head and shoved a knee against his rear end. Madobe, my wiry persecutor, glanced into my room with derision and fear. Dhuxul pulled the chains tight, Madobe winced in pain, and Dhuxul shoved him back to the other room.

It appalled my conscience to see a man chained and smacked on my account; but there was no room for such fine feelings in Somalia. The pirates were poor but vengeful bullies who wanted to acquaint me with hunger, with the prospect of death, above all with the rule of force. The soul of the country's social order was still violent, even autocratic, and there was no contradiction between the disorder of its anarchy and the power of violent discipline.

"Okay, Michael?" Bashko repeated.

The boss had made his concession. I had to respond.

"Okay," I said.

And Madobe, for a while, quit thwacking me.

IX

The bosses' demand for money tumbled in the first half of 2013, from eight million dollars to six million, then flirted with five. Mom kept track of everything in her notebooks, the FBI saved recordings;

there was a sense of progress. She bargained with Fuad, or some proxy for Fuad, by email and phone. "I told them I was a retired person, I was on a fixed income, and I had sold property and I was raising as much as I could," Mom said.

She'd assembled money for my ransom through various circles—family, friends, magazines I had worked for, various U.S. and German institutions. But the fund was limited. Western hostages have a rough price on the world market, but it's a function of guesswork, of global rumor and bluffs, of sheer illusion and sometimes accurate journalism.* In Somalia, the shipping industry had distorted the hostage calculus, because the largest cargo ships carried massive insurance plans, and every day a vessel full of oil or steel rested at anchor off Somalia represented a dead loss for its owners. After a certain amount of time, it made financial sense for the owners to splash out and recover both hostages and ship. This logic didn't apply to human beings on land. But pirates pretended it did.

For a year and a half, Mom's life had revolved around the mess on the kitchen table. She'd spent most of it struggling with a brick-wall demand of twenty million, so the momentum in the spring came as a relief. Since our last phone call in January she had asked for another conversation with me. "I would say, 'I need to talk to my son; I need proof of life.'" she said later. "We were dealing with 'Abdi Yare' . . . and he would say, 'I will do that as soon you have the money.' Meaning *his* amount." So a long period of no telephone contact began.

In late spring, Fuad, or Abdurrahman, put my mother in touch with a mysterious Sa'ad elder calling himself Sheikh Mohamud,

---

* Whatever ransom had sprung Rolly and Marc a year earlier would also have set expectations for mine.

who promised to work as an intermediary. Under his ministrations, the ransom demand seemed to collapse. "He mentioned $1.5 million," said Mom, "and I said, 'Okay, I can work on that. I don't have one point five, but I will do my best, and maybe we can reach an agreement.'"

Until then, her offer had rested at one million dollars. "But he retracted a few days later," Mom said. "He came back and said, 'No, you misunderstood—it was coming *down* $1.5 million, from six.'

"Of course, we listened to the recording, and we had not misunderstood," she said. "He was very clear about it. But now it was different again, and it bounced back and forth, and on our next conversation it was five million again, and it stayed there for a while."

The odd part of this story is that I had a similar conversation with Abdurrahman in June 2013. One afternoon, he came into the compound in a happy fog of smiles from the whole team of guards. "Michael," he said, "you will go free. The demand is down to $1.5 million. You will fly to Nairobi in seven days."

The news was so sudden I thought he was telling the truth. Eight million dollars was ridiculous, but $1.5 million—from what I knew about hostage negotiations—did not seem out of range. I didn't know how Mom would pay, but it was the first time I'd heard a story from Abdurrahman that was not an obvious lie. So I allowed myself a flutter of optimism, which carried me along on a dream of freedom that fit with the chronology Mom had indicated on the phone—"Another couple of months!"—and I was nicer to the pirates, and everyone got along, until, after seven days, the excitement faded, there was no sign of change, and, when I saw Abdurrahman again, he seemed unwilling to talk.

I asked him about the pirates' demand, and he mumbled, "It is four point five."

"You said one point five just over a week ago."

"No, I said one point five *less*," he insisted. "You have misunderstood."

X

The devastation I felt was foolish and brutal, foolish because I should have known better and brutal because hope had become a psychological risk, something worse than a frustrating cycle. It was a breaking wheel, an emotional indulgence with a treacherous downward slope. It could fuck me up for days. I had to detach myself like a Buddhist from my own desire to be free, the way I had to detach myself during a hunger strike from my profound desire for food. I had to quiet my raging thoughts and quit hoping for any future at all. The discipline was monkish but not large hearted; I just learned to adjust to the shifting currents of indignity with as much quiet loathing as I needed to keep myself sane.

Sometime in the summer a new pirate named Farhaan joined the group of guards. I woke up one morning and a fat, jolly-seeming man with dull eyes and a scruffy goatee, who spoke some English, introduced himself with a gentle handshake, pointing to a little scar on his wrist.

"From Mogadishu," he said. "Nineteen ninety-three."

"*Black Hawk Down?*"

"Yes."

I squinted. Bashko was about twenty-five; Farhaan seemed a little older.

"What happened?" I asked.

"Shooting-shooting," he said.

"Twenty years ago," I noted.

"Yes," he said, and walked away.

Bashko sat in the doorway with his gun. "How old is Farhaan?" I said, and Bashko flashed me a number with his fingers and hands. "Thirty!"

"So in Mogadishu," I said, "he was ten?"

He laughed and said something down the hall to Farhaan, who answered in an irritated rattle of Somali.

"Thirty-five!" Bashko corrected.

Somalis called the Battle of Mogadishu "the Day of the Rangers," and it had mythic status in my pirates' minds. The two-day battle in 1993 was a low point for the American military as well as the U.N., whose good-hearted mission to feed Somalis in the first years after the fall of Siad Barre now stands as "the greatest failure of the U.N. in our lifetime," according to one UNICEF official. The author Aidan Hartley, who first applied the word "warlord" to Somalia's belligerent ex-generals and tribal leaders, has been more colorful and direct. "International forces swiftly picked a fight with one of the Mogadishu warlords, and the development goals were all swept away in a bloody feud that led to the mission's failure," he wrote in an afterword to Gerald Hanley's *Warriors*. "And so it was that U.N. peacekeepers . . . ended up machine-gunning civilians from helicopters."

The battle, in that sense, exposed the worst contradictions of international aid. Food aid is not just largesse between nations; it's a political tool, and Siad Barre had relied on it during his regime—first from the Soviet Union, then the United States. When the collapse of Communism ended any political need to shore up distant African dictatorships, Western aid to Somalia dwindled, and generals rebelled. The most powerful upstart was a Sa'ad leader of the

Habar Gidir,* Mohamed Farrah Aidid. Warlords need political support no less than presidents, and sacks of U.N. grain, for Aidid, were
one way to shore it up.

The civil war after Siad's collapse was bloody enough to shock
world leaders to attention, and a swarm of U.S. Marines swept onto
beaches near Mogadishu in late '92 with the goal of stabilizing Somalia. The elder President Bush intended the mission as a grace note
to his first term in office. He hoped for reports about Western medical care and international aid, and the self-contradictory doctrine
of "humanitarian force" did manage to bring most warring Somali
clans to the peace table. But "trucks with food," as a German Red
Cross worker pointed out at the time, "are like trucks full of money,"
and Aidid simply rerouted them. It was straightforward corruption.
The unequal distribution spoiled high Western talk about nation-
building, and when the U.N. tried to break Aidid's stranglehold on
the grain, America had to back up its demands with guns.

Aidid hated the U.N. He wanted to lead Somalia, but the U.N.
had tried to push him out of the peace process without considering
that his wider clan, the Habar Gidir, held crucial influence. Violence escalated between Habar Gidir militias and U.N. troops for
several months while presidents changed in the White House. Finally an American group of special forces in helicopters captured
two of Aidid's lieutenants in October '93 (under President Clinton).
The mission went wrong. Somalis shot down two Black Hawks over
the streets of Mogadishu, angry Somalis closed in on the wrecks,
and international forces fought a two-day street battle to rescue
the trapped Americans. It turned into the bloodiest quagmire for

---

* The Sa'ad are a subclan of the Habar Gidir, who in turn are a subdivision of the
Hawiye.

the American military since Vietnam. Hundreds of Somalis died, maybe a thousand were wounded, and the Army lost eighteen troops, including two Delta Force fighters and one Black Hawk pilot whose corpses were dragged naked through the streets and paraded on Somali TV.

This mess *did* help explain what I was still doing in Somalia. Sa'ads had not forgotten the Day of the Rangers. For them it was a humiliation, a day of murder they still failed to understand. Aidid died in 1996, but some of the Sa'ad guards I met still considered themselves embroiled in a clan war with the United States.

(Some pirates thought of Germany as a "subclan" of Europe, and some accused me of having clan relationships with "ruling families" in the United States—the Bushes or the Clintons. The reason they could get away with such a weird but convenient misunderstanding was that last names have a different meaning in Somalia. Every Somali, in fact, has three first names: one personal and the other two cascading down from the father's side, indicating recent parentage but not advertising clan or family membership.)

What the pirates said around me, in any case, played up the supposed clan tensions, including Ali Tuure's ridiculous claim of cannibalism and anything Farhaan uttered. Farhaan wasn't even Habar Gidir. But he came into my room one morning with his phone to show me a Somali documentary about the disaster. It included clips of President Bush making promises on TV, spliced with bloody scenes of Somalis wounded or killed by helicopters. He squatted near my bed and watched me watch the movie.

"George Bush—criminal!" he said after a while.

"No good," I mumbled, frowning at the scenes on his phone. But it was odd and complicated to hear this criticism from a pirate.

Some liberal opinion held that Western aid to developing nations amounted to neocolonialism, a soft imperialism that allowed poor nations to grow addicted to charity while rich nations told them what to do. The Day of the Rangers was Exhibit A.* My pirates wanted aid anyhow. They didn't think too hard. Bashko felt that rich countries should help destitute places like Somalia with no strings attached. But there were always strings, and the odd part was that aid didn't even seem to cross Bashko's mind when he thought about the Day of the Rangers.

I finished watching the movie and decided to probe for my guards' version of events.

"Farhaan," I said, "why? Americans came to Somalia, why?"

"Oil!" Bashko shouted from the doorway.

"Yes, oil," said Farhaan, in a deeper, more sober-sounding voice.

"Iraq war, same-same!" cried Bashko.

"Hang on," I said, to clarify. "America wanted oil from Somalia in 1993?"

"Yes! Yes!" said Bashko.

"Yes," declared Farhaan.

"Oh, boy," I mumbled.

XI

I woke up on the first morning of Ramadan in July 2013, and two guards, Farhaan and a young pirate named Xalane,† watched me disappear into the bathroom without stirring themselves to make

---

* See *The Road to Hell*, by Michael Maren.

† Full name Xalane Ma'lin Dare, though he tried to go by "Mohammed."

beans. Someone had lit a cooking fire on the patio, and eventually Farhaan brought a thermos of tea, which he set near my mattress with elaborate and gentle courtesy. But no sign of food.

"*Digir?*" I said, and Farhaan explained, in a hushed deep voice—thick with pious correctitude, as if he expected me to understand—that I was in a Muslim place.

"Michael, no *digir* this morning."

Xalane watched us from the corner with fervent eyes. "Ramadan!" he said, in a voice gone whispery with outrage. It offended him that an infidel should even ask his friends to cook after dawn during the holy month. Fired by an equal and opposite outrage, I resorted to the loud conversational voice the pirates preferred for me to avoid. "Somali bullshit!" I said, and Farhaan made a calming motion with his hand—"*Okay, okay.*"

I kept complaining. "I refuse to starve because you're being Muslim," I said in irritated English, oblivious to whether he understood. "If it's a problem for you, then you can fucking well set me free."

"Ramadan!" answered Xalane.

I declared a hunger strike. If I had to go hungry, I would do it as an act of will. I'd learned to convert any skipped meal into a protest: "Michael no *chum-chum*," I shouted, "Michael no *chum-chum!*" which was not just a refrain of mine but also a koan for the guards to ponder: *If Michael doesn't eat, Michael won't eat!*

They understood it very well. Farhaan hurried out of the room.

Xalane stared with his hurt, puppyish, adolescent eyes. He was a teenager, and he'd taken lessons from Madobe in treating me like a herd animal. "Ramadan!" he hissed again after a while, with the same passionate wounded pride.

Muslims are supposed to show kindness during Ramadan to the poor and unfortunate. The fast forbids indulgent consumption between dawn and dusk—food, sex, cigarettes, drink—to cleanse the body and nudge the believer toward God. Handling food, or sitting in the same room as an infidel having a meal, is objectionable but not strictly forbidden. A subtle Muslim can work around the contradiction. Waiters and cooks show up for work during Ramadan; Muslim office workers have been known to attend lunch meetings. But divine consciousness was hardly the point for my pirates. Islam, for them, was a group activity, a set of rules they adhered to through pious observance of ritual. Islam, like all the major monotheisms, had spread as an antidote to tribalism, a transcendent solution to the warring profusion of local polytheisms in the ancient and medieval Middle East; but Islam, for my pirates, was a clan of its own.

Dhuxul had a fat young relative named Abdirashid, a plush-lipped pirate princeling who strutted around in military gear and sometimes lounged in a yellow sarong, irritating the other guards with his air of privilege. Abdirashid was no more religious than Dhuxul; in fact both men had a taste for gin.

But Abdirashid knew how to cook, and that was how they worked it out. On Dhuxul's orders, during the long, fast-somnolent Ramadan afternoons, Rashid cooked me decent meals. He carved chunks of mutton and served them in a thin pool of spiced gravy, and when I said I liked hot food, he ground the spices freely, using a wooden mortar and pestle. The other guards watched with a mixture of wariness and amusement and hunger. They couldn't even chew khat while the sun shone, so they acted uneasy around Rashid's delicious-smelling meals, and they laughed when the heat of the chili made me sweat.

After a few days of this new meal, I added Rashid's recipe to my collection:

Garlic
Ginger

Dates
Onion
Tomato
Small red chili
Chop, sauté in stock, and mash.
Serve with meat.

It represented a gesture of Ramadan mercy from Dhuxul, who also ordered his TV moved into my room. For months I'd asked for a shortwave radio so I could listen to the BBC, and I liked handheld radios because you could switch them on and off. But a TV was a massive, blaring complication. As soon as Dhuxul's gift blinked on, five pirates filed into my room and settled in the far corner with their clanking weapons. Abdinuur, Farrah, Madobe, Hashi, and Xalane sat gazing at the screen like kindergartners. The satellite package at Dhuxul's had programming in Arabic and Pakistani; for news in English, there was only Press TV, the Iranian propaganda channel. I could tolerate about five minutes of Press TV each day, to glean headlines, but once the screen came on in the morning my guards would watch the news, or anything else, for hours. So Ramadan became a daily negotiation of TV rights, a constant (armed) struggle for the remote.

The channel I liked best was FTV India, a subcontinental edit of FashionTV. The sight of women startled me; I hadn't seen any in fourteen months. Now, on TV, I could watch a parade of graceful, refined, bloodless, long-legged women wearing outlandish clothes. As a free man I never followed fashion, but I had gone all these months without contemplating creative work of any kind, so I paid attention, not just to the alien beauty of each model, but also to the cut of each skirt and dress, to the thumping music and colors, the whole spectacle. The pirates found it uproarious. Bashko mocked the stiff way the women had to strut. (He wasn't used to seeing high heels.) Part of me would have laughed with him, but these glass menageries in Paris and Milan now felt impossibly fragile, a delicate counterweight to my stinking underworld, and I couldn't believe they existed. They belonged to the old civilized hypocrisy, the glitter and sexual froth of Western cities, which I missed.

"Shut up," I said. "This is fucking great."

XII

Islam imposed some limits on my pirates' cruelty. I find that sentence hard to write. Unbelieving bosses like Dhuxul may have manipulated their foot soldiers by spreading the story that infidel hostages ate pig, which was true but an excuse to dehumanize us; but individual guards could be kind. Bashko and Hashi and Abdinasser the Sahib listened to my requests. They replaced notebooks and pens. Whenever they felt chipper, I could ask for sambusi, and they called the runner and ordered a batch from the mysterious Indian or Pakistani shop in Galkayo. I never forgot that each pirate was here to steal my money, but there were limits to the horror in the sense that none of them wanted to torture, or kill, the infidel.

The guards appeared to waver between Sufism and Wahhabism. They listened to sermons recorded on their phones and scoured the Koran to see who was right about what. Pirate gangs and al-Shabaab represented separate, lucrative, highly taboo career opportunities for young Somali men. Both groups had established corporate-like structures in a country with almost no jobs. A gunman who joined a pirate or terrorist network could earn a salary, make friends across clan lines, distinguish himself with basic military training, and move up in rank. Very few Somali enterprises offered so much opportunity, and I sometimes had the feeling that my guards thought and debated about the religious doctrines dividing pirates from terrorists while they sat around in these barren rooms. One afternoon Bashko felt so bitter about news of an American air strike somewhere in the world that he threatened to join al-Shabaab. "America, fucking!" he said.

The Wahhabi challenge in Somalia was modern, oddly, the way Protestantism had once been modern in the Christian world. Wahhabist fundamentalism dated from the eighteenth century and urged Muslims toward a literal analysis of the Koran, motivated by a desire to keep Islam pure from corruption. Its founder, Muhammad ibn Abd al-Wahhab, took the razor of rational skepticism to certain traditions, including the idea that Sufi ancestor saints might intercede, like ghosts, in the fates of living men.

He never took a razor to the woolly notion that the Koran might be anything besides the direct and immutable word of God. This belief has frozen in stone the most violent verses of a scripture completed in about 632. The word "Muslim" means "one who submits to God," just as "Islam" means "submission," and from that point of view it's undeniable, even to dull believers like my guards, that a non-Muslim has failed to see the light of a single, all-knowing, and universal power.

Even more universal than the word "God," though, is the image of light itself, which started to seem curious to me in Somalia. The ancient Jewish levels of the soul (*nefesh, ruach,* and *neshamah*) that underlie the Christian model have near-exact parallels in Hinduism, Buddhism, Sufism, and even the Platonism of Plutarch. In every instance the higher levels are associated, somehow obviously, with light and joy. The most evanescent level of the self in certain branches of Buddhism and Hinduism goes by the name "body of delight," a level of consciousness that you might think would be incomprehensible to a dirty, wretched piece of human filth stuffed into the dim corner of concrete prison house.

People have a natural religious instinct, an intuition of forces greater than themselves, a need to appease and understand. I doubt any religion has clarified the forces of human fate except in shadows. In Somalia I could apprehend these forces as something terrible but merciful, a fantastic punishment for my ignorance that stopped short of murder. I was still alive, though not because of my own wit—and I was susceptible to unexpected moments of joy. There were mornings in Somalia that felt so brilliant and warm, so limpid, that my emotions rose to the occasion. In King Solomon's language I had lived in the house of mourning for a year and a half; I had quit working for mirth.* But mirth came and went on its own. Which told me that human creatures had the power to thrive in foul circumstances precisely because of the consciousness bubbling up from our limpid core. I had nothing else. Of course I had to keep that idea near the front of my mind, it wasn't always clear. But the only source of strength in my hot and desolate prison houses was internal. If I'd focused on circumstance, I wouldn't have lasted long.

The fierce American thinker and satirist Richard Mitchell once made a point in an essay about language and the limits of words:

> We can usefully say of "hatred" and of "love" and countless
> other intangibles as well, exactly what Augustine said of
> Time: We know exactly what they are, except when someone
> asks us to explain what they are. This is not a defect in our

---

* "The heart of the wise is in the house of mourning, but the heart of fools is in the house of mirth" (Ecclesiastes 7:4). Not that I felt wise.

language any more than the failure to indicate relative humidity is a failure in a clock. Countless such words stand as markers at the boundaries of vast mysteries pointing back over their shoulders and saying no more.

Words, like religions, just point and suggest. They're markers at the boundary, not vessels of absolute truth. To focus on the words and not the mystery in the distance is a form of idolatry—a mode of worship supposedly rejected by Muslims—although some fundamentalists indulge in it to the point of murder. Literalism is a common but fatal error that even Sufis can make, apparently, and it was miserable for me to sit around in a prison house where the word of a religion felt all-important, and my own language so useless. It didn't help that I had no pride to fall back on. Boodiin was right when he said, "You have made a mistake." But "Mistakes are human" was no consolation. I thought about suicide every day.

Death would have been easy in Somalia. AK-47s lay around like junk. In Galkayo, the notion of grabbing a rifle to shoot a few pirates, and then myself, started to seem not just desirable but moral, because it would have saved a lot of people a great deal of trouble. It would have spared any SEAL team the dizzying risk of a mission. I knew that my family and colleagues were working to get me out, but thinking about so much money and trouble devoted to the cause of my freedom brought me close to violence. It still haunted me that "Mustaf Mohammed Sheikh," the pirate we'd interviewed in Hobyo, may have been present at Rolly's ankle-hanging. It haunted me that Rolly had been abused after my leap from the ship, that Digsi might have turned on Gerlach to arrange my kidnapping, that Digsi and "Mustaf" may have planned everything from the start. Other journalists had made similar runs from Galkayo to Hobyo without getting nabbed. God knows I'd screwed up; God knows I shouldn't have come. Now I had a long time to stew over my mistakes, the way a prisoner has years to consider his crimes.

But still. Why me?

"A suicide is always a bankrupt, always a human being in a blind alley," wrote Aleksandr Solzhenitsyn in *The Gulag Archipelago*, marveling at the number of Soviet prisoners who did not commit suicide. "If these millions of helpless and pitiful vermin still did not put an end to themselves—this meant some kind of invincible feeling was alive inside them. Some very powerful idea."

I steered around the question of suicide on some days only by cold logic. An adult who committed suicide "did not obviously love you"—I returned to this idea more than once while I brooded about my dad. I understood the corollary, sometimes with gritted teeth. Killing myself would have meant defeat for everyone I loved.

I remembered the flaming monks in Vietnam, the discipline and detachment that expressed itself in fire. I remembered what I'd read in the Bible—the Book of Job, the Gospels—and I remembered my Stoicism, not straight from the philosophers but from an essay about Epictetus, also by Richard Mitchell. In one chapter of his book *The Gift of Fire*, Mitchell revived the ancient but surprising idea that a victim suffers only by his own consent. Whining and self-pity do nothing but screw up the pain. "To be sick, or to suffer, is inevitable," wrote Mitchell, "but to become bitter and vindictive in sickness and suffering, and to surrender to irrationality, supposing yourself the innocent and virtuous victim of the evil intentions of the world, is not inevitable. The appropriate answer to the question, Why me? is the other question, Why not me?"

This idea helped in Somalia. A sense of victimhood and self-pity in those prison houses was as easy to contract as a contagious disease. But remembering Epictetus, however secondhand, boiled a good deal of neurosis away.

XIII

By August, I hadn't spoken to my mother in more than seven months, and in the poisonous environment of those pirate houses I couldn't tell the difference between punishment and brutal caprice. It occurred to me, with a sense of horror, that my mother might die while I languished in a concrete room. A lot of people might die. Relatives, friends, presidents, popes. The pirates offered me scraps of information about the world outside, but the hot, anonymous days had smeared the distinction between life and death, fact and lie, punishment and ordinary suffering. When I asked Bashko for a shortwave radio, he said, "Okay!" but nothing happened. Scabies developed on my thighs. Abdinuur brought some kind of salve, but the condition never cleared up. Nothing connected, nothing made sense. Even though I made hesitant friendships with two or three guards, I could never expect a pirate to tell me the truth, and a diet of lies can wear you down like a diet of Big Macs.

Late in August, we returned to the Pirate Villa, where I learned that the phone-call blackout was in fact a very specific punishment. "We are trying to pressure your mother," Abdurrahman said with an easygoing smile, as if sense and logic were on his side.

One afternoon in September, Dhuxul and Yoonis turned up at the Pirate Villa. I had never seen Dhuxul there before, so for most of the morning I felt jittery. He lay sideways in the entry hall, wooden prosthetic leaning behind him, and chewed khat with his men where I could see him. I thought, *He's here for a reason*, and sure enough, we piled into Land Cruisers late in the morning for a long trip to the bush.

"We will make a video," Yoonis explained. "But this time the men will have to beat you up. Then you will finally go free."

"Oh, sure," I mumbled.

We drove for an hour. The tediousness of these excursions into the Somali waste was interrupted only by Dhuxul's cruel imagination. We stopped near a stand of bushes and thorn trees, and the men wrapped their heads in keffiyehs, walked me around to a particular branch, and forced me to squat so they could tie my hands in a stress position behind my back. Madobe looped the rope around the branch and shoved his bare foot into the base of my spine to tighten it. I shouted. Abdurrahman aimed his digital camera.

"You people are insane," I told him.

No one looked me in the eye. Yoonis interrogated me: "What is your full name?" "What is your father's name?" and so on. When they released me, I quivered with rage. We sat for a while in the autumn sun and waited for the sky to darken. Dhuxul told me, through Yoonis, that my mother was in the last stages of negotiation. She'd flown to Europe, he said; she was waiting there now. "It will not be long before your suffering is over." I thought about it all the way back to Galkayo, where we settled in Dhuxul's house, and I decided they wouldn't have placed me in a stress position to make a dramatic video if they were so confident of a ransom.

Therefore, I wasn't on the verge of liberty.

So.

Why did Mom fly to Europe?

Assuming Dhuxul hadn't lied, I could think of two reasons. One would be a wedding. My cousin in Cologne must have postponed her marriage to her longtime boyfriend because I had vanished in Somalia. Maybe she'd quit waiting; maybe Mom had traveled to Germany for the reunion and the champagne.

The other reason would be a funeral. Oma was eighty-nine.

I spent several days having a slow emotional breakdown, because I couldn't tell whether I should mourn my grandmother or not. I studied the men with fierce mistrust, the way a child might focus on sometimes friendly adults who also flog him. I looked for omens in the yard. I studied a spool of razor wire installed on Dhuxul's compound wall and watched the planes rumbling across the cobalt sky for clues to whether Oma was alive or dead. The trade-off between a book about these cruel and ridiculous people and a few more hours or days with my grandmother felt like an ashen contract with the devil, a stupid thing to entertain, and the panicked unawareness of whether I had *any* more time, or whether that sweet woman was already gone, racked my heart. I hadn't loved her enough. I hadn't loved anyone enough. I couldn't come close to repaying the lifetime of love I'd received, and what could I do about it now? Hurl myself through Dhuxul's razor wire? Murder pirates? Howl? I wanted to howl, and just recovering from an evil video in the bush on a grim, sweat-sodden mattress felt insufficient. I raged in silence. I had a core of burning hay. The sorrow tensed the fibers of my skinny muscles and I was unable to sleep for hours, until I just passed out.

I demanded a radio again from Dhuxul, thinking, *I really deserve something from these fuckers now.*

The fat boss mumbled something in his bleak voice and limped away on his wooden leg. The men must have noticed my distress. To cheer up their obviously sour hostage they ordered restaurant food, and we all ate spiced and greasy rice with vegetables and goat, as well as sambusi, which came wrapped in newspaper. The sambusi shop happened to send big scraps of some English-printed newspaper, which we used for napkins, and I spent the afternoon piecing together torn broadsheet pages from the *Gulf News*. For the first time in a year and a half—since my radio had disappeared when we first boarded the *Naham 3*—I started to collect scraps of insight into the disheartening course of the planet.

The disconnect is strange to think about now. Four months

earlier, my grandmother had fallen asleep in her house in Holland after complaining about a stomach flu. She'd placed a glass of water on the bed stand, rolled down the shutters, and closed the door. In the morning, my aunt, who lived in the house, woke up to do an hour's worth of kitchen work before she suspected a problem. Another aunt in Cologne dreamed on the same morning that Oma had invited her to open a window. "You'll like it," Oma had said in the dream. "The fresh air is nice."

My good-humored grandmother died on her bed in May. I had no way of knowing that, no way of divining that Mom had already flown to Holland to see her buried in a cemetery on the north edge of the village, where my grandfather had rested for years; or that Mom had spent three days in Europe without giving a number to Somalis or hinting to any pirate that she had left Redondo Beach. So the idea that she was waiting around for my imminent release in September—this wild idea that led to a fanciful, but not irrelevant, emotional rupture—must have been dreamed up by Dhuxul.

XIV

Several mornings later, after a bleak dream, I scribbled in my notebook:

CHICKEN SATAY

Crushed peanuts, coconut milk, red chili, soy sauce,
shallots, lime
Rice

Bashko served me a breakfast of sullen beans and oversweet tea. Someone had cooked them with well water. I stretched out on my mattress afterward with stomach cramps, and the dream made me want to see my grandmother again. The doubt that I would, and the grief, came in long uncertain waves.

I was trying not to let the guards see any emotion when Dhuxul limped into the room and handed me a battered shortwave radio.

Part 8

STRONGER THAN DIRT

1

Over a year and a half, I had missed a new pope, a new president of France, and Syria's deepening civil war. Young terrorists had bombed the Boston Marathon, and Hurricane Sandy had flooded New York and New Jersey. Philip Roth had announced his retirement. Chinua Achebe, Margaret Thatcher, and Gore Vidal had died. All of it had rippled in the distance while I rotted on my mattress. It shouldn't have mattered, but writers are social animals, whether they like it or not, and now, by holding the radio to my ear and pacing the floor of my room, I could pick up faint programs from the BBC.

My sense of the current date had weakened after the fistfights and confusion over the *Naham 3*'s calendar pages; it had never recovered. By listening to the World Service, I figured out the real date and compared it with tentative guesses I had scratched in my notebook. I was seventeen days off.

The hour of news in the morning added an interlude of distant conversation to my daily routine. On some days I caught another broadcast, Radio Sultanate of Oman, and I gathered from the existence of this station that Oman had an expatriate scene large enough to demand English-language programming. The music hour featured awful top-forty hits and an odd British host who read the local papers out loud. He gave us tales of cars washed away in wadi floods, twins abandoned in a Muscat park, a fisherman killed by a leaping stingray, and the beneficent public-spending habits of certain Omani princes—all recited in a rakish Midlands accent over the galloping, whistling theme from *The Good, the Bad and the Ugly*.

His name was Fike, apparently. He called himself "Fike on the

Mike," and he interpreted his top-forty mandate with a loose sense of time, digging back twenty or thirty years to play hits from the same week in 1986, or 1979, which didn't always improve the song list but sometimes reminded me of home.

Blondie, Donna Summer, a band called M (which had one big hit, "Pop Muzik"), and Rod Stewart had dominated the radio in 1979, while various car-pool moms drove me and a pack of other kids to and from elementary school. Their songs playing over my tinny shortwave radio conjured the cracked asphalt, the square un-graceful cars, the fluorescent-lit supermarkets, and the cinemas sticky with spilled Coke that I still associated with 1970s L.A.

A few months before my father killed himself, we went to see *Cannonball Run*, a screwball comedy about street racers driving across America. The film was retrograde in every way, from its gen-der politics to its celebrity cast, but Dad loved it. Burt Reynolds was his favorite actor, and the jumpsuited women must have distracted him from his addictions. I loved it, too. Thinking about the movie in Galkayo loosened something, a resistance or a mistrust, maybe a lifelong defensive posture against the innocent, corrupted, awk-ward, hopeful, stagnant, sun-beaten suburb of my childhood.

I had astronaut wallpaper in my bedroom, and I liked model rockets, those cardboard tubes with plastic fins and parachute-loaded nose cones. We would set up the spindly launchpads in a brush-grown field behind our house in Northridge, and Dad came out to make sure we found a dirt patch sufficiently clear of weeds to avoid starting a brush fire. The rockets went *Pssssssssssssssstt* like a deflating balloon and shot into the cloud-streaked firmament over L.A. They popped apart near the top of the arc and came floating down, or twisting, depending on the state of their easily tangled chutes. The tangled ones landed hard and bounced in the weedy dirt.

I don't know what Dad dreamed about back then, and I never asked. While he sank into addiction I was too busy resenting him. I remembered the bitter criticisms and the shouting, but at the same time, of course, he would have tilled his own dreams into my head. He wanted me to study science. I almost *did* study science. Maybe the instinct I had from age twelve that something besides a heart attack had sabotaged a man I considered all-powerful was what drove me to books. He would have been disappointed—he didn't even like to read. His late notes to me were misspelled and half-coherent, either from booze or a pain-distracted mind, and for his son to become a *writer* would have been a catastrophe for his Northridge dreams, for all the love he had tried to express.

Maybe every suicide is an apocalyptic gesture, a last-ditch howl at the moon. Even the disciplined self-immolation of Thich Quang Duc had an element of drama, and sometimes I plotted the best way to go out in glory and gunfire. I had strong urges to do something irreversible. But it occurred to me that Mom didn't deserve to have two men in her life die by suicide. An adult who committed suicide "did not obviously love you," by my own definition, and on some afternoons this line of thinking was all that kept me alive. (Even such clear-sounding logic took an effort of will and cognition to arrange in my head. I wasn't entirely sane.)

Around this time I started to pray. Reading the Bible on the *Naham 3* had not returned me to strict religious belief, but prayer did help me articulate my most self-destructive emotions, so it became a way to balance my brain and remind myself of the forces raging overhead. It let me sort out what was, and wasn't, within my power.

Writing in notebooks had the same effect, and I remembered that the poet Derek Walcott had once compared composition to prayer. "Any serious attempt to try to do something worthwhile is ritualistic," he said in an interview. "If one thinks a poem is coming on—in spite of the noise of the typewriter, or the traffic outside the window, or whatever—you do make a retreat, a withdrawal into some kind of silence that cuts out everything around you. What you're taking on is really not a renewal of your identity but actually a renewal of your *anonymity,* so that what's in front of you becomes more important than what you are."

This detached but inward-turning concentration became the most important aspect of prayer for me in those prison houses, rather than the belief in a personal God who could hear and intercede. "Renewing my anonymity" maintained my sanity. Epictetus meant nothing else when he wrote about removing your self from suffering. "If you regard yourself as a man and as a part of some whole," Epictetus told his students, "it is fitting for you now to be sick and now to make a voyage and run risks, and now to be in want, and on occasion to die before your time. Why, then, are you vexed? Would you have someone else be sick of a fever now, someone else go on a voyage, someone else die?"

II

Sometimes I heard uncertain, hovering noises at night, and I woke up to find my guards listening in dead silence to a staticky phone for signals and interference. I was never in favor of cutting-edge surveillance technologies before I became a hostage, but now I fantasized about stealthy, invasive aircraft of any kind, even insect-size drones, those insidious but supposedly still experimental flying robots that could imitate beetles or dragonflies and cling to ceilings to spy on people.* On quiet, nervous nights when some force appeared to be listening, I would cross myself on my mattress and pray in a silence-breaking, conversational voice. The Somalis never interrupted. They respected prayer, though my noisiness made them uneasy. They thought drones could pick up voices. I decided to accept the pirates' superstition and use this perhaps fanciful technology to my advantage. (Just in case.) During each prayer I included an explanation, in clear German, of my whereabouts and added a description of the house and yard and the specific location of my room. (Just in case.)

My prayers, in other words, had a practical side. The miseries of Somalia hadn't stripped away a fundamental cussedness about my situation. Good and bad were reversed for hostages, as Rolly had pointed out—"We are like the devil, they are like God"—so a "Fuck you" mental orientation kept alive our sense of right and wrong. It was hard to balance this justified rage with the pirates' arbitrary behavior, and it made nonviolent resistance tricky to practice. I wanted very much to be violent. So did my guards.

One day during Ramadan, for example, the men had confiscated my TV to watch it on the porch, where it blathered at high volume.

"Hey, can you turn that thing down?" I said in a loud voice.

"Michael! Be quiet!"

I lay in the heat on a thin woven mat in my sun-shot room; Dhuxul had gone to work. The TV was a constant source of tension. I couldn't see why this supposed gift from the boss should make my life miserable while it eased the tedium for my guards.

---

* Seen two years later in *Eye in the Sky*, a fictional thriller about an American drone strike in Eastleigh, the Somali neighborhood of Nairobi.

"Can you turn it down?" I said again after a while.

"Shut up!"

Someone turned up the volume.

"TURN IT DOWN," I roared, and Bashko came charging in with his rifle cocked. I felt ornery enough to fight him, just out of my head enough to leap to my feet and do whatever damage I could, so it took a deliberate act of will to keep myself quiet on the floor and watch to see how far Bashko would let his temper carry him. Violence unprovoked by a physical threat was against the rules for these men, and to test their limit I had to "renew my anonymity," or remove myself from the equation, mentally, so I could locate a fulcrum point between my temper and my self-control.

Near the end of 2013, Nelson Mandela died, and the BBC's coverage of his funeral lasted several days. The news electrified my guards. He was *their* hero, an African resistance leader who'd stood up to white supremacy. They sat there with rifles, like jailers, but identified with Mandela, who'd sat in jail. His greatness, of course, consisted in transcending both tribe and race, and the radio coverage led with his remarkable line from an interview after his release from prison in 1990. "As I walked out the door toward the gate that would lead to my freedom," he said on my battered little shortwave, "I knew if I didn't leave my bitterness and hatred behind, I'd still be in prison."

Rage remained my natural element in Galkayo, so forgiveness was elusive. Mandela had noted in his autobiography that white South African lawyers and judges under apartheid considered him a *"kaffir* lawyer." *Kaffir* is a nasty term in Afrikaans, close to *nigger* or *coon*; it derived from the Muslim slave trade. Arab traders used it to refer to non-Muslim African slaves, people it was halal to capture. The word had spread through European colonies in Africa as an epithet for slaves as early as the 1600s. I couldn't compare my situation to Mandela's—he'd suffered for the color of his skin over the better part of the twentieth century, without even leaving his country—but while I lived in Somalia, the label for me was *galo*, *kafir*, infidel, and in that sense I noticed a parallel.

Forgiveness for Mandela meant putting down a great deal of pride. Even when he was right, he'd learned to relinquish rage. He was a Methodist, but radio reports pointed out that he never trumpeted his beliefs, and by the time he died, no one could say in public where he went to church or how often. So the forgiveness he referred to as his real liberation from prison was nondenominational, human rather than distant, not mystical or in any sense out of reach.

I had time to think about that while I lay on the floor.

III

One day in early November I sat on the mattress at Dhuxul's house and leaned over some scraps of newspaper, waving away flies in the hot afternoon. Bashko sat in front of his pile of khat. He looked hopped up and bemused. At last he asked a question.

"Michael," he said. "America—*dukhsi?*"* *Are there flies in America?*

I shrugged. "Yes. But not like this."

"Europe?"

"No same-same."

He thought for a while and said, "Why? Nuclear?"

"Hah!"

Bashko wanted to know if the United States and Europe had

---

* Pronounced *dersi*.

rid their countrysides of insect pests by detonating nuclear bombs. "Interesting idea," I said, and tried to explain that the real reason was less apocalyptic. Cleaner bathrooms and kitchens, I told him; no goats in the street. "Of course, parts of America still have many *dukhsi*," I said. "But conditions are different."

"Malaria?"

"Small-small. It depends on the health of the animals. And the people."

Bashko asked me about camels, mules, cows, and goats, which led to questions about the most common meat. We discussed how to say "cow" and "chicken" in Somali—*lo* and *digaag*—and I may have drawn a sketch of the edible bird.

"Okay!" said Bashko.

This unusual conversation had consequences in California. Word swept the rumor kitchen that Michael's favorite food was *digaag*, that I missed *digaag* more than anything, and Fuad informed my mother that I had made a special request for chicken, so the pirates would slaughter one for me if she wired a quick five hundred dollars.

"I told him no way," Mom said.

Dhuxul's prison house stood in an urban-pastoral part of Galkayo, next to houses as well as open fields, and it was common for us to hear bleating herds of goats, fussing pigeons, donkeys, chickens, and mating cats. After lunch that afternoon I heard a kitten cry and glanced up from my notebook. I'd never heard such a helpless noise inside the compound.

"*Bisad?*" I asked Bashko. *Cat?*

"Yes."

"Mother?"

"Finished," said Bashko.

I didn't want to interfere if the mother had just left on a hunt. But I had fish and powdered milk.

We listened to another hour of ragged crying before I asked to see the animal. Bashko disappeared into a garbage-strewn kitchen in one corner of the compound, semidetached from the house. He returned with a frightened young cat the size of my hand, with orange, flea-ridden tiger fur.

The men watched in fascination. I opened a can of tuna and set it on the floor. The kitten caught a whiff, buried his face in the meat, and let out a growl of pleasure so profound it made the pirates laugh. Good sign. A cat with an appetite for solid food was no longer a suckling. I thought he might like some milk.

There was no bowl or dish, so I asked Hashi to use a kitchen knife to cut the bottom off a plastic water bottle and make a small, rough-edged plastic tray. I mixed some milk and served it to the kitten, who lapped it up, shoving the plastic around the floor.

The cat must have been three or four weeks old. Male or female, I couldn't tell—everything was too furry—but I named the creature Jack because his fur was orange and the date was close to Halloween. After his can of unexpected tuna fish, Jack settled at one end of my mattress and fell asleep.

A stray cat was vermin to the guards, so Bashko, Hashi, and Farrah found my sentimentalism amusing. Madobe came out of his room and stared at me in disgust.

Once Jack had lost his innocence about seafood, we became good friends. He listened for my chains in the mornings; after my dawn visits to the toilet, he would mew and come running. Dhuxul noticed, but instead of banning the animal, he scolded the men in a dead and droning voice. The kitten could stay for now.

On the third night, Jack angered Madobe by creeping back and forth across the pirates' mat. When, inevitably, he crouched on the porch for a shit, Madobe swiped him against a wall. I slept through this commotion, but in the morning I noticed that Jack looked ill, or at least off-balance, and Bashko told me what had happened. He insisted on tying up the cat.

"You're kidding," I said. "Restrain him?"

"*Haa*, yes," he said. "Nighttime, only."

I glanced around the room. "Using what?"

There was no answer, so I let Jack roam free. When night fell, I told the Somalis to let him go where he pleased. The next morning, of course, he was gone. Bashko tried to explain that the mother cat had returned, so the guards had set Jack free. But later I heard an alternate story from Hashi. He said Madobe had thrown Jack over the wall.

"Because why?" I said.

"Because—Madobe."

"Fucking," I said.

No young animal had much of a chance in Galkayo; I knew that. I had also understood that Jack's term as a pet would be limited. But caring for a stray had reminded me of the pleasures of ordinary life.

Three days later, we heard a thin wail outside the compound wall. Someone opened the door and the kitten raced into my room.

"Jack!" I said.

He looked frantic, frightened, and thin. He hadn't found much to eat. *It sucks out there.* I opened a can of fish, and he feasted like a lion.

I'd missed him keenly. I tried to stifle my emotional reflex the way I tried to stifle my disgust at the flyblown filth in my room, or my urges for revenge, but even while I suppressed these instincts I knew it was a muffled and white-knuckled way to live. The kitten got to me. He was the only creature I had met since my leap from the ship who seemed to like me. Now that he'd returned, I decided to keep him around. I dug in my bag for a pair of underused long pants, which had a belt improvised from a frayed strip of sarong cloth; I tied this soft rope around Jack's middle, like a harness, and fastened the other end to a door handle. The fabric was long enough to let him sleep on the foot of my mattress, on a flattened part of the mosquito net. Bashko threw a rag behind the door for use as a kitty toilet. This system worked. Jack established a spot and slept there. At night sometimes he attacked my feet through the net, which woke me up, but he kept out of trouble with the guards.

At last I subjected him to a bath. I carried him to the shower room in one hand, with my soap and shampoo in the other, to give him a lather and a rinse. He didn't appreciate this treatment at all. But in the Somali heat his coat dried quickly, and his color changed from dun and foxlike to something like furry peach.

IV

Jack had a long Abyssinian face, and he could be clumsy as well as ridiculously cheerful. He grew like a weed. But his furry nether regions failed to develop like a boy's, so I started to think he was female.

"What should your name be?" I asked the kitten. "If you're a girl and all."

I decided to call her Julianne, after the actress Julianne Moore (another redhead).

One morning when Yoonis turned up at the house, I made a joke to Bashko—out of Yoonis's earshot—about the cat returning from the chaos outside to eat free meals at the house. Bashko's eyes lit up.

"Yoonis, same-same!" he said, and I laughed out loud.

The joke distracted me from an obvious fact. Yoonis, as a translator, showed his face only when the bosses had organized a phone call or a video. Bashko caught me unprepared the next day with an

order to pack my things. "Video, video," he whispered. He promised
we would return to Dhuxul's, so we left Julianne in the room, har-
nessed, with a supply of milk and an open can of fish. We drove out
to the desert bush for another pointless act of pirate theater in front
of another arching cluster of thorns. These excursions took hours;
they were object lessons in wasted time. But under this particular
cluster of thorns, I first heard the name Abdi Yare, which the pirates
had used in phone calls to California. It was a shape-shifting name,
a label applied to more than one pirate, but the rumor in California
was that my guards were tired of holding me—"Abdi Yare" had run
short of cash—so he seemed willing to bargain.

We returned to Dhuxul's and idled in the compound while the
men packed our things. Hashi found Julianne in my bedroom and
handed her to me in a blanket. "*Bisad*, okay," he said, and instead
of staying at Dhuxul's, we drove to the Pirate Villa with the kitten
trembling in my lap.

That night I heard swirling sounds in the sky, an erratic and
maddening noise like a turboprop landing and taking off. Galkayo's
airport lacked runway lights—it closed for business after dark—so
I think all of us had visions of SEALs using the airport for a staging
area. The rolling-thunder sound continued for a week and filled me
with a strange and hopeful trepidation. It frightened the pirates, and
one of them woke up in such a state of nerves he needed pills to
calm him down. The next morning he sat against a wall in the en-
tryway, smoking a cigarette with sagging lips, and the others made
fun of him. They told me to call his name. "Xiiro," I said,* and he
just looked around, glassy eyed.

By now I just wanted freedom or death. I was ornery enough to

* Pronounced *hero*.

suffer until my price fell to something manageable—I refused to yearn for a sudden, splash-out ransom of many millions—but my patience had shriveled, and I would have welcomed violence. I wanted pirates dead. These weren't my rules. Death, and threats of death, were currency in Somalia; pirates wielded them for profit and fun.

One morning I happened to ask Bashko for news about the *Naham 3*, and he came up with a surprise.

"*Naham 3* finished!" he said. "*Albedo*, sink!"

"What happened?"

"Finished! All crew, Somalia."

I didn't understand the sequence of events, but apparently the *Naham 3* had been moved from the *Orna* and tethered to a new ship, the *Albedo*, which had sunk. The bosses had tried to run an emergency skiff to save the hostages and pirates from the foundering ship. But several of the original twenty-three hostages from the *Albedo*, and about twenty Somalis, had drowned.

"All died," he said.

"Jesus." I squinted. "Pirates no swim?"

"No."

I nodded. "*Naham 3* okay?"

"Yes, okay. Not died."

"All crew, Hobyo?"

Bashko hesitated. "Eh—Hobyo, Harardhere," he said.

Bashko's details were off, but overall he'd told the truth. The *Albedo* sank in the summer of 2013, because parts of the hull had rusted through. The *Naham 3* stayed on the water, somehow, for another month, but by late summer the Somalis had abandoned both vessels.

"One Chinese," Bashko admitted, "is died."

"What? Who?"

He described Jie, the young Chinese crewman, and said he had died after a hunger strike. Jie was the good-humored, fey-looking kid who had made the joke about "cargo" when I showed him my new soccer jersey. One part of grief is fear, and the proximity of death—news of a fellow hostage, even if he was miles away—left me grim and melancholy.

"He go crazy," Bashko said.

"I wonder why."

V

Julianne was a pain in the ass, like any decent kitten. When she wandered free of her cloth rope during the day, she drove Madobe nuts. She scampered around the Pirate Villa yard to inspect laundry buckets and potted plants, and more than once I glanced out to see Madobe's tall shape lumber after something unseen, like a ballplayer trying to field a tricky grounder. He would bring in Julianne and dump her in front of my mattress with a fierce, hissing complaint in Somali, shaking his splayed hands in frustration. *That thing won't sit still.*

One night, a plane made a deep arc over Galkayo, and I heard the pirates whisper, "AC!" They went quiet and tense, and I fell asleep with Julianne perched on the foot of my mattress. Around midnight, Issa woke me up. "Michael, come on. Go out." Groggily, I let him unlock the chains. I had to gather my things and roll up the mosquito net. Pirates packed the car while Julianne stood in the middle of the concrete room, looking confused, tethered by the long cloth to a window shutter.

Bashko led me into the courtyard while the pirates emptied the house.

"Bashko," I said. "*Bisad.*"

"*Bisad*, no," he said. "*Bisad* free."

I squatted next to the car, draped in my blanket, looking up at the black, starry sky. For months I'd felt like a man underwater; for months I had drowned the most subtle and human feelings of sympathy and hope because they would have exposed me to emotional destitution. The cat had revived them. Bashko came over to explain that we were moving back to Dhuxul's, but he would stay behind to clean things up. He would feed the cat. Then he would set her free.

"Okay, Michael?"

I shrugged. It was long expected, but not okay.

We drove to Dhuxul's in a hurry and I had to sleep somehow in the humid concrete room. Through the doorway and the arabesque arch I could still see a spatter of stars. The pirates had feared a raid. I wondered if surveillance had traced us to this house. Weird feelings asserted themselves. *Can they find me, or not?* I had no idea what the military wanted, I couldn't tell why I was still here, and there was no way to measure my own losses in character and ordinary love except by the numbness in my blood. Grief overwhelmed me—not just for Julianne, but also for Jie and all the crewmen and the stupid waste of lives and time that seemed to trail these pirates like a stink. I'd never seen such a powerful human force of chaos at such close range. Pirates had blinkered, selfish habits—they had a weaker instinct for cooperation than any group of humans I had ever met—and they were too shiftless and khat-addled to clean up their own mess in Galkayo, which resulted in a stupid and self-aggrandizing pirate society, a suicidal culture in which gunshots rang in the street and gunmen were winners, as Fuad had written to my mother, "while educated ones are losers in life."

I'd read a theory somewhere that pirate behavior tended to increase during lulls between empires, because when tension between great powers existed, bands of pirates or guerrillas had less room to operate. They tended to fall under the ordered influence of one side or the other. In periods of transition—let's say after the fall of Communism—the center gave way, and more forces acted on their own. The French historian Fernand Braudel had noticed this pattern when he studied the Mediterranean of the 1570s. The Spanish Armada had overwhelmed Ottoman imperial ships at the Battle of Lepanto (where Cervantes had fought), and tensions had slackened. "The end of the conflict between the great states," he wrote, "brought to the forefront of the sea's history that secondary form of war, piracy." The theory held for Somalia because Siad Barre had collapsed after his Cold War sponsorships dried up. But it couldn't quite account for the century and a half of relative peace on the oceans *before* the Cold War, the surprising lull in piracy that had started only under pressure from a minor breakaway republic (the United States) in the early 1800s.

I came up with another theory in the hot concrete room. Barbary pirates were a fringe expression of a long-simmering war between Christians and Muslims. They had existed before the Battle of Lepanto, and they had existed afterward. Tensions between empires may have let up after that battle, but the struggle didn't end for good. Mediterranean piracy was a "secondary form of war" that also flourished during eras of primary war, not unlike our own, when imams find political reasons to fire up their people by emphasizing Verses of the Sword.

"Man, who in his own selfish affairs is a coward to the backbone, will fight for an idea like a hero," says Don Juan in Shaw's marvelous play *Man and Superman.* Sure. And ideas about the Koran gave my guards an excuse to hold me captive. But they weren't unique in the history of human rights abuses. An Argentinian journalist named Jacobo Timerman had counted the number of high-minded and lethal ideas fueling violence in his country while he sat in a government prison during the 1970s.

> Rural and urban Trotskyite guerrillas; right-wing Perónist death squads; armed terrorist groups of the large labor unions . . . terrorist groups of Catholic rightists organized by cabals who opposed Pope John XXIII . . . Hundreds of other organizations involved in the eroticism of violence existed, small units that found ideological justification for armed struggle in a poem by Neruda or an essay by Marcuse.*

Ideas were just indicators, like words. They could inspire a person to great heights, or they could stodge the flow of instinct and love. Some ideas worked as excuses for tribal violence. Even fine ideas could drive people nuts, which meant that the foliage of an idea depended on its mental and emotional soil. There was entropy and violence in the world, I thought, and that was interesting. But there was also entropy and violence in the human heart.

One morning Issa leaned against a wall and fiddled with his phone. He always looked pensive, so I sometimes thought he was clever, or at least less gullible than the others. Now he said, "Michael," and showed me a doctored photo of a smiling African man with a single, centered eye in his forehead. He'd found it on the internet.

"Real?" he said.

"A one-eyed man?" I said, and he gave a bashful laugh. It wasn't a joke—he really wanted my opinion.

"No, no," I said, a little startled by the question.

---

* From *Prisoner Without a Name, Cell Without a Number.*

He nodded and went back to browsing through pictures on his phone.

"Issa," I said after a while, "what will you do if I go free?"

"I will go out," he said, and waved his hand. "From Somalia."

"With your money?"

"Yes."

"When Michael is free, Issa will be free?" I said with a crooked smile.

"Yes."

"Where will you go?"

"To Italy," he said. "Boat, from Libya."

Stories had mounted on the radio about a fresh push of migrants to Europe. Issa stood to earn several thousand dollars from my ransom, and with that kind of money he could live well in Somalia. Did he really dream about a complicated voyage to Italy? The overland route through Ethiopia and Sudan to Libya would be dangerous and long.

"Somalia to Libya—how?" I said.

"No problem."

Maybe he had good smuggling connections; maybe he was just being coy.

"You're crazy," I told him.

This was the end of 2013. Chaos in Libya had opened paths for smugglers to move more people across the Mediterranean, and lethal capsizings had become regular news. I thought of the humanity pouring into the sea as a mass of strangers, a class of people called "migrants" who would be unknowable until you met them, here and there, in Europe. But one of them sat right in front of me. Calling my feelings "mixed" was an understatement. My feelings whistled and pissed like a tropical storm—resentment, fury, pity, alarm. Issa held violent power over my fate, he could kill me if I tried anything funny, and both of us wanted out of Somalia. But his captive would move home to the relative privilege of Berlin—if I got out at all—while my Kalalshnikov-armed jailer harbored the grand dream of moving to Europe on a tottering Mediterranean boat.

VI

Near the end of 2013, negotiations budged again, and Mom had reason to hope the pirates would capitulate. She had to wonder for the first time about the logistics of my release. "We thought they might come to an agreement for $1.5 million," she said, "and we thought we'd better have a plan in place to get you out of there." She contacted a retired British officer in Nairobi, Colonel John Steed, who knew how to organize transportation for pirate hostages once a ransom had been paid. Steed ran a charity within the U.N. Office on Drugs and Crime called the Hostage Support Program.* "Fair degree of trust required," he wrote to my mother. "Pirates do sign a faxed agreement, and have only gone back on agreements twice."

Steed put Mom in touch with a pilot named Derek, a charter flight operator who lived in Nairobi and had long experience with missions in Somalia and other parts of Africa. He named a steep fee, but added, "Take note that I will be totally exposed and on my own."

While Mom considered this offer, her mysterious intermediary, Sheikh Mohamud, insisted on receiving his own fee of one hundred thousand dollars, effectively raising the ransom. Derek asked

---

* Now the Hostage Support Partnership, not part of the U.N.

questions among his contacts in Galkayo and reported that he could verify the bosses involved in my case, including Ali Duulaay and "Abdi Yare," but he couldn't establish a credible identity for Sheikh Mohamud. "He does not fit in," wrote Derek. "Sheikh Mohamud is also the name of the current president of Somalia.* So that does draw some suspicion."

To me, "Sheikh Mohamud" also resembles "Mustaf Mohammed Sheikh," the supposed name of the pirate we interviewed in Hobyo. Maybe the resonance was deliberate. But "Sheikh Mohamud" is also a clichéd and common name in Somalia, almost like "Fred."

Several days later, Mom received a phone call from this shadowy Sheikh Mohamud, saying he was no longer in Galkayo and did not want to see Abdi Yare or any of the other bosses again.

"They have insulted me," he said, and disappeared.

VII

I knew nothing about these negotiations. But Bashko and Issa insisted that my family, and my governments, were the causes of our constant location changes. We were still locked up together because of *my* clan's intransigence. Around New Year's the pirates drove me through the streets of Galkayo in broad daylight, blindfolded, to a house protected by extra-high compound walls, with words painted over the doors indicating it had once been an office or a school. We

---

* Hassan Sheikh Mohamud became president of the Federal Republic of Somalia in 2012.

called this new villa Abdi Yare's House. No one told me the meaning of the move, but a left-behind sheet of paper taped to the powder blue wall in the largest room had cartoonish, classroom-style computer graphics and several lines of Somali, along with a slogan in English:

TO BE A PIRATE IS TO BE IN DANGER!

Someone had a sense of humor. Abdi Yare's House had previously served as a pirate reeducation center.

Outside the front window I could see a minaret heavy with loudspeakers. By evening, after two calls to prayer, it was obvious that the blaring sacred song would vibrate through our concrete walls, like an AC/DC concert, five times a day. It reminded me of a story credited to Kabir, a fifteenth-century Hindu poet from a Muslim family who once wrote a whimsical dialogue between himself and a fictional mullah. "Why must you shout," Kabir asks the mullah, "as if Allah is deaf?"

Bashko talked in vague but optimistic terms about my ransom negotiations, as if he expected fabulous wealth to rain down from several glittering cities at once—Los Angeles, Berlin, Washington, D.C. His optimism threw me for a loop. Before my kidnapping, I had believed that professional kidnappers all over the world knew that America, in particular, maintained a strict no-ransom policy. But it was news to Bashko.

One day, after Somali negotiators evidently tried to lower the pirates' expectations by telling them no money could be expected from Washington, Bashko stalked into my room and said, "Why?" with a look of mocking sarcasm. "America no money?"

I shrugged.

"America, no money for thieves," I said, and tried to explain the rationale: if governments paid out for every hostage, thieves would keep taking more. "Criminals, everywhere," I said, and mimed a person nabbing a hostage.

But I was no longer sure I believed it. Ransoms did fund more kidnappings, and a no-ransom policy could slow them down. But not deter them: Americans, like Europeans, were targets no matter what. Greed was too fundamental. Relative wealth was its own incentive. My kidnappers were romantics who thrived on dreams of a life-changing fortune dropping from the sky. To Bashko it seemed the height of American evil that helicopters might arrive before a bundle of cash, because he listened to reports on the radio every morning about billion-dollar bailouts, catastrophic Wall Street losses, interstellar arms deals, and trillions in public debt. When they did the math it seemed incredible that some slice of that action couldn't be wired to Somalia. The gulf between my privilege and their poverty was so vast that my own vile state—bearded and filthy and chained every night, rotting into my mattress like a castaway—was readable as the price of a poor man's ambition.

These justifications did not make me mellow. They did not ease my mind. I didn't want my guards to move to Europe, and I didn't think they deserved a cent of my cash. I even thought a no-ransom policy worth its salt in Washington should require a consistent military response. Otherwise, criminals like Issa or Bashko, not just in Somalia but throughout the world—young men who heard about the fantastic wealth of the West but spent little time boning up on divergent hostage policies, who hardly knew the difference between Britain and France, and who, in any case, had seen enough government corruption to scoff at principled statements by the State Department—would never learn how dangerous it could be to kidnap a Westerner.

"Michael," Bashko said, his temper heating up. "Because, *adiga. Aniga*—no America, no Europe!"

Because of you, he was saying, *I can't go to America. I can't go to Europe.*

"Because of me?" I said. "Why?"

Drones around the *Naham 3* had photographed him while he guarded us on the upper deck, he said. He was a recognizable pirate; his face would be in databases, and for the rest of his life he would have to stay out of the most promising nations on earth. Bashko's international prospects were dimmed, and it was all Michael's fault.

"I did not kidnap me," I told him. "I did not make you a pirate."

"Because—*adiga*—Somalia!" he shouted in our broken language. *Because you came to Somalia!* "Fucking!"

"Fucking," I agreed.

One afternoon I glanced up from my mattress at Abdi Yare's House and noticed that Bashko had left the room. His rifle lay on a mat. I considered grabbing it. The room was large and empty, with a glare of sunlight streaming in from the concrete yard. I tried to judge from the sound of movements and hushed voices where the guards were. They would have bedded down in two separate rooms.

Bashko came in, noticed the gun, picked it up nimbly by the muzzle, and sat down with a brilliant smile.

"Problem!" he said, meaning the unattended firearm.

I smiled back.

The house was silent that afternoon, because an Orion had flown overhead. Bashko rested his rifle behind him. He locked his elbows around his knees and munched a stem of khat. His eyes were fervid. I had just been wondering how many of the guards I could shoot before they got to me.

"Michael," he said. "America, coming—*adiga* finished."

If the Americans come, you will be killed.
"I know."
"Why no money?" he asked.
I shrugged.

VIII

From my mattress at Abdi Yare's House I could sometimes see the moon, large and blurry, like a fat silver lantern over the compound wall. The light spilled in through a metal screen. Moon sightings were so rare for me in Somalia they came as a shock: the prison houses kept me locked away from the drama of the natural world. I couldn't count the number of clear, moonstruck nights I had missed in Somalia, or (even worse) the number I had left to enjoy. Somewhere in Paul Bowles's novel *The Sheltering Sky* the lead character wonders the same thing. "Everything happens only a certain number of times, and a very small number really," he says. "How many more times will you remember a certain afternoon of your childhood, an afternoon that is so deeply a part of your being that you can't even conceive of your life without it? Perhaps four, five times more, perhaps not even that. How many more times will you watch the full moon rise? Perhaps twenty."

I wondered if Mom could see the same full moon from California. No reason why not. I was lost, but I hadn't left the planet. I had just quit indulging in hope for the future. I wandered, instead, in the underworld of the past, and on one of these nights I remembered my father, just before he died, picking me up from a guitar lesson wearing his clothes from work, chewing a toothpick, broodily distracted behind a pair of plastic sunglasses. In spite of his mood he was full of enthusiasm for something I had written to commemorate my sixth-grade graduation. Those few sentimental lines had melted him. He wanted a copy. I can't remember what they said. But this memory in Somalia disrupted the story I had continued to tell myself, all these months and years, about our relationship. I wondered if we would have fought like hell over my career.

Not loving enough was the crucial failure, like not appreciating the moon. I never told Dad how much I wanted him home when I was twelve, because I was twelve, and because I had no idea that I would see him again maybe four, maybe five times more in my life.

His alcoholic sense of waste in Northridge must have been a powerful distraction from the simple thrill of living. My childhood memories were charged with that thrill. The dry tedium of the suburbs hadn't beaten it down. It occurred to me in Somalia that I lacked my father's problem. I was learning to thrive in an ugly atmosphere. In spite of foul circumstances I had found a way to live. It's still hard to describe. Dad's disillusion sounded like bare-knuckled realism, but it proved to be a stubborn chemical ignorance of a beauty that surrounded us every day. Northridge, after all, could also be beautiful—a once fertile part of Southern California still dotted with sycamores, pines, and liquid amber trees, even cactus and banana trees. It had wildlife: possums and cougars, rattlesnakes and owls. The relative bleakness of Somalia had revived colorful memories of an awkward American boyhood, a chorus of strange people and cracked-asphalt schoolyards, graceless restaurants, dusty baseball diamonds, of polluting cars and stifling schoolrooms that were beautiful, too, and this weird superhuman beauty, like the power of the sun, had not even wavered when Dad shot himself in the chest.

After one of these horrible nights I woke up feeling shaken, frightened, but somehow cleaned out. I remembered that one point of a sublime poem by Saint Francis called "The Canticle of Brother Sun and Sister Moon" was love for the unlovable, an opening of the soul toward beauty as well as the ugly abomination of death.

A pirate tossed the clinking keys. I unlocked my chains and shuffled to the bathroom. I came back and waited for breakfast. Bashko, replacing the night-shift guard, delivered my ration of beans and sat against the wall, wrapped in a sarong. He listened to news on his phone.

A few stray flies showed an early-morning interest in the sugared beans. I waved them off.

"Michael," said Bashko after a while. "America, no money?"

I didn't want talk about it.

"*Bur'ad*, finished!" he went on. *Pirates are done for.*

"Oh, yeah?"

"*Bur'ad*, no ships," he said, cryptically.

I shrugged and finished eating, then retreated under my mosquito net and listened to the radio.

Bashko had placed his finger on an unpleasant fact. One reason I'd languished so long in Somalia was the decline of piracy off the coast. The *Naham 3* turned out to be the second-to-last vessel hijacked during the dramatic upswing in Somali piracy, the heyday between 2005 and 2012, and now the bosses invested money elsewhere—in foreign real estate, drug running, weapons smuggling, even human trafficking. Shipowners now sent cargo vessels past Somalia with armed teams on board; navies were helping to keep the peace. Hijackings off Somalia had all but ended in 2013 and '14, and the gangs clung to what they had. Including me.

On the radio I heard about a U.N. report announcing precisely what I had flown here to investigate—that piracy in Somalia had employed thousands of people in certain regions and towns. Illicit business had attracted capital to industries like boat repair, restaurants, and housing, and I wondered if turning the illicit movement of goods into something legitimate might not be far behind. While I rotted in Galkayo, in fact, work had started on the Hobyo waterfront to build a small port and to grade the dusty bush trails leading from the town. Members of the Galmudug government were even working to renovate Mussolini's Farmhouse. It was a comical act of whitewashing, and I wouldn't learn about it for months, but Hobyo elders and investors had started to convert the ruin where Rolly and Marc and I had lived into a quasi-government building known as the Villa Galmudug.

Also on the radio, I started to hear familiar voices. A Somalia expert I knew from the Hamburg trial, Stig Jarle Hansen, talked about al-Shabaab. A BBC reporter from Berlin, a friend named Damien McGuinness, now reported from Latvia. People's lives had moved on. Hearing Damien's voice unstuck my habit of resisting hope. It reminded me of busy restaurants in Berlin, of low lights and music, cigarette smoke and half-crumbled East German tenement buildings, especially the bar in one of those buildings where I used to gather friends for casual dinner and drinks. It cracked my practiced indifference to think about that life, and I missed them all with a crushing, lonely desire.

IX

During the first half of 2014, we moved between Abdi Yare's House and Dhuxul's house every four or five weeks, depending on aircraft noise, and Dhuxul decided to stash me in the corner of a larger, dimmer room at his house, away from the door, so I no longer had a view of the sky. My guards shut the bottom half of the steel shutters in this room, all day long, so I had to squint when I wanted to read or write. At night they closed the shutters completely.

I thought my colorful clothes could still flag the attention of planes, so I did laundry often. The outdoor bathroom at Dhuxul's was a semidetached chamber with no windows, and the pirates had to stand in the yard holding Kalashnikovs while I plunged my shorts and soccer jersey into a bucket of water and sudsed them up with Top-O-Mol. Sometimes they wouldn't let me out because of a plane in the sky. I started to wonder if the presence of armed men in the yard, on its own, was a clue to my location.

Laundry became a comforting ritual. My brain wandered to strange places while my hands did the work. Every African I'd met—Rolly as well as the pirates—referred to Top-O-Mol detergent as "O-Mol," which struck me as weird, because the company promoted the opposite nickname on each plastic satchel: TOP! I remembered Ahmed Dirie sitting under a thorn tree one afternoon in the bush, staring at a plastic satchel of the powder and coming up, finally, with "Top!"—which produced a rotten-toothed grin of surprise, as if he'd never studied the package before.

It dawned on me during a laundry session that they were echoing Omo, a brand of detergent African kids grew up with from Senegal to the Seychelles. That made me think about the pop-cultural power of a simple brand of soap, which reminded me of old Ajax detergent ads in the United States. They predated my childhood, but they'd left such an impression on a generation of American kids that both Tom Waits and Jim Morrison had made fun of the jingle in their songs. The old black-and-white commercials featured a knight in shining armor riding to the rescue of plumbers, diner cooks, and suburban housewives, while a jarring ridiculous chorus in the background sang, "Stronger than dirt! Stronger than dirt!"

I hummed this jingle to myself while I worked.

One day, Bashko denied me permission to wash my clothes. "Tomorrow!" he said, but the next day he also said no. This petty restriction moved me to rage. It eroded my slim but established set of rights. I stood up to mount a protest on my woven-plastic exercise mat. I said, "Washy-wash," in the same calm and patient tone I used to insist on trips to the bathroom before dawn. The tone must have irritated Madobe, because he stepped over in a quick fury to pull the mat from under my feet. I went straight down. Most of my weight landed hard on my twisted right leg, and there was intense pain from the top of my shin to my ankle, like a crack in wood. I took this rich opportunity to yell and swear. Bashko hollered back, brandishing his rifle. He ordered me to sit on my mattress in silence, and my next trip to the bathroom involved an excruciating limp.

By dinnertime I had declared a hunger strike.

"No *chum-chum*?" said Bashko when he tried to serve me food.

"No *chum-chum*," I said. "Because Madobe."

He sighed and left the room. These strikes were a ritual now, like the laundry. Bashko and the other guards pretended not to care. But the next day, after I refused a second meal, they asked for my demands.

"I must see a doctor," I said and pointed at my shin. "X-ray."

Any clinic in Galkayo with an X-ray machine would have to be run by a real doctor. I doubted the pirates would present me to one. But I saw good reason to hold out for a demand just beyond the bosses' reach: I wanted to force them to let me go. This cloudy design was a far more serious proposition than protesting a missing bowl of beans, and it had to be approached with care, since the bosses would shut down any protest that posed a direct threat to their ransom. I thought a defiant, showy strike would invite beatings or torture. But I could imagine escalating a small misunderstanding to a justified, disciplined protest.

From stray reports on the BBC I had gathered that a human could last a month without food, given water to drink. Without water I would die in three days. I wondered if the pirates would confiscate my liquids. But the injury to my leg went against every rule, as Dhuxul and Madobe both understood.

I navigated the first day with water, tea, milk, and mango juice. I just rationed supplies. Half a bottle of juice and one cup of milk per day, plus one bottle of water, felt right. I could anticipate the gnawing hunger, and I handled the panic.

On the second day I felt a heavy, hollow depression from the moment I woke up to pee. The panic returned. My brain went groping for a way to rationalize my self-starvation, but all it found was a stubborn refusal to let Madobe off the hook.

By the end of the third day the men had begun to worry. Abdul, the effeminate guard, came in to hand me a greasy package of sambusi.

"No," I said.

"No problem!" he whispered. *Our little secret.* He motioned for me to hide them, so I ate one and hid the rest. My body sponged up the nutrition and I felt better for about two hours.

Abdul and Bashko came in the next morning and said, "Michael! Doctor tonight! *Chum-chum* okay."

"Mm-hmm."

It was a ploy, but I noticed my advantage. I had demanded an X-ray. I could take them at their word, eat a snack, and if I still had no X-ray "tonight"—which seemed unlikely—I could resume the protest in the morning.

"Okay," I said, and let them serve me a bowl of beans.

My leg had improved, and I knew the bone was only bruised, not fractured. But I limped convincingly to the toilet, which kept

Madobe's sarcasm in check. He always watched me with alert, half-mocking eyes for evidence that I was just fine.

That evening, I went to sleep without knowing the state of my own hunger strike. No doctor had arrived. Bashko pretended we were back to normal in the morning and delivered a bowl of beans. With my stomach rumbling, I said, "No doctor, no *chum-chum!*"

"Fucking!"

The hunger intensified every day. It made me scrappy and mean. During my fierce and starving afternoons I nursed every old, familiar prisoner's grievance. I resented the guards' resentment, I loathed their guns, I hated their religion. I thought of them as enemies who lived on such a deep circle of hell that they owed me a profound moral debt from the first sluggish hours of the morning, when they unlocked my chains, opened the clanking shutters, and granted me permission to pee. These grievances weren't new, but the hunger stripped them raw, and the longer I turned them over in my head the more I had to face my own mistakes, until the emotional balance I nurtured to survive an average day seemed to burst into black smoke and spiral like a crashing plane. On these occasions I could screw myself into the ground with memories of my capture in President Alin's car and my warm swim in the ocean off the *Naham 3*—my feelings of guilt, my suffering mother, my helpless relatives and friends—and this easy lurch from righteous anger to self-recrimination made me rotten-minded with rage. Part of me still begged for vengeance. Part of me still wanted suicide. I still pulled at my chain, psychologically, like a junkyard dog.

On day five, I had to review my motivations. I felt weak. I wanted the struggle to end. The pirates hinted that liberty was imminent—"*Chum-chum*, okay!"—but in my undernourished state I thought their wispy gossip and promises of freedom were more maddening than the raw passage of time. I learned to listen with distant bemusement, the way an old man watches TV.

By day six my body had started to consume itself. I looked, and felt, like a scarecrow. I let Bashko convince me that a doctor would soon pay a visit. He called the runner and ordered sambusi, and I indulged in a greasy feast before bedtime, but I saved one, wrapped in plastic, for the morning.

In the morning I asked Bashko about the doctor.

"No doctor," he said.

"No *chum-chum*!" I said.

"Fucking."

On day seven, I refused breakfast, then lunch. In the afternoon, two bosses arrived. Dhuxul and one elder who went by "Abdi Yare" came in, looking stern, followed by Yoonis and a strange new Somali they introduced as a doctor, a small-featured young man with glasses. He listened while Yoonis translated my complaint. He palped my shin and tried to look knowledgeable. But everyone could tell I wanted to hold out for some concession, just as I could tell this young Somali had no medical degree.

"The leg is not broken," he said. "You will be fine."

He handed me a small pot of Tiger Balm ointment to rub into my skin.

"Okay, Michael?" said Yoonis.

I said nothing.

"The doctor says you are fine," Yoonis insisted, with the bosses staring me down. "You do not need an X-ray."

"Mm-hmm."

"You must eat."

I said nothing.

X

_____

Sheer frustration after the failed hunger strike brought me to a pair of contradictory, dead-end realizations, neither one liberating or, in fact, very helpful. The same puzzle had ruled my captivity for more than two years, but now I felt it in my gut like the dull point of a pike.

I wanted to die; I did not want to die.

These feelings were compounded by the blanket of desert heat that pressed on Galkayo during an average afternoon. "It is almost impossible to describe the malaise, the very special weariness of spirit," Hanley wrote in *Warriors*, "which eats into one after the sixth month in the midst of the tension and the hot silence." Six months! "I know of fifteen cases of madness in that wilderness." Hanley wasn't reassuring to think about, and the worst part about not wanting to die was facing this malaise every day.

But my hunger strike had rattled the pirates. It forced them to wonder what might happen if I died and denied them a ransom. Farrah, the long guard with a gentle manner, who had a sharp chin and large teeth, seemed impressed with my stamina. One afternoon while he sat alone on the mat, watching me in the room, he said, "Two years!" with a broad, lazy smile, as if he were tired of the routine, too. *"Adiga."*

"Haa," I said.

"Two—years," he repeated.

A bit longer, in fact. By now it was late March 2014. Two years and two months in captivity. Farrah kept smiling, as if it were some kind of achievement.

I liked Farrah. He was a lank and quiet man, unsure of his role as a pirate. Sometimes I caught him deep in brooding pleasure over the music he played on his phone. He played air oud like a teenager—he followed the twanging notes with his long fingers, nodding his head—and he'd boasted innocently about K'naan as a clan brother, a fellow Sa'ad, before the others had shut him up.

In case of a violent rescue, I didn't want Farrah to die.

In case of a violent rescue, I didn't want *me* to die.

One morning I listened to an hour-long program from Rome about the new pope, Francis. My shortwave was fickle in the hour before the World Service—usually it tuned in to Radio Sultanate of Oman, sometimes it preferred Vatican Radio. On this particular morning, I heard Francis compare human sin to the stars, and his simple image had an uncommon persuasion for a hostage lying on the floor of a prison house.

"At night we look at the sky, and we see many stars," the English reporter translated, and in the background I could hear the pope give his homily in Italian. (*"Tante stelle, tante stelle."*) "But when the sun rises in the morning, the light is such that we can't see the stars. God's mercy is like that: a great light of love and tenderness."

This homily was the first stirring and relevant idea I had heard in many months. It reminded me of the Unforgiving Servant, the petty man in the Gospels who walked into the street after pleading for mercy from a king, only to hassle another servant for a much smaller debt. I noticed that if the pirates were in debt to me, morally, then I was in moral debt, too—up to my neck in it. Rotten with obligation. To my mom, above all; to my entire family, to all the institutions working to set me free. It would have been idiotic, hypocritical, to maintain some persecuted notion of myself. I was still alive, for one thing. In spite of my nasty circumstances it struck me as basically *good* that I hadn't drowned myself off the ship. Therefore, I shouldn't kill myself now. All the personalities from Epictetus to Pramoedya, from Thich Quang Duc to Derek Walcott, who had sustained me so far—all these different ideas of liberation from the self—seemed to congeal in the pope's image of the sun, and a strange feeling of gratitude spread in my blood. I had nothing but a quiet throb of life, which itself was a gift, like the power of thought, and the simple poetry in the pope's words unfastened something, so I could feel how bitterness and anger were acts of will, like suffering itself, and how a slight step backward, an unhooking of the mind, could let in a flood of mercy and light.

XI

So I called a private truce. I stopped treating the pirates like persecutors. I talked as pleasantly as possible to the men during the daylight hours when we had to sit in a single room among crumpled leaves of khat and kettles of oversweet tea. When they asked for mango juice, I gave them a bottle, without wondering to myself why they didn't just go to the goddamn store.

"Good—morning," Hashi would say when he opened my steel shutters in the morning.

"*Subax wanaagsan,*" I answered in his language, and meant it.

My routine hardly changed—I listened to the radio, I drafted a novel in my notebooks, I raised my voice now and then to let any hypothetical drone discover my location—but I no longer cursed myself, or the pirates, every morning. My hair and beard were wild as a hobo's, with startling new streaks of gray, but I no longer felt the strain coming from within.

By now I had abandoned hope as a decadent indulgence, a fine flapping of the spirit that ended too easily in desolation. When I thought about my friends in Berlin, my family in Cologne, my grandmother in Holland, or my mom and my friends in California, I thought of them as shades from the past. I assumed Mom had packed up my apartment and stuffed everything into storage. I hadn't spoken to her in fourteen or fifteen months. I knew there was a chance this dim existence in Somalia would end in gunfire, or with an unexpected hostage sale to al-Shabaab, who wouldn't mind having an American to destroy in public. I assumed the past was gone; I just moved from one moment to the next.

Epictetus said in more than one of his lectures that real human freedom is moral choice, the skill to choose good over bad and not to be distracted by "impressions." This turned out to be a lot of work. By "impressions" he meant not just prejudice, reflex, and the first impressions we all form about strangers who might be enemies or friends—the usual bending of the light through a cognitive prism that modern psychologists also teach their clients to see—but the basic wrong impression that good and bad can be discovered *out there*, among the hordes of uncontrollable other people. "Sectarian strife, dissension, blame and accusation, ranting and raving—they all are mere opinion, the opinion that good and bad lie outside us," Epictetus said. "Let someone transfer these opinions to the workings of the will, and I personally guarantee his peace of mind, no matter what his outward circumstances are like."

One afternoon I noticed two guards, Issa and Rashid,* absorbed in a movie on a sleek new phone. Everyone else at Dhuxul's had gone to sleep. The voices of the actors coming from the phone sounded American, and I wondered which American film could hold these men so rapt. The BBC had been full of Oscar coverage of the Tom

---

* The Pirate Princeling.

Hanks movie *Captain Phillips*, which followed the famous naval standoff between pirates and SEAL snipers in 2009.

I listened for a while and thought, *Fuck me, that's Tom Hanks.*

"Issa," I said with a sour grin. "Movie okay?"

"*Haa.*"

A week or two later, Farhaan, the youthful veteran of Mogadishu, came to squat heavily beside my mattress with the same smartphone.

"Michael, look," he said, and showed me a scene from *Captain Phillips.* To my surprise, he handed me the phone. While we watched parts of the movie—early scenes set in Oman and on the cargo ship MV *Maersk Alabama*—my nerves woke up from their slumber of the past few months and an idea arrived with a faint, stirring hope. *What if I just called home?* The pirates tried to keep their phones out of my reach because they worried about that possibility. Now I concocted a plan to dial Mom's number without alerting Farhaan. I'd have to blurt something in German; then I would hang up, pretend I had shouted at the film, and curse and swear and apologize for somehow screwing up the phone. *Oh dang where'd the movie go?*

Farhaan's number could then be traced from America, and I could be rescued.

For the first time in months I had a real alternative to my dull and hopeless prison life. My heart thudded. It *could* work, but the idea ran the considerable risk of leaving an American number behind in the phone's software, which a pirate might see.

Farhaan retreated to his mat. He chewed khat and talked with Farrah. I found the volume button. To dial a number I wanted a silent keypad. I killed the volume slowly, waiting for my guards to think about other things.

Instead Farhaan blurted, "Michael."

"Hmm?"

"Problem, telephone?" he said.

"I don't know."

"Volume, volume."

"Mm—yeah. Hit the wrong button," I mumbled.

He came over to fix it.

"Thanks."

He returned to his corner, and I watched a little more. After a while he stood up to leave. Farrah, who spoke less English, remained in the corner with his pile of khat.

Deciding whether to use this tool for my physical freedom was also a moral decision, discerning better from worse. I might die; the guards might die. But those were the terms of our existence here, imposed by my captors. I had not turned into a saint.

I fiddled with the volume again.

Farrah said, "Michael! Problem."

"What? No problem."

"Sound, sound," he said.

"Hmmm."

The whole house slumbered. Farhaan came back and the guards exchanged words. Farhaan, heavy and patient, came to squat on his haunches and stare.

"No problem," he said.

"No problem," I said.

Flies buzzed. Afternoon light poured through the door. Farhaan squatted about a yard away. To distract us both from what was on my mind I pointed at the main Somali character, the pirate who would survive the movie and go on trial in New York.

"This Somali," I said.

Farhaan nodded. "Abduwali," he said, referring to the real pirate Abduwali Muse. "He is my friend."

"Really?"

"Yes, my clan brother. My friend from childhood."

"Darod?" I said, referring to the clan. Farhaan had said he came from Puntland, where the Darod dominated.

"Yes," he said.

"Abduwali is in America now," I said. "In prison."

"Yes."

I don't know why Farhaan showed me *Captain Phillips*. I think he was just being kind. It seemed like a morbid film for pirates to watch, since we all knew how it ended: three simultaneous bullets from the stern of a warship, three mutilated pirates; blood, horror, and a rescued American. No doubt they felt entangled in the same drama. (Maybe they were watching for tips.) The spectacle of Somalis in a Hollywood film also held a druglike fascination for them, and smartphones, even more than TV, had delivered the distant, narcotic world of pop culture straight to their hands.

After forty-five minutes, long before the climactic sniper fire, Farhaan grew tired of squatting near my mattress in the buzzing heat, watching me watch the film.

"Okay, Michael," he said, and took his phone away.

XII

One afternoon in May, while I wrote in my notebook, Bashko came in and set a bottle of liquor on the concrete floor with a clink.

"Alcohol?" I said. "Why?"

"From *taliyaha*,"* he said, which was our word for Dhuxul.

---

* Pronounced *taleeya*, meaning "commander."

"Why?"

"Good!" Bashko said.

He lifted his thumb and went away.

The bottle, from Ethiopia, had a yellow label showing a juniper bush and a brand name in Amharic, along with the English words DRY GIN. Dhuxul drank the same stuff. Since I was working, I saved it for sundown, when I would need help falling asleep. The bottle had an electric effect on my guards. Every time a new pirate came in and spotted the rare, clear, potent, forbidden liquor on the floor, he looked unnerved and tempted. A few words exchanged in Somali would explain the mystery—a gift from Dhuxul—but no guard was immune to the luxurious allure of the gin.

First Abdinuur, the machine gunner, came in to beg with a plastic cup.

"Sahib," he said in a rough and pleading voice. "*Aniga*, gin, okay."

I laughed and poured him a little. He'd never used the word *sahib* with me before.

"*Adiga* Muslim?" I said. *Aren't you Muslim?*

"*Haa*," he said, and downed the shot.

Later in the afternoon, Rashid, the Pirate Princeling, tried his luck. "Sahib," he said. But Rashid had cheated me out of limes and sambusi and other little treats, and I liked him less than Abdinuur. I wagged my finger.

"Muslim, no," I teased him, though I knew he wasn't observant.

"Sahib," he insisted.

"No."

That evening, I mixed a cup of gin with mango juice to drink before going to sleep. It tasted vile. Abdinuur came in to wrap the chains around my feet and expressed, in a mixture of Somali and pidgin, that I should be happy about the gift from Dhuxul, because a bottle of Ethiopian gin could run twenty dollars.

I felt real surprise. "It shouldn't cost ten," I said.

The next day the pirates were no less surprised that my gin still existed. Why hadn't the booze-starved Christian emptied his bottle? They paraded in, one by one, to stare or beg for more. I traded Rashid one slug for a lime, and in the evening I asked Bashko to cut my lime in half.

I squeezed it into a tin cup of cloying tea from my thermos, and this concoction was tolerable. I made a note:

<u>SOMALI GIMLET</u>

One part Ethiopian gin
Whole fresh lime
Two parts sweet black tea
Adjust gin content as necessary

The pirates pooled their allowance to buy gin of their own, and one day, while Dhuxul was gone, a runner delivered an identical bottle. Abdinuur tilted it up to drink in great bubbling gulps. Four or five others gathered around with plastic cups. Bashko and Farrah both abstained, at least in front of me. But it was interesting to watch the others abandon Islam for an evening.

A few days later, in early June, Hashi woke me up by opening the metal shutters at dawn, as usual, and said:

"Michael? *Adiga* free."

"Hmm?"

"Today," he answered, with the flying-airplane hand gesture I had learned to loathe. "*Adiga* free."

"Really?"

"*Haa.*"

I went to the bathroom, returned, and ate my bowl of beans. Afterward Hashi and Bashko both told me to pack.

"Why?"

"*Adiga* free!"

"Bashko, what's going on?"

He squatted near my bed and explained that sometime in the afternoon I would be driven "to Galkayo," where I would board a plane for Nairobi. I couldn't just sit here with my towel hanging on the shutter, my skin disinfectants on the windowsill, my bottled-up toothbrush and steel cup all waiting on the floor. I had to be ready to leave.

I didn't believe him, but over the next hour I watched the pirates pack their own clothes into plastic sacks. My heart started to race. At last I packed my faux-leather bag. I even separated a few snacks and mango drinks into a plastic bag as a carry-on. The idea that my ridiculous satchel, which had to be tied with a dirty rope, would survive transshipment in a luggage hold was delusional. But for the first time in months I allowed myself a few inches of optimism. I imagined a U.N. plane, a skinny turboprop with a dozen seats. I wondered what to say to strangers.

Around noon, Abdurrahman, the urbane translator, came to Dhuxul's house with his telephone and showed me a text message in English:

Tell Michael we will bring him back to Dunckerstrasse in Berlin.

It also gave the correct house number. Astonishing. A current of hope stirred in me again.

"You must answer this person," said Abdurrahman.

"Who is it?"

"He has come to help you." He handed me a notebook. "Please write your answer here. I will send it."

"I should write to him?"

"Yes."

But Abdurrahman didn't want me to type into his phone. He wanted to transcribe the message later and send it from a different location.

"I see."

For the rest of the afternoon Dhuxul sat with his men on the porch, ruminating over piles of khat. His wooden leg lay next to him on a mat, suited up with a sock and shoe. Dhuxul's moments of fatherly kindness to his men had a menace that reminded me of Indonesia, about ten years earlier, when I had visited a Koran school in Java. It was a plain but sweltering, banana-shaded dormitory where young Muslim radicals had lived with their teacher. "He is not like other leaders," one of the boys had said. "He sits and eats his meals with us." The teacher was a fringe-bearded ally of al-Qaeda named Abu Bakar Ba'asyir, who had masterminded the bloody 2002 bombings in Bali. This implosion of class difference and hierarchy was a technique of pirates throughout history—not just idealistic, not just admirable, but also a simple way for criminal bosses to win the devotion of poor young men.

Late in the afternoon, Dhuxul's phone rang. The last thing I remember hearing from the commander that day was "Ahhhhh. *Maya*." No.

Night fell, and Hashi came in to wrap the chains around my feet. I asked him, full of fragile and almost childish hope:

"*Aniga*, free?"

"*Haa*," he said. "Tonight."

XIII

I woke up at the first muezzin on the same filthy mattress. I thought I heard the thrum of a drone. The guards acted tense and ignored my requests for more drinking water and shampoo. All morning they maintained an uneasy quiet.

In the afternoon, I asked permission to use the toilet while Abdinuur sat in a chair in my doorway. He just stared into the courtyard and ignored me.

"*Abdinuur*," I said. "*KADI*."

He gave me a filthy look.

"What's the problem around here?" I said, very loud, which brought Bashko darting into the room with his rifle. He told me to shut up and argued with Abdinuur. For a minute I watched in disbelief. The pirates were like Keystone Kops. At last my bladder asserted itself: "*KADI*," I roared, and then all the pirates were arguing.

They let me walk to the toilet, but I had shattered the uneasy quiet. Hours later, in the dead of night, a car arrived to drive us to Abdi Yare's. The men tossed my things on the floor. They seemed resentful and bitter. When I lowered my mosquito net in the dark, Bashko came in to lock up my chains, and I whispered at him for an explanation.

"Because, *adiga*," he said. *Because of you.*

The translator and runner at Abdi Yare's House was a slithery, oily man with a long face and close-set eyes. He came in with deliveries of khat and necessities from the market. He looked no older than most of the guards but acted calm and superior. He did seem well informed, so I asked Bashko if this man, Hassan, could offer me news. He minced into the room, with careful disparaging eyes, and seemed to answer every note of defiance in my voice with a qualm of infidel hatred, as if I were too stupid to understand why I had to sit in a room.

I asked about our day of near freedom the previous week. "A man came to give us money for you," he said. "His name was Joe. Do you know him?"

"I don't think so."

"He came with seven hundred thousand dollars, but we told him the price was three million. We told him, 'Go back to your motherland.'"

"How odd."

"He wore the uniform of your military. You say 'fatigues'? He came here with three people. They did not have proper visas, and we do not know how they entered the country. We referred them to the minister of the interior. They were under arrest for two days."

"'Interior minister' for Galmudug?" I asked.

"Yes."

"Mm-hmm."

"We have evidence he came from Djibouti. We do not know what he intended. He spoke like an American. We think this man was a commando."

"What a peculiar story," I said.

"Do you know him?"

"I don't know anyone named Joe."

At least not anyone who would come to Somalia. It did seem possible that a contractor might try to get me out, but I couldn't fathom why someone like that would startle my kidnappers by wearing fatigues. The only fact I could rely on was my street address on Abdurrahman's phone. Someone had spelled it correctly. A pirate wouldn't have been careful about the c in Dunckerstrasse, which suggested that my apartment was intact, which suggested that no one had packed it into storage, which suggested that someone expected me to return, which suggested that my family and friends were more than just shades from the past. The more I wandered down this road in my head the more the wheel of hope and disappointment racked my emotions, lifting me for a while but leaving me, for a while, in even worse condition.

My guards must have moved through the same cycle. I think it gnawed at their morale to think that a ransom had landed in Galkayo, briefly, but flown off again into the clear blue sky.

XIV

When Ramadan started later in the summer, we lived in Dhuxul's house again, and someone liberated the TV, again, from his bedroom, though not for my benefit. The World Cup was on. The men watched it on the porch. I went to sleep every night with the glare of soccer matches flickering through the door. They played after dark in Somalia, beamed across the planet from Brazil, and since I had to be chained and quiet on my bed by sundown, I followed the tournament every morning on the BBC.

World Cup soccer woke up a powerful nostalgia for Berlin. The commotion of a European city during a soccer tournament is unlike anything in America, where people retreat to backyards and living rooms for the Super Bowl or the World Series, leaving the streets deserted. Berliners collect in bars and cafés on summer evenings for the World Cup—men and women, young and old—to drink and chatter and holler at big outdoor screens. People wander the sidewalks with flags. They chant national songs. When I worked late in my apartment I could keep an ear on the score just by listening to the crowd. If opponents scored a goal, a few people cheered. If Germany scored, the sidewalk erupted. Mounting tension toward the end of every match expressed itself in the wavering noise, and you could actually hear the ball approach a goal, or the release of pressure when it changed sides, or the sound of agony when a player missed a shot. To follow a good game, you didn't even need to watch TV.

Germany advanced to the semifinals in 2014, to play Brazil, and I asked permission to watch. My body still felt the aftereffects of my weeklong hunger strike. Not only had my muscles wasted; my immune system had broken down. Boils had grown on my skin from a staph infection, and I suffered some kind of cyclical fever. These afflictions possibly helped my case. Dhuxul consented, but no one knew what time the game would air. I stayed up for the early time slot and the men let me sit, wearing chains, on a plastic chair in the doorway. But the early game was a rerun, so the men sent me to bed.

In the morning Bashko woke me up with exciting news.

"Michael!" he said. "Germany—seven points!"

I scowled and shook my head. Obvious pirate bullshit. Who scored seven goals in a professional soccer match?

"Seven points!" he insisted. "Brazil, finished!"

"Hmmm."

The story led the World Service. Germany had knocked out the host nation with seven goals, humiliating Brazil while a billion people watched on TV. The sheer impertinence reminded people on the radio of the 1950 World Cup, also in Brazil, when a player from Uruguay hushed the vast crowd by scoring a goal against Brazil in the final minutes of the deciding match. The Maracanã Stadium—almost two hundred thousand people—fell silent. I heard an interview with the Uruguayan player as an old man on the BBC, and he gave a memorable summary of his own career.

"Only three people have silenced the Maracanã," he said. "Frank Sinatra, the pope, and me."

By now some friends in Berlin were starting to wonder if I'd learned to sympathize with my pirates, in the strange fashion of hostages who survive by adopting the viewpoint of their bullies. Therapists had named the Stockholm syndrome after the behavior of Swedish captives in a bank robbery in 1973. The hostages defended the thieves' behavior to the police after a six-day ordeal. It wasn't like that for me. Most of my comfortable and civilized self had stripped away, but the core of it, my will, had sharpened. I would have escaped in a second if I'd spotted a chance. My mother, in California, knew the World Cup was on, and she encouraged the FBI to suggest a military rescue during the tournament. She thought my guards might be distracted at night. "Soccer is kind of universal," she said, "so I figured they would be watching, since they didn't have much else to do."

She was right. But she didn't call the shots. Mom had no direct line to the president. "I wrote a couple of letters to the White House, but I never heard back," she said, and after more than two years this reticence upset her.

I wouldn't have minded. I was sane enough to welcome another way out, but it was crucial—for my own mental health—to quit straining for vengeance. Stockholm syndrome and forgiveness were not equivalent: I'd learned to forgive, but I hadn't forgotten the nature of the game.

Germany advanced to the final, and guards let me sit in the plastic chair again, well after dark, in the doorway. I wrapped myself in a blanket and thought our festivities looked like a sinister imitation of a World Cup party in Berlin. Eight or nine Somalis sat cross-legged on the cold patio, where no light shone but the flickering screen. Someone hung tarps across the arabesque arches of the patio to hide the TV glare, and Farhaan passed around a plastic bottle with some bootleg gin. We kept it hidden from Dhuxul, who lounged at the front of the group with his wooden leg against the wall. During the game preview, the TV flashed an up-close shot of the actual trophy, the World Cup itself—thick molded gold and malachite. Dhuxul's hand reached up to swipe at it. His men laughed. I felt a wave of disgust. The gesture was pure instinct on Dhuxul's part; a thief wanted anything that glittered.

XV

We moved back and forth between the houses, Dhuxul's and Abdi Yare's, throughout that summer. We never returned to the Pirate Villa, and Bashko insisted the reason was "drones," but I think it had more to do with pirate-gang politics, because we heard furtive, indistinct humming at night no matter where we lived.

In late August I woke up to hear that terrorists had decapitated a freelance journalist in Syria, James Foley, in a gruesome new style of video. For months my radio delivered bizarre news about the Islamic State, which rose like a gas from the Sunni provinces of Iraq and Syria in 2014 to establish a patchwork "caliphate" where callow and criminal men tried to live without conventional law, like the pirates who had strung Rolly from a tree, and who, like their predecessors in al-Qaeda, used Islam as a license for blood-thirstiness.

I'd never heard of Foley. He'd been kidnapped in 2012, during my long news blackout. But his story sounded familiar—a freelance excursion to a dangerous country, some lapses in judgment, a world of shit. The radio report had me paralyzed. I didn't know yet that the image of a hostage in an orange jumpsuit in the desert, kneeling before a robed Islamic State executioner holding a knife, would become a new gauge of mayhem in the world, an updated emblem of entropy.

News of Foley's execution agitated my guards. When Bashko brought my beans for breakfast that morning, he said, "Michael! James Foley. Killed!"

"I heard that."

"Daesh, no good," he added.

I didn't know the term, but to Bashko the name Daesh was as common on the radio as "Islamic State" was to me. He explained the derogatory Arabic nickname.

"Ah, okay," I said. "Fucking," I added.

I must have looked angry and grim.

"*Adiga*, no," he said, meaning it wouldn't happen to me.

"Hmmm."

Until now al-Shabaab had expressed only a low-voltage desire to buy an American hostage. I hadn't been worth the money. Otherwise Garfanji would have sold me in the two or more years since his threats in the wilderness. But when Daesh started to win territory and fame in the Middle East, there was a faction of Shabaab fighters who wanted to shift allegiance to them, from al-Qaeda, and one way to draw their attention was to behead an American. So, among certain members of al-Shabaab, my market value went up, which may have encouraged one pirate faction to consider selling me off.

Foley may have died under similar circumstances—kidnapped by one group, but sold to murderous Islamists. Mom was sheltered from the worst possibilities by the FBI. She learned nothing of these nuances at the time, although she'd exchanged emails with Jim's mother, Diane, for moral support. Now Jim was dead. "When I first heard the news, I had a bad feeling," she said later. "Then I heard the name 'Foley.'" Mom, with a feeling of dread, had to send her condolences.

The news in 2014 seemed to describe a new, wobbling twenty-first-century world order. I heard about the rotting out of nation-states, the spread of transnational groups like the Islamic State and Boko Haram, which had started to dissolve borders in Africa and the Middle East and mock the power of some national militaries as a mirage. Russia had invaded Ukraine, using the U.S. war in Iraq as a justification to ignore a sovereign country's borders. ("Good!" Bashko had said when he heard about Putin's annexation of Crimea.) Entropy had picked up speed. A noticeable number of interviews on the BBC featured people from both the left and the right who ridiculed the idea of national sovereignty, as if old ideas naturally had to be dumped in the garbage. But it was hard to see a shimmering vision of justice and peace in the distance to replace these old ideas. Instead the world was rolling back to factionalism, to violent opportunism, to old swamps of chaos and crime.

One brilliant late-summer morning I plotted another hunger strike under my mosquito net while the radio murmured beside my ear. The net indicated my mood. When it was down, during daylight hours, I felt depressed. Bashko sat alone in the room and watched me.

"Sahib," he said.

I glanced up.

"Mango," he requested.

I wanted nothing to do with Bashko today. But I sighed and crawled out from the net. I pulled a bottle from the clanking case of juice and tossed it to him. For this favor I expected information.

"News," I said.

"No news, sahib," he said.

We had just moved back to Abdi Yare's House again. I felt weary and disgusted with the old routine.

"This house—why?" I said.

"I don't know, sahib." He shook his head.

"*Aniga*, no free. Why?" I said.

"No news," he repeated.

I scowled and crawled back under my net. I resumed my position—one arm thrown over my face, listening to the radio—and this time I meant it as a direct personal snub.

After a minute Bashko hissed, "Hey! Michael!" and waved at me to sit up.

He did have news? I opened the mosquito net and sat on the edge of my mattress. Bashko told me a wild story. He said the guards would stop work if the bosses couldn't cut a deal—they were tired of changing houses, too. For two months they'd received no allowance.

"All group," he said, meaning all the guards, "stop work."

I nodded, uncertain of what to say. "A labor strike?"

The BBC had recently mentioned a miners' strike in South Africa, so I said, for clarity, "South Africa, same-same?"

"Yes!" Bashko answered and laughed.

I nodded again and asked if a hunger strike by the hostage would help.

"Okay, sahib!" He lifted his thumb. "Slow-slow. Two weeks."

XVI

Several days later, Abdinuur—who was the senior guard, although he didn't act like it—came into my room and announced to Bashko and some other men that he had quit. Bashko celebrated, throwing his hands in the air. Evidently Abdinuur had told "Abdi Yare" on the phone about his intention to strike. Abdi Yare had fired him on the spot. For some reason that was a good sign. The same evening a car arrived in the darkened yard with an ominous rumble, and Abdinuur disappeared. I found it blood chilling. Bashko reassured me that the rest of the group would stay and guard me—by his reckoning we were on the verge of freedom—but I didn't dare believe him. I saw no reason Abdi Yare couldn't replace the whole team, one by one, and leave me in the hands of new and more dangerous men.

On the first day of September, Yoonis came to squat beside my mattress. He said there would be a phone call to a man called Robert, "from the U.N." He gave me a list of simple facts to mention and said, "Do not tell him where you are."

"I don't know where I am."

What was going on, though? I wondered if "Robert" would be the same man who had failed to show up with a U.N. security team at the airport. Or if "Robert" was the real name of "Romeo"—the nickname of the calm-voiced negotiator Garfanji had called in the darkened bush over two years before.

I decided to rehearse a few lines in German to describe my location. I concocted a sentence explaining that I was in a house near a mosque with a (rather loud) minaret, which I could see from my east-facing window. I practiced weaving it into English phrases for "Robert," so the Somalis wouldn't notice. My heart raced.

Before lunch, Yoonis ordered me to throw my blanket over my head. Six of us had to walk out and sit in a hot Land Rover in the courtyard, with all the windows sealed. The call would be routed somehow from Mogadishu, and Abdi Yare would listen in. The phone rang. Yoonis spoke in rough Somali and handed it to me. "Michael, my name's Robert," said a self-assured, but unfamiliar, American voice.

I answered a security question and gabbed about my health. Since Yoonis had ordered me to be dramatic, I also gave my whereabouts in half-hollered, desperate-sounding German. It seemed to work. I got every bit of information out to Robert, or Bob, who I gathered was not from the U.N., and I told myself that if the whole thing was a trick by the Pentagon—as Yoonis half believed—the Pentagon would have what it needed.

Robert connected me somehow to my mother. She asked in an urgent voice how I was. "We're trying to get you out!" she said. Hearing her again after nineteen months was a miracle, a memory of a lost life, but I couldn't let it raise my hopes, because her language hadn't changed—after all this time she used the same questions and the same vague, encouraging optimism. I spent the rest of the day in a haze of panic and confusion. I couldn't tell whether negotiations had budged, or how much German my pirates had detected.

For lunch Hashi cooked flat, crepe-like pancakes called anjero instead of pasta. I used the pancakes to sop up a potato-and-onion mixture with my hand. We'd been eating like this for weeks, if not months. The pirates had noticed that I refused plain spaghetti but didn't mind anjero. Bashko asked if I knew anjero from the United States. ("Yes, from Ethiopian restaurants.") Their treatment of me, I thought, had improved since my weeklong hunger strike. Maybe I'd convinced them I was crazy enough to commit suicide.

Now Bashko watched me eat, with wary, questioning eyes. He asked if my mother had promised a ransom. She hadn't mentioned money at all, but I said, "Of course."

He seemed to relax.

"Bashko," I said carefully, between bites. "Abdi Yare speak—phone call good?" *Did Abdi Yare say it was a good phone call?*

Or, more to the point: *Are we cool, even though I just ratted our location in German?*

"*Haa*, yes," he said.

"Okay."

I tried to relax but couldn't.

XVII

The next morning we heard on the radio that a leader of al-Shabaab, Ahmed Abdi Godane, had been killed by a drone while his convoy paused near a village in southern Somalia. Godane had organized the siege of the Westgate Shopping Mall, in Nairobi, where dozens of shoppers were slaughtered by Shabaab terrorists in late 2013. The gunmen had ordered some of their victims to recite the *shahadah* before they died ("There is no god but Allah") so they could distinguish Muslims from *kuffar*.

Bashko heard about the strike while he sat wrapped in a blanket, beside his rifle. "Michael!"

"Hmm?"

He gleefully whispered the news about Godane's death, held up his thumb, and smiled. "America, good!" he said.

Later in the week, I woke up to an almost extraterrestrial noise over the courtyard, an electromagnetic hum, intense but unplaceable, and I wasted no time uttering a prayer in conversational German to describe my location to any nearby snooping drone. The guards mumbled to one another in the dark, and Bashko shuffled out to the courtyard. It occurred to me in a half doze that he and I both had inconsistent views about military drones. As long as they helped us, we didn't mind.

Bashko's rifle banged like a cannon, and I twitched in bed.

The next morning I asked why he'd fired his weapon. Bashko's typical answer to such a question would have been "Because, thief!"—meaning a stranger, some lurking Somali—or else flat denial. This time he told me, in a tense excited whisper, that five drones had circled the house for two hours. He'd looked up to see faint lights reflected on a layer of cloud. The lights, he said, were blinking on top of the drones. He had noticed them only because of the weather.

"Five?" I said skeptically, using five fingers.

"Five," he said, flashing the same gesture.

I wondered if it was a fairy tale. Then I wondered if my German outbursts on the phone had done some good. Then I wondered if we were all about to die in a raid. But Bashko didn't even wonder why the drones had paid a visit.

"Because, *adiga*," he said. *Because of you.*

"No," I dissembled, with a smile. "Because, al-Shabaab. We are in Harardhere?" I said. "Al-Shabaab is in Harardhere."

"Okay, sahib," he said.

The whole month of September was a weird fog of rumor and fear. In spite of the new stirrings I hoped for nothing, trusted nothing. I heard a rumor from the guards that someone had arrested Mohamed Garfanji in Mogadishu. Then I heard he'd gone free again. I mulled a hunger strike to force the bosses' hand. But I wondered whether open defiance would worsen my situation. I thought a labor strike by the guards could easily bring a fire sale of the hostage to another pirate group, or even to al-Shabaab, and if that was true then a hunger strike might bring nothing better. The whole process could start over.

The swirl of uncertainty nauseated me, and I put no faith in rumors of freedom.

One morning in late September—the 23rd—Yoonis came to my room with his phone for another conversation with Bob. This time he let us talk for thirty seconds. "Okay, do you have any idea what's going on?" Bob said, and managed to explain exactly nothing before Yoonis snatched the phone from my hand.

"Proof of life, only!" he said, and I lost my temper.

"What the fuck are you doing? You should have let me finish!"

"Why?" he said. "Tonight, you will go free."

"If you're lying, Yoonis, I swear I'll stop eating tomorrow."

That was a hot flash of temper. I tried to keep hunger-strike plans to myself. Later I caught Yoonis joking about the conversation to Hashi, and I assumed he was proud of fooling me, of trying to raise my hope when my real fate was to be shifted like a sack of millet to some terrorist's Land Rover.

Around noon I had to use the bathroom. Before I finished, the main compound gate swung noisily open and a Land Rover rumbled into the yard. My limbs swamped with fear. Cars came at night, as a rule. Hashi stood outside the bathroom with his Kalashnikov and said:

"Michael? *Gari.*" *Michael, your car is here.*

"What *gari*? I'm busy."

"No problem," he said.

My other guards buzzed in the hall like excited schoolboys. Abdurrahman the translator, Madobe, and a runner had arrived in the Land Rover with a sealed clear plastic sack of bound hundred-dollar bills.*

"You are going free!" said Yoonis when I came out.

I studied the bills to see if they were fake. Hard to tell. It was a lot of money, but al-Shabaab would have paid in dollars, too (not shillings). It says something about my flinty frame of mind that in spite of the cash, I couldn't believe I was about to go free. I'd shut down everything in self-defense, and I still had a hair-trigger temper, an animal mistrust of the mysterious changes upending my comfortable prison world.

"You must pack your bags," Abdurrahman said. "You are going to the airport."

I dropped a few things into my faux-leather bag, in a desultory

---

* Probably one hundred thousand dollars, for about ten guards.

way, and tied it all up with a dirty rope. The day felt bright and warm. I had time to make a journal entry. "I'm sick and stuffed-up, with clogged ears and blurred eyes, lungs full of bronchitis and a heart full of rage." One of the guards had given me a bottle of potent Egyptian cough syrup to calm my bronchitis (or whatever it was) and help me sleep. I'd been sick for weeks. Boils thrived on my skin. By now it just felt normal.

I packed my notebooks away. No one seemed to care about them. A few men wanted to shake my hand. I submitted, but looked away: I did believe I would never see them again, but I thought somebody else would just deliver me to another part of the bush and transfer me to a more dangerous gang.

I climbed into the car with only Yoonis and Abdurrahman, the two translators. No weapons in sight. That was oddly encouraging. But when the car pulled out of the compound, Yoonis changed his story.

"We will not go to the airport now. We will give you to some other Somalis," he said, which was the wrong thing to say to a hostage in my frame of mind. I nearly bit off his head, thinking *You just sold me to another gang.* I felt blind with practiced mistrust, fierce as a cat piled into a traveling cage.

The heat and dust of Galkayo seemed pleasant, though. I saw school compounds, semifamiliar houses, and medical clinics. Robed women with children moved along the road. Driving in a car without a tight contingent of armed men felt almost civilized, and it was such a surprise to see everyday life in a Somali town without squinting through a blindfold that I began to notice a different fear, an unexpected panic that all my wound-up defenses might be useless now. I might have to unwind. *What if these guys are serious?* The streets bustled with people and goats, and trees threw a spangled, fluttering shade. Plastic litter had collected around the bases of the houses and walls, which had painted advertisements and logos, and I wondered, with a stir of nausea, how it would feel to walk these streets like a normal man.

I'd grown used to being a hostage and I didn't know how to stop.

We drove some distance into the bush, where a white sedan waited beside a gnarled acacia. "Get out. You are free," said Yoonis, and that was it.

My atrophied arms began to tremble.

A pirate I recognized climbed out of the sedan, leaving the passenger door open, and climbed in with Yoonis and Abdurrahman. They drove off in a hurry. I found myself alone in the quiet waste with a new driver, who looked almost as nervous as I was. Dust blew up off the bush. There was no other gang. This new man spoke American English. He described a wild plan to deliver me to a hotel in North Galkayo, where I would meet my mother.

"Oh, sure," I said, trembling with fury again, fangs still dripping with sarcasm. "My mother's in Galkayo."

"She is in the hotel."

"I thought we were driving to the airport."

"We are driving to the hotel first," said this Somali.

Fuck off, fuck off, I thought.

"Great" is what I said out loud.

While we drove to town he recommended lying far back in the seat and draping my blanket over my head.

"It's better if people don't see you in this car."

"Can you tell me what's going on?" I said.

"You are okay now. You are free."

"I want to talk to somebody."

"I will call Bob," he said.

He dialed a number while he steered along the dusty road, and on the phone I heard not just Robert, or Bob—the negotiator—but my mother. That confused me. Were they in the same room?

Her voice sounded musical and happy.

"Where are you now?" I said. "Not in a Galkayo hotel room?"

"No, we're in California," she said.

"Your driver will take you to a hotel," Bob said, "and another man will drive you to the airport. Your pilot's name is Derek."

The fierce pessimism I had applied all morning to these unusual events opened its grip a little. I just wasn't sure what to feel instead. Freedom seemed as bizarre as a Thanksgiving feast. I was too racked and shattered to face a pleasure like that. While we steered through Galkayo my driver made small talk, chatting like a guarded American, a melancholy kid who wanted to show some friendliness but preferred not to expose too much of himself. (I could relate.) We pulled up in front of a small but tidy hotel under the withering sun, and we spent just enough time indoors to call Bob and switch drivers. Then I rode with another Somali to the Galkayo airport.

This dry airstrip with a few low buildings was so mythic to me, such a magnet for my fantasies and dreams, that it felt odd to see it in real life. On the square of tarmac where I had shaken Ashwin's hand before his flight to Mogadishu I now saw a single-engine Cessna. A bantam, leathery pilot wearing mirrored sunglasses stepped out, paused under the wing, and snapped photos of me emerging from the car.

"For your mother," he said.

"You must be Derek."

I gave him a real but weary smile. Derek was the first competent man I'd met in two years (since I'd left the *Naham 3*). He shook my hand and offered me a cheap blue backpack stuffed with clothes. One of my rubber Thai sandals broke as I stepped into the plane—

just in time—so I was pleased to find a fresh pair of sandals in the backpack. Also a tube of Dramamine.

Derek rearranged some bags in the cramped space behind our seats while I rooted through my new belongings.

"Flew in with my own fuel," he chatted, pointing at large plastic tanks in the hollow tail section behind our seats. He'd emptied the tanks into his plane while he waited. "For the return trip." Galkayo's airport lacked reserves of the right kind of fuel, he said, so he'd buzzed up from Mogadishu in this little plane like a flying bomb.

The backpack also contained a new shirt, protein bars, toiletries, a pair of glasses with the wrong prescription, and a pair of waterproof safari slacks with a tag from the Djibouti NAVEX. I blinked and remembered the feeling of hot sun pressing down on the air-conditioned shop, and I noticed an unexpected rush of gratitude for the cheap racked clothing and the thousand brands of shampoo.

Derek chatted away in fluent and reassuring English. He sounded Scottish or South African. His plane had an old-fashioned instrument panel—crowded with black meters and dials, no digital screens. He climbed in and slammed his flimsy door. I fastened my seat belt. We put on headsets, ready to go. The tarmac in front of us lay empty, but a Somali guard asked us to wait "just half an hour."

"What for?" Derek asked him.

"A journalist is coming; he wants to take your picture," said the Somali.

"No," I told Derek.

My head felt cramped; my body felt limp and weak. I would feel cramped and weak for months. People have said, "You must have been overjoyed," but joy wasn't on the menu that afternoon. Any ransom is a filthy compromise, and I'd lived like a hated castaway for so long it was hard to imagine that anyone wanted me back. I blinked in the hard sun and tried to unstick my brain.

"Galkayo tower, Galkayo tower," Derek radioed, and gave his call sign. "Request permission to take off," he said. "Two souls on board."

No response from the tower. He let the plane roll forward.

"Galkayo tower, Galkayo tower," Derek repeated, and I felt another tremble in my atrophied muscles. *Two souls on board*, I thought. *He has a point.* A living dog was better than a dead lion. I had sometimes wished for the moral clarity of a rescue, but violence would have been a compromise of a different sort; it would have endangered the people who came to get me. It would have killed Bashko and Hashi and Farrah. It might have killed me. The bosses, in any case, would have survived.

"Sometimes they don't answer," Derek mumbled.

My daily sense of terror and waste had started to scatter like a fog, and the changes panicked me. *Oh God oh God what now.* After years of halting speech in one kind of pidgin or another I wasn't sure where to put the things I felt. *Gratitude* was too weak a word. Maybe Lazarus led out of the tomb was no less tongue tied. It just felt fine to sit in the warm cabin of a functioning plane. I looked at the cracked and sun-beaten white buildings of the airport—these objects of fantasy for two and a half years—in mute animal wonder.

"Galkayo tower, Galkayo tower," Derek repeated. "Request permission for takeoff. Two souls on board."

At last there was noncommittal noise from the radio.

"Yes, okay," crackled a voice, and Derek lined up his plane for takeoff.

Part 9

FUGUE

I

We wore sunglasses because of the glare, and we spoke through mouthpieces on our headsets because of the propeller roar.

"I know two of your friends," Derek said.

"What?" I said, still disoriented by the series of events.

"I flew a pair of Seychellois fishermen out of Somalia the same way. From Adado."

"Rolly and Marc!" I said.

"That's right."

Most of my past felt like such a thin fantasy that it overwhelmed me to hear about people I knew.

"When did they go free?"

"That was in November 2012, I believe."

"My pirates said there was a ransom of four million dollars."

"I imagine they did say that."

We soared over the sere, flat, hot desert bush, over clusters of villages and roaming packs of camels. The plane wobbled in a headwind. Derek said, "We've got two and a half, maybe three hours to go, depending on wind. We might hit turbulence—you normally do near Mogadishu in the late afternoon. I was getting nervous there at the airport, to be honest. Much later and we would've had to spend the night."

I took a Dramamine.

I didn't know how to hold sustained conversations.

"You do this for a living?" I said.

"Oh, yes," Derek said. "Spent seventeen years in the military, nine in the SAS.* Afterward I started my charter business in Nairobi. I thought, *You've got to use the training.* Otherwise, what is it for?"

Derek showed me his right hand, which lacked part of an index finger. "Lost that in Oman in 1975," he said. "I've got a metal knee, too. Jumped from a plane with the Americans near Fort Bragg, through two layers of cloud. Conditions perfect, but my knee happened to come down on a sharp rock. Broke the kneecap."

"Ouch."

"Gotta be careful of that."

Derek was Scots by heritage, but he spoke with a mild South African accent. He'd lived much of his life in East and South Africa. An old breed of bush pilot.

We approached Mogadishu from the north and circled over long lines of surf near Lido Beach, the city's public waterfront. Clear weather let us see the whole jumbled sprawl of what used to be a grand African city. We came down over the water to land on an exhaust-scarred runway, where a pair of SUVs waited along the edge. Men wearing beards and mirrored sunglasses gave directions with their arms. When I climbed out, four of them hustled me, like pirates, into a baking Land Rover.

The guys in the car were American and German, from the FBI and the BKA. One of them took my blood pressure. I showed them the boils on my skin and the Egyptian cough syrup I'd been drinking. They said a military plane would land soon and fly me to Nairobi. I sat like a castaway in that hot car, swathed in my pink flowered blanket, relieved to be out of Galkayo but nervous not to be out of Somalia. After twenty minutes, an olive-green cargo plane landed with an incredible wind and roar. It was a C-130, not very different

---

* Special Air Service, a special forces unit of the British military.

from the big planes I'd heard in the air as a hostage. It lined up near our Land Rover and lowered a tail ramp, showing a greenish interior outfitted for medical care. I sat on a stretcher fixed to the floor of the plane. An Air Force doctor quizzed me and took my blood pressure. He asked if I wanted to spend the flight lying on the stretcher.

"No, it's not that bad," I said.

He gave me a sleeping tablet "for later tonight," and warned me not to down it with alcohol. I hadn't been in the presence of so many well-meaning people in too long; I wasn't sure how to behave. Without my glasses I couldn't make out individuals, but wandering back and forth in the hollow, dim-lit fuselage were placid-faced young airmen wearing khaki jumpsuits. Soon we strapped ourselves to seats along the inner wall, and one bearded man, an FBI agent named Kevin, sat next to me.

"We're happy to see you, man," he said with a smile. "There's some sandwiches at the front, if you want. Once we take off, you can walk up there."

Absentmindedly I let my pink blanket drop to the floor. He pointed and smiled through his beard.

"I've been lookin' at pictures of that thing for a couple of years," he said.

I brightened, but it was too early for penetrating questions.

"It feels good to be in one of these big planes," I said, "instead of hearing them over the house all the time."

Kevin laughed.

We flew north again, to Djibouti, for some bureaucratic reason. "We have to fly to Djibouti first because . . ." Kevin tried to explain over the roaring noise. "Then we'll go to Kenya." I just nodded along. A young blond airman sat next to me. The knees of his khaki suit had thick padding, which reminded me of what Derek had said about sharp rocks.

"You guys paratroopers?" I said.

"Yep," said the young airman.

They'd landed within twenty minutes of us in Mogadishu; the C-130 must have shadowed Derek's plane. Someone had prepared for shit to go wrong.

This plane ride lasted deep into the evening. For paperwork reasons, I crisscrossed East Africa twice—up to Djibouti, down to Nairobi—and hurtling through the darkness like that, free but bewildered, unsure of how the next few days would look, elevated my blood pressure and made my heart slog with excitement and uncertain hope.

We landed in Nairobi after dark. I stayed with a BKA officer and his family in a quiet, banana-grown suburb. This BKA man—I'll call him Heinrich—had stocked the fridge with German beer. "Men always want beer when they get out," he said. Heinrich saw me coming from miles away.

His compound had a sunlit garden thick with fruit trees and flowers. I lived in a guest room outside, detached from the main house, where I could take a shower and shave, sleep when I wanted, and make real coffee in a little machine. Two turtles roamed the yard and coupled in the sunshine.* I moved through this gorgeous place with the shocked eyes of a zombie, not quite trusting it, hoping it was more than a dream. My blood pressure, which had already impressed two doctors, refused to go down. Even in this lush corner of Kenya I woke up with my heart racing three or four times a night. I made a note in my journal: "I move from one thing to another like a fish. My brain is prone to cramp, and so is my chest. White-hot rage grips me sometimes." But in this house I began to relax.

---

* Without yelling.

An FBI psychologist who had boarded the plane in Djibouti stayed near me for three days. He was African American and sweet tempered, a bulky former Marine, and he had the rumbling, dry sense of humor of a combat vet. When we went out in public for lunch, at the Westlands mall, my brain wound up like a spring and I started to scrutinize every stranger with a fierce and panicky alertness that I couldn't seem to control. This adrenaline clarity reminded me of a veteran I had interviewed years ago in California, an ex-soldier who'd tried to explain his mental condition to me. "The first thing I noticed when you walked into my office," he said, some thirty years after his tours in Vietnam, "is that you were unarmed."

I turned to the FBI shrink, whose name was Carl.

"Am I hypervigilant?" I said.

"Maybe!" he said with a wide grin.

After considering this for some time, I said, "Are you here because I might have PTSD?"

He answered, "We don't like to put a label on anything."

I called my mother and we had an early, excited reunion on the phone. TV trucks had surrounded the house in Redondo Beach. Since she had kept the story quiet, my release took the L.A. media by surprise, and even now, except for a simple statement from her, they had little to report. I was in no mood for interviews. I wouldn't have known what to say. I felt easily overwhelmed, and my powers of decision making had atrophied. I didn't trust myself at all. Even the simplest choices posed by the FBI and BKA people were confounding. The puzzles had started before we left Mogadishu: Did I want to lie down? Was I hungry? Did I need a tranquilizer? Did I want to fly home to Berlin, or California? A State Department representative during our layover in Djibouti had waited for me in an office tent, eager to show me a "privacy waiver." Did I want to sign this form or not? (How the hell did I know?) Did I want to talk to the media, or should the government make a statement on my behalf? For a man who'd lived in the corner of a concrete room for more than two years, who'd lost his knack for interpreting ordinary social cues, who had felt the burden of making the world worse whenever he *did* make a choice, treading back into regular life was not like taking wing but like walking through a thick substance, like moving through water on the ocean floor.

Someone from Heinrich's house ordered a pair of provisional glasses for me from a Nairobi optometrist, based on what I could remember of my own prescription. My numbers were off, but the glasses sharpened the garden and let in a flood of baffling, vivid detail whenever we drove into town. I could see the ocher volcanic soil crumbling along the roadsides, the deep-shadowed banana groves, the beat-up cars in dusty shimmering gridlock when herds of brown oxen crossed Mombasa Road; the brilliant, burning Kenyan sky.

I preferred not to wear my glasses.

II

A reporter from *Der Spiegel* named Matthias Gebauer met me at the German embassy in Nairobi on the second day, to see how I was. He happened to mention a shootout, as if I had heard about it, a massacre among my pirate bosses that had killed several people.

I blinked.

"When did this happen?" I asked.

"In Galkayo this morning," he said. "I just read it on Twitter."

Der Spiegel had involved itself in my case and helped my family from the first day, although they never had to, legally speaking, and

Matthias was considerate and kind. He told me what he knew about the shootout.

Two days after I left Galkayo, several pirate bosses held a summit meeting at a yellow house belonging to "Abdi Yare," a house I didn't recognize, although it had a typical steeply raked blue metal roof and an arched gate squeezed between two businesses, recognizable in photographs as an urban building, with ads painted on the yellow walls. Dhuxul and Abdi Yare[*] were evidently inside the house when the incident started. A second group of bosses "rolled up heavy" in SUVs, according to people who described the scene to me later. Ali Duulaay and Ahmed Dirie, the rotten-toothed man from my first months as a hostage, stepped out, along with Ahmed Dirie's brother and a fourth man called Abdi Ganeey.[†] They had belonged to my kidnap team, and they'd overseen my guard team for most of 2012. But after my leap from the *Naham 3*, another faction had watched me, led by Dhuxul and Abdi Yare, and these men had received $1.6 million in ransom cash. Duulaay and the others were outsiders now.

Each faction had a loyal group of guards. Rival pirates aimed their weapons at one another in a complicated standoff, for mutual security. One of them, Farhaan—the pirate who'd let me watch *Captain Phillips*[‡]—aimed at Duulaay's head. For reasons I still don't understand, Farhaan pulled the trigger. So the sadistic boss who had

---

[*] Named by the American and German agents in Nairobi as Ali Qoryare, aka Nuur Jareer—the man in charge of my kidnapping. Neither name helped me place him, and other pirates used the name "Abdi Yare." But the man in this story was a top boss in my case.

[†] Bakayle's brother.

[‡] Different from another man called Farhaan, a midranking boss, who may have been present, too.

tormented Rolly with a cigarette while he dangled upside down from a tree, who had clouted me more than once for no reason—maybe the cruelest man at a gathering of cruel men—died on the spot. Gunfire unleashed by the others killed Ahmed Dirie, his brother, and Abdi Ganeey. Abdi Yare was injured. Dhuxul, on his wooden leg, pulled him to safety. "Farhaan the petty pirate ran away," a source in Somalia wrote. "He is on the run for fear of a clan vendetta (hunted by Ali Duulaay clan mates)." Some rumors placed him afterward in South Africa. "He scraped off a few thousand dollars for offering his guard services."

Friends of Abdi Yare drove the injured pirate leader to Mohamed Garfanji's house in El Hur, on the Galmudug coast, to recuperate. But within three days, Abdi Yare—whoever he actually was—died of his wounds.

Five men who had tormented me for almost three years had vanished like a wisp of steam. I felt staggered, bewildered, relieved. A raid killing Bashko or the other guards would have weighed on my conscience, but hearing about this shootout left no trace of grief. The bosses had excused themselves from the world; the scent of cash had roused them to an ecstasy of self-destruction more precise than any American raid.

III

I flew home to Berlin with two BKA agents and three people from the FBI, and we stopped first for a layover in the Vegas-like circus of the airport at Abu Dhabi, with its faux-mosque architectural fantasies and its murmuring midnight crowds. The weird stimulus of this airport put me on edge. While we waited near a food court, I wondered how it would be to see Mom again, and I wondered if I would see Oma at all.

From Abu Dhabi we took a late flight to Berlin, and the attendants served a two-course meal. Between courses, mine asked, "Would you like a change of silverware?" and the question lay so far outside my recent experience that I just sort of wagged my jaw; I had no idea what to say.

I was in a fugue state, dissociated from my old life and self even while I returned to it. We landed around dawn at Tegel Airport, on a gray, fogbound morning in Berlin, where the German government had set up a small reception with snacks and drinks. My mother was supposed to land around the same time, and we were going to be reunited among various FBI and German government officers; but Mom's plane was delayed. So after some nosh and paranoid chitchat—I had absolutely no idea who anybody was—a BKA man drove me to my apartment.

The familiar streets of Berlin were fog- and drizzle-smeared, like a flickering dream from a prison house. I had trouble believing they were real. For three or four days I had used my natural languages again, and the flood of detail they brought to my brain was overwhelming, like the detail through my provisional glasses. Suzy met me at the door with a key, and it seemed incredible that she still existed, incredible that my friends and apartment were still intact. My uncle in Cologne had maintained the expenses. I just opened the door and sat down. A group of friends had emptied my clothes from the drawers and closet, for some reason that Suzy explained but I found hard to understand. But the brownish cobblestones and the Space Age street clock on Helmholtzplatz hadn't moved, and the neighborhood looked almost unchanged. The thick trees outside my kitchen wavered in the autumn drizzle.

Suzy had left a postcard, which helped me understand about

the clothes: "MIKE! This is your housekeeping team—Suzy, Daryl, Aimee, John, and Desmond. We are in the middle of removing MOTHS from your worldly goods. All the textiles in the flat need to be either drycleaned or washed at 60 degrees + C. Some of your clothes are with us, being laundered. We are so happy you are home and can't wait to see you and give you your clothes back."

My friends had cleaned the place in early 2014 and finished off the chore with an improvised but melancholy celebration—they got drunk and left a bunch of bottles behind. These bottles remained in the kitchen until the BKA called Suzy a few days before my release. The housekeeping team returned, to clear the bottles, but Berlin moths had turned my apartment into a summer breeding ground, as Berlin moths will do. So the housekeeping team took some of my clothes home to throw into their washing machines. Out of startled gratitude and delight, I invited everyone out for drinks—the first coming-home party full of nonstrangers that I navigated in my weird fugue state—and it was wonderful. Suzy, Daryl, Aimee, John, and Desmond each presented me with a massive bag of clean laundry at the bar.

Seeing my mother again, at a Berlin hotel, was a system shock. Part of me couldn't grasp that someone I loved and remembered from so long ago could stand there again in real life. She looked older, but spry and flushed with emotion, vulnerable as a girl. I looked wraithlike and hollow eyed. One of the first odd stories she told was about seeing the moon in California. "I used to look up at it at night and wonder if you could see it, too." I smiled and told her about the handful of times I had noticed it from Abdi Yare's House. For two years and eight months we had shared no other common reference.

She had lit candles for me in church; she wore a new crucifix. Like several hostages I'd met, she had leaned back on her childhood religion. For two years and eight months, my mother had been captive, too.

It was weird to think, in the sterile room of this brand-new Holiday Inn, how close I had wandered to suicide. I didn't mention it, but I remembered the years we had gone to church in Northridge, the hot suburban streets, and the neighboring apartment complex where Dad had ended his life. Mom had remained so evenhanded on the phone for 977 days because her primary instinct was to protect me—the same reason she had maintained a falsehood about Dad's heart attack. She hadn't told a malicious lie. But the line of logic that kept me alive on my worst days in Galkayo—that Mom didn't deserve to have two men self-destruct—made it fortunate, for both of us, that I had bothered to figure things out.

Her psychological strength had faltered only near the end, so a professional negotiator had stepped in. Robert, or Bob, was a Californian who worked on missionary-hostage cases in Africa. He'd helped liberate a group of Kenyan medical workers from Ali Duulaay earlier in 2014. So he knew the right personalities, and at the FBI's instigation, he had volunteered to help. "Abdi Yare came down really quickly at the end with his demand," Mom said. "We still don't know why. Until July he was still demanding four million."

I told her about the stirrings of labor unrest among my guards, and she nodded. "We didn't know if it was some disagreement, or if things were maybe not going so well for all the pirates, but when they went down like that in September, we knew there was some kind of urgency."

Mom said Denis Lyon had followed my case with energy and intelligence as a healthy man in his midseventies, but a stroke had disrupted his brain in 2012, and he'd spent more than a year at a rehabilitation center. "His speech was totally gone," Mom said. "He could only utter noises. He would recognize his family and friends, but he couldn't talk to them."

Denis died, after a second stroke, in 2013. Unbelievable. I'd spent countless hours with family and friends in my imagination, and the only surprise more intense than coming home to find everyone alive was coming home to find some of them dead.

"How is Oma?" I said lightly.

"Michael, she died last year. She wanted so much to hold on."

I started to cry.

Oma had slipped away while I baked in a hot prison house on a sweaty mattress, while my guards lit cigarettes and fussed over their fucking khat. Part of me knew it, part of me had already grieved, but the news still made me want to rip up the ground and go looking for her. I wasn't done with my grandmother. There were no words powerful enough. Pirates did the same thing to seafarers from all over the world, of course. Untold stories of hostage families from Senegal to Vietnam, from Argentina to India, involved quiet tragedies like these, and such intimate losses were the real ransom extracted by kidnappers and other traffickers in human flesh.

IV

Those early weeks of freedom consisted of drizzle as well as beautiful, crisp days with a fine autumn sunlight. Living in Berlin again was like pulling on an old pair of jeans. It felt familiar, even though certain changes were hard to miss. A grim, gravelly matter-of-factness about the city had retreated; my neighborhood had more lights, and fancier restaurants, and people were obsessed with fantasy-minded TV shows I had never heard of, like *Game of Thrones*. Along with the posh and flashy changes in Berlin there was an air of dissatisfaction and rebellion, as if the West had never moved through this cycle before, as if it were all new again, and no one could even imagine that the prosperity of the sixties had had something to do with its hipster discontents. Young men wore beards like the one I had just shaved off.

Berlin is a walking city, and when I tried to run errands on my emaciated legs, my ankles and knees swelled up like balloons. Underexercised ligaments protested like creaky hinges. For a month I felt crippled; I kept to a walking radius of about two city blocks. But the FBI wanted a long series of debriefings to bulk up its file against my kidnappers, so I had to answer questions every day for the first three weeks at the embassy in central Berlin. I couldn't even walk to the subway. So they arranged a driver, and the man who picked me up every morning was a genial field agent who'd spent time as a paratrooper in Afghanistan. He told me about jumping from C-130s and doing mountain training in the snow. He seemed to have symptoms of post-traumatic stress, because he ran at the mouth, and after a day or two, frankly, I learned to do the same. We jabbered at each other in the car, and it was therapeutic as hell.

The FBI and the BKA both wanted to hear my version of the story, to fill in gaps in evidence they had gathered, and to prosecute pirates if they could. I was happy to tell it. Discussing the nightmare with people who knew it from a different angle was useful. I learned to talk at length in English again; I learned to express things I had only witnessed or felt. Some days, of course, were exhausting, and after one difficult debriefing, I sat slumped in the FBI car, feeling dazed and numb. "When you've told it a hundred times," my friend at the wheel said, "you'll get better."

I came out of Somalia with a quick temper and a tendency to panic in social situations—my fugue state included a flaming protective mental boundary, a firewall to limit stimulation. The easiest remedy, at first, was exercise. Emotion is a form of energy, as I'd learned in the ocean on the *Naham 3*, and pouring sorrow and rage into a regimen at the gym was the readiest way to use it up. I felt hair-trigger delicate for at least three months, not beyond the reach of suicide. But body and mind are not separate creatures, and physical recovery helped uncramp my brain.

Carl's refusal to label my condition "PTSD" also helped. "We don't wanna pathologize anything," he said, and for me it was healthier not to intellectualize my recovery, not to turn the rage and grief into a separate complex to recover from. I focused on growing stronger, not on being "happy." Mirth was no longer the point. A great change had rolled through me in Somalia that I still found hard to articulate. Parts of me felt shriveled and twisted, and sometimes, when I untwisted them, I fell under a foul depression that was like a stench coming out of a cave. But I knew better than to order my feelings around. In Somalia I had learned to take moments of happiness however they arrived. The Latin term *amor fati*, or "love of your fate"—phrased by Nietzsche, stolen from Epictetus,* a principle developed over thousands of years of European philosophy—happens to turn up, again and again, in traditions from Buddhism to Islam. Love your fate or get bulldozed by it.

A small example of this idea, from Muslim Africa, occurs in an essay on Morocco by Paul Bowles. Somewhere in the desert during the 1950s he watched an impatient city Muslim slam a car door on the hand of an old man from the country. "Calmly the old man opened the door with his other hand," Bowles wrote. "The tip of his

---

* "Seek not for events to happen as you wish, but wish for events to happen as they do," Epictetus said, "and your life will go smoothly and serenely."

middle finger dangled by a bit of skin. He looked at it an instant, then quietly scooped up a handful of that ubiquitous dust, put the two parts of the finger together and poured the dust over it, saying softly, 'Thanks be to Allah.' With that, the expression on his face never having changed, he picked up his bundle and staff and walked away."

That wasn't the version of Islam I encountered in Somalia. It was also not the Islam of Salafi terrorists in Europe. Public debates about Islam rumbling in both Europe and the United States before I left for Somalia had grown harsh and manic while I sat around as a hostage, and they were no closer to resolution when I got out. The debate itself had coarsened, in fact—there was a stink of tribalism. The great, aging poet of Gerlach's generation, a Somali camel herder born in the 1940s named Hadraawi, has fiercely beautiful poems against tribalism, which he calls "this baleful malaria" infecting Somalia, and in the West we were learning to enjoy (all over again) the low and feverish heat of the same disease.

I thought about the drumming, trumpeting parades held centuries ago in Italian villages whenever a batch of captives came home from the Barbary Coast, with their songs of liberation belted out by Catholic choruses in the sunshine. They celebrated the difference between Christian Europe and the Muslim enemy. My ordeal in Somalia introduced me to the shape of those differences, the underwater contours of a cultural chasm that many people in the West would like to exaggerate or ignore. Neither approach does much good. It's ridiculous to hear that Somali pirates "aren't really Muslim," when most of them are nothing else, and excuses to abuse the infidel are there in the Koran for anyone to read. On the other hand, a pirate interviewed in a Kenyan jail by U.N. researchers in 2012 put the problem very well. "If I go back to Somalia," he said, "I would like to pursue an education. Because right now I don't know what is right and what is wrong. In Somalia people are born Muslim and they know how to recite the Koran. But everybody forgot what the actual principles are."

V

In November, I noticed a Facebook message from Mohammed Tahliil, the boss of my guard group in Hobyo. I recoiled from the message and ignored him at first. But Tahliil had been gentle, even good humored, so eventually I wrote back.

"Hi Mohammed."

"How are you Michael," he wrote. "I am at Hobyo. I hope u are fine. The pirates who held u hostage killed each other over group vendetta and money issues."

"Which pirates got killed?" I wrote.

He listed them, and when I asked for details about Abdi Yare, he wrote, "Abdi Yare was supervisor/pirate action group leader. . . . He collected the ransom money. Abdi Yare team was attacked by Ali Duulaay team at Galkayo over the ransom money."

He went on:

Many youth members were sympathetic with your pain in bondage. We're happy that you came out alive. The local community members had no power to rescue you, but the youth, women, area folks and faith leaders strived to plea on your behalf to reduce harm to you, and redeem the good name of the native people and the land.

The native communities, the individual persons in youth and women groups, and faith leaders who pleaded for your

freedom and safety will remain a silhouette and unknown
ghost to you. Just know that you were not alone, and you had
many friends in the darkness. . . . Every society / community has a few good persons in a sea of evil men.

Tahliil's English had never been so fluent. I wondered if someone else was typing into his phone. When I asked for a picture of
Abdi Yare, he suggested looking through my "old friend's" material.
I contacted Ashwin and culled some frames from his video footage.
Ashwin lived in an old brick house in a German town not far from
my uncle in Cologne, and we met more than once just after my release to exchange notes. We'd made a number of tactical mistakes in
Somalia, but there was no bad blood; the risks had been clear before
we landed.

While we drove to the airport, Ashwin said, he had spotted Somalis on a technical in the distance, among the rocks, waiting. We
had taken a detour through town, which led us to an alternate road
to the airport, so it's possible the pirates were hoping to catch us
both on the more obvious road, before Ashwin boarded his flight. "I
think it is just dumb luck that they didn't catch me," he said.

One startling image from his footage was a close-up of one
guard, a shapeless and sullen-looking man squatting behind the
antiaircraft cannon on the technical that drove with us to Hobyo.

"Jesus, it's Dhuxul," I blurted.

Seeing his face again lit a cold, raging fire. It explained why
he'd looked so familiar to me in Galkayo. He'd ridden with us to
Hobyo. "He is a high-ranking pirate," Yoonis had bragged when I
first moved into Dhuxul's house as a hostage, and now my anger at
the men who'd hired him—the gap-toothed "security chief" called
Nuur, but also Digsi, Hamid, and ultimately Gerlach, who bore re-
sponsibility for our safety—seethed in my blood like acid. (I still

kept anger in a storehouse like that, whole barrels of it, corroding in the shade. The question was how to dispose of it.)

"Abdi Yare" remained an important puzzle, though. Too many pirates went by that name. The one who mattered evidently was the mastermind behind my capture, a boss who also went by "Qor-yare" and "Nuur Jareer." Still working on a hunch, I sent another frame from Ashwin's footage to Tahliil, a picture of the pirate with a keffiyeh-wrapped face whom we had interviewed in Hobyo, "Mustaf Mohammed Sheikh."

"Mohammed, what is this man's name?" I wrote.

Mohammed wrote back, not entirely to my surprise:

"His name is Nuur Jareer."

I remembered the way this pirate had stared at me through his keffiyeh in the hot room in Hobyo—his supposed fisherman's an-ger, his portentous unsteady eyes—and it startled me to think he was dead. He'd meant me nothing but harm. The Sa'ad elder, Digsi, may have cooperated with him: he'd organized the interview, and I believe Digsi had wanted to trick us into an ambush in Garacad, on our way back from Hobyo.

Gerlach was also, at best, an incompetent guide. Hamid and Digsi had hired pirates to serve as "security" under his watch, and he should have vetted those decisions. It was my own mistake to trust him. But Ashwin and I both had the impression that Gerlach and President Alin were speaking for their clan in Galmudug when they welcomed us. Evidently not. It's possible that Gerlach himself was betrayed, and of course it never escaped my attention that the evil in my captors' minds had proliferated in a furnace of victim-hood, of resentment and bottomless blame. So heating up similar passions was no way to recover.

Gerlach and I met several times in Berlin, over lunch—alone or with other people—to exchange information. At last I showed him

Ashwin's picture of Dhuxul. He became incoherent, and confused. When I told him how upset I was with his services, he stood up and left.

We no longer speak.

VI

The mysterious American who'd landed in Galkayo to release me in June was real: Mom had hired him. He went by Joe, and parts of the wild story Hassan had told me were true. Joe had a military background. He worked for a private contracting firm in Somalia. As a Navy SEAL during the Battle of Mogadishu, he had forged connections among the Sa'ad clan, so he thought he could help.

Joe contacted my mother in the spring of 2014, and with her permission he talked to a faction of the gang. By June he had made a deal, and he flew to Galkayo with seven hundred thousand dollars from her ransom fund, and a great deal of her trust. "What I'd heard, and what everybody had heard, was that the pirates were broke," Joe told me. "The creditors wanted money, the guards were sick of it, they were ready to be paid, and so your price went down," meaning that Dhuxul, at least, had offered to let me go for a bargain.

Armed with a pistol, accompanied by a doctor and a Somali police colonel he trusted, Joe met a pirate representative in a Galkayo hotel. Joe doesn't know the man's real name, but he went by Abdi Yare. He was an accountant for the group, and I believe he kept in telephone contact with Dhuxul during the meeting.

One day before Joe landed, the surviving crew from the *Albedo* had walked free, so a ransom had slopped through the Galmudug pirate community. Joe worried that something might go sour. Sure enough, in the hotel, the accountant felt bold enough to demand more cash.

"What do you mean you need more money? We've discussed this many, many times," Joe said.

The accountant was alone, without weapons. Joe had a pistol, a knife, and two assistants. "When I leave here," he said, "either Michael's coming with me or I'm gonna kill you in the bathroom. This isn't a case of 'If it doesn't go well, we'll both go home.'"

The phone rang. Probably Dhuxul. Joe wouldn't let the accountant answer.

"I'm just a middleman," the accountant protested.

"I don't care," said Joe.

"Allah knows I haven't done anything bad," the accountant said.

"You're about to have a chance to explain it to him."

The phone rang again. Joe warned him not to answer, since there was too much risk that the accountant might ask for armed help. The accountant answered anyway. Joe lost his temper. He pulled his knife and dragged the pirate to the bathroom, intending to kill him, but one of Joe's assistants, the Somali police colonel, persuaded him to stop.

I met Joe one spring night on the coast of Virginia, where he told me this version of the story. He was an unassuming man with a shy smile and a mustache. He'd volunteered for the mission because he'd found a way in. This was his line of work, but it still astonished me that anyone cared enough to dream up such a difficult job. But hearing sketches of plots to retrieve me from Somalia—imagining the sacrifices required by rescuers in case anything failed—still buckles my knees.

"The pirates told me you showed up in fatigues," I said.

"No, I was in civilian clothes."

"They said you spent a couple of days in jail, because they couldn't verify your Galmudug visa."

He chuckled. "I left the same day."

"But killing the accountant," I said. "That was part of an official plan?"

"Well, it was *my* plan. I was on my own on this." He smiled. "I wasn't representing anybody."

I went to Somalia with a stubborn and fairly proud streak of individualism, which my experience has tempered with oceans of gratitude. I'd built a personal ethic of taking calculated risks as a journalist, of trying to burden no one but myself, so relying on people to come get me was a disgrace. But when you need help, you need help. And showing gratitude was the way to manage my corroding barrels of anger. Joe knows I'm grateful, but the anonymous members of the military ought to know it, too. I've heard rumors in the meantime of a SEAL plan to remove me by force from the *Naham 3*, and I've heard a rumor that the SEALs who rescued Jessica Buchanan were also looking for my sorry hide. The story goes that U.S. intelligence had placed me in the same bush camp. I can't see much further into these stories, and the rumors might be wrong. The Buchanan raid probably did lengthen my time in Somalia. But so did pirate politics; so did my own boneheadedness. I can't regret the results of the raid if it freed Jessica and Poul and denied the pirates a second ransom, and what else is left, besides my own reaction?

"Seek not for events to happen as you wish, but wish for events to happen as they do," Epictetus said, "and your life will go smoothly and serenely."

VII

In late 2015, I flew to the Seychelles to see Rolly. His daughter Maryse decided not to tell him beforehand. "We were thinking that we will give him a surprise," she wrote. Even as a retired former hostage, in his seventies, with a pension, Rolly took a fishing boat out for weeklong trips around Mahé, so Maryse would have to find an excuse to keep him on land.

"He has stopped drinking for a while now," she advised me.

"No problem, I'll buy him a soda," I wrote.

"Haha! The minute he sees u he is going to drink."

Victoria was a modern city built around a harbor, with lush and beautiful palm-grown hills, pirate-themed restaurants, and a feeling of lassitude and sweat. Maryse met me at the airport and drove me up from the bright and busy town to a hillside community with vast shade trees and long concrete bungalows. This was Belvedere, a planned-housing estate. We walked between two of the bungalows and found Rolly on his doorstep, muttering something cranky in Creole.

When he spotted me, he shouted.

"*Eh!*" he said. "Mi-*chael!*"

"Rolly!"

We spent a good two hours on the porch while daughters, grandchildren, sons-in-law, friends from up the road, and neighbors came and went. I reminded him of the promise we'd made in Somalia, to have a reunion drink "under the mango tree," wherever that was. I offered to buy him a Coke. But in the afternoon, he took me to a neighborhood liquor store for a round of beer, then found a crowd of buddies in the front yard of a house across from his bungalow, under a massive, drooping, wide-spreading mango tree that was so large it had escaped my attention. "*Bonswar,*" Rolly said to each man as we clinked our bottles. They called him "Ti Rolly"— short for Petit Rolly, since he was short.

"I'm not enabling you, am I?" I said to Rolly.

"Eh?"

"It's okay if you drink?"

"Is okay, Michael. Sometimes I stop, for my health. Is not a big problem."

I nodded.

"We do it like this in Seychelles," he said.

The house and the giant mango tree, the whole slope of Rolly's road, overlooked a grass-grown cemetery with white monuments and stone crosses. The men around us mumbled, and we heard laughter from the children and grandchildren in front of Rolly's bungalow.

"You have a nice family."

"Yah. Thank you."

"How are you doing?" I said.

"Me, I'm okay, Michael."

"You sleeping well?"

"Yes, yes."

"No nightmares, nothing like that?" I said.

"No, no."

In Somalia we had both slept poorly. In Berlin I still woke up at night with my heart racing. Nightmares weren't the problem—I could count my Somali nightmares on a single hand—but as a hostage I had picked up the habit of bolting out of sleep around three or four in the morning to listen for drones. Now I slept with mild sedatives.

"Me, I hear this fat man get arrested," Rolly said.

"Garfanji? I heard the same thing." The Somali government had put him in jail for a month or two near the end of my confinement, in 2014. "It didn't last long."

"Oh yah? He go free again?"

"He's got too many friends in Mogadishu."

"Ahh," said Rolly, in weary contemplation. "But Ali—he dead now, eh?"

"Ali Duulaay got killed in a shootout, from what I hear. Over my ransom," I said. "Same with Ahmed Dirie."

"Yes, I hear that."

One of Rolly's friends interrupted us to say that Marc was coming over—we would see him any minute.

"How is Marc?" I said.

"He's okay, Michael."

Rolly and Marc had been free for two years, and when Rolly said they were okay, I believed him. But *okay* was a deep intangible for us, and its meaning bent away from the usual one. It meant living above a certain waterline, surviving on the right side of self-destruction.

We sat in silence for a while.

"But the children," he went on. "They still in Somalia?"

"Yes, the whole *Naham 3* crew," I said, "minus two men. Jie and Nasurin have died."

We'd known both of them, but not well. Nasurin was a short Indonesian with a wispy mustache. Jie was the witty Chinese kid. The rumor about his death wasn't true after all, but I didn't know that yet, and the uncertainty over who was dead or alive was a perfect illustration of the quicksand I had slipped into, the mire of obscurities and half-truths that had almost swallowed me whole.

"Bakayle's in charge of the children now," I said. "With Ali gone."

"Which one?" said Rolly.

"You know Bakayle—'Fifty Million.'"

"Oh, Jesus. This man? Oh, Michael."

"I know."

We sipped our beer. I'd been out for more than a year, but my freedom wasn't complete with the *Naham 3* crew still in Somalia.

"I got this Bible the children give me," Rolly said. "I take it with me from the boat."

"The one the pirate kicked?"

"Yah! It falling apart now. But I tell my family, 'When I die, please bury this Bible with me.' On top of my coffin, like that."

The graveyard down the slope was called Mont Fleuri, and on Sundays it teemed with life. Children and families moved among the white monuments, holding flowers or balloons.

Recovering from captivity is different for every hostage, and Rolly had benefited from a large and boisterous family. He swore by fishing and religion; his family loved him. Nothing else mattered. The president of the Seychelles invited him and Marc to an annual presidential birthday party, at a mansion in Victoria, which made Ti Rolly cocky and proud. A former hostage needs social support, no less than a soldier returning from war.

"Me, I very happy to see you here, Michael."

"I'm happy to be here."

We didn't even mention the grief and gratitude we both must have felt in the meantime, the gratitude that was like a reminder to love "enough," whatever that meant. During my week in the Seychelles, I tried to buy gifts for Rolly and Marc, but they returned them in the form of other gifts, and we wound up just having a big family cookout with grilled snapper and fresh octopus salad.

"Well, now you in the Seychelles," Rolly informed me, "I take you out in my boat tomorrow."

"Right, what are you fishing in?"

"I got a friend, he let me take his boat," he said. "Is like the *Aride*. 'Bout the same size. He the owner, not me, but he know I like to fish."

"I'd love to go out on the boat."

"Just around the harbor, Michael."

"Right, not out toward Somalia."

Rolly chuckled. "No, no."

"I think your family would kill us."

VIII

If a debt was too large to pay back—ethically, practically, emotionally—then you paid it forward. That was my current working method: humility before the monstrous past. Near the end of October 2016, I waited with several people in the dull, overcast light at Nairobi's international airport while Indonesian, Vietnamese, and Filipino diplomats talked on their phones. A group of Chinese embassy workers waited in a black van by the curb. The *Naham 3* men had spent almost five years in Somalia, longer than any group of pirate hostages but one,* and I was here trying to put some of my gratitude into action.

I'd sent some of my own money to the crew's ransom fund. Then, out of frustration, I'd collected more from a small group of friends. The money amounted to a fraction of what the pirates expected, and I wasn't eager for Bakayle or his clansmen to have more of my cash; but I had gathered that none of the six governments involved were planning to mount a military raid. There was no other way to set the men free.

Journalists referred to the *Naham 3* men as "forgotten hostages," seafarers left behind from the peak days of Somali piracy. A British security firm called Compass Risk had negotiated their release for

---

* Four Thai hostages from the fishing vessel *Prantalay 12* were held two months longer.

a sum that amounted to "covering the costs" of holding the men—
that is, making sure Bakayle's gang could repay its loans to the
surrounding communities in Galmudug that may have provided
food, water, or khat. A charity called the Hostage Support Partners,
run by John Steed,* had coordinated the mercy mission. A maritime
law firm based in London and Hong Kong, called Holman Fenwick
Willan, helped with logistics and legal advice, and they'd been kind
enough to fly me to Nairobi.

The men emerged in two groups. First the Chinese diplomatic
van closed its doors and hurried around to a distant airfield gate, followed by some straggling TV cameramen. When the van emerged
again from the gate, with little red Chinese flags flapping on its front
hood, a bus with curtained windows followed, shuttling part of the
crew to the Chinese embassy. We never saw them. I heard a rumor
that Beijing wanted to spirit away the Chinese-speaking crew—
including Taso, from Taiwan—to control the story of their release
and thwart the patriotic Taiwanese press.† A sturdier rumor held that
Cao Yong had suffered a stroke almost a year before: he and several
others needed quick medical treatment. The reedy, efficient, stern-
seeming young man who had shut down my idea for a rebellion on
the ship was now paralyzed along one side of his frame. A violent mutiny might not have ended any better; but it was a hard thing to hear.

The rest of the men came out of the terminal building in a quiet
mass, looking careful and gaunt. Arnel, who'd started as a skinny

---

* The retired British colonel who had helped my mother find Derek, the pilot.
He'd also hired the second Somali driver on the day of my release. Steed helped
with many long-term pirate cases in Somalia.

† But Taso returned to Taiwan a few days later, and there was no lack of patriotic
and emotional stories.

man, resembled a broomstick. Hen was no longer a squat Cambo-dian muscleman; he looked haunted and deflated. Sosan had lost a tooth, as well as the flowing, sarcastic anger I remembered in his eyes. None of them knew the officials and journalists who had turned out to greet them, and none of them expected to see me. All day long, I had wondered if they would be sour or wounded, or just antisocial—since I had felt antisocial on my first day out of Somalia—and I wondered if I had done enough to help.

I tapped Sosan on the shoulder. His face lit up, and he shouted. The others noticed and said, "Michael!" They swarmed me and cried out in unbelievable pleasure; they almost knocked me to the ground.

We spent several days together in a clean, glass-sided hotel that must have seemed miraculous to the men after so much misery. Tony Libres teased me for being "fat"—I'd gained back my forty pounds—and over meals they told me horrible stories in sudden, collective gusts. They talked about living in "the Forest," a wooded valley that sounded not too different from the valley where Rolly and I had lived in 2012. Sosan had lost his tooth when he bit into a piece of field-cooked ostrich. Korn Vanthy was recovering from a gunshot wound.

They'd lived on the *Naham 3* until late June 2013, when the *Albedo* started to sink in a monsoon sea. It went down over several days, while the pirates ignored warnings from the crew. The rusted hull took on water near the bow and truck-size steel containers started to clang and slide. On its final night, in early July, the ship tilted in rough waves, the containers tumbled into the ocean, and seven of the *Albedo* hostages leaped and swam for the *Naham 3*. Four drowned. But Nguyen Van Xuan, the Vietnamese fisherman, jumped into the dark water with a roped life preserver attached to his wrist by a fishing line. He swam it to a struggling crewman. The *Naham 3* men, holding the rope on deck, pulled the *Albedo* hos-tage up the side of the ship the way they had rescued me; then they tossed the preserver back to Xuan, in the water, and by this method he saved three lives.

"That's amazing," I told him.

Xuan shrugged, with extreme Asian modesty.

"For me, it is ordinary," he said.

The *Albedo* tugged on the *Naham 3* while it went down, but the water was shallow. The cables and tethers remained intact, and the *Naham 3* didn't sink. Pirates had moved several other *Albedo* hostages to shore in a skiff, alive, and after a night of terror and confusion, the massive cargo vessel rested on the seabed, with its high bridge tower lifting over the surface, and from then on it functioned as a pier. The *Naham 3* stayed moored to it for a month. Members of both crews lived in crowded, filthy conditions on the work deck until the *Naham 3*'s half-repaired generator finally rumbled to a halt. Then, with everyone on board, the pirates detached the tethers and let the fishing vessel drift on the long northerly current. It stranded at Idaan, lodging its deep keel in the sand a few hundred yards from the beach I had seen with Ashwin and Gerlach. The pirates ferried everyone ashore in skiffs.

From there the crew members split up. The *Albedo* men moved to Adado, a town well inland from Harardhere. The *Naham 3* crew spent most of its time in the Forest, where pirates improvised a shelter from a tall thorn tree. To keep rain off, they patched together some thickets and tarps. "We called this our 'House,'" Arnel said, and they lived in it for most of their three years on land, although sometimes the pirates stashed them in real houses in Budbud. They lived on anjero, tea, rice, and beans. To bulk up their diet, they hand-tied traps for rats and small birds out of rope and tree bark. "We put rice on the ground," said Arnel, with a sad, twisted smile, "a bird came down to eat it, and we pulled the rope."

They roasted the meat in secret, because the pirates didn't trust them to catch their own food. (The pirates who'd placed them in such a dire situation evidently worried about disease.) "When they caught us, they punished us; they tied us up," Arnel said. "So we hid the meat."

One afternoon a pirate ordered Korn Vanthy, the young Cambodian, to cook a pot of rice. Korn Vanthy was playing a card game. He refused. They argued, and the next time Korn Vanthy stood up to pee, the pirate fired a rifle round through his bare foot. The other men closed up the tree shelter for twenty-four hours in protest, keeping the pirates outside while they mounted a hunger strike. "Rebellion!" Tony said with a smile. "Twenty-four hours, only. We were very angry."

I noticed no international resentments among the crew in Nairobi, no whiff of old tensions from the ship. From what they said about the Chinese, I gathered that the whole group had consolidated against the pirates. It was odd and wonderful to see them together. By now they were even more accustomed to living as a crew than I was to thinking of them that way; but the arrangement was artificial, constructed by staffing agencies like Step Up. They had homes and families all across Asia. After a few days' recuperation, they would never meet again in one place, in such a complete gathering. So going home was also melancholy.

"Did Step Up pay you?" I asked Ferdinand.

"No, Michael."

"Not at all? Not even wages for your families?"

"No."

But Steed's organization had raised a small amount of money for all the men to start new lives.

I mentioned Jie, the Chinese kid, and asked Tony how he had died.

"Jie did not die, Michael! It was Wang Zhao."

"Oh!"

He meant a young, quiet Chinese crewman who used to sit above us on the conveyor belt, a boy with full black hair cut in jagged angles, like a stylish mop. His large eyes had seemed to accept everything they witnessed—the Chinese karaoke, the Hong Kong action films, and the *Tom and Jerry* cartoons no less than the weird and violent behavior of the pirate guards—with a childlike equanimity. He died one day in 2013, during an outbreak on the ship of a bizarre blackened-skin disease, something like black gangrene. "They gave us medicine, but not the right one," said Tony.

Wang Zhao fell unconscious on deck after carrying a tray of cleaned fish to the kitchen. The crew attended to him for a night. But his neck had swollen, which obstructed his breathing. "Around ten o'clock in the morning, he lost his life," said Tony. "The pirates said, 'Take him inside the freezer.' Like that! No other comment."

Wang Zhao was twenty-four. Contrary to Bashko's report, he hadn't starved himself. Several other men suffered for weeks from the fever and the blackened swelling, but no one else died until the spring of 2014, when the Indonesian, Nasurin, fell sick in the Forest. After a rainstorm, he complained of a fever and remained ill for two weeks. Arnel and Tony suspected malaria. "He said the inside of his body felt very hot," Tony recalled. Pirates threw drugs at Nasurin—acetaminophen, antibiotics—but the young Indonesian died in their outdoor camp in May of 2014. "No medical treatment!" Tony said, with a look of disgust.

So two human bodies, Wang Zhao's and the captain's, were lying in the freezer when the *Naham 3* gave out. I asked what the pirates had done with the contents of the hold.

"They dumped all the tuna!" Arnel said, in his high and musical voice.

"All of it? A hundred tons or so?" I asked.

"Yes, all of it," said Tony. "But the other bodies stayed inside."

"You're kidding."

"The pirates are crazy, Michael."

I could imagine the final shudder of the engine, the silence on the water and the fear among the crew. On their last day at sea, they noticed a warship on the horizon, and some pirates arrived on a skiff, leaving it tethered to the rear of the doomed vessel. After sunset, Jian Zui—the most adventurous Chinese hostage, the sarcastic but good-humored man who'd mimed jumping into the water—pretended to fall ill and slept outside, on the work deck. Late at night he crept back to the skiff. Pirate guards had drifted off, and he wanted to motor out to the distant warship. He slipped over the side and cut the rope with a knife. But a wave knocked the boat away before he could climb in. Jian Zui panicked; he swam for the beach in the blackened water, against the tide. To reduce his weight he stripped naked. When he crawled up on shore—exhausted, thirsty, with a coral-sliced hand—he decided not to grope around in the dark; instead he went to sleep. He intended to wake up before dawn, Arnel said, "but when he wake up, the sun was shining"—Arnel laughed—"and he was nude!"

"What did he do?" I said.

He found dry clothes in an empty pirate skiff and walked a long way inland, without water. At last he came to a nomad's hut, where he begged for something to eat and drink. A young woman offered him milk and goat. "But while he was eating, this woman call Bakayle on the phone," Arnel said. "And Bakayle come in a car."

"With a gun," said Tony.

So Jian Zui answered a question lingering on the edges of my conscience ever since I had left Somalia. What if I'd escaped on land? Suppose I'd thrown myself at the mercy of strangers in Galmudug?

"Bakayle beat him?" I said.

"He say, only slapped," Arnel answered. But a magazine report from China would later describe a long scar on Jian Zui's scalp, from the butt of Bakayle's rifle.

I never saw Jian Zui in Nairobi. I could only guess at his condition. From proof-of-life pictures taken in the bush, I thought he looked no worse than the others. These Asian sailors tended not to complain, so in the muted-festive atmosphere of the hotel it was hard to find psychological wounds. But I recognized the long silences, the gaunt faces, the frozen anger and pent-up sorrow, and I could guess how long it would take them to recover.

When I came out of Somalia, I had no tolerance for the broad ambitious tendency of the mind to dream up ideas and distant plans; I lived in a brutal animal-survival mode, and I had to let myself recover. Body and mind know how to do that, and they revive one fiber at a time. Animal survival is also not opposed to the dreaming world of ideas—we inhabit both selves at once, at the very least—but I mistrusted big ideas, and distant plans, for a long time. Ideas had gotten me into trouble. Ideas could easily go wrong. Even in Nairobi, more than two years after my release, I was wary of long-term plans. But I also had a glimpse of something I find both irresistible and hard to describe.

I couldn't speak Tagalog or Ilocano, the Filipinos' main languages, and their English had rusted in Somalia. We had the old problem of finding the right words. I thought about the way Rolly and I had used "okay" as a stand-in for whole libraries of mutual language. It was a deep pleasure to see the crew again on the balcony of a sun-drenched Nairobi hotel, to watch them eat well and drink decent coffee, but the obstacles to recovery for men who have been captive for so long made it painful, too, and there was no contradiction, no cancellation of one extreme by the other—bleakness by joy, or vice versa. The opposites intensified each other. When I thought about my own swim in the black ocean off the *Naham 3*, I saw that disentangling the exhilaration of those moments of freedom from their lingering horror was impossible. Absolutely no way. And when the men talked about returning to rural jobs in Vietnam or Cambodia or the Philippines—the tattooed Buddhist, Phumanny, mentioned selling hot chilis from his parents' farm—I sensed the ragged uncertainty of the future, blended with elation that we had one at all.

"Jian Zui tried to escape, like you," Tony said with a grin.

"Yes. But, uh—"

Oh, good grief.

"He's okay now?" I said.

Arnel nodded and smiled.

"Yes," he said. "He's okay."

Later we celebrated at the Philippine embassy in Nairobi: a church service, a buffet dinner, karaoke. We spoke ship's pidgin to one another, and it felt awkward to use such a stunted language on land, in an almost formal setting. Of course I wouldn't have missed it for anything. I'd lived on a thermal of happiness ever since the news of the men's release, and the world felt ordered again, at least for a while. I sensed that core of inane excitement, the irrational "body of delight" I had gleaned in Galkayo, which pointed toward a durability of the soul that I had found so elusive on the ship. But I lacked the vocabularies to express this idea to anyone at the embassy. I could hardly express my gratitude—or not just gratitude but also rage, hunger and horror, the long paralysis of hope. Death, renewal, grief, and love. The parching sun on the desert bush, and the astonishing tonic of the sea.

Afterword: My Life as a Camel

When I first traveled to Somalia, part of me was drunk on Bruce Chatwin's fascination with nomads, his suspicion that humans had evolved to wander, not to sit still. (I felt nomadic myself.) But once I was a hostage of nomads, or the descendants of nomads, that romanticism burned off pretty fast. Ahmed Dirie made a bitter joke during my first week as a hostage—"*Adiga, giil!*" or *You are a camel!*—which cemented my place in the hierarchy. I would not be allowed to talk to pirates as a man: I was an outsider, an infidel, and they would be pleased to trade me as livestock.

Ahmed Dirie made the joke in our Land Rover, after he and the other pirates dragged Rolly and me out for a random, day-long motor tour of the desert bush. (The U.S. military had just rescued two other hostages in a distant part of Galmudug.) The Land Rover bounced in circles across a ridged, grass-grown plain of mud while black-and-white goats bleated and trotted away. Ahmed Dirie pointed at them and asked Rolly for their name in English. They urged Rolly on until he bleated, which made all the pirates laugh.

"*Adiga, ari!*" Ahmed Dirie said. *You are a goat!*

After a while he prodded me to bleat like a goat, too, but I played dumb. When we passed a herd of camels, Ahmed Dirie said, "*Adiga, giil!*"—*You are a camel!*—and the pirates laughed again.

Camels are valued livestock in Somalia: one camel costs several times the price of a goat. I understood the joke and glared.

Later, in a room in Mussolini's Farmhouse, both Ahmed Dirie and Mohammed Tahliil separated me from Rolly and Marc, to offer me extra food. I gathered I was on a separate budget. They watched me eat a meal of salty goat liver, which tasted awful, so I asked for a drink of water.

Ahmed Dirie scowled. He was a midlevel boss who knew how to practice the sneering attitude that even a privileged hostage deserved punishment and abuse. He challenged me with his water bottle—full of yellowish, septic-looking dreck. The earth in some parts of Somalia was so full of human and animal waste that the wells were diseased, and the top pirate bosses understood that foreign hostages ought to have bottled water.

I shook my head. Tahliil went out to find a sealed plastic bottle. But Ahmed Dirie lost his temper.

"*Adiga!*" he said—*You!*—holding the foul-looking water in my face and lecturing me in Somali. He unscrewed his bottle and tilted it up for a long swallow, without moving his furious eyes from mine. His lecture resumed. *He* could drink the water. It was good enough for *him*. What was my problem?

Evidently I was a prissy hostage who had started to cost too much. Ahmed Dirie gestured at the junk food piled in the corner, which I received on a regular basis: bottles of sugary mango juice and vanilla sandwich cookies called *biskit*, which also constituted privileged treatment. Who else received such goodies? Why did I need clean water?

Ahmed Dirie looked ready to hit me.

"If I drink that," I said, pointing at his bottle, "I'll get sick." I mimicked vomiting. "*Aniga*, no Somali." *I am not Somali.* "No same-same."

He stared with a slack mouth. Ahmed Dirie grasped my tone, but not my rationale. He didn't know a damn thing about bacteria, foreign immune systems, or native disease. You might think international hostage-takers ought to learn such subtleties; and the top bosses, who shaped the budget and enforced the rules, probably did.

But not Ahmed Dirie. Somalia had lacked a national school system for more than twenty years.

These stories wound up on my cutting-room floor, like dozens of others. They impeded the flow of the book. Whole scenes, clutches of vivid detail, went missing for the same reason. When I left Somalia, I knew days' and weeks' worth of memories had vanished from my mind, but the process of debriefing with the FBI, then sitting down to write, showed me that I had a whole torrent of violent and wretched recollection, more than enough for a book. The nightmare had fixed the most important details in my brain.

But storytelling, by its nature, is an act of selection, and the selection has to be impressionistic or emotional if it will resonate. It has to leave the reader with what Tolstoy called "infection," a lasting visceral sense of how things felt. A good book also has to be dramatic, so I steered through the torrent of terrible memories by selecting moments that drove the narrative forward or left an emotional brand: memories that burned, memories that stank of flesh.

One character I decided to leave out was a guard who watched me during the first three months, but never again. He was a middle-aged, sweet-tempered man with a prosthetic leg (like Dhuxul). He said two memorable things on the day of Ahmed Dirie's camel joke.

Around lunchtime, we stopped in a house with delicate walls made of tall, twisted, bending twigs. An ocean breeze blew across the soft dirt floor. Other pirates unpacked a pasta meal while this man sat down and took off his leg. He let it rest beside his rifle, an AK mounted with an aluminum-looking grenade.

I felt rotten. He must have noticed.

"Michael," he said. "Problem?"

"Yes," I said. "I want to go home."

He made the motion of a plane with his hand. "Free?"

"Yes."

"Do not worry," he said. "God is one."

I squinted and felt a bolt of rage. I wondered what to call a kidnapper who thought he could ease his prisoner's mind with religious pronouncements like that. I studied the man's face, which had creases beside his nose and white-flecked stubble. But I cooled my temper because he seemed to be a decent man, not cut from the same sarcastic cloth as Ahmed Dirie.

Later the same day, during more idiotic wandering in the car, we got stuck in the dust. Most of the pirates piled out to push the Land Rover while Rolly and I stayed in the rear. This one-legged pirate stayed in the front seat, guarding us in his genial way.

He asked, in English, about my "subclan."

"What do you mean?"

"America, Europe?" he said.

"Europe," I said. "For now."

"Subclan Franza?"

"France? No, Germany," I said.

"Germany, good!"

I was surprised.

"Good, why?"

"Yes, Hitler!" said this decent and gentle-seeming pirate, who made a sieg-heil sign. "Hitler good!"

"No!" I said.

But, yes. A similar anti-Semitism was common in Muslim countries from northern Iraq to Indonesia, and I would hear it more than once from my pirates. A surprising number of Somalis had a positive impression of Germans precisely because of the Holocaust. No Jews lived in this part of the world, so Hitler had a good reputation in the bush.

Another trimmed scene:

Bashko listened to news about the annexation of Crimea on the Somali BBC in early 2014, after Russia's President Vladimir Putin rolled his proxies into Ukraine.

"Putin, okay!" he said with a mischievous grin, lifting his thumb.

I scowled. I'd listened to the morning news, too. The World Service had reported that Russia's Black Sea fleet was blockading Sevastopol's harbor, effectively holding a third of the Ukrainian navy hostage.

"Putin *bur'ad*," I said sullenly. *Putin is a pirate.*

Bashko laughed. Somali pirates admired Putin as a strongman—someone who used violence at will, who refused to put up with guff from the hypocritical Western liberal order.

Do these little slices change the larger story? Sure. Not much, but some. Every woven detail changes the look of the rug. A writer can make the difficult choice to cut such vivid scenes if the same information comes up elsewhere; but even if they're chopped from the manuscript they belong to the writer's sense of self—the larger, shifting, more terrifyingly subjective sea of emotion and memory that the book seems to fix in stone.

The kidnapping tweaked my original ideas for a book and spirited the story off in a new direction so quickly the reader forgets about the German pirate case. But I was enthralled with the trial in Hamburg. Germany has a modern constitution, drafted after World War II, and its laws reflect the relative lack of high-seas piracy in the mid-1900s. The United States and Spain, with older systems of law, still have draconian punishments for piracy on the books from two or three hundred years ago, including death sentences and life prison terms. This clash between a liberal modern state and an archaic, almost zombie-like crime—risen from the dead after two centuries of relative quiet on the high seas—fascinated me.

Twenty public defenders filled the courtroom, two lawyers for each pirate. Most of them insisted their clients were innocent fishermen who had been press-ganged at gunpoint in the deserts of Puntland and Galmudug, or the backstreets of Mogadishu, to ride out in motorboats and attack foreign cargo traffic. These defenses were smoke screens. But the court had to give them the benefit of the doubt, because the Somalis' lives weren't well documented. All ten pirates received jail sentences of about seven years; the court subtracted time spent in prison before and during the trial—almost two years—and more for standard good behavior. By December of 2014, shortly after I returned to Berlin, all ten would-be hijackers of the MV *Taipan* walked free in Hamburg.

That bothered me. But what seemed even worse was that a German court couldn't deport them to Somalia. Sending even a convicted criminal back to an unstable nation like Somalia would have violated European human-rights norms. The German word for this policy is *Abschiebestopp*—a blanket halt to deportations—and it's an expression of humane European tolerance, of erring on the side of mercy. I'm not against it in theory. But of course the Hamburg pirates were pleased: "Staying in Germany is a reward in itself," Stig Jarle Hansen, a Norwegian expert on Somalia, told me in 2011. "That's the second-best thing to ransom."

In the weeks and months after my long nightmare in Somalia the notion of sharing the same continent with the Hamburg Ten spiked my blood pressure. I was still traumatized. My heart and brain were so constricted from hostage-rage that I had spasms of defensive mistrust. I've calmed down in the meantime, and the knee-jerk response to migration in European border countries like Hungary strikes me as chaotic and paranoid. (Rage and fear are poor motivations for policy.) Of course, there's nothing wrong with deporting convicted criminals, and I think European countries need to adjust their laws and ship home anyone who uses the comfort and relaxing quiet of the West to commit a serious crime, to cool their heels afterwards, or—of course—to plan attacks on European soil.

I wasn't wrong about the pirates' pastoralism, though. Very few of them were former fishermen. Only one pirate in a boatful needs the maritime skills to run an outboard motor or navigate. It's a far more important talent for a pirate to aim and clean a gun. Most pirates I met were clan militiamen, descendants of nomads, bred far from the coast. The more refined or city-bred guards made fun of the rougher men by saying, "He is nomadic," or, "He is from bush." They said that about Ahmed Dirie.

While I still languished in a Galkayo prison house in about 2013, the pirates told me a rumor that Ahmed Dirie had moved to London.

"Really?" I said.

"Ahmed Dirie! Go out. London," said Bashko.

They thought he'd married a Somali woman there. I doubted it. Western surveillance planes had photographed my guards, and the pirates knew very well that the EU, as well as the United States, kept vast collections of snapshots of known or suspected criminals. It would have been foolish of Ahmed Dirie to board a plane for London. And by late September of 2014, of course, I learned that he was shot dead on the ground in Galkayo, two days after I left Somalia, in a dispute over my ransom.

By then a great migration to Europe was in full swing, and it included a percentage of Somalis. The headlines made me think of Issa, who had suggested on a hot afternoon that he wanted to move to Europe. When Mohammed Tahliil tracked me down on Facebook Messenger,

I asked about Issa, and Mohammed responded with a photo of my formerly sullen, dirty guard wearing a stiff dark suit, standing beside a two-layered wedding cake and his white-dressed Somali bride.

"He has been living in Mogadishu," wrote Mohammed.

"Does his wife know he was a pirate?" I answered drily.

"Yes, she know what piracy is."

So Issa hadn't split for Libya. That was reassuring. But I wondered how much of my ransom had paid for that wedding cake.

On the surface it should have been easy for me to line up with Donald Trump or PEGIDA (Patriotic Europeans Against the Islamization of the West), or some other reactionary movements that protested the "Muslim invasion" of refugees in Europe from war-torn places in Africa or the Middle East. I do think Western progressives have a weird habit of underestimating the power of Islam as a force for separation among Muslims just arriving in a strange new (industrialized, Christian) place. But the fact is that most Somalis who leave for the West aren't pirates or terrorists. They're trying to get away from pirates and terrorists. Most of them want to escape the consequences of clan warfare that still wastes and beggars their country. I know enough other Somalis—journalists, translators, businessmen in Nairobi and New York—to distinguish between hard-working immigrants and the men who held me hostage.

In the spring of 2015 I read about a Somali teenager who made the journey Issa had aspired to. "Ismail" had traveled hundreds of miles across East Africa, through Ethiopia and Sudan, and over the Mediterranean to Italy, where he was taken in by Save the Children. Smugglers had detained him in Sudan, treated him poorly, and called his family in Somalia to demand more cash.

He was held hostage, in other words. Ismail went from being a willing migrant—paying smugglers to deliver him to Europe—to suffering as a trafficked person, held against his will. These detentions were common along the migrant trail. Traffickers are happy to hold migrants for free labor, for ransom, or for sex work if they're female. Such violent exploitation has become a normal aspect of life on the way to the West. When Ismail described his ordeal to a British newspaper, he said his brutal traffickers had offered him insufficient food. All they gave him to eat during the day while he languished in Sudan was, he said, "Biscuits and mango juice."

Hang on.

Sound of screeching brakes.

The U.N. had documented reports of pirate gangs dabbling in the migrant business by moving Somalis across the Gulf of Aden, from northern Somalia to Yemen, where they might find work, using little white skiffs. Was it possible that pirates, or former pirates, helped to move migrants overland, across East Africa, toward Europe? Maybe the real scoop wasn't that some pirate foot soldiers wanted to leave Somalia for greener pastures (of course they did); maybe Issa had entertained a trip across East Africa to Libya because his bosses also invested in migration routes.

A pirate gang and a human-smuggling gang needed the same tools, after all: Kalashnikovs, SUVs, and cheap food to keep their clientele from starving.

"Mohammed," I wrote to my Somali correspondent on Facebook, "are pirate groups in Somalia involved in other business now? I think some pirates help drive migrants now to Sudan or Libya. Is that true?"

"Yes, it is true," he wrote.

"Pirates help Somalis get to Libya?" I repeated, just to verify the point.

"Sure, they help drive migrants to Libya to go European countries."

Eventually I wrote a *Businessweek* piece about a Somali ex-pirate who organized human smuggling along the East African migrant trail.

My hunch was right, even if pirate involvement wasn't necessarily common. I also learned about a surprising link between the Arab Spring and migration from Africa—a simple, if not obvious, connection between Middle Eastern wars and the flood of people on the Mediterranean. After Muammar Qaddafi's death in Libya, the Syrian civil war and the rise of the Islamic State in both Iraq and Syria drove middle-class Arabs to the Libyan coast for cheap trips across the water to Europe. This new traffic lit up old smuggling networks in North Africa. The higher prices paid by Syrians lowered prices for everyone else. The waves of immigrants crossing the European countryside in 2015—Syrians, Afghans, Nigerians, Ghanaians, Eritreans, Ethiopians—were therefore a direct result of smooth-functioning criminal networks, as well as Western wars. Angela Merkel tried to show leadership within the EU by opening German borders, but her strategy backfired. Because of disorganization, and garden-variety racism, the EU missed its chance to respond to the problem properly as an organized bloc. So the former Somali pirates who jumped in on the East African action were opportunists in a more sweeping, historical trend.

It's important to point out that Immigration with a capital *I* has always fired up ferocious hatreds and self-righteous indignations, hot passions for and against, which only complicate a complicated issue. The topic is never as clear as one side likes to claim. My research for *Businessweek* involved a two-week ride on a German naval vessel called the *Frankfurt am Main*, which cruised the Mediterranean in 2016 as part of the European Union's effort to deter smuggling gangs in Libya. The cruise demonstrated the EU's profound dysfunction when faced with a complex, historic humanitarian problem.

Around 2:00 a.m. on May 15, 2016, a white rubber dinghy left Libya with over a hundred West Africans. The *Frankfurt* learned about it through a satellite phone signal, and we stopped about twenty-four nautical miles north of Tripoli while German special forces kept track of the boat. The sun rose, and the migrants cleared Libyan waters. Germans went out to rescue them in semirigid inflatables. The Africans were lined up on their listing rubber dinghy by the Libyan smugglers in orderly fashion. When they had all been moved to the *Frankfurt*—also in orderly fashion—the Germans set the inflatable on fire, probably to rob the smugglers of a cheap but reusable resource. Journalists weren't supposed to photograph the fire, but the bulbous white boat sent up thick, oily billows of dead black smoke, which diminished into a patch of bright orange flames, flickering and heaving on the surface of the sea.

Most of the people came from West Africa: Nigeria, Mali, and Ghana. I watched the Tyvek-suited crew feed them a thin gruel of rice and vegetables in plastic bowls. The men and women were quiet, wary, but relieved to be on the ship. I talked to one enthusiastic kid named Ahmed: "It make me so happy that I forgot all the struggle it took to get me here," he said. "I thank God."

He was a Muslim from northern Nigeria, with narrow eyes and a broad nose and lips. He said the little rubber dinghy, floating in the shore break in Libya, had surprised him. "On that boat, it was different from what they said," he told me. "They tell me I gonna ride a ship all the way to Europe."

But now he *was* on a ship. Later in the afternoon the Germans transferred him and everyone else to the *Aquarius*, a private vessel run by the humanitarian group SOS Méditerranée, which would land them in Sicily. So many people had migrated to Europe from war zones like Afghanistan and Syria that Ahmed's asylum claim, when and if he gained a hearing, wouldn't be very strong. His most logical choice would then be to go underground. Plenty of migrants tried to stay in Europe as unofficial workers, rather than submit to a deportation order and start the migration cycle again.

Rescuing migrant dinghies on the Mediterranean followed the pattern I saw. European ships, for legal reasons, waited beyond Libya's twelve-mile territorial limit, then rescued the smuggled Africans from drowning and shifted them to Italy, the nearest stable country, according to humanitarian convention. EU vessels—doing what they could in place of coordinated policy from Brussels—did not deter the gangs. They helped the gangs. Lives were at stake, so they finished the smugglers' last mile. Everyone on the water understood it very well. More responsible smugglers waited for good weather, then ran out in fishing boats to the twelve-mile limit, pretended to fish, and counted the waiting vessels—from EU navies, from NGOs like SOS Méditerranée or Médicins Sans Frontières, from Frontex. "Rescuers and those that have made the journey note that vessels often lack enough fuel to reach Europe, suggesting that smugglers are deliberately creating a Safety of Life at Sea (SOLAS) scenario where rescue is imperative in order to save those on board," wrote the authors of a report by Sahan, an African NGO, on the Libyan crossing in 2016.

An official total of 1,115 people were pulled from inflatable boats by that legion of ships in calm, sunny conditions on May 15, 2016; we saw 10 percent of them.

"Today we had rubber-dinghy weather," said Lieutenant Janine Pirrwitz, the *Frankfurt*'s press officer. Not without dry wit.

Mohammed Tahliil has since been arrested for his involvement in my captivity, and until the case works through the U.S. courts I can't say much more about him. But my life as a camel left me with a complicated emotional response to mass migration.

On the one hand, of course, I was a trafficked person, which meant I felt something for people coming across the Mediterranean. On the other hand, I didn't want ex-pirates moving to Europe. I also didn't want ex-pirates to *profit* from moving people to Europe. The best way to reduce both was to take migration out of criminal hands.

The proper humanitarian solution—a traditional American solution—was to let a certain number of people apply for asylum from destitute or war-torn regions without leaving home. People vetted from overseas by the State Department, for example, could fly safely to America. It wasn't a perfect system, but it had been used before to help end the "boat people" crisis caused by the Vietnam War. It was a decent way to regularize a messy, dangerous, criminal problem. The United States had fewer terrorist attacks by radicalized immigrants than the EU precisely because it interviewed and selected asylum-seekers from across the water.

There's a moral difference between "smuggling" and "trafficking," as Ismail's story indicates. A smuggled person has paid for passage, hoping for asylum. A trafficked person is held or used unwillingly. The roles can blur on the migrant trail, and most willing migrants on a long voyage may also be exploited, including former pirates. The point was not how to ease the mind of a single European, like me, who'd found himself abused for a while in that dirty twilit world. The point was how to face the near-permanent problem of human migration and integration. "Shutting it down" doesn't work. People move because of wars, weather, and economic distress. They have for thousands of years.

"No matter what you do, people are going to be fleeing Syria right now," Jason Pack, an expert on Libya, told me in 2016. "Yes, there are some economic migrants from sub-Saharan Africa, and there are some small pull factors you could address (including rescue ships on the Mediterranean)—and then Nigerians or Ghanaians wouldn't come. But for Eritreans and Syrians, it doesn't matter. They don't care how dangerous it is. If you're a young man determined to come in this way, you're not gonna be deterred."

But in America, by 2017, the ruling party had declared a cultural war against immigrants, especially those from Muslim countries. This partisan project was a deliberate attack on classical liberalism, the Enlightenment tradition that evolved into both branches of American politics: traditional rock-ribbed conservatism as well as the progressive Left. Both branches had powerful enemies, from Moscow to the Horn of Africa. The great irony to me was that my pirates' dazzling lies, their bully-boy behavior and naked will to power—their incompetence at treating outsiders like human beings—was echoed in the rise of Mr. Trump.

I hope this book will serve as a cautionary tale, not just for wandering journalists. The temptation to dissociate yourself from whole groups of other people is powerful, as more than two decades of civil war in Somalia will demonstrate. The United States could go the same way if it's not careful. Human beings like to think they have nothing to do with certain other human beings. That's a scurrilous lie, a cliché that needs some experience and discipline to see through, but forgiveness will teach you more about good and evil than a thousand fervent preachers of hate, whether they come from a windswept Muslim village or a glittering Western capital.

"If only there were evil people somewhere insidiously committing evil deeds," Aleksandr Solzhenitsyn wrote in *The Gulag Archipelago*, arriving at a similar conclusion from his time in a Soviet prison, "and it were necessary only to separate them from the rest of us and destroy them. But the line dividing good and evil cuts through the heart of every human being."

Acknowledgments

Thanks above all to my mother, Marlis Saunders, and the FBI agents who supported her during the long and frustrating negotiations to get me out.

Thanks to Lou Saunders, her husband, who suffered through everything, too.

Thanks to Mathias Müller von Blumencron, Georg Mascolo, Holger Stark, Matthias Gebauer, and Wolfgang Büchner at *Der Spiegel* magazine, as well as Daryl Lindsey and Charles Hawley at *Spiegel Online*, for both moral and practical help.

Thanks to Jon Sawyer and Tom Hundley at the Pulitzer Center on Crisis Reporting for their engagement throughout the ordeal, especially supporting my mother in California.

Thanks to Sara Miller-McCune at what is now *Pacific Standard*, to David Bradley at Atlantic Media, to Mel Leshowitz and Ellen Beaumel, and to John Keenan of Keenan & Associates.

Thanks to Ashwin Raman, Derek Seton, Bob Klamser, John Steed in Nairobi, and of course to Joe for excellent logistical help.

Thanks to David Rohde for all kinds of help.

Thanks to Olivia Judson for introducing me to "Courage Under Fire," James Stockdale's fine essay about his time as a prisoner of war in Vietnam. Stockdale's ideas about Epictetus have informed mine, and I think it's remarkable that we arrived at similar conclusions in captivity by very different paths.

Thanks to Susanna Forrest in Berlin, and thanks to the rest of the cleaning crew—John and Aimee and Desmond—and to all my friends, in Berlin and elsewhere, who agonized while I was a hostage.

Thanks to Nicole Busse, and thank you to Blanche Schwappach.

Thanks to the circle of FBI and BKA agents who supported me just after my release, and for the memorable meal of Königsberger Klöpse in Nairobi.

Work on this book was aided by grants from the Logan Non-fiction Fellowship, based at the Carey Institute for the Global Good in upstate New York, as well as the Pulitzer Center on Crisis Reporting in Washington, D.C.

Thanks to my readers: Susanna Forrest, Stig Jarle Hansen, Rasha Elass, Taran Khan, Mark Kramer, and everyone in the winter 2017 class of the Logan Nonfiction Fellowship.

Thanks to my wonderful surfing editor, Karen Rinaldi, and my fabulous agent, Kathy Robbins.

Thanks to Hannah Robinson and Nate Knaebel for their close attention to the manuscript.

Thanks to Abdi Warsame's entire family in Wiesbaden and Berlin for their moral support, and for Abdi's Somali-language translations.

Thanks also to H., a Somali who worked on my behalf and corroborated some of the stories in this book.

And, of course, thanks to Anna Noryskiewicz for help with Chinese translations and pinyin spellings.

Glossary of Names

ABDI WARSAME—a Somali court translator in Hamburg, Germany.

ABDI YARE—nickname for the top Somali boss in the author's hostage case, used by more than one pirate.

ABDINASSER—a blustery and good-natured pirate guard who declared himself the author's "sahib."

ABDINUUR—a pirate machine gunner and nominal leader of the author's guard group.

ABDIRASHID—the "Pirate Princeling," a guard who claimed to be the son of the boss named Dhuxul, also known as "Rashid."

ABDUELLE—unofficial mayor of Hobyo, living in Hobyo.

ABDUL (GUARD)—a slight, effeminate-looking pirate guard.

ABDUL (TRANSLATOR)—a Somali ransom negotiator aboard the *Naham 3*.

ABDURRAHMAN—a Somali translator and assistant negotiator in Galkayo, also known as "Mustaf."

ABDUWALI—an older pirate guard aboard the *Naham 3*, with good English: a de facto translator.

AHMED DIRIE—a pirate group leader with rotten teeth, unfriendly to the author, belonging to both kidnap and guard teams.

AIDID, MOHAMED FARRAH—a Somali ex-general and warlord who clashed with U.N. forces during the Battle of Mogadishu in 1993.

AKES—a quiet Filipino crewman aboard the *Naham 3*.

ALI'S BROTHER—a pirate group leader prone to violence, brother of Ali Duulaay.

ALIN, PRESIDENT MOHAMED AHMED—president of Galmudug state in Somalia, 2009–2012.

ANDERS—a Norwegian negotiator with good Somali skills. Name changed for this book.

ANGELO—nickname for a pirate guard who treated Rolly well and loaned the author a leather coat.

ARNEL BALBERO—a Filipino crewman on the *Naham 3*, "promoted" because of his English skills.

ASHWIN RAMAN—Indian-born documentary filmmaker in Germany, the author's partner in Somalia.

AWALE, MOHAMUD—official but nominal mayor of Hobyo, living in Galkayo and London.

BAKAYLE—nickname, meaning "Rabbit," for a pirate leader with large ears. Also nicknamed "Fifty Million" by Rolly.

BASHKO—diminutive for Bashir, a pirate guard who helped the author.

BIG JACKET—nickname for a guard-team leader on the *Naham 3*.

BOODIIN—a pirate translator in Hobyo.

BUCHANAN, JESSICA—a U.S. aid worker kidnapped in Somalia and rescued by Navy SEALs.

CAO YONG—a wiry Chinese engineer on the *Naham 3*, often fixing the generator.

CHORR—a pirate friend of the boss called Bakayle. Chorr kicked Rolly's Bible aboard the *Naham 3*.

DAG—a pirate guard in Ali Duulaay's gang, often stoned on khat.

DEREK—a bush pilot and contractor based in Kenya.

DHUXUL—a pirate boss in Galkayo with a wooden prosthetic leg.

DIGSI—a respected Sa'ad clan elder in Galmudug.

DUULAAY, ALI—a top-ranking pirate boss, leader of the group that captured and held both Rolly Tambara and the author.

FARHAAN—nickname for a plump pirate guard who let the author watch *Captain Phillips*.

FARRAH—nickname for a tall and shy-seeming pirate guard in Galkayo.

FATXI—a pirate boss with a mansion in Hobyo.

Glossary of Names

FERDINAND DALIT—a Filipino crewman on the *Naham 3*.

FUAD—a Somali ransom negotiator in and around Galkayo.

GARFANJI, MOHAMED—a top pirate financier in the Hobyo-Harardhere pirate network.

GERLACH, MOHAMMED SAHAL—Galkayo-born elder in Berlin who served as a fixer in Somalia.

HA, NGUYEN VAN—a Vietnamese crewman on the *Naham 3*, a former rice farmer.

HAMID—fixer who assisted Mohammed Gerlach and the author in Galkayo.

HANLEY, GERALD—author of *Warriors*, about Somalia during and after World War II.

HASHI—nickname for a kind pirate guard in Galkayo.

HEN, OR "HAYLE"—nickname for Kim Koem Hen, a Cambodian crewman on the *Naham 3*.

HERSI—a slightly comical young guard in Hobyo.

ISSA—nickname for a tall, loping pirate guard who watched the author in Hobyo, on the *Naham 3*, and in Galkayo.

JIAN ZUI—nickname for a Chinese crewman on the *Naham 3*. Real name Leng Wenbing.

JIE—a young Chinese crewman aboard the *Naham 3*.

JOE—a U.S. military contractor based in Mogadishu. Name changed for this book.

K'NAAN—a Somali-Canadian rapper.

KIM KOEM HEN—real name of Hen, or "Hayle," a Cambodian crewman on the *Naham 3*.

KORN VANTHY—a Cambodian crewman on the *Naham 3* who hooked his hand while line-fishing.

LI BO HAI—the first engineer aboard the *Naham 3*, a senior leader of the crew.

LYON, DENIS, AND SYLVIA—friends of the author's family.

Glossary of Names

MADOBE—nickname for a pirate guard who disliked the author. Real name Abdisalaan Ma'alin Abdullahi.

MARC SONGOIRE—a hostage fisherman from the Seychelles.

MOWLIID—a machine gunner in the author's security team during the trip to Hobyo.

MUSTAF—a nickname for Abdurrahman, a Somali translator and assistant negotiator.

MUSTAF MOHAMMED SHEIKH—a false name for the pirate boss interviewed by the author in Hobyo.

NGEM SOSAN—a sarcastic Cambodian crewman aboard the *Naham 3*.

ÖZYURT, CAPTAIN HASAN—captain of the *Gediz*, a Turkish counter-piracy frigate.

PHUMANNY, EM—a sweet-tempered Cambodian crewman on the *Naham 3*, with a back covered in Buddhist tattoos.

PRAMOEDYA ANANTA TOER—Indonesian novelist and political prisoner, interviewed by the author in 2004.

QIONG KUAN—Chinese first mate aboard the *Naham 3*.

RASHID—the "Pirate Princeling," a guard who claimed to be the son of the boss named Dhuxul. Also "Abdirashid."

ROBERT—a California negotiator who helped conclude the author's case. Also "Bob."

ROLLY TAMBARA—a hostage fisherman from the Seychelles.

ROMEO—pseudonym for a U.S.-based ransom negotiator.

SAUNDERS, MARLIS—the author's mother.

SAYYID MOHAMMED ABDULLAH HASSAN—a Sufi firebrand and revolutionary leader in British Somaliland, lived 1856–1920.

SHEIKH MOHAMUD—nickname for a Somali elder who tried to intervene in ransom negotiations.

SIAD BARRE, MOHAMED—Somalia's last strongman president, deposed in 1991.

STEED, COLONEL JOHN—head of the Hostage Support Partnership in Nairobi.

STEVE—a California-based FBI agent assigned to the author's case.

SUZY—the author's ex-girlfriend in Berlin; Susanna Forrest.

TAHLIIL, MOHAMMED—a mild-mannered pirate guard leader in Hobyo.

TASO—nickname for a Taiwanese engineer aboard the *Naham 3*. Real name Shen Jui-chang.

THICH QUANG DUC—a Buddhist monk in Vietnam who immolated himself in 1963.

THISTED, POUL—a Danish aid worker kidnapped in Somalia, with Jessica Buchanan, rescued by Navy SEALs.

TONY LIBRES (ANTONIO)—a Filipino crewman on the *Naham 3*, also the ship's cook.

TUURE, ALI—nickname for a Somali pirate leader on the *Naham 3*.

XALANE—a young pirate guard who tried to pass himself off as "Mohammed."

XUAN, NGUYEN VAN—a Vietnamese crewman on the *Naham 3*, a career fisherman.

YAŞAR—a naval officer aboard the *Gediz*, a Turkish counter-piracy frigate.

YOONIS—a pirate translator in Hobyo and Galkayo.

About the Author

MICHAEL SCOTT MOORE is a literary journalist and novelist; the author of a comic novel about L.A., *Too Much of Nothing*; as well as a travel book about surfing, *Sweetness and Blood*, which was named a best book of 2010 by the *Economist* and *PopMatters*. He has worked as an editor for *Spiegel Online International*, and he's written a column on transatlantic policy from Berlin for *Pacific Standard*. He's received grants and fellowships from the Carey Institute's Logan Nonfiction Program, the Fulbright Foundation, and from the Pulitzer Center on Crisis Reporting. He divides his time between Los Angeles and Berlin.